CROSSCURRENTS
PURSUING SOCIAL JUSTICE AND INTERRELIGIOUS WORK
SINCE 1950

CrossCurrents (ISSN 0011-1953; online ISSN 1939-3881) connects the wisdom of the heart with the life of the mind and the experiences of the body. The journal is operated through its parent organization, the Association for Public Religion and Intellectual Life (APRIL), an interreligious network of academics, activists, artists, and community leaders seeking to engage the many ways religion meets the public. Contributions to the journal exist at the nexus of religion, education, the arts, and social justice. The journal is published quarterly on behalf of the Association for Public Religion and Intellectual Life by the University of North Carolina Press.

The Association for Public Religion and Intellectual Life (formerly ARIL) is a global network of leaders, scholars, and social change agents who explore religious life, engage in intellectual inquiry, and lead ethical action in the world today. Their primary objective, especially through annual summer colloquia and *CrossCurrents*, is to bring together leading voices of our time to advocate for justice and to examine global spiritual and interreligious currents in both historical and contemporary perspectives.

A membership to APRIL includes access to *CrossCurrents* starting with Volume 58, 2008, though our partners at Project MUSE, monthly newsletters, early access to summer colloquium themes, a 40% on UNC Press books, and more. For more information, including membership and subscription rates, visit www.aprilonline.org.

This reissue of *CrossCurrents* was one of four issues published in 2017 as part of Volume 67. For a current masthead visit www.aprilonline.org.

© 2017 Association for Public Religion and Intellectual Life. All rights reserved.

ISBN 978-1-4696-6691-4 (Print)

CROSSCURRENTS

BLACK RELIGIONS IN BRAZIL

6
Introduction
Cláudio Carvalhaes and Marcos Rodrigues da Silva

15
An Afro-American History: Paths for a Theological and Epistemological Afro Reflection
Marcos Rodrigues da Silva

35
Toward a Black Theology in Brazil
Leontino Faria dos Santos

55
Black Theology in Brazil: Decolonial and Marginal
Ronilso Pacheco

65
Being a Black Pastoral Agent in the Context of Brazilian Reality
José Geraldo da Rocha and Cristina da Conceição Silva

74
Black Pastoral Agents and The Bible in the Afro Context: A Hermeneutic of Years of Enchantment
Obertal Xavier Ribeiro

86
African-Indigenous Jurema: The Greatest Common Divisor of the Brazilian Minimum Religion
Nancy Cardoso and Cláudio Carvalhaes

105
Christians and Yorubá People Eating Together:
Eucharist and Food Offerings
Cláudio Carvalhaes

145
The Importance of the Intersectionality in the Studies of
Gender and Religion: A Short Analysis of the Ogum Omimkayê in Salvador, Brazil
Sílvia Barbosa

157
Liberation Theology in Brazil: Some History, Names and Themes
Cláudio Carvalhaes and Fábio Py

180
Notes on Contributors

About the Cover: Zabumba Black Musicians from the State of Maranhão in Brazil
Title: Pandeirinhos ou Repinicadores
Photographer: Marcos Palhano
http://marcospalhano.wix.com/fotografias
https://youpic.com/photographer/olhodobturador/marcos-palhano
olhodobturador@gmail.com

RELIGIÕES NEGRAS NO BRASIL

183
Introdução
Cláudio Carvalhaes and Marcos Rodrigues da Silva

192
Uma História Afro-Americana: Caminhos Para Uma Reflexão Teológica e Epistemológica Afro
Marcos Rodrigues da Silva

213
Por Uma Teologia Negra no Brasil
Leontino Faria dos Santos

233
A Teologia Negra no Brasil é Decolonial e Marginal
Ronilso Pacheco

243
Ser Agente de Pastoral Negros no Contexto da Realidade Brasileira
José Geraldo da Rocha and Cristina da Conceição Silva

252
Agentes de Pastoral Negros e a Bíblia no Contexto Afro: Uma Hermenêutica de Anos de Encanto
Obertal Xavier Ribeiro

265
Jurema Afro-Indígena: O Máximo Divisor Comum da Religião Mínima Brasileira
Nancy Cardoso e Cláudio Carvalhaes

284
Os Cristãos e Yorubás Comendo Juntos: Eucaristia e Oferendas
Cláudio Carvalhaes

327
A Importância da Interseccionalidade nos Estudos de Gênero e Religião: Uma Breve Análise Sobre o Ilê Asé Ogum Omimkayê (Salvador, Bahia)
Sílvia Barbosa

340
Teologia da Libertação: História, Temas e Nomes
Cláudio Carvalhaes and Fábio Py

365
Autores

About the Cover: Estilo Zabumba Maranhão
Título: Pandeirinhos ou Repinicadores
Fotógrafo: Marcos Palhano
http://marcospalhano.wix.com/fotografias
https://youpic.com/photographer/olhodobturador/marcos-palhano
olhodobturador@gmail.com

CROSSCURRENTS

GENERAL INTRODUCTION. BLACK RELIGIONS IN BRAZIL

Cláudio Carvalhaes

Brazil has never been a paradise where races could live together in peace and harmony. The myth of the "cordial man"[1] in Brazilian society, an archetype of the common Brazilian citizen who, while not made necessarily of kindness, was surely made of affection. This belief in this affection covered, like an ideological leaf, the cruelty and the historical vicious violence of Brazil's deep-grounded racism. Thus, as we believed in the Brazilian affection, we created the image of a harmonious and peaceful country. However, this apparent form of being Brazilian was the pride for some and death for others. Even though racism, corruption ande class strug-gle have been present throughout Brazilian history, it has only recently that, for many, it became evident in the recent political upheaval that Brazil is facing and its consequent fights everywhere: anger, hatred, division and confusion on the streets, schools, churches, and within families. Once the wealth of some and the power of dominance started to shift hands, the concept of the "cordial man" was thrown into the abyss. What we see today in Brazil is a ruthless abandonment and persecution of the black and indigenous populations and other minorities.

The fact that Brazil has never had a civil war/civil rights movement to wrestle with its racist history, as if there was never a kind of "in your face" ongoing historical violence to be grappled with, made people "feel" that Brazil was not/is not racist. The white washing ideology of a cordial country allowed Brazilians to ignore its deep-seated forms of racism, but the colonial history of Brazil can be told under one single word: racism. Brazil was the last country to sign the law against slavery. The white elite that came to Brazil, and who continue to control the country, is the same elite that rules the economic financial market, the creation of the laws, and the political power. In the deep veins of Brazil's colonial history runs the thick blood of indigenous and black people.

I believe that the discovery of how I was individually formed and shaped by blackness mirrors in some ways what happens in Brazil as a whole. Through the denial of blackness, emotional, physical, and intellectual erasure of black roots, fear of anything black, demonizing of black religions, and the self-denial of my own racism, I never had to engage my own blackness and could hide under my accepted whiteness. I could easily pass as simply white. In the same way, liberation theologies still owe a debt to black people. Liberation theologies could easily pass (and often do) as a white male heterosexual theology under the tropics.

In the same way, liberation theologians failed to grasp the depth of the racist oppression in Brazil. While liberation theology appeared in Latin American in late 60s, the work of black theologians did not start to appear until the 80s as Latin American theologians did not fully engage with racism as a fundamental form of oppression in the continent. The U.S. theologian James Cone spoke often at EATWOT, and repeatedly criticized Latin American theologians for their racist blind spots, but even now theological and religious departments in Brazil are filled mostly with white males. The work of Black Liberation Theology happened through small movements in different places around Brazil but without any institutional support for male and female black scholars. The result is that the theological production of a Black Theology has been small, sparse, and yet to be developed.

Despite the slow and stubborn start, recognition of Black Liberation Theology in Brazil is growing. The religious, cultural, political, and economic scenario is now very different. A new social order, with new challenges, religions and religious formations, social religious actors, feelings, forms of socialization, technologies, communication formats, economic neoliberal formations, transnational partnerships, sexualities, desires, and material needs, has created new demands, new forms of oppression, new challenges, and new forms of violence. These are hard times, demanding new forms of black thinking that are yet to be imagined.

Surely, the scope of this journal is much smaller than the challenges of our time. What this journal offers is a short historical account of liberation theology in Brazil and the (small) place in which Black Theology has been historically developed. This journal suggests potential: a sense of what has been done, what is possible and yet unimagined, and the complex intersectionalities of interreligious black thinking in Brazil. This journal brings together the work of several black thinkers who are developing black forms of thinking within a very hostile, anti-black environment. That hostility extends especially to black women, who are some of the most marginalized groups in Brazil. Even in this collection, we have only three women. This I believe is the biggest weakness of this journal, and we pledge as theologians to leverage more space for women as the conversation continues. We invite the critique, knowing that we have so far failed to fully examine our own racism and sexism and that we too perpetuate oppression. The patriarchal weight on the formation and development of liberation theologies in Latin America has made invisible the voices of black women in particular! Feminist voices, movements, and spaces have been suppressed and invisibilized. I invite those with strong critique to enter into dialogue with the texts and/or to submit their own essays for further work. We need more people publicly engaging this work, especially women, queer, and indigenous people, to begin as soon as possible another further volume.

There is much work to do! This project is a beginning, a conduit for a few voices, a reaching out to companions in this work, and a sharing of the public platform we collectively have established. This journal offers itself as a small volume of essays as a starting point for conversation, an invitation to deeper study and further reflection. We expect this is just the beginning and that more voices will pick up and continue the work that needs to be done. The future is pregnant with a new mo(ve)ment that examines what has been done, expands, breaks, and takes it to other communities, other social needs, with other forms of praxis and theories, and surely new forms of liberation! We must continue to blacken our theologies so that our black theologies will also blacken the class struggles. Our work cannot continue without extensive consideration of the intersection of race, class, gender, indigeneity, ableism, sexualities, and ecology.

The challenges of translation were huge, and it was nearly impossible to fully convey culture and context in a language that is not of the people. My gratitude to Tiago Chiavegatti, Alice da Cunha, and Josefina Terrena for translating these texts into English, to Katie Mulligan who edited as much as possible, these articles in English, and to Mercia Carvalhaes for editing the texts in Portuguese. We were all limited by the difficulties of translation, and not every word is explained or nuanced in a way that the English readers might need or want. Retaining the nuanced voices of the authors across translation requires some additional effort on the part of you, the reader, to grasp what is meant. We thank you, as well. I am also very grateful for the many ways we received support from Union Theological Seminary in New York City. Without Union, this project would have not come to fruition.

Finally, I am very grateful to the capable and brilliant writers who participated in this journal. I am delighted to edit this volume with Dr. Marcos Silva, who is part of one of the most critical groups of black thinkers in Brazil called Atabaque. He initiated this project and I have been honored to help put it together. To him my deepest gratitude for this gift!

Gayraud S. Wilmore defines the history of the African American people in United States this way: "Three dominant themes or motifs stand out as foundational from August 1619 Jamestown, Virginia, landing of the first forced arrival of Africans to the present. They are: survival, elevation and liberation."[2] I believe we could recount the history of all African people in the Americas in this way. Engaging in this project for me has drawn me deeper into this same history, into the same forms of survival, elevation, and liberation. Surely, this project has provided a way of learning to love more and better a people I call my own!

Introduction

Marcos Rodrigues da Silva

The cultural diversity and the elaboration of an Afro epistemology from Brazil constitute fields of studies where theological and philosophical thinking can hardly be delimited due to the innumerable and tenuous and tense borders within many fields of knowledge. However, this is our intent for this journal as we begin a reflection based on the historical Afro movements of struggles and the social and ecclesial commitments from various traditions of faith and knowledges. It is not our aim here to work from or defend a hypothesis that is clearly delimited by one form of knowledge or thinking.

We start in the second half of the 20th century, when the theological movement to emphasize the realities of the poor in Latin America emerged, and when the method of analysis and thinking had an Eurocentric foundation.[3] This Eurocentric form of thinking offered narrow and specific markers for the interpretation of acts and behaviors of the poor. In this journal, we focus on contributions from beliefs and knowledges made by black peoples of the Afro-American diaspora, as well as from universal knowledges, scientific and technological reflections. All of these knowledges can offer, in their own way, references for the survival of the planet and new possibilities for the relations between individuals, groups, and societies.

We take the notion of diversity as our first premise. We are diverse. This fundamental truth is always endangered by individual and collective actions of intolerance. We are historically, ethnically, and linguistically diverse, as well as religiously diverse.

Our religious diversity is profound. Our diversity is everywhere: It exists among atheists and religious people, among distinctive religious traditions such as Christians, Buddhists, Muslims, followers of African religions, and so on. It also exists within religious branches that share a common bud, such as Judaism and Islam, and Christianity, or even culturally different as expressions of the same faith in different places and periods, like Spanish and North-American Catholics. Our diversity is also present within traditions and religions built upon orality, such as Native Americans and Afro-Americans.

As Albert Memmi says, "While every colonial person finds itself in the condition of a colonizer, not every colonizer is irrevocably destined to become a colonialist. And the best ones refuse to do so."[4] Memmi's distinction between being a colonizer and asserting oneself as a colonialist is a dialectic relation that involves the being and living together of oppressed and oppressor. In this sense, Memmi finds a connection between a notion of a hierarchy based on race and the control of the many forms of material and symbolic production in the colonized regions.

At the same time, Memmi makes warns of the consequences of being black colonized and enslaved: "This excitement towards colonizer values would not be so suspicious, however, if it did not carried in itself its very opposite. The colonized does not merely seek to enrich himself with the colonizer virtues."[5]

And Memmi stresses that repression is one of the catalysts for producing knowledge of the colonized people, with their symbolic universes and their referentials of sense. The author also points to a struggle for self-affirmation during the process of destruction of a people, identities, and histories: "The colonized accepts and affirms himself, claim himself with passion." But who is this colonized? It is certainly not the regular man, holder of universal values that are common to every man.[6]

Finally, we can see in our liberation theologies the partial imposition of the culture of the dominators, since it was necessary to the control and instrumentalization of local cultures according to the logic of the new standard of power.

Contextualization of the subject

Our aim is to look at the study and reflections of Afro-Brazilian researchers and analyze the journey travelled in their practices and studies. We intend, with these articles, to bring forward and systematize what this exercise of elaboration means in the context of the Latin American theology. Everything takes place from a communal practice, modeled from family communities, terreiros, sanctuaries, supplemented by other practices that come from academic studies. Several factors were brought together for that, including many elements of an Afro epistemology in the second half of the last century to our current moment.

We do not take this starting point as a limit, but we focus on a large territory that allows movements of encountering the significant theoretical productions that arise from there. This territory comprises the environment that acknowledges the traditional African religions, the various religious practices of the Western Christian tradition that are, first and foremost, marked by their cultural diversities. The approximation of this study means to understand the place (or places) in the Afro religious landscape, recognizing the "others" not as competitors but as true partners in an existential adventure of faith/religion.

Among the universe of productions and systems we focus on here, we would like to develop the investigation on how discourses express themselves and manifest symbolic and/or disguised forms. We verify the identity character of Knowledge, what has been experienced and lived, and how it can be grasped. In order to do that, it is necessary to be able to identify things, people, events through naming, describing, and interpreting, using appropriated concepts and language.

Currently, the studies on religion and Afro religion value religious phenomena in various ways. There is a recognition of religious issues that permeate daily life like folk religion, under the many forms of spirituality, that provide elements to build identities. They are the building material of collective memories, mystical experiences, and cultural and intellectual trends that are not limited to the realm of organized and institutional churches.

Using this recognition as a landmark, the central objects are the epistemological elements for an Afro-American Theology and a dialogue with the theological discussions to affirm an Afro-American Theology.

There is a construction of a new set of interpretation tools based on the experiences of the Afro people of the African diaspora in Brazil and on their particular way of living, knowing, and being amidst secular adversities. It is critical to remember respect for diversity as one of the most important values to fully exercise one's citizenship. Only with absolute respect for diversity is it possible to understand and overcome assertions that sects do not exist (since there are large and small religions), nor syncretism (because a pure religion, devoid of influence for not religions, does not exist), and above all, to insist that no religion is better than the other from the perspective of historians, philosophers, and religion scientists. Each religious experience contributes to a portion of the religious thinking; each systematization of religious practices expresses the vision of a particular group, and each behavior witnessed had and has its own specific value, precisely for being and making clear the difference.

Theological reflection in the context of Afro experiences and practices has been conceptualized in different ways: Black Theology in the United States.[7] Incultured Theology in some African regions; Black Liberation Theology and Theology in Context, in other African regions[8] ; Afro-American Theology, in Latin America; Antilles Theology on the Caribbean.

On a personal level, it is essential that the individual recognizes himself as the maker and actor of his own history. In terms of blackness, this means to accept oneself as black. On a community level, the exigence is to accept the traditions, myths, and celebration practices, with their particularities and similarities. To accept that is to recognize the struggles of everyday life, expressed in poverty and practices of exclusion.

We present a view on "Being Black Pastoral Agent in the context of Brazilian reality" by the theologian Geraldo Rocha and the PhD candidate Cristina da Conceição. The biblicist theologian Obertal seeks a biblical–theological look on the practices of black pastoral agents and the Bible in an Afro context; Cláudio Carvalhaes writes about "Christians and Yorubá People Eating Together—Eucharist and Food Offerings", and offers possibilities of dialogue between two often distant religions; Marcos Rodrigues points to elements for "An Afro-American History: paths for a theological and epistemological reflection"; Nancy Cardoso and Cláudio Carvalhaes, departing from the Afro-Native-Brazilian religion of Jurema, propose a dialog with the possibilities of Black Theology regarding all the shades of native peoples as a task of the whole Liberation Theology, particularly regarding the life and struggles of women; Rev. Leontino Farias dos Santos presents a script "For a Black Theology in Brazil" using as a starting point the persistent racist practices in Brazilian society to point to the necessity of developing a Black Theology that causes us to think about racism under the light of biblical–theological premises of liberating and prophetic intent; Silvia Barbosa and Maria Gabriela Hita develop the intersectionality of race, class, gender, age/generation in the Candomblé Ilê Asé Ogum Omimkaye in Bahia and help us see the ways in which blackness is shaped/developed in a Afro-Brazilian religion. Finally, the theologian Ronilson Pacheco shows that

"Black Theology in Brazil is decolonial and marginal" in a context of violence, racism, and the fight for rights and for recognition that profoundly marks the life of blacks in Brazil.

The paths of Afro-American and Caribbean theology, more than merely pointing to a theological itinerary, have the obligation to reflect, emphasize, and highlight all those who are touched by the struggles of the black people. This is hardly a theological novelty, but a deepening of a reflection anchored on a singular reality that intends to reveal the witness, the compromise, and the solidarity of the black community regarding the changes in the reality in which they live in Latin America.

Notes

1. Buarque de Holanda, Sérgio, Raízes do Brasil (São Paulo: Companhia das Letras, 2015).
2. Wilmore, Gayraud S., "Historical Perspective," The Cambridge Companion to Black Theology. Edited by Dwight N. Hopkins and Edward P. Antonio (Cambridge: Cambridge University Press, 2012), 19.
3. Three sources will be essential to understand this period. Freire, P., Hassmann, H., Malumba, E., and Cone, J. Teologia Negra—Teologia de La Liberación, Ediciones Sígueme, Salamanca, 1974; CONE, J. and WILMORE, G. Teologia Negra, EP, Sao Paulo, 1986. ASETT (org.) Identidade Negra e Religião—Consulta sobre Cultura Negra e Teologia na América Latina, CEDI/Edições Liberdade, Sao Paulo, 1986.
4. MEMMI, Albert, Retrato do Colonizado precedido do retrato do colonizador, Civilização Brasileira, Rio de Janeiro/RJ, 2007, p. 55.
5. Idem. p. 165-164.
6. Idem, p. 173-174.
7. James H. Cone expresses as following his understanding about making Black Theology in North America:[...] Comenzaré mi exposicións dando uma deficición de libertad, historia y esperanza. Examinarédespuéslasconsecuenciasteológicas que de ahí se deducen.[...] VV.AA. Teologia Negra-teologia de La liberacion, Ediciones Sígueme-Salamanca, 1974, p. 63.
8. In Africa, since the times of the Second Vatican Council, Vicente Mulago and others already talked about "Black Theology and cultures". During the 70s, James Cone had already demonstrated that it was not only legitimate but necessary and timely to reflect on theology using blackness as a key, or vice versa. During the last two decades of the last century, both in Africa and in the diaspora, the legitimacies and the necessity of Black Theology were recognized.

CROSSCURRENTS

AN AFRO-AMERICAN HISTORY
Paths for a Theological and Epistemological Afro Reflection

Marcos Rodrigues da Silva

Introduction

At the Round of Talks on Ethnic Territorialities and Intercultural Relations, a series of reflections was raised. This convocation was part of the Second Seminar on International Culture and Development (SICDES), which took place at Unochapecó, Santa Catarina (Brazil), in May 2014, and also as part of the Thematic Symposium on African, Afro-Latino, and Latin-American Issues and their Contemporary Challenges in the Second International Congress of EST Colleges on September 2014. These meetings were critical moments that opened a dialogue to share our reflections on a significant topic for the entire Afro-American community.

Drawing from these meetings, our task in this chapter is to present an inventory of the history of Afro-American thought worldwide, derived from the contributions of Black movements that emerged in the 1970s, 1980s, and 1990s of the 20th century. These meetings and the reflections that came about provide us with a database of significant elements that support theological production, and open up a path for reflection capable of signaling new scenarios for the first years of the 21st century.

The congresses on black culture in the Americas

The initiative to organize the Congress on Black Culture in the Americas arose from the need for a multidisciplinary examination of the social and cultural problematics of Afro-Americans by various professionals, such as historians, sociologists, anthropologists, artists, writers, theologians, and scientists of religion (ACTAS..., 1989). The program for these Congresses was inspired by thematic lines arising from the different contexts of Latin America and the Caribbean.

The first Congress on Black Culture in the Americas occurred in Cali, Colombia, from August 24, 1977, to August 28, 1977. This congress was convened and supported by the Colombian Foundation of Folk Researchers (ACTAS..., 1989). Its goal was to promote a reflection by Afro-Americans on the political cultural, economic, and religious obstacles and barriers imposed by settlers, and still in force against Afro-Americans. Participants were divided into four working groups. The first group dealt with the political, religious, aesthetic, and moral issues. The second group focused on issues related to socioeconomic structures. The third group analyzed art and technology. Finally, the fourth group reflected ethnicity and miscegenation.

According to the participants, several countries seek to decrease the Black population, using strategies that include forced miscegenation as artifice. It is not our intention today to make a full report of the entire Congress, but it seems fundamental to bring up two recommendations approved at this event. First, to denounce that most History, Sociology, Economics, and Politics textbooks from American countries omit, cripple, and deform the authentic participation of Black people in the development of the countries that they are a fundamental part of. Second, the realization that the history of Black America cannot continue to be disseminated, written, and internalized on as a chronicle of slavery (ACTAS..., 1989). In addition to its substantial content, the first Congress on Black Culture was important in itself as a truly historic event.

With the theme "Cultural Identity of Black People in the Americas," the second Congress was held in Panama City from March 12–21, 1980. The event brought together over three hundred delegates from America, Africa, and Europe. Four subthemes concerning issues related to the Black community were debated: (1) social identification in the class structure; (2) cultural identity of Black people in their formal and informal education; (3) cultural pluralism and national unity; and (4) the prospects of Black people in the future of the Americas.

Among the topics discussed, the most relevant was the Cultural Issue of Afro-Americans, from which three points emerged: (1) the urgency of formulating an educational project in which the participation of the Black diaspora culture is as relevant to the construction of a Black identity as the dominant culture has been to the fragmentation and denial of social identity of Black people; (2) to redeem the underlying worldview of these cultural manifestations, taking into account the updated experiences of Black resistance; and (3) the articulation of political action with a cultural dimension as a starting point.

The issue of sociopolitical movements was discussed during the Congress, indicating some areas where reflection and action are needed, such as socioeconomic and cultural marginalization, abandoned children, political parties, agrarian issues, unemployment, women's status, police violence, and the extermination of Black people (ACTAS..., 1989).

Four other issues were also discussed: (1) a project for an international organization of Black people; (2) the creation of an international association of Black people; (3) Africa and Latin Afro-American relations; and (4) the presence of Black women. The women present at this Congress declared as follows:

> We, Black women in particular, are the best example of overcoming personal challenges, of character and moral integrity, despite living in completely hostile societies that exploit our labor, gender and race. It is therefore time to recognize our merits, since the trend of minorities in power in subdued societies is to ignore us or to neglect us. It is time to recognize the pivotal role we play in transmitting the cultural values of our ancestors, and our decisive participation in the accumulation of wealth in the new American societies. We realize that in this struggle, the African, Caribbean and Latin American Black woman is fighting for a new social order that seeks to destroy all forms of economic privileges, originating in racial, sexual, intellectual and class discriminations. Thus, our struggle aims at the destruction of the domination exercised by imperialist people over colonized people (ACTAS..., 1989, pp. 111–112).

Revisiting the records and analyzing the results from these Congresses on Black Cultures, we can see how these meetings signaled an important phase in the Afro-American movement. They represented the evolution of this movement in each country and acted as a driving force for it. Furthermore, they also helped increase Black awareness at the continental level.

The Brazilian black movement: significant experiences in the Latin-American and Caribbean contexts

The Black Movement in Brazil, of course, is not homogeneous. It is actually a conglomeration of many different practices and stances that share the primary goal of fighting racism and the struggle for full participation of Black people in society. It is important to highlight three significant experiences in the latest phase of the rise in public recognition of the Brazilian Black Movement, namely the Unified Black Movement (MNU), the Group of Union and Black Consciousness (GRUCON), and the Black Pastoral Agents.

The MNU emerged in the context of the late 20th century. It is recognized as a landmark in the struggle for a national Black consciousness in the 1970s. Upon its emergence, there was a general state of police violence against the impoverished population. This violence intensified and became widespread in the peripheries of the cities of Sao Paulo and Rio de Janeiro, as well as in other major cities. We must add that Black people were the most affected as they were blamed preemptively for bank robberies, thefts, and any sort of misconduct in that sociohistorical and economical contexts. The motto "to be Black is to be suspect until proven otherwise" always prevailed.

The intense police persecution of Black children and youth caused revolt among the Black population. More than 3,000 people organized themselves and protested at the steps of the Theatro Municipal in the afternoon of July 7, 1978. This demonstration against violence and racial discrimination led to the organic initiation of the Unified Black Movement.

One key platform of the MNU at the end of the 1970s was to establish November 20th as a national day for Black Consciousness and against racial discrimination in honor the anniversary of the killing of Zumbi, a legendary leader of the Palmares Quilombo. This action was effective and resulted in the mobilization of the Black population toward gaining greater awareness of what it means to be Black in Brazil.

MNU's main audience consisted of Black university students and those linked to students' movement, which shows both its scope and its limits. It refrained from employing a strategy of popular penetration in its early stages. However, with the help of social and political sciences, MNU militants sought to establish a dialectical reading of class relations and to deepen the reflection on the mechanisms of exploitation and the violence inflicted on Black women and Black men. Despite its academic character, the MNU gathered many supporters in the 1970s and the beginning of the 1980s and even became the greatest expression of the Brazilian Black movement during that period.

Another group of equal importance was the Group of Union and Black Consciousness (GRUCON), which was directly involved in preparing the Puebla Conference.[1] Since the Church of Brazil was required to present an analysis of the situation experienced by African-Brazilians, a group of scholars (sociologists, anthropologists, theologians, pastoralists, and pastoral workers) met in Sao Paulo.[2] As a result of the exchange of observations drawn from various scientific approaches, the group reached the following conclusions: (1) It was important to not understand Black people as individuals who practice a non-Catholic cult; (2) it was unimportant to find ways to bring those individuals to the Church; (3) it was necessary to look at the global reality of the Brazilian community as a social, political, economic, and religious whole; and (4) the historical background of their current realities mattered.

The participants believed that their first task was completed, but it was in fact the beginning of a new and long process. Realizing how difficult the topic was, the group took steps to identify itself with the reality of the Black people. Since most activities fell into the ecclesial and pastoral fields, the participants became aware of the extent and the evangelical commitment posed by this challenge, and opted for an analysis of the global context in an attempt to recover the identity of the Black person. In this way, they avoided a superficial analysis of data and facts.

The historical retrospective also aided the understanding of the path traveled thus far. Often, elite scholars and religious figures traveled alone, with little influence on the daily life of local communities. Still, a social, political, cultural, and religious assessment from the point of view of Black communities highlights the presence of the message and experience of the Gospel in all its gestures and attitudes. In addition, the presence of traditional African religions is noticeable. These religions, when respected and practiced, offered guidance to the teachings of the Orishas, especially to traditional African religions in the diaspora.

The founding of GRUCON on December 5, 1978, created the Reflection and Study Group, which approved a series of activities and projects to be undertaken pursuant to the National Conference of Bishops of Brazil (CNBB). The Group rapidly grew in various states of the federation by holding thematic meetings at the national, state, and local levels. From this group, the CNBB Line II,[3] supported by the representatives of Black Pastoral Agents,[2] took a prophetic attitude and put forward a joint action.

In 1979, the Task Group met in Sao Paulo, to plan the execution of this project, and a meeting of Black pastoral workers was scheduled for February 1980. On this occasion, it was decided that the meeting would not be restricted to priests and officers of the church, but would also welcome laity and Black Pastoral Agents. Similar to previous meetings, it was an inquiry on the reality of the Black community. Another urgent issue raised by Black Pastoral Agents was the need to reflect on the reality of Black communities, African religious traditions, and African religiosity in different parts of Brazil. At first, the concern was the situation and the practice of Blacks in the Church. However, throughout the meeting, the organization of Black people in different sectors of the community was stressed.[4]

Another extremely important group for the expansion of Afro reflections was the Black Pastoral Agents (BPAs). In their first meeting, these agents gathered people from various regions of Brazil and offered some concrete suggestions for the pastoral care of the Catholic Church:

1 to stimulate and encourage contact with other colleagues who have already produced material on the subject of Black people;
2 to create a group to collect news and circulate experiences and information between groups;
3 to form Black study and action groups in the states;
4 to establish contacts with existing Black groups and participate in them;
5 to discover, enhance, and encourage Black leaders and their pastoral work in the community;
6 to contact Africans living in Brazil for integration and exchange.[5]

The path to the formation of the Black Pastoral Agents (BPA) became unavoidable. The seed spread quickly throughout the country. A message of Black awareness began to spread from the church sector to cultural, political, and popular organizations. Everywhere, the debate from the viewpoint of Black people began to be enhanced and enriched by the practice of militants. It is out of respect to the grassroots organization and to Black people that these steps were carried out.

This movement recovered the struggle of Blacks within the Church, from its ancestors to the Basic Ecclesial Communities. Furthermore, the Black Pastoral Agents were committed to work with other Black segments already existing in the country and who also prioritized the popular movements.

The first activities began in Sao Paulo, with features that resembled the movement of Black Christians. Soon, they felt the need to reflect on the experiences of the Basic Ecclesial Communities, where Black people often were a majority. Black women were major protagonists in the organization of focus groups and the mobilization of public action.

Seventy people were present during the first meeting of the BPAs[6] held on March 14 and 15 of 1983 at the Immaculate Conception Church in Sao Paulo. Most of them were pastoral workers and leaders of the Catholic communities. The theme of the meeting was as follows: "The reality experienced by Blacks and their participation in the Church of Brazil."[7] The activities at this meeting were divided into two groups: the first one, Black people in the Church of Brazil, presented by Father Antonio Aparecido da Silva,[8] who sought to situate the reality of Black people in Brazilian churches. The second group, themed "Church, power, and Blackness," was coordinated by Fr. Mauro Baptista,[9] who tried to locate the experience of Black people in society and in the Church, and analyzed the experience of Black people in capitalist society, upholding the thesis that the entire Black community is the product of not having, not being, not being able and not knowing.

From this first meeting of the BPAs, several propositions emerged as follows: (1) develop a focus on grassroots work as a way to raise awareness and promote liberation; (2) as pastoral agents, be aware of discrimination, denounce it, and assume one's own Blackness; (3) bring people together, form groups, and pass on the experiences gained to create awareness; (4) broaden the discussion about discrimination and marginalization of Black people with families, work colleagues, acquaintances, etc.; (5) awaken the conscience of White people as recipients of a discriminatory and racist heritage; (6) learn and study the origins and critically delve into the events of the community; (7) seek to raise awareness among Black couples and especially children, leading them to embrace their own Blackness; (8) enhance local and regional meetings and larger conferences; (9) create a team to elaborate sources from the reality of Black people; and (10) hold two annual meetings for pastoral agents, preferably Black, to touch upon the subject of Blackness.

Six months later, on September 6–7, 1983, the second meeting of the BPAs took place at the Immaculate Conception Church in Sao Paulo. This meeting was attended by approximately 100 people, among them pastoral agents, lay people, priests, religious men and women, and representatives of other Black movements. The discussions revolved around routing and resolving actions in the face of a liberating pastoral movement. Furthermore, they addressed the actual concern of how pastoral workers could take on their identity and liberation with their brothers.

The exhibition of Candomblé set up for the occasion unveiled the deep ignorance and racial prejudice from Black Pastoral Agents toward Afro-Brazilian cults.[7] Another significant moment was the formation of think tanks that gave rise to three basic questions: What is the specific task of Black pastoral workers? Is Christianity a religion for Black people or does a coherent Blackness require conversion to Candomblé?

The helpful formation of a liberating catechesis where Black people were perceived from their own reality followed these points: (1) connecting the Black struggles with various popular struggles; (2) raising awareness among priests, pastors, religious, and seminarians and encourage them to embrace their Blackness and the struggle of being Black; (3) using the pastoral as a space for awareness on the Negro question; (4) taking advantage of strong periods in pastoral activity (like the devotion to Our Lady of Aparecida in October) to raise broader awareness; (5) including the issues of Black people in the Christmas novena, in the Fraternity Campaign, etc.; (6) promoting masses and liturgical celebrations with African-Brazilian rituals; (7) emphasizing the 20th of November—Black Consciousness Day—creating a foundation to denounce racism; (8) putting together those resources for the work of the different groups; (9) taking advantage of the Month of the Bible to use the resources, revise the facts, maintaining as a central theme the bondage of Black people and their hopes of liberation; (10) helping the Church become "Blacker" by taking on the struggle of Black people and also by Blackening its own ranks (more Black community leaders, seminarians, nuns, pastors, priests, bishops); (11) ensuring that the meetings of Black pastoral workers continued to be a space to share experiences.[10]

The following year, the third meeting of the BPAs took place from April 30, 1984, to May 1, 1984. Approximately 150 people participated. The topics discussed were as follows: (1) educating Black people in the Brazilian educational system, (2) Black people in the history of Brazil and official textbooks, (3) the effects of formal and informal education on the learner, (4) Black children in the renewed catechesis, and (5) popular religiosity from the perspective of those living north of Minas, in Gerais, and in Bahia.

From August 7 to August 9 of the same year, the BPAs had their fourth meeting in accordance with the proposal to hold training meetings for the participating agents. Work groups and panels explored these themes: (1) the Brazilian economic crisis and Black people; (2) the reality of Black people; (3) the situation of Black women in popular media. Always using a model of presentations followed by a discussion and a reflection, the meeting achieved its proposed objectives: an opening to the presence of Black people, in concrete situations of the Catholic Church, and society in general; a dynamism and organization of the Basic Ecclesial Communities and the popular movement. The conclusions of the meeting were summarized in the following proposals: (1) a deepened understanding of the topics; (2) an expansion of the reflections on African religions; (3) discussion of the meaning and experience of African-Brazilian culture; (4) Black people in the current society and police violence in the context of racism. At each encounter, agents became progressively more engaged and expanded their reflections; additionally, a greater number of people were reached.

At the opening the fifth meeting of BPAs, a special tribute was paid to Fr. Antonio Aparecido da Silva, director of the Our Lady of the Assumption Faculty of Theology in Sao Paulo. His presence in that institution enabled the next meetings of BPAs. In this fifth meeting, a training course for BPAs was designed to analyze in depth the racial issue. As opposed to the other courses that happened every six months, this new training took place annually.

The first one was held on May 4–5, 1985, with "Constituent Assembly and Blackness" as the theme. With about 250 attendees, the event included a significant presence of first-time participants. They were Black pastoral workers who wished to put forward their questions on the topic approached from the perspective of the Black community. There was a reflection on a pedagogical proposal covering the difficulties encountered by these agents during their pastoral work with the Black community. One suggestion was to prepare a booklet written in a simple and accessible language that conveyed basic notions of the constitutional process and the role of Black people in politics. This participatory meeting strengthened the activities of the agents in their own communities, and enabled discussions for a new constituent assembly, which would be enacted in 1988.

The sixth meeting occurred on September 15–16, 1985, at the Faculty of Theology, Our Lady of the Assumption, where approximately 300 people attended. The methodology and themes were divided into three groups: The first dealt with two topics, "The reality of Black people in Brazil," and "Liturgy and Blackness." The working group was intended to include those people considered to be newcomers to the movement. The second group worked on the theme "Blackness and a Constituent Assembly," as a continuation of the fifth meeting. The third group was intended to gather the more experienced members, who debated on the subject of "Blackness and Agrarian Reform." At this meeting, the implementation of the Central Quilombo, as a gathering space, was reinforced.

The seventh meeting of BPAs took place at the Faculty of Theology, Our Lady of the Assumption on April 19–20, 1986. The themes discussed at this meeting were as follows: (1) Black people and the land (in tenement houses, in slums, in the rural area); (2) the martyrs of the walk; (3) the identity of Black Pastoral Agents. Besides the debates and the study groups, participants also experienced the joy of one another's company which strengthened the fight against racism and the embrace of Blackness in every participant. During the closing, a rich liturgy was celebrated.

The Training Course for BPAs took place between June 29, 1985, and July 3, 1985, at the Faculty of Theology, Our Lady of Assumption. The content was developed in response to the common difficulties of Black Pastoral Agents, in their regular pastoral work within CEBs (Base Ecclesial Communities) with themes involving Afro-Brazilian religions. Thus, the course's topic was "Worship and Faith: the Black community celebrates faith." The reflections were conducted by Fr. Mauro Baptista, who sought to highlight the issue of the African-Brazilian religiosity within the complexity of popular religiosity. There was also the effective participation of Fr. Antonio Aparecido da Silva, who emphasized the Black religious manifestations in Brazil within popular Catholicism.

As a Candomblé practitioner, Prof. Dra. Maria de Lourdes from the Federal University of Bahia (UFBA) analyzed the values present in the Candomblé rite and the secrets of African-Brazilian religions. Later, Fr. Edir, theologian and founder of the BPA, gave a seminar titled "Black People and Liturgical Celebration."

The results, like on previous meetings, were presented as proposals asking communities to deepen their understanding of the topics discussed and, at their pace, materialize them in their pastoral actions or popular movement. The following proposals were presented: (1) intensify the studies on Candomblé; (2) carry out black liturgy in our communities and homes; (3) search for festive dates; (4) seek to work with priests; (5) prepare resources for black liturgy; (6) promote debates in the communities; (7) take advantage of other liturgies beyond the Eucharist; (8) expand the issues and concerns of the black; and (9) reflect on the history of black people in grassroots groups.[11]

In parallel to the biannual meetings, the second BPAs training took place from June 29, 1986, to 30 June, 1986, with about 120 participants. Study topics were assigned to the three panels: (1) Black people in the current sociopolitical and economic contexts; (2) Blackness and faith in Candomblé; and (3) Blackness and faith in the Methodist and Catholic churches. An agenda was built to guide pastoral workers and leaders of base communities, Black clubs, sororities, congadas, and Black neighborhood associations. In this process, the Atabaque Center was created with a summary of the proposed content to be researched and elucidated.

The BPAs today are recognized as an organic Afro-Brazilian institution in society, one of the most widespread in the country. Its members are people acting in diverse sectors of society and the Church with the primary goal of reflecting on the status of Black people, with a commitment to seek social change together with other poor people. They take on the mission to "blacken" the Church, which means, to work through the Christian faith in communities scattered throughout Brazil, from the standpoint of Afro cultures and religious practices.

The movements of the Black Pastoral Agents in central and Latin America and the Caribbean

The Afro-American Pastoral Meetings arose from the desire and the need to articulate the working initiatives carried out in Black communities of Central and Latin America and the Caribbean. Although the term pastoral gives the connotation of an initiative linked to the Catholic Church, the meetings have convened at the discretion and will of the leaders of Afro pastoral groups, active in different countries, who were not welcomed or guided by the Church's hierarchy.

The first meeting discussed popular religiosity and Black culture. It was held in Buenaventura, Colombia, in 1980. Although representation was not as broad, the meeting kick-started a process that gradually gained greater official participation from the Church. Among the conclusions from this meeting, we highlight the following: (1) the need for scientific research on Afro-American culture; (2) the value of an increased awareness of the cultural problematic of Afro-American communities; (3) the need to challenge churches to a pastoral commitment that includes the Black community; and (4) the need to seek appropriate ways to use religious expressions from Black culture. Participants also warned against the shallow folklorization of the Afro-American culture.[12] The reports and published material based on the discussions from the meeting were eventually distributed to the participating countries.

The second meeting was held in 1982 at Esmeraldas, Ecuador, with the theme "Identity and history of Afro-American people in light of the history of salvation" and included a larger number of participants. They debated and addressed in depth the historical fact of widespread denial of Black identity and other oppressed people in the continent. They insisted on the need to collaborate with the processes of affirmation of Afro-American identity. Moreover, they found that there was a lot of misinformation regarding Black people and emphasized the importance of a deeper reflection on the model of integration of people and cultures toward a greater egalitarian society.

As reflections were made based on historical elements, the discussion of values and anti-values was certainly considered. It was important to factor them in. This second meeting reaffirmed the need to discover and analyze in depth the liberating power of the Word of God in the Afro community in order to understand, both in history and in our present times, the signs of salvation. As a way forward, it was proposed that theologians should work on a theology based on the Gospel that reveals the Afro-American face of God.[13]

The third meeting took place in Porto Belo, Panama, in 1986. The theme chosen was "Afro-American Identity and pastoral care." At this meeting, they discussed how the Black population greatly contributed to diffuse popular religiosity in Latin America and the Caribbean, from an angle of joy and celebration. The participants affirmed the importance of keeping the identity of Black communities through the valorization of the historical memory that would prevent the dilution and loss of the Afro-American and Caribbean specificities.

The fourth meeting took place in Puerto Limon, Costa Rica, in 1989. The theme of this meeting was "The Afro-American family," an attempt to look deeper into the way of life and structure of families in Black communities, as well as its particularities. The Black family has values that reveal its deep commitment to the defense of life, with some key features: (1) blood relationship (parents, children, relatives, and cronies, etc.); (2) listening and respect for elders; (3) broad understanding of family; and (4) openness to the collective good. These characteristics of Black families should form the basis for pastoral action. Although deeply affected by slavery in the past and marginalization in the present, the Black family is one of the landmarks of the resistance of Afro-American people.[14]

The fifth Afro-American Pastoral Meeting was held in Quibdo, Colombia, in June 1991. The presence of two hundred and twenty delegates from different countries, representing various Black organizations, was very significant. The theme was "Pastoral and Afro-American Education." The goal was to encourage the development of a project for Afro-American education, calling for a debate on the Black cause in churches and governments. Another goal for the meeting was to bring about a genuine Latin-American reflection on the Afro-American Pastoral Meetings.

According to the participants' evaluations, the meeting was fruitful and positive since the debates were clarifying.[15]

For the sixth meeting, participants went once again to Esmeraldas, Ecuador, on September 19–20, 1994. This meeting was attended by 180 people from 14 countries: Brazil, Colombia, Costa Rica, Ecuador, Haiti, Honduras, Mexico, Peru, Dominican Republic, Benin, Mozambique, Uganda, and Zaire. The discussions on issues addressed at previous meetings were resumed. Reflecting more deeply on the topic of Afro-American spirituality, the meeting strengthened Black Christian communities, pulling from their own spiritual experiences rooted in cultural and religious traditions of African origin.[16]

We can conclude that Afro-American and Brazilian movements in the 1980s and 1990s drew attention to the different forms of organization of the Afro-American community. Another mark from this period was the unforgettable Black Front, which was active precisely when the military dictatorship was coercing Black organizations, arresting its members and closing their meeting places.

From the Ecumenical Consultations of Afro-American and Caribbean Theologies and Cultures comes the concept that Afro-American people are the living and challenging face of the suffering servant who calls Christian churches to account and is systematically put through a state of exclusion by the intricate relations of Latin-American society.

During the final three decades of the 20th century, Christian churches found in their pastoral experiences new challenges and paradigms that came from Afro-American communities demanding a new way of living and announcing the Gospel. Among the new challenges and paradigms are the racism, prejudice, segregation, discrimination, and violence against Black people that, in a way, are already institutionalized and internalized into daily life.

This encounter with the reality experienced by Black communities is clearly apparent in the documents and attitudes of lay Christian leadership and in an outspoken faction of the ecclesiastical hierarchy. Although shy and timid, the first steps were taken to bring to light scandals present inside and outside the churches.

Some questions were raised for a theological-pastoral reflection, in order to understand and to seek the proper evangelical attitude to overcome the evil that restricts the rights of the Afro-American population.

We know that theology happens through the spontaneous experience of God's revelation, but it is complemented by human words seeking to demonstrate the purpose of faith, a gift from God. Every theological reflection arises from the limits that people—the faith communities—encounter while seeking to understand the divine purpose.

It is from these experiences of faith experienced in Afro-American communities that we can, from the perspective of religious studies, ask some questions about the Afro-American theological reflection: How do we facilitate and create opportunities for Afro-American people to reaffirm their spaces and autonomy in their practice of faith, specific cultures, and full citizenship rights? What sort of interventions could be used to foster an ecumenical dialog among traditional African religions: Candomblé, Tambor de Mina, Reisados, and Congo, for example, and Christian churches? What ecumenical liturgical practices can answer this common desire within communities of faith to celebrate the God of life? When are we going to be able to take part in the great feast of the Lord gathered around the common values of Afro-American traditions? Which prophetic course of action must be taken to put a definitive end to certain attitudes within the churches that degrade women at all levels, especially in ministry?

These are some of the pertinent questions that permeate the dialogue and the practices of syncretism and ecumenism, of an Afro-American and Afro-Brazilian perspective and experience. Thus, the agendas of the churches will be enlarged to take on a new pastoral practice and to insert themselves into Afro-American realities. The specificities of this particular population must be recognized and protected. In this way, Afro communities will affirm the value of self-esteem as a sign of dignity of the Afro-American population.

In a search process for the assertion of these ideals came the Atabaque Center—Black Culture and Theology,[17] through the reflections of its members in a space for discussion, reflection, and proposals from the experiences of all these organic movements of the Black community in Brazil. The Atabaque received the important task of putting together the Ecumenical Consultation on Afro-American and Caribbean Theology. The First Consultation was held from July 8 to 12, 1985, in Nova Iguaçu, a suburb on the outskirts of Rio de Janeiro, a place of concentration for Black communities in southern Brazil. These communities, besides suffering great racial discrimination, were victims of police violence (Neves 1986). Because this was an ecumenical consultation in a time when the Afro theme was starting to appear more often in discussions, agendas, community celebration, spaces of theological training, pastoral work environments, and in the hierarchies of the churches, they felt obliged to reflect on their own historical and institutional roles regarding the Afro-American population.

> The meeting was attended by thirty people, of which twenty-five were Black (eighteen men and seven women) and five were white. In addition to the Christians (among whom were Roman Catholics, Methodists, Presbyterians, Baptists, Lutherans and Episcopalians), there were also people who practiced Voodoo, Candomblé and Lumbalu. People came from Haiti, Dominican Republic, Curacao, Costa Rica, Panama, Colombia, Peru and Brazil (Neves 1986, pp. 13–14).

The purpose of the consultation was to clarify the role the Church played in the submission and domination of the Afro-Latino American sector. From this evaluation, the intent was to deduce the current role of the Church in the tasks of social justice with the people.

The second Ecumenical Consultation took place in São Paulo on November 6–12, 1994. Mirroring the success of the first consultation, it sought to add to the research and production efforts in the areas of social and religion sciences and Theology of Liberation to deepen, discuss, and develop contents on the theme "Afro-America: Culture and Theology," in light of the practices experienced in Afro-American communities. The objectives of the consultation were as follows: (1) to pool the various social and theological aspects from the reality of Afro-American communities and emerging Caribbean in recent decades; (2) to analyze and deepen theological reflection in light of the great challenges present in the pastoral reality of Afro-American and Caribbean peoples; (3) to encourage greater articulation between theological reflection initiatives that have emerged in the various regions of the continent concerning the Afro issue, creating an exchange with similar proposals in other continents; (4) to enlighten, at a theological level, the challenges posed by the Christian Churches and by the Santo Domingo Conference and develop the requirements of an inculturated evangelization; (5) to make an assessment of emerging theological aspects of Afro-American and Caribbean Pastoral Care; and (6) to reflect further on ecumenism and macro ecumenism from the cultures and religions of African origin (Silva 1997).

This second consultation included the participation of social scientists, theologians, pastors, priests, babalorixás and ialorixás, and researchers of Afro-American issues, representing eleven Latin-American countries, South Africa, and the United States. Six workshops were set up to deal with the following themes: (1) Black Latin-American Feminist theology; (2) Blackness, political projects, and new world order, (3) Liberation Theology, faith and African religious practices; (4) Ecumenism of Black faith communities; (5) Liturgical experiences; and (6) the Bible and Black communities (Silva and Santos, 1997).

The third Ecumenical Consultation on Afro-American and Caribbean Theology was held in São Paulo (SP) on October 20–25, 2003. Similar to its previous editions, it gathered theologians, social scientists, educators, and pastoral agents from several Latin-American and Caribbean countries. Also present were representatives from the United States, Republic of Congo, and Angola. The theme was "Afro-American Theology: Advances, Challenges and Perspectives," giving the participants the opportunity to continue, and broaden, the discussions from previous consultations. As a result, a variety of thematic texts that propitiate a valuable illustration of Afro-American theology was offered to the readers.

The consultation was held with four main themes: (1) a reading of the Afro-American situation; (2) the context of theological production; (3) thematic workshops; and (4) progress and challenges. The Third Consultation achieved its purpose, generating an excellent published document that maintained its relevance in spaces where Afro-American and Caribbean theological discussions take place and resonate to this day. Members of various groups of the Black movement, including the Atabaque, participated actively in these consultations. In this sense, the group was organizing and establishing itself and being structured.

Final considerations

Over time, the Atabaque Center left a significant legacy. Its members had a very significant dimension in the education and empowerment of Black identity in Latin-American and Caribbean communities. An analytical examination of the intervention and elaboration process of Atabaque Center members shows relevant epistemological elements. We can highlight the development of a Black theology from the other side of the story; that is, a theological reflection in its entirety includes insertion practices in day-to-day life of the Black community.

The space of the Black community provided members of Atabaque Center with a potential environment of historical and religious elements and a different economy that is capable of questioning and of being questioned on the premises of an Afro-American and Caribbean theology. This practice of sociohistorical and theological insertion cannot be abstract. It must be linked to actions lived in the historical, ecclesial, and communal contexts. In this chosen environment, the intention is to make a biblical election committed to mediations and conditioning that should trace a face of God, increasingly Blackened and committed to the practices of liberation of Afro-descendant populations.

Many are the obstacles to complete the task proposed by Atabaque Center members, given the importance and scale of the theme. It is necessary to eliminate the prejudices against traditional African-Brazilian and African religions. We must seek convergence, never generalization, in the foundations of faith, and in the expression of these foundations.

In the Christian religions, the foundation of faith is sought in Jesus Christ and the history experienced by the Hebrew people, whose testimonies are recorded in writings of the Bible. In the case of African and African-Brazilian religious traditions, that foundation comes from the history of the Orishas, whose testimonies are transmitted within a strictly oral tradition.

The studies carried out by the members of the Atabaque Center include an exercise of careful analysis of the terms of the congadas of the Moçambiques, the quicumbis, and practices of Creole drums, among many other manifestations by Black people. The paths for an Afro-American Theology and the deepening of a Latin-American Black epistemology are enabled by all the reflections of the specialized sciences.

Notes

1. The III General Conference of the Latin American Episcopate took place in Puebla de Los Angeles, Mexico, from January 27 to February 13, 1979, with the theme "Evangelization in the present and in the future of Latin America."

2. Meeting of the Black Pastoral Agents in Sao Paulo, Brazil, 1980, p. 1.
3. This is how the Missionary Action Line was called in the organizational structure of the CNBB.
4. Ibid., p. 2.
5. Ibid., p. 3.
6. BPAs (APNs in Portuguese) is how other organizations of the Brazilian Black Movement refer to the sympathizers and members of the Black Pastoral Agents association.
7. Cf. I Encounter of Black Pastoral Agents, Sao Paulo, 1983.
8. Ordained in 1979, he was the parish priest of the Church of Our Lady of Achiropita for 10 years. He was also the Provincial Director of the Congregation of Orionine Priests and Rector of the Faculty of Theology of the Pontifical Catholic University of Sao Paulo, and president of the Society of Theology and Science Religion (SOTER). Founder of the Atabaque Center, he was present at the creation of the Black Pastoral Agents association in 1983. He also campaigned for awareness and fight against racism while working with the Episcopate during the Conferences of Puebla and Santo Domingo, and was one of the most important leaders of the afro Pastoral in the last 30 years.
9. Priest at the Parish of Our Lady of Fatima in Vila das Belezas, a poor neighborhood in Sao Paulo, from 1963 to 1995. Member of the Society of the Divine Word, he was ordained in 1959 and then studied Theology in Rome during the four following years. He was the first Brazilian to obtain a doctorate in Missiology from the Gregorian University. A very conscious black priest, his love for the Afro-Brazilian people is manifest in his thesis dedicated to the Afro religion in Brazil. He was one of the first to suggest the use of epistemological elements for a Black Afro-American and Caribbean Theology during the Consultation on black culture an theology in Latin America in 1986.
10. Ibid., p. 26-7.
11. Cf. Reporto f the V Encounter of Black Pastoral Agents, 1985.
12. Cf. Relato do primeiro Encontro de Pastoral Afro-americana. In. Palenque—Boletim Informativo, Quito, 1980.
13. Cf. Relato do segundo Encontro de Pastoral Afro-americana. In. Palenque—Boletim Informativo, Quito, 1982.
14. Cf. Relato do terceiro Encontro de Pastoral Afro-americana. In. Palenque—Boletim Informativo, Quito, 1989.
15. Cf. Relato do quarto Encontro de Pastoral Afro-americana. In. Palenque—Boletim Informativo, Quito, 1991.
16. Cuadernos de Pastoral Afroamericana 5/6, Quito, 1995, p. 25.
17. The Atabaque Center, an interdisciplinary group of reflection on theology and blackness formed by people from Theology, Philosophy, Pedagogy, and other fields and from different religious backgrounds, was founded in 1990 in Sao Paulo. The group is connected to the Theology and Afro-American Cultures of the EATWOT. The group is named after an Afro-Brazilian hand drum, manifesting the desire to become a channel of communication between the many communities of faith, a voice that calls to worship and justice, dance and fraternity, a society without discrimination.

Works Cited

Actas del Primer Congreso de La Negra Cultural de las Americas, 1989, in Notebooks Black Americans, Quito: Abya Yala.

Neves, Amelia Tavares C. (ed.), 1986, Identidade Negra E Religião. Sao Paulo: Associação Ecumênica de Teólogos do Terceiro Mundo (ASETT), CEDI/Edições Liberdade.

Silva, Antonio Aparecido da and SANTOS, Sonia Querino of (eds.), 1997, Teologia Afro-americana: II Consultation Ecumenical Theology and Cultures African American and Caribbean. Sao Paulo: Paulus/Atabaque/ASETT.

CROSSCURRENTS
TOWARD A BLACK THEOLOGY IN BRAZIL

Leontino Faria dos Santos

Taking in consideration the insistent practice of racism in Brazilian society, it is easy to imagine the need to develop a Black Theology that calls upon us to reflect on this phenomenon, in light of biblical-theological presuppositions of a liberating and prophetic nature. We use as reference the Black Theology that developed in the United States as a theological movement that emerged among black Christians in the second half of the 1960s, focusing on the theological reflection on the struggle of black Americans under the leadership of Martin Luther King jr. In Brazil, the great reference to understand better this theological movement are the works published by Edições Paulinas, written by James H. Cone (God of the Opressed, 1985), one of the most important works on Black Theology; and the collection of documents on the first phase of the history of Black Theology from 1966 to 1979 by Gayraud S. Wilmore (Black Theology, 1986).

Regrettably, we find that the Liberation Theology that developed in Brazil and in Latin America (although its focus was more on a Marxist social-economic analysis than on the liberation of an oppressed race) in the 1980s and 1990s explored, as it was hoped, a relevant Black Theology that was impactful and that would arouse the attention of Christians in Brazil. Initiatives with a liberating bias were not enough to make the general populace think about the problems of blacks in Brazilian society. It is admirable to consider the fact that the leaders of North American Black Theology sought to maintain a certain dialogue with the leaders of Latin American and Asian liberation. The effects of this effort were not enough to impact Christian religious segments or Brazilian society. It is appropriate to consider, therefore, that Black Theology distinguishes itself from Latin American Liberation Theology by avoiding the use of Marxist social-economic analysis and by focusing on the liberation of an oppressed race rather than a social-economic class.

However, the effort undertaken by the Roman Catholic Church, which was more committed in the twentieth century to the problems of blackness than the Protestant Churches, deserves a positive mention. Among these Protestant Churches, there are some that never have addressed the black question satisfactorily, from a liberating and prophetic reflection.

Basic assumptions that justify a Black Theology in Brazil
Historical retrospective of racism in Brazil
Racism in Brazil results from the same causes that determined it in Spanish America. Unlike what happened in ancient times, in which discrimination was based on religious, national, or linguistic differences, this type of discrimination in Brazil was made in relation to culture and being different, including here the marked differences of physical traits and skin color. In the beginning of the sixteenth century, the colonizers who arrived in Brazil (Portuguese), brought in their cultural baggage, ideologies from the social, political, economic, theological, and pseudo-scientific explanations, considered by them logical, to justify the origin of racism. They had the same characteristics, foundations, and principles already used in Europe, which were also based on theological misconceptions based on some Old Testament biblical texts, which were themselves transformed into a biased doctrine that developed among fundamentalist theologians.

The European theological misconception of racial discrimination became a strong motive for defending black slavery in Brazil. Already in 1520, it was said that the Amerindians were not descendants of Adam and Eve. The biblical foundation for this was found in the story of Noah who was intoxicated with wine and got naked in front of his children. Ham, one of Noah's sons, in seeing his father in this situation and mocking him, was therefore cursed along with all his offspring. Racist theologians then concluded that blacks are the descendants of Ham, therefore cursed and condemned to permanent servitude and slavery. Other biblical quotations (Ephesians 6:5 and Ecclesiasticus 33:26–28) have also been the subject of misleading interpretations, always with the purpose of justifying black slavery and the need to be docile and servile.

It validated in Brazil, what was already happening in Europe, since the end of the Middle Ages, in the beginning of the sixteenth century, that is, the division of the population into "the clean of blood" and "the infected." Blacks, Mestizos, New Christians, and Indigenous were prevented from holding positions of trust or honor, on the grounds that they had no Catholic tradition and titles of nobility. The arguments were almost always of a theological and social nature. The Negroes belonged to an "impure race," whose blood was "stained." The unfolding of all this in Brazil resulted in a practice already known among Europeans, which required that, in order to exercise certain public functions in Brazilian society (court clerk, tax collector, outside judge, councilor, among other functions), all of them should prove that they were "clean of blood," that is to say, that they had no member of the races considered impure in their family.

In the nineteenth century, what was called the "Aryan myth," with its roots in the Iberian Peninsula, had also prevailed in Brazil, when in the middle of the century, scientific experiments with human and simian brains were held, which gave rise to a number of Treaties on racial differences. Here, Africans are targeted as biologically inferior beings.

There was an incorporation in Brazilian society of the theory of Count Arthur de Gobineau[1] that had had great impact in Europe. In Gobineau's work, it is worth mentioning that the Aryan race is considered superior to other racial groups. In this way, Gobineau classifies the Semitic race as inferior to the Aryan one, which would be considered the pure European. The idea that the Jew is Semitic, and as such a foreign and inferior race, has become a basic principle of anti-Semitic Aryans. Coupled with Goubineau's theory was the contribution of Houston Stewart Chamberlain, who applied the concept of "superior race" to the Germans in order to support them in their nationalistic aspirations and proclaimed the Jews as a degenerate race. It is in this context that Adolf Hitler appropriated these ideas and used them to demonstrate the Nordic superiority and to justify the extreme anti-Semitism of Nazism, which was responsible for the death of more than six million Jews. The ideas of Goubineau and Chamberlain had significant effects in the United States and Brazil where they served to exalt and "affirm the superiority of white

Americans over blacks and to justify the segregation and subjection of blacks to the dominant white group."

It is worth mentioning, however, that America was already populated by blacks who were sent to the United States and Brazil. The so-called "negro traffic," begun in the middle of the fifteenth century by the Portuguese, first in Europe and then in the newly discovered lands of the new world as slaves, at the same time "blessed" by the Church, thanks to the misinterpretations of the sixteenth-century fundamentalist theologians. The Church legitimized colonization and slavery with its practices and preaching of resignation and subservience. The layman and the religious, the theologians and the hierarchy even justified slavery and enjoyed it. Some pontifical documents of the time, especially from the Popes Nicholas V (1452) and Leo X (1514), authorized the Portuguese Crown and then the Spanish Crown to conquer the lands of the Saracens, pagans, and unbelievers, enslaving their inhabitants. The false notion of "its just war against the enemies of the faith" brought with it the legitimation of enslavement of the vanquished.

It can't be denied that prophetic voices within the Roman Catholic Church also rose against the enslavement of natives and blacks. Brother António de Montesinos, Bartolomeu de las Casas, Bishop António de Valdivieso, Fathers Manoel da Nóbrega, José de Anchieta and António Vieira are among them. One of these priests, referring to the omissions related to the problem, wrote: "The priests who go to Brazil are not going to save souls, but to condemn theirs." It is worth noting the teaching of Paul III against the slavery of the Indians; but the enslavement of the blacks was not always rejected with the same intensity!

Protestants only established themselves in Brazil from the second half of the sixteenth century. The majority of missionaries sent to Latin America were North Americans. Especially those from the southern United States that arrived in Brazil defending slavery and using blacks for housework in their homes. It is worth remembering that somehow these missionaries have always been in favor of black slavery, one of the reasons behind the strains of the American Civil War, between southern and northern states of the United States.

It is important to consider that among Brazilian Protestants, Rev. Eduardo Carlos Pereira, a Presbyterian pastor, was noted for his strong protest against racism and slavery. In 1886 Pereira published a booklet entitled The Christian Religion in its Relationships with Slavery, in which he severely criticizes the fundamentalist interpretations of the Bible on racism; draws the attention of the Presbyterians to their silence in dealing with the problem; challenges the pulpit to abandon the silence; asks the faithful to restore freedom to slaves. This was because at that time it was proven that Methodists, Baptists, and Presbyterians were slave owners.

As we have seen, Goubineau's ideas also had much influence in Brazil. Between 1869 and 1870, he visited the Brazilian Emperor, Dom Pedro II, at which time they started a great friendship and even discussed the abolition of slavery and immigration policy. It was at this time that he predicted that in less than 200 years the Brazilian inhabitants would disappear, condemned by the increasing miscegenation.

Tavares Bastos, an Alagoan deputy, defended the need for a renewal of the Brazilian population by encouraging white immigration. He believed that ending the slave trade was not a matter of compassion; it was a way of averting the losses that the blacks brought to Brazil. He maintained that science had already confirmed that the black was the root of the evils of the nation and a bad worker. The coming of the white would be a step toward progress and a symbol of civilization. He is more productive, affirmed the deputy!

Besides blacks, the Asians were also victims of racism in Brazil. In 1880, the permanence of Chinese in Brazil was ardently discussed. São Paulo politicians questioned Chinese cuisine; some thought that cats, rats, caterpillars, larvae were part of their typical dishes. The Chinese were called "square face," and young Brazilians were advised to avoid marriage to these Oriental people. The Japanese also suffered discrimination, especially during World War II. They were considered, besides from an impure race, to be traitors, spies, enemies.

Main characteristics of racism in Brazil

Currently, there is a great diversity of races in Brazil. Apparently it is said that there is a peaceful coexistence between the races, even naming this coexistence: racial democracy. However, in practice, discrimination is notorious, especially in relation to blacks. In fact, demographic statistics still provide inaccurate data on the various ethnic groups in Brazil. Because of social pressures, many people of the black race deny their identity and define themselves as "mixed race" and even as "whites." This makes the data collected by the official organizations relative.

Although official data do not always reflect the truth of the facts, we can say that the Afro-descendant population today is close to 50%. This makes Brazil the second largest country in the world with a majority black population, surpassed only by Nigeria. In any case, they are people who live in inferiority compared to other races.

The living conditions of the blacks in Brazil today are worrying. From the socioeconomic point of view, their financial income in the workforce is very unequal. It is still more frequent to have the presence of the black in subordinate functions and more disqualified, socially. In construction work, for example, blacks are the majority while whites usually act as master builders.

As for schooling and culture, it is noticeable that the degree of schooling of Brazilians reinforces the inequality in which the black population of Brazil finds itself. The illiteracy rate of the economically active black population is very high relative to the white population. The average years of study of whites are far superior to those of blacks. To exemplify, we note that currently (2016) blacks are less than 1% in the courses considered forward looking of the University of São Paulo (USP). In approximately 5 years, USP's Medical, Law and Engineering courses enrolled only 77 black students. These data represent 0.9% of enrollments made between 2005 and 2011, according to a source at the University of São Paulo.

To make the situation of disparagement and inequality of the black race worse, many textbooks reinforce the black's inferior position. In Brazilian history books, almost always written from the perspective of the white, the black appears almost exclusively associated with slavery. The idea that is in the mind of those who study this history, is that black is equal to slave and consequently, the black is considered inferior. In historical accounts, in the gallery of its heroes, the black is almost never remembered. The reference to Zumbi dos Palmares as the leader of a resistance movement against the exploitation from the whites, for example, is almost never made!

It is worth mentioning that the cultural highlights in relation to the black race, when they appear, are almost always linked to aspects considered peripheral or folkloric, as with musical manifestations, eating habits and linguistic contributions. Let us recognize that in many situations, in the white culture's standards, the black features are considered as subculture and an expression of the exotic.

Discrimination includes the criteria of beauty, culture, and civility toward white standards. Not even indigenous culture is taken into account. Similarly, in relation to the black, the indigenous culture is also considered exotic, befitting those who are uncivilized. It is clear how the media and its opinion makers confirm what we affirm. Novels, reporting, and films almost always show blacks in subaltern roles, as domestic servants, in secondary roles, or in deeds that injure social ethics.

There is no way to dismiss the situation of the black woman, probably one of the biggest victims of all this history of discrimination. She has played a variety of roles always as a subordinate. She was a slave, object of pleasure of the masters in the mills, reproductive being, used to increase the human capital of the slavers, exploited in domestic activities and in the field work.

As a reproducer, the woman was demeaned in her dignity and encouraged to reproduce more than 10 children in order to obtain her freedom. Despite this degrading her honor and being disrespectful, she resisted heroically and refused to gain her freedom in this way. This is what Roger Bastide says in "The African Religions of Brazil": "The whites encouraged the procreation of his slaves: the woman who had put 10 children into the world was freed; later the number was lowered to 7."[2] Despite the advantage, women almost always refused to produce child slaves for society in return for her freedom. Many voluntary abortions were practiced as a form of resistance. In many cases, these women, without any medical assistance, during the practice of abortion, were also victims of death. That is why the birth rate among black women was low. The result of this type of treatment, nowadays, is that black women still form the largest contingent of the population living in favelas or "communities," besides being poorly remunerated as domestic workers or peasants. They are still three times the victims of discrimination: as women, as poor, and as black.

According to Agência Brasil, with data published on June 25, 2012, black and poor women are more vulnerable to risky abortions. According to research done in 2010, 22% of Brazilians aged 35 to 39, living in urban areas, have already had an abortion. "The most common characteristic of women who perform their first abortion is to be up to the age of 19, black and with children" says the anthropologist Débora Diniz, of the National University of Brasília and the Institute of Bioethics, Human Rights and Gender (ANIS), and the sociologist Marcelo Medeiros, also from the National University of Brasília and the Institute of Applied Economic Research (IPEA).

Discrimination also occurs with black children when, at risk, they are sheltered in nursing homes, in the expectation of some form of adoption. Waiting for some charitable family, many of these children always believe that someone will arrive, accredited by the Justice Department to take them. But adoptions of black children are rare! When they are not adopted, many stay in shelters until the age of 17 and 11 months when, depending on the situation, they are forced to leave this environment, thus being subjected to indigence, delinquency, prostitution, psychic and social imbalance: life without a future!

Influences of racism on culture of the people
All this past violence against the black race left in Brazilian society historical legacies that still remain. In relation to work, blacks remain in the background. Because of their low schooling, they have not had great chances. Few, as we have seen, have access to university or to complete a college degree. Most are devoted to manual labor, coarse labor, and are often victims of wage injustices. Racial prejudice, under new forms and zealously guarded, is present in language (many still refer to the black as "a man of color"), in textbooks, in education, in religious expressions of Christians, in popular music, in Brazilian culture in general.

In the Protestant religion, for example, the message of the pulpits continues to bring into their rhetoric expressions such as "the black and rude sin"; in songs we can find such phrases like "black battalions," "my heart was black; but Christ has come in; with his precious blood; and made it his target." The Alliance for the Evangelization of Children (APEC), for example, adopts in its didactic work, the so-called "Book without Words."[3] Among the colors referred to in this material is the use of black, which can induce the child to reject themselves when he or she is black. Black appears here as a symbol of sin. Considering the criticisms regarding this position, APEC replaced the word "black" with "dirty." It makes us think black is dirty, dirt! In books on Christian ethics and theology the phrase "men of color" continues to appear, even in writings against racism.[4] Certainly, there are authors and translators who believe there are men without color, whites!

Other terms such as "mulatto," "negro," "black," and "blackness" have generated feelings and complexes of inferiority, giving the individual a sense of non-being and of not being equal to the other. A significant change in language and literature would allow, we believe, changes in the meaning of the word "black" in order to achieve a positive and worthy sense of the term "black."

Racial prejudice has been a permanent practice that creates obstacles to the social participation of a particular ethnic group and to the exercise of their rights as citizens. It alienates the black and, in a masked way, sometimes makes him believe in the so-called "racial democracy." This is to hide the inequalities that exist between blacks and whites. Those who defend "racial democracy" make an ahistorical reading of the slave period and believe in the so-called "innate cordiality" of Brazilians, in the idea that opportunities are equal for all, blacks and whites and that, therefore, there is no distinction of race, color, sex, religion. A partial and naive view of such a complex problem!

Movements of resistance against racism

Despite all this, great efforts have been made by blacks and sympathizers, so that there is a change in the racial situation in Brazil. The struggle for black conscience in the face of this reality is gradually managing to impose itself on society. Although it is not as it should be, the search for recognition of the record is sought in relation to the ideological representations that continue to mark the discrimination of the black race. It is part of the struggle of blacks for their dignity and their rights in society. It is a necessary struggle for the awareness of society. It is recognized as fundamental that blacks are aware of what they represent in society and that everyone is guaranteed access to specific information and the creation of a "critical mass" for the struggle to become viable.

Various forms of articulation of "black consciousness" have emerged in African American communities.[5] It is worth highlighting the movement "Black Brazilian Front" (FNB), which emerged in 1931, with the aim of denouncing racism, fighting for equality of rights, especially in the labor market, for the right to education and for right of land and housing law. Another fighting front, which emerged in the 1950s, is the Movimento Vento Forte Africano, under the leadership of Solano Trindade, who advocates the idea of combining racial discussion with the class struggle. Add to this the contribution of Abdias do Nascimento, with a more black-African vision, working on the idea of quilombismo, which was a black space of reinvention of their own black culture and a dialogue of negotiation and confrontation with society.

Specifically in Brazil, it is worth remembering three important experiences linked to the Black Movement. Prof. Marcos Rodrigues da Silva, in a study on "Afro-American Communities," cites the "Unified Black Movement" (MNU), which emerged in the late 1970s, and faced police persecution of black youths, often blamed for bank robberies, robberies and marginal practices, without proper verification. It was this Movement that secured that November 20th would be considered the "Day of Black Consciousness" and of the fight against racial discrimination, in honor of Zumbi, from the Quilombo de Palmares. Prof. Marcos also mentions the "United Black Consciousness Group," organized in 1981 under the leadership of laity, religious people, and priests of the Roman Catholic Church, linked to the missionary work of the National Conference of Bishops of Brazil. Finally, Prof. Marcos mentions the work of the "Black Pastoral Agents" in the 80's, with the ecumenical opening to welcome, value and better understand Afro-Brazilian religions and cults.

Prof. Antonio Olimpio de Sant'Ana, one of the voices of the antiracism movement in the Brazilian Methodist Church and organizer of the National Ecumenical Commission to Combat Racism (CENACORA), in his entry on "Racism" in the Brazilian Dictionary of Theology, believes that "a strong, objective, inclusive ecumenism, which encourages truth, reconciliation, and justice, which results in a spirituality that strengthens the love of neighbor"[6] can be one of the means to combat racism. The work of CENACORA—organized in 1987 by representatives of Evangelical Churches, the Roman Catholic Church and the Syrian Orthodox Catholic Church, is also worth mentioning. Having as its objective to discuss racism biblically and theologically; to reflect on black and indigenous spirituality; to promote and encourage activities that empower people to combat and eliminate racism; to challenge churches to examine the existence of racism in their communities.

Other civil social organizations have emerged to strengthen existing movements, with actions of some relevance in Brazilian society. We mentioned the National Commission against Racial Discrimination (NDRC), the Central Única dos Trabalhadores (CUT), in Brazil; the Inter-American Trade Union Institute for Racial Equality (INSPIR), organized in 1995. The purpose of this Institute is to train and enable trade union leaders on racial discrimination and prepare them to negotiate clauses on the promotion of racial equality and to encourage the organization of black workers. The three Brazilian worker's organizations (CUT, CGT, and Força Sindical) are involved in this struggle.

Fragments for a Black Theology in Brazil

The certainty that God hears the cry of the oppressed

In the history of the people of Israel, God is the One who sees and hears the cry of His people. It reminds us, in this story, of the suffering of the Israelites under the oppression of the Egyptians; they treated God's people as slaves. Speaking with Moses in the wilderness, God said thus: "I have indeed seen the misery of my people in Egypt. I have heard them crying out because of their slave drivers, and I am concerned about their suffering. I have come down to rescue them from the hand of the Egyptians ..." (Exodus 3: 7–8). Here, we see God's dissatisfaction with the oppression and the anguish of the people of Israel. God promises deliverance for that people and desires to count on human collaboration in the struggle for liberation. Explicit is the condemnation of God to any kind of exploitation!

It is believed that God continues to want to intervene in all social reality where there is oppression, discrimination, misery, and death threats. Because God, both in the history of the liberation of biblical Israel and in the ministry of Jesus, always appears alongside, in defense of the poor, marginalized, discriminated, the oppressed!

In Jesus's ministry, He is visibly sympathetic to the victims of discrimination as was he with the situation of women in the society of His time; He also acted against those who discriminated against the poor, orphans and widows, foreigners, and others who were marginalized at that time as was the case with the sick, the slaves, and those of other races.

It's worthy to remember in the history of liberation, the event of Pentecost (Acts 2:1–12) in the life of the Church. There we have examples of how the new world must be. The Holy Spirit descends upon the Church gathered in Jerusalem and overturns the cultural barriers of language and race, and all people, at the same time, are able to understand and accept the message of the Kingdom of God! There lies the great sign for the possibility of life, of unity in diversity, against the total denial of any kind of discrimination, whether of peoples, races, or nations.

The testimony of the Christians from the first century serves also as an example for our practice against discrimination. One of the most striking examples is perhaps the conflict between Judaizers and Universalists, when the Roman centurion, Cornelius, was converted. Cornelius is a Gentile, but the Holy Spirit descends upon him; Peter is convinced by God that people should not be welcomed by discriminating against them (Acts 10: 17–18); the action of the Holy Spirit was decisive at that time in the history of the Church so that the doors would open to non-Jews the experience of baptism. In the Pauline Epistles to the Romans and the Galatians, the recrimination is clear to any kind of discrimination, whether it was cultural, religious, gender, social class, or even slavery.

Writing to the Galatians, the Apostle Paul says: "… So in Christ Jesus you are all children of God through faith, for all of you who were baptized into Christ have clothed yourselves with Christ. There is neither Jew nor Gentile, neither slave nor free, nor is there male and female, for you are all one in Christ Jesus."(Galatians 3:26–28). In other Letters, the Corinthians and the Colossians, besides the Letter to the Romans and Galatians, Paul is incisive, even repetitive, about this teaching.

The question and answer to this interrogation
To what extent has the Church of Christ heard the cry of the oppressed? —We must recognize that, despite the evidence from the Holy Scriptures on discrimination, it has been difficult to overcome the problem. At certain moments in the history of the Church, the institution itself became an agent of discrimination and missionary projects of an oppressive character. This is what one sees when one reads the history of the Church in the Middle Ages and, in modern times, when the Jews were discriminated against. Also missionaries who accompanied the colonizing expeditions of the Portuguese and the Spanish had difficulties in accepting without

discrimination the peoples that were to be evangelized. Many Christian leaders were advocates of black slavery brought from Africa.

In Racism in Brazilian History, historian Maria Luiza Tucci Carneiro, from the University of São Paulo (USP), Brazil, says, referring to the situation of Brazil during the colonial period:

> Segregationist ideas were conveyed through sermons, tales, songs, chronicles, poems, anecdotes, theatrical texts and painting. In all these forms of expression the figure of the black emerges as that of an inferior, animalized, servile being; and the Jew emerges as the enemy of humanity, identified with the incarnation of the devil, with the 'Antichrist'.[7]

In all this, the existence of the force of the discriminatory mentality, of an ideological character, and the complicity of the Church (both in Catholicism and Protestantism) is undeniable.

The struggle for theological misconceptions to be condemned

From a "biblical and theological point of view" (Gen. 9:25), there is no basis for the claim that the black race, for example, results from Noah's "curse" cast upon Canaan following his drunkenness with wine in the face of his son's expression of irony when he saw his father without clothing: "Cursed be Canaan! The lowest of slaves will he be to his brothers." There is no biblical foundation for racist theologians to believe that all blacks not only descend from Ham but are also condemned to permanent servitude and slavery. The Spanish priest Juan Bautista Casas claimed in 1869 that the black race suffers from the curse, according to the Pentateuch and that this inferiority was perpetuated throughout the centuries. But Gardner's commentary on "Biblical Faith and Social Ethics" about this misinterpretation is appropriate when he said:

> A careful reading of this passage, in its own context, shows that it was Noah and not God who laid such a curse upon his son, Ham, and that Noah was in a bad condition to be the mouthpiece of the Lord under those circumstances (EC GARDNER, 1965, p. 406).

If the curse had been established by God, it would be difficult to believe in His redemptive will in relation to human life and in the divine possibilities to change and transform intragroup relationships. God would be inconsistent and contradictory to His redemptive nature.

The religious movements of resistance against racism in Brazil understand that it is necessary to prophetically denounce the fallacy of the so-called "scientific racism"

This denunciation is necessary because many people still believe that everything that is apparently scientific is worthy of belief. The thesis of early social scientists is still held by many people. These were conclusive in arguing that the original man was white; in contact with the tropics, however, he underwent a process of degeneration, making him black. Several thinkers defended this type of fallacious thinking: Voltaire, Linnaeus, Kamper, Buffon, in order to demonstrate the hierarchy of the races. All this, although without sustainable foundations, aimed at the sacralization of colonial domination.

Until the end of the last century (1995), several publications circulated pointing to multicultural intolerance. In "Alien Nation," Peter Brimelow defends rigid control of the immigration to the United States in defense of the hegemony of whites in that country. Two other authors, Richard Hernstein and Charles Morray, published a year earlier in "The Bell Curve," the claim that because of genetic factors, the IQ of blacks is inferior to that of whites and Asians.

Until the nineteenth century, theological pretexts prevailed for the justification of racism. Science has advanced sufficiently to disqualify the arguments of those who think that there is superiority between the races or those who have used Darwin's theory of evolution to misrepresent it to justify racism. But, as Maria Leuiza Tucci Carneiro (USP, 1994) says,

> Although they do not match the scientifically proven reality, racist theories have served to justify the frustration of society against "undesirable" groups, covering economic, political and social interests. We can say then that prejudice is based on false ideas, leading to the configuration of imaginary dangers.

It is necessary to unmask the ideology of racism

Its origin is in the past, when it was intended to justify inequality in relation to the development of the populace. This ideology served the ideals of colonialism to make slavery and oppression of blacks, Australian Aborigines, and Native Americans legitimate. It served, equally, to deny the equal access of these peoples to the cultural goods (material and spiritual) of all ethnic groups and nations.

The idea that *the Church needs to acknowledge and confess to collaborating with the development of racism in the history of humanity* has been considered as unequivocal. Catholics and Protestants are accomplices in this story. It is not enough for the Church to recognize that in many situations it was silent and, at certain times, its members defended servitude. Cardinal Gonzalvi, papal representative (1815), for example, refused to censor the slave trade in order not to offend the "Catholic States" where such trade was permitted. Pope Leo XIII, in a pastoral letter sent to the Brazilian bishops in 1888, when slavery was abolished in Brazil, declared that slavery is not essentially evil and that it can be constructive, provided the master is "good."

Many Protestants, following the example of the Catholics, were also in favor of slavery. Moravians, Methodists, Anglicans, Baptists, Presbyterians, Quakers of Europe were slave owners.

More than confessing, Christians need to apologize to black and indigenous people for not having fought against racial discrimination and for their liberation from oppressive powers throughout human history!

The Church has been encouraged to accept the challenge of inculturation from the perspective of black communities

We take as a basis the text of Father Antonio Aparecido da Silva (Father Toninho),[8] published in "Black Community: Current Challenges and Perspectives" (Atabaque—ASSET, São Paulo, 1995). In this text, Father Toninho mentions "cultural reluctance in the European community" in relation to black immigrants since the thirteenth century. It points out that for Europe, although considered modern, the non-European world was classified as "savage" and prehistoric.

In the face of this scenario, the cultural question became more notorious in reflection on the 500th anniversary of the conquest of America (1992), especially in the study of the encounter between European, indigenous and black cultures and the problems arising from then on. It is recognized that black culture in particular is emerging in Latin America and that despite the predominance of a Western cultural pattern established from colonization, there is not just one people and one culture. There is a cultural plurality that has become evident, especially from the cultures of blacks and indigenous people.

Considering this cultural reality in Latin America, the Church in particular is challenged to develop an inculturated pastoral, mainly from the perspective of the black community. Father Toninho explains:

> In order for the Church to become a meeting of different peoples, united and harmonious, a deep, sincere and respectful dialogue between the Gospel and Cultures must be undertaken and intensified in order to preserve the legitimate identity of the various peoples.

This has been one of the great challenges with serious problems to overcome in the journey toward black culture, not always recognized in its various aspects as legitimate enough to be assimilated by the Church, especially among Protestant churches in Brazil.

Father Toninho sees inculturation as a dialectical process, where the evangelical proposal "... lived and adopted through cultural forms not incompatible with the Gospel, is returned, expressed or re-expressed according to the modus-vivendi (culture) of that people." Conclusively, Father Toninho says that the black people in the diaspora assimilated from what they already knew before; and integrated the evangelical proposal into their own trajectory. " In this way, the process of inculturation in the black community has shown that evangelization is not simply the communication and reception of the historical legacy of Christianity, but that "The recipient of the Gospel can only receive it by recreating within himself, by himself" .

In short, the Church has been called upon to accept the permanent challenge of moving toward the blacks and their culture, so that they may know the saving action and the liberation of God, with a new look at themselves and the world.

It is recognized at present time that the Church has tasks to fulfill in race relations

The Church has "a responsibility to make clear the relevance of the Christian faith to issues of social concern and to intragroup relationships," Gardner says. The Church is a witness and, as such, must be faithful in the proclamation and interpretation of her faith to the world. It can't shy away from concrete actions involving aspects of economic, political, moral, and religious life in society. More than rhetoric, the Church needs to be practical, take positions, denounce the evil that compromises the well-being and dignity of brothers in society.

The Church's mission before the world must be clear, objective, transparent. Its discourse should be prophetic and present in the lives of the oppressed as "salt of the earth" and "light of the world." People who are victims of discrimination need to see and feel this! It is the task of the Church to manifest in its own life the unity and fraternity it proclaims.

As part of its responsibility, the Church must work toward the implementation of justice in an integral manner within social reality. Moved by love, it must seek change, renewal, or even reconstruction of the institutional structures through which human needs can or should be met. There are many problems that emerge from racial discrimination. Whatever may be the character of these problems, the Church can't ignore the obligation of concrete actions to combat discrimination. Take for example the black missionaries and churches of Jamaica in 1783, defined as centers of subversion by the colonial authorities of the time. These churches were burned and missionaries were arrested and sentenced to death, but the emancipatory movement did not die.

For a Black Theology in Brazil, it is necessary to strengthen the ecumenical effort

The problem of racial discrimination has been on the agenda of the Assembly of the World Council of Churches (WCC) since its meeting in Amsterdam. At the time, several documents drew attention to the fact that the eradication of racial discrimination and hatred was necessary. The appeal was for the Churches to eliminate any form of racism from their practices. In 1961, three churches in South Africa withdrew from the WCC for disagreeing with this antiracist stance. In 1969, the WCC recommended boycotting companies with investments in South Africa and then created the Program to Combat Racism.

Already in Amsterdam it became clear that racial segregation in the Church is "scandal" in the Body of Christ. The Church that wants to be "Church of Jesus" in the world, cannot be segregationist like various Christian groups have remained throughout history.

In 1957, the Catholic bishops of South Africa recognized that there was racism within the Church; in 1967, Pope Paul VI pronounced through the Encyclical *Populorum Progressio* censorship of racism, referring to the practices of the past, the present, and future.

Despite these efforts and many others, it is recognized that racism should not be considered only the problem of a few religious people, fighting isolated against such evidence. As Rev. Antonio Olímpio de Sant 'Ana wrote, "The struggle against racism depends ... on a strong ecumenism ... that encourages the churches to feel part of the suffering, the anguish and the misery of the dispossessed..."[9] We regret, however, that ecumenism today is not so strong and active in determining the change of mentality and course in the history of humanity with the effective participation of the Christian Churches for the ideals of the kingdom of God.

That the Black Theology in Brazil has a liberating character

For a liberating Black Theology in Brazil, it is necessary, at first, a *re-reading of the Holy Scriptures*, from the reality of the blacks in the historical process, keeping in mind the biblical texts that are the foundations of the Christian faith, in a relevant element in the liberation dimension. With a new look, realize that blacks, when oppressed by the rebellious powers of this world, embodied in self-sufficient rulers, have been victims of abusive capitalist systems. In this way, the scriptural texts will reveal that historically oppressed blacks are to be regarded as subjects and not objects in the ideal of liberation of the Kingdom of God. It is necessary to recognize in this new attitude that until now the reading of the Holy Scriptures has been of the priestly type, from the interests of the powerful of this world or simply of those who participate in the assets of capitalist civilization (many of them also represented in the ecclesiastical structures of our time). It is worth considering that the re-reading of the Scriptures from the perspective of the oppressed blacks, of a prophetic character, will, at the same time, be of a liberating nature.

With the re-reading of the Holy Scriptures from the oppressed black's perspective, it is necessary to *re-read the contents of Theology* in search of their liberation. This re-reading must be of a prophetic nature, which will be decisive for these contents to also become impacting, since it should take into account the analysis of the reality of the black people and their yearnings for liberation.

Black Theology in Brazilian society must take into account the reality of the black person in this society that it contemplates the contents of theology in what they have of liberation. It is fundamental, therefore, to take into account the social and even utopian dimension, which contemplates, in the socio-political context, aspects that are relevant to the liberation process. Under this liberating bias one must re-read values of the Christian faith which concern the life of the oppressed human being as the mystery of God, of Christ, of the Church, of grace, of sin, of the sacraments, of eschatology, of anthropology and of the notion Of God's Kingdom in a world of rebellious powers and death threats. This re-reading will bring us closer to the liberating character of the Gospel of Christ, so present in His ministry in proclaiming and carrying out the liberation of all kinds of marginalized people (women, sick, foreigners, possessed, slaves, Samaritans) of any race, social class, religious origin, culture.

Echoing considerations from the Boff brothers (Leonardo and Clodovis Boff),[10] it seems pertinent to observe the need for a *re-reading of history* from the point of view of the marginalized, including blacks. The goal is the discovery of new sources, new interpretations and perspectives, in order to give historical awareness to these people to strengthen the struggle for liberation in all dimensions.

How could a Black Theology be constructed without taking into account a *re-reading of the Holy Scriptures*, a *re-reading of the contents of Christian theology*, and a *re-reading of historical reality* in the struggle for the liberation of an oppressed race?

Notes

1. Gardner, Edward Clinton, *Fé Bíblica e Ética Social* (São Paulo: ASTE, 1965), p. 4001.
2. Bastide, Roger, *As Religiões Africanas no Brasil*, Volume I (São Paulo: Livraria Pioneira Editôra, Universidade de São Paulo, 1971), p. 98.
3. dos Santos, Leontino Farias, Educação: libertação ou submissão?: a ideologia da educação protestante na perspectiva da APEC" (SãoPaulo: Sociedade Religiosa Edições Simpósio, 1989), p. 118.
4. See in E. C. Gardner, "Fé Bíblica e Ética Social", São Paulo, ASTE, 1965, p. 402. Also in the text "Albert Schweitzer por ele mesmo", published by Martin Claret Ltda., São Paulo, 1995, p. 29, among others.
5. dos Santos, Leontino Farias, *In Dicionário Brasileiro de Teologia* (São Paulo: ASTE, 2008), p. 182.

6. de Sant'Ana, Antonio Olímpio, *"Racismo"* in *Dicionário Brasileiro de Teologia* (São Paulo: ASTE, 2008), p. 845.
7. Carneiro, Maria Luiza Tucci, *O Racismo na História do Brasil* (São Paulo: Ática, 1994), p. 11.
8. Father Antonio Aparecido da Silva, also known as Father Toninho, is a Master in Moral Theology from the Pontifical Alfonsian University of Rome; Master in Philosophy-PUC / SP; Founding Partner of the Brazilian Society of Theology (SOTER) and the ATABAQUE Group.
9. de Sant'Ana, Antonio Olimpio, *Dicionário Brasileiro de Teologia* (São Paulo: ASTE, 2008), p. 845.
10. Boff, Leonardo e Clodovis, *Da Libertação – o teológico das libertações sócio-históricas* (Petrópolis: Vozes, 1980).

CROSSCURRENTS

BLACK THEOLOGY IN BRAZIL
Decolonial and Marginal

Ronilso Pacheco

The place of the Exodus

Exodus has always been an important reference for liberation theology. The history of the Hebrew people being exploited and martyred in Egypt became the starting point, the hermeneutics par excellence of theologians who sought an engagement, in Latin America, with the liberation of the continent from the modernized exploitations of capitalism: exploiting work, creativity, land, production, nature, all this with profit and the maintenance of power being the main goal. From this comes the understanding of the comparison with the Exodus. But for this purpose Exodus ceases to be the understanding of a narrative that speaks of a displacement, a crossing from one point to another. It is necessary to call attention to what constituted the period of servitude in Egypt and to what this exploitation recalls in our condition here and now.

Black theology is included as one of the "liberation theologies." The name came to be used in the plural because what was once only the so-called liberation theology opened the way to a plurality of theological perspectives that came to claim place and emancipated voices. For black theology, which emerges in the United States in the 1960s, the place of the Exodus is central because of the condition of the oppressed and of their exploitation, but an aggravating factor marks it: the emphasis on racism and slavery. We are not just talking about people whose work and workforces are exploited. We are talking about slavery, and all that it can mean in countries like the United States, Haiti, Colombia, and, of course, Brazil.

Black theology is still incipient in Brazil, but it's gradually proving its need and place, revisiting, due to efforts of a small new generation of theologians, the reflections made by James Cone, Jacquelyn Grant, Cornell West, Gayraud Wilmore, Allan Boesak, Desmond Tutu (the last two in the South African context), among others. The reflections of many of these theologians, brought to light here by people like Peter Nash and Nancy Cardoso, are now beginning to be gradually reclaimed by new faces that are more present in a context of political action, street practice, resistance uprisings in defense of the life, and dignity of blacks in the context of violence and racism in Brazil, all of which point to the contribution of black theology in problematizing the various inequalities in the country with the way bodies and territories are treated. Here the Exodus continues to be a starting point, among other things, because the cry of the black people, the young blacks, the black women, continue to be cries of pain and silencing.

The period of servitude of the Hebrew people in the land of Egypt narrated in the Exodus should not be thought of as a romantic story of heroism where God is the protagonist operating miracles, signs, and wonders. Rather, it must be thought of in the context of the pains and violations that are present in the condition of a slave, or in the context of the lives of those who are made slaves in colonized territory. This means that the historical context of the Hebrew people in Egypt bears similarities to the process of colonization undertaken by Europe that also reaches Brazil. In a colonized territory, as Brazil had become, its history begins with men and women murdered daily, women raped, black bodies whipped, tortured, disappeared, and subdued.

The silence maintained under the weight of violence and fear is never without the Christian religious investiture. As Riolando Azzi well describes:

> Even though black populations already lived in Africa in a stage of greater development, generated by the sedentary life and the practice of agriculture, the reduction to the situation of slaves in the Brazilian colony had diminished in many of them the capacity of resistance and fight for the dignity of life. Few horizons opened up

to people who were treated like animals exposed to the trading market, and as "parts" in the great gear of the machine. For them labor lost its value, due to its imposed and forced character, being considered as an unjust punishment, or, in a more Catholic perspective, as a form of atonement of sin.[1]

It is in this sense that a black hermeneutics would necessarily pass through the Exodus. In identifying with a narrative that begins in a territory of subjugation, capture, oppression and the construction of a mentality, and the various forms of resistance, another hermeneutical horizon emerges, which foments other narratives and looks and thinks from another place.

In Egypt, the Pharaoh makes use of his power. He makes use of his governmentality. The Hebrew people became a threat. If they continued to grow, the ruler's fear was that they would threaten his power, subvert the order, and, if they were offenders, panic would take hold of Egyptian society. Of course, there were alternatives. They could be integrated into society, not as slaves, not on the sidelines, not confined in the territories of containment and constrained by social control, but as subjects with a much wider range of opportunities. They could still transgress, it is true, but it would not be a very different possibility from the legitimately Egyptian youngsters. But this was too much work.

So the Pharaoh's solution was to reduce the penal age to zero—the first "criminal" age was the age at which a Hebrew, a slave, had the strength to do heavy work. If he was born a boy, he must die. It was not worth risking a child who, when he grew up, had on the horizon the possibility of threatening the safety of the Egyptians, killing, perhaps, because of hatred of his slave condition. But two midwives felt uneasy concerning the Pharaoh's decree. The decree contradicted their own office, which was the defense of life, those who welcomed the born, those who listened close to the cry, the scream, the mixture of physical pain and joy of the soul of the mothers. Sefra and Puá, in a book in which women and subaltern characters are largely anonymous, have names and faces. They have subverted an order and inspired an awareness of resistance and struggle for freedom and life, culminating in the Exodus.

It is then possible to think of the Exodus not only as an exit, but also as a rescue, a driving of the people that leave the place of the centrality of the power of an empire to the margins. Exodus then becomes, first and foremost, a figure for the margins. God the symbolic power of the empire of its coercive potential, controls and exploits the people, by making them move toward the periphery. So here is more than a geography, the episode portrayed in the Exodus is also a kind of declarative locus, because the exit, the resistant escape of the places under control and the intervention of the oppression of the empire, is a necessary condition for the construction of new alternatives and possibilities to glimpse freedom and autonomy.

Here the Biblical Exodus and the Quilombola communities meet. In the context of the struggle and resistance of the black people in Brazil, the quilombos[2] were "the promised land" whose symbolism had the power to move blacks out of the place of control and oppression of the colonial "empire" of Portugal. The flight to the quilombos, territory of hope of a free way of living, autonomous and communitarian, was not a crossing without pain, tricks, conflicts, and losses along the way. It was not a crossing without betrayals and constant attacks of sabotage (inside and out), but it was the movement that instigated the freedom that was possible, the uprising, the unlocking of the center's oppression, to a rebuilding from the margin.

Hence Exodus having its strong trajectory narrative in the desert in which, for being a desert, everything must be rethought, repositioned, replenished, collectively created, and where the daily distribution of the manna falling from heaven is the perfect metaphor for the criticism against accumulating and yet at the same time the furtherance of equal sharing. This sharing that unites in resistance, that feels the same pain, was fundamental for black people to survive the exploitation and the executions that happened in the slave regime.

The multitude that takes refuge in Jesus, a new escape to the margin
Another important narrative model in guiding black theology is the famous episode of the multiplication of loaves and fishes, in Mark chapter 6. It's inspiring due to, at least, three moments:

The first is the death of John the Baptist, murdered at the request of the emperor. This is emblematic because John the Baptist dies for a trivial reason, a gratuitous demonstration of the empire's strength and violence against a subject that denounced the empire. He was a peripheral wanderer, a body independent from the management of the empire, and the death of John the Baptist also disrupts the capacity that power has to decide life and death. That mentality, typical of the colonial power, is one that a black body knows all too well. In Brazil, the body of John the Baptist could very well be replaced by the body of the mason Amarildo.[3] It could be replaced by black peasant leaders confronting land settlers. The death of John the Baptist causes frustration, fear, discouragement. It represents the threat of this homicidal and torturing power that also chases away the peripheral black population. This is the moment of helplessness.

The second moment is Jesus's withdrawal with the disciples and the crowd following them to a place that is remote, far away (here again the prospect of flight, of exodus). With Jesus goes a multitude of helpless men and women; it is a hopeless escape and withdrawal, surrounded and pressured by an oppressive empire. Here is a new departure from the centrality and power of the empire to the construction of other possibilities of existence and experiences of resistance from the margins. Facing a crowd without much direction, the disciples suggest Jesus discharge them so they can get food, feed themselves, and come back later. But the proposal is rejected by Jesus, with a simple phrase: "you give them something to eat." In other words, do not force the crowd back into dependence on the controlling empire which controls access to food in order to demand labor exploitation, absurd taxes, and silent obedience. The confrontation and overcoming of the colonizing power necessarily passes through the common resistance to the disintegrating capacity of the invested ones of the colonial power, a sort of "collective subject" not given to fragmentation. This is the moment of community empowerment, and this is the moment when this episode is very reminiscent of the quilombo resistance strategy of the black people.

The third moment to be highlighted is the episode of the miracle of the five loaves and two fishes that are presented to Jesus as the only food in the community to be consumed. But more than the literalness of having fed (or not) about five thousand people, it becomes the great metaphor of the creative and innovative power of the multitude that is able to surprise the empire. This act of feeding surprises the empire, the colony, the state, the lord and his ingenuity, and the many systems, both institutionalized and informal, that repress the collective. The miracle of multiplication is the unexpected, which may be the struggle itself or the communion that sustains the rebels in the struggle, but it can also be the subversion of the given, ready, supportive hermeneutics of the status quo. In the multiplication of small hermeneutic fishes, black theology fed famished blacks, confused and confronted hermetic, historical, and hegemonic hermeneutics. Or, quoting Peter Nash:

> When speaking of an European type of theological thinking, it is clear that one is talking about a stereotype, but stereotypes often have their origins in some form of reality. Few of us on the western side of the Atlantic have read the works of all European theologians, but those whose works are widespread in the Americas believe and teach that there is an absolute disembodied or universal truth independent of everyday experiences. Postcolonial theologies, in general, oppose this rejection of humanized theological data.[4]

Black theology and decoloniality

Here we can start a dialogue with a proposal (not given as definitive and established) of black theology as a decolonial theology. Following the definition of Ramón Grosfoguel,[5] decoloniality enhances not only pure reflection, but the epistemic response of the subalterns to the Eurocentric-U.S., hegemonic project, be it in theology, in politics, or in social relations and forms of presence in the world, but, always, kept to the border (in the margins). In the perspective of the decolonial project, borders are not only a space where differences are invented, they are also enunciated loci from where knowledge based upon perspectives, worldviews, or experiences of subaltern subjects are formulated.

But this "epistemic response," this "enunciated locus," this "formulated knowledge" should not be understood from the addictive academic comprehension. All this is present in the margins, in the peripheries, in the territories that are daily oppressed and silenced, in cities such as Rio de Janeiro and São Paulo. This knowledge is formulated, for example, from the resistance of mothers, almost all of them black, whose children were victims of state violence. Here the *enunciated locus* becomes the pain.

It is the pain territorialized, the place of those who speak from loss, confrontation, longing that is strength and memory that is faith and perseverance.

I had the opportunity to accompany some mothers who were victims of violence in Rio de Janeiro, and I reproduce here one of the reports heard in a circle of talks by a human rights group and a network of mothers who were victims of violence:

> Every day I think that if I lived near the Rio-Niterói bridge, I would have thrown myself from there to end this suffering. Since the state took the life of my son, my life at home with my husband is hell. Only among you, in acts, demonstrations and encounters like these, I have a little happiness.

It is embarrassing, for those who constantly listen to their reports and follow the struggle, to have to hear them repeat the same stories of loss in the various meetings in which they participate, a cycle that seems to have no end. We hear, feel undignified and weep—I cried during two or three statements—and it feels like inhabiting a hell materialized around us. It is embarrassing to have to hear them speak again about the death of their children: of the shots that crossed the head; of torture with a bag and drowning; the humiliation before dying; the ignored body; of the crime scene that was violated and forged to simulate a confrontation; the precipitated accusation by society of "bandits" and "involved with the trafficking"; the decent funeral that was denied; the refusal to help. Each time these mothers tell what happened, they die a little. But their resurrection comes every time the memory of their children calls for justice.

When the armed wing of the state kills one, we have no idea how many dead (living without any life) the officer left behind. And every victim of the "drug war" is never just one "victim." Black youth of the favela. Young black police officers living in the same favelas. The state kills where, when, and how it wants, without getting its hands dirty, as it uses the hands (and faces) of others to squeeze the trigger and shout while it shoots. The weeping of each mother at the genocidal violence that consumes the youth in the Brazilian peripheries is generated from the State. Who will stop the state? With these women, the academy must learn to be affected, beyond its instrumental rationality, data, well-crafted Power Points, and well-explored and interpreted concepts. With them, churches need to learn to have faith, perseverance, and indignation through an alienating environment that does not approach their members from the real world; they need to cry, feeling the same pain. With each of these mothers, NGOs need to learn not to be coopted, not governed by the state, but to guide, demand from, and face it. With them, we all need to learn to be supportive, less ideological, more subversive, more firm, and for the sake of love and justice, to have the courage to look into the eyes of the state—with its founding racism—and tell it with the strength of a mother: "We will bring you down." It is the same reaction as the Hebrew midwives. It is the same reaction of black mothers enslaved or embedded in a racist society, which protect sons and daughters from the pain, and prepares them for the pain and the hostility that will come.

Black theology in Brazil, although it has not prospered contemporaneously with black theology in the United States and South Africa, for example, is inserted into a set of "reactions" with new readings made from the margins. It goes along with other narratives that are disputing the liberation of the watched and conditioned subjects. In the decolonial perspective of Grosfoguel, everything must be provincialized, that is, to lose this centrality that pushes to totalitarian control, to suffocating and repressive homogeneity. I would also state, closer to us as Latin Americans, everything must be peripheralized, made peripheral, with no place at the center, moreover, critical of the centrality and hierarchy of places of power and their forms of access. Black theology is in this narrative dispute, conscious that a hegemonic hermeneutics, "from the center," will always demand veracity, legitimacy, or, in other words, "explanations." But it would respond calmly, as James Cone:

> It is obvious that, because white theologians have not been enslaved or lynched and have not been placed in ghettos because of color, they do not think color is an important starting point for theological discourse.[6]

Conclusion

I would like to conclude by proposing an invitation to an effort, nothing new, perhaps similar to what Rudolf Bultmann called "demythologization." Provoked then by black theology, I am inspired to demythologize the many myths that we have and that we construct in a society of "colonial functioning," those centralizing, totalitarian, hegemonic thoughts, that guide our daily life.

I propose that we demythologize public safety, and its advocating aura of "keeping order." The public security programs in Brazil in particular are the continuity of control and intimidation of black and poor bodies, of curtailment and confinement in precarious and equally criminalized territories. We should demythologize the great media and its construction and maintenance of the stigma against the poor black youth of the favelas. We must demythologize the elections, which remain the only form of popular participation, but which, nevertheless, restrict, block, and neutralize all forms of popular participation. We must demythologize the left, when clothed with intellectual purism, guiding the organization and the course of the oppressed that it intends to defend without allowing itself to be affected by its narratives. We must demythologize Justice and how it is used in defense of the interests of those who concentrate power, of who approaches the centrality and how it is used as an instrument of oppression and control of those who are at the margin—a permanent judicialization of life. We must demythologize the primacy of economics, which makes every subject or product, or consumer either invalid (therefore disposable), or productive (therefore necessary to the primacy of productivist pragmatism), the selectivity of the lives that matter (hence the need for movements such as Black Lives Matter).

Notes

1. Azzi, Riolando. A Cristandade Colonial: Mito e Ideologia (Rio de Janeiro: Vozes, 1987), p. 111.
2. In Brazil, Quilombo is the name given to the places of refuge of the escaped slaves from the cunning and farms of the masters during the colonial and imperial period. In the quilombos, slaves tried out an experience of freedom and of community practices. In Brazil, the most famous quilombo was Palmares, located and still preserved today in the State of Alagoas, northeast region of Brazil. Palmares rose to prominence in the second half of the seventeenth century and endured for more than a century. Its most legendary figure is the black Zumbi.
3. The well-known "Amarildo case" is the story of the man, the black, Amarildo, a resident of the Favela da Rocinha, one of the largest favelas in Rio de Janeiro, who was approached by police officers in front of his wife in 2013, taken by them and never returned. The investigations pointed to death and disappearance of the mason after being tortured by the

police, who believed that he was part of, or had information about, drug trafficking in the favela. The phrase "where the Amarildo?" gained international repercussion and was one of the most quoted during the famous "June 2013," when a series of gigantic demonstrations took over the entire country.

4. Nash, Peter. Relendo Raça, Bíblia e Religião (São Leopoldo, RS: Cebi, 2005), p. 33.

5. Grosfoguel, Ramón, and Joaze Bernardino-Costa. Decolonialidade e perspectiva negra. In Revista Sociedade e Estado – Volume 31, number 1 January/April 2016, pp. 15–24.

6. Cone, James. O Deus dos Oprimidos (São Paulo: Paulinas, 1985), p. 64.

CROSSCURRENTS
BEING A BLACK PASTORAL AGENT IN THE CONTEXT OF BRAZILIAN REALITY

José Geraldo da Rocha and Cristina da Conceição Silva

Introduction

Being members of the association of Black Pastoral Agents (BPA), we are connected with ourselves and with our ancestors' faith history. Throughout its ecclesial journey, the BPA gave birth to a protected space for growth in faith and blackness, brought about by people involved in the process of transforming the world through the constitutive elements of Justice. Black consciousness operates in this space as a key element in strengthening the fight against racism, despite the great challenge for its development in Brazil. The history of BPAs has taught us that the achievements of black people need to be fostered every day, always considering the different social and political contexts. To be a BPA is to be committed on a daily basis to the implications of having faith in a God who is with the poor people and has a black face, and whose spaces of expression are also associated with terreiros (sacred houses). Our commitment to the values of Africanness discovered in the terreiros will drive a new way of being in the world and a new way to fight for the justice of the Kingdom.

As we reflect on the invitation and the challenge proposed by the Ecumenical Association of Third World Theologians (EATWOT), the first thing that came to mind was a song that nurtured the journey of the Black Pastoral Agents. "I am so black, as God created me I know how to struggle for life, to sing for freedom and to like that color."[1]

In this song, whose author is unknown, the first element is the affirmation of blackness. This affirmation was very difficult to accept due to racism and the association of blackness with the ugliest and worst things in the world. Therefore, black consciousness erupting is a cry for justice, and with it the certainty that we are children of God, because we are created by Him, with our black color. From this certainty, the struggle for life and freedom will be generated, without denying our blackness.

In order to respond to the proposed challenge, this text was drawn up in three sections. The first section elucidates the obstacles faced by the BPAs in Brazil at the beginning of their journey due to racism and prejudice against all things related to blackness. The second section touches on some of the history of the organization, highlighting the relevance of Liberation Theology in promoting hope among the poor and, consequently, Blacks. Finally, in the third section, we present an overview of the current situation of Black Pastoral Agents and the relevance of the activities of this organization for the fight against racism, discrimination, and religious intolerance. These three elements characterize the meaning of being a BPA today.

It takes awareness

The subtitle suggests that one of the first necessary statements in this text is that it is not easy to be black in Brazil, it is not easy to be black in the Americas, it is not easy to be black in the diaspora, and it may not be easy to be black anywhere in the world. Our proposition requires us to reflect on the difficulties of affirming oneself as a black person in Brazilian society, and also as a Black Pastoral Agent in an ecclesial context where Christianity, wrapped in the cloak of Eurocentric culture, overvalued a notion of God which relegated to the back burner other cultural notions of God, particularly those of African origin. Therefore, to be a Black Pastoral Agent in the context of our Brazilian reality is a matter of asserting a certain identity. This identity is marked by faith, which acts as guidance for our actions against racism, and in the promotion of racial equality. To be a Black Pastoral Agent in this context requires the sharpening or the uprising of consciousness, which, according to Ardunini, can be understood as follows:

> Consciousness is to know that we know. It is self-recognition. There are human beings that ignore that they are humans. And there are

those who do not explicitly know that they are human beings. What makes the difference is consciousness. (...) without consciousness, human beings are equal to objects. They become as disposable as objects. (Ardunini 2002: 84)

This consciousness enables the transition from object to subject of history. Black people acting in history as subjects, and not as mere objects, is the result of the enhancement of consciousness crafted within black groups. This black consciousness, acquired by Black Pastoral Agents, has become a major disruption in ecclesial life. Becoming a subject of history, something that black consciousness has taught us, makes us stand differently in the face of racism and discrimination in the churches and in the daily practices of Brazilian society.

Our God is a God who makes History with us. We are certain of God's presence nearby, walking with us, hand in hand, and encouraging us amidst the hardships experienced by the black community in their daily lives, both in Brazil and the Americas. Racism and discrimination are attacks against human dignity that confront the magnitude of God expressed in the features of black people in the diaspora. The cry that rises from the ground echoes as a loud groan of the spirit. To be a BPA is to find in this reality a refuge for the deepest human aspirations. It strengthens the fight, for just like He did in the Exodus, God hears the cry of blacks. So, as subjects of history, BPAs begin to see themselves as people with a mission containing and expressing the beauty and richness of blackness manifested in black identity. Blackness then, begins to be understood as a gift from God.

> The discovery of blackness as a gift from God awakened the Black Pastoral Agents to the need to place it at the service of the cause of the Kingdom among the impoverished. The values derived from blackness are fruits of divine goodness, and no one receives a talent for himself, but to serve the cause of the Kingdom of God through the community. To act in the perspective of negritude, as a gift, is to act moved by the Holy Spirit of God. (Rocha 1998: 156)

As a gift, blackness must be at the service of the black community. We affirm that "BPA-ness" is a prophetic dimension of blackness. To be a BPA in the current context of Brazilian society is to face courageously the challenges of the materialization of God's justice among the poor, and particularly among the black community, making every effort to overcome discrimination, racism, and all forms of related intolerance.

Patchworks of our history

A little history will help us understand the meaning and significance of BPAs in Brazilian society. The stories of the Black Pastoral Agents begin in the early 1980s, where they primarily worked in Ecclesial Base Communities, pivotal places of life, and hope for the poor in Latin America, founded and supported by Liberation Theology. Inspiration for BPAs was based on the belief that blacks working in the churches and social movements faced a reality that was not always considered in all the social struggles of the black movement.

The BPAs were initially apprentices of Liberation Theology. They taught us to become aware of the rights and the challenges that our faith placed in a socio-ecclesial context. Since then, they have triggered many important discoveries, among them the great wealth of resources and culture in black communities. This discovery triggered a boom in the Black Pastoral Agents organization, which required a meticulous networking of grassroots groups and commissions at a state, regional, and national level, as well as the election of a board that operated institutionally. It was a time of discovery, of the "good news of blackness," and suddenly, what was black, was now also beautiful and had value. It was a time when faith and church were blackened.

Initially, black priests guided this process of reflection and organization. Faith and blackness, the place and role of black people in the churches, were subjects that have always been present in the early discussions of the organization. The growth of the organization required new ways of responding to demands at a national level, leading to the establishment of an executive board. In the beginning, this board was closely linked to the black ecclesiastical ranks of the church. This was reflected in the election of Father Toninho as president of the Black Pastoral Agents organization. The ecclesiastical affiliation of the priests directing the organization, and their ties to religious congregations, reduced the difficulty in obtaining resources for the organization. The BPAs were structured in large regional quilombos as a way to revive faith and blackness in black groups and communities. The quilombos were our networks for education and training about blackness.

Times changed, as did the ideas on the organization of the BPAs. The role of the laity began to gain momentum, leading non-ordained people to be elected as president of the Black Pastoral Agents. The rise of laity caused some black priests to withdraw, and consequently, some funding sources also pulled back. The diminished revenue inaugurated a new era for the institution. The large gatherings that took place in the early years suddenly became unaffordable, as our people did not have, nor they do to this day, the resources available to support the entity. Numerous attempts to reorganize themselves have been pursued in order to reduce costs. However, the long-awaited sustainability remains a problem far from being solved. This difficulty, coupled with many others, influenced the organization of the entity's grassroots groups.

An overview of the current affairs of BPA

Today, Black Pastoral Agents are organized in fourteen states of Brazil. The context of affirmative action policies implemented in Brazil from 2003 onwards caused many social actors struggling against racism to gain greater visibility and recognition, and the same happened with the BPAs. Currently, the work of the BPAs is noticeable in different contexts of social struggles in Brazil. However, in recent years, there has been a noticeable shrinkage of achievements and greater inability to gain the kind of political access that would make the interests of the black community relevant at a national level.

This new situation urges us to reflect. Factors to consider include changes in the ecclesial setting, but also in the political landscape of Brazil. Many basic issues black people fought for were incorporated in the social demands of the policies implemented by the state. Entering the labor market for many of us dramatically changed our availability for militancy. We are not denying this is a good thing. However, in this new framework fewer people feel compelled to gather and discuss issues, such as the need for running water, since they already have it. Those who sought to have electricity, asphalt, employment, sanitation, among other basic state services, now have access to it. Moreover, some people within our group took positions in the executive or legislative branches and even in the private sector, creating a split within the organic nature of the BPA. Simultaneously, many of us took our first steps within the ecclesial grassroots communities sustained by Liberation Theology. This ecclesial practice was assaulted by the conservatism of the church, which discouraged many black people from discussing their rights within church groups. The disintegration of social movements also reached the BPAs, and nowadays, the grassroots groups are almost extinct in many places. The conscience of a BPA remained in the individuals: once a BPA, always a BPA. Nonetheless, the dynamism required to strengthen the fight no longer occurs in the same manner that it used to.

The entity needs to find new ways to organize itself. It may no longer be worthwhile to think in terms of a massive organization, but rather to keep the flame alive for individuals who are fighting against racism, religious intolerance, and discrimination and promoting racial equality, as these are guiding elements in the struggle of our faith and our ancestry. It is worth considering that the BPA's main thread has always been the idea that our role as black people must be present in all areas where we operate on a daily basis. This idea was the subject of much debate at the foundation of the black pastoral work, as it relegates blackness to a segregated space for consideration, a model that is incompatible with the concept of the BPAs. If there are BPAs in the Pastoral of the Land, in the Catechesis, in the Pastoral Worker, in the Daughters of Mary, in the Cebs, and in many other places in the church, as well as in the Terreiros, at the schools, at the universities, in public institutions, and so on, a ghetto model is clearly not the most appropriate way for the BPAs of implementing a mode of action and intervention.

The traces of an ancient faith increasingly become a reality in the daily life of black groups in Brazil. The God of life is revealed and expressed through religious practices and experiences in African-Brazilian cultures, whose privileged place of manifestation is the terreiro (a Candomble house). The recognition of Candomble houses as spaces for the manifestation of God added new meanings to the BPAs' practices in their fight against racism and discrimination in Brazil.

For many centuries, the Church's action was based on the need to evangelize black people. The struggle of BPAs, however, has shown that black people are the true evangelizers in the churches. God is already among the black community. The experiences in the groups of Black Pastoral Agents throughout these decades have been clear evidence of the God of life making history with us. The signs of the presence of this God can be perceived by all those who manage to extricate themselves from ethnic, cultural, religious, and social prejudices, and remain open to the action of the Spirit, which enables everyone to understand and discern what the other one is speaking in his own language.

The journey of Black Pastoral Agents has resulted in progress for anti-racist struggles, leading black people to dive into themselves, taking the history of it for themselves. With this history comes also the awareness of Afro-ethnic belonging, which contains an ancestral cultural tradition from a historic, cultural, and religious point of view and, consequently, the legitimization of different views on black people and their relations in Brazilian society.

Christianity in Latin America, particularly in Brazil, experiences a certain discomfort with the African-Brazilian communities, especially in regard to how historically it has dealt with the African religious matrices. According to Hoonaert, the way Christian religions have connected with the black community in Brazil is characterized by a systematic process of institutionalized violence. From the first "religious gesture" of Catholicism during the colonial period, which was the baptism of black people arriving to Brazilian ports to be enslaved (Hoonaert 1978, 1983), to the present day, where the most diverse forms of religious intolerance have disrespected black people in their religiousness and diminished their human dignity.

The political project of the Brazilian state, associated with religion, spared no effort to implement the system of slavery, one of the most abominable practices of violence that mankind has known. The slave regime as a political system made use of violent methods and practices to submit and subjugate black people to forced labor. In this subjugation process imposed by the system, the religious expressions linked to African traditions were viewed and treated as an affront to the interests of white colonizers, since they functioned as physical and spiritual strengthening elements of the enslaved black people.

The way black people experienced their religion in the colonial period was perceived as a threat to the system, which is why it was understood that they should be persecuted, fought, and exterminated. Authors, such as Eduardo Hoonaert, state that the manner in which Christian churches relate to the black community in Brazil is marked by a systemic process of institutionalized violence. From the first "religious gesture" in Catholicism to baptize black people who came from African to be slaves during the colonial period (Hoonaert 1978, 1983), till the present days with diversified forms of religious intolerance, black people have been disrespected in their own religious views and practices, and diminished in their human dignity.

In this socio-ecclesial context, the action of BPAs, who from within the Christian churches are harsh critics of the racist and discriminatory behavior of the churches, will expose and intensify conflicts. On the other hand, the recognition of the values of blackness present on the terreiros eventually leads Black Pastoral Agents to participate effectively and affectively in the religions of African origin.

The significance of the presence and experiences of many BPAs in these areas has contributed substantially to opening up new possibilities for dialog. No longer as evangelizers, but as heirs and participants of an ancestral tradition of African origins. That understanding drives a new mystique, where religious values of "Africanities" act as strengthening elements in the fight. The ancestral faith, so often denied and silenced in the country's history, and preserved with African zeal in the terreiros, has been assumed, by BPAs, as a dimension of its own existence as black men and women.

The commitment to the values of Africanities discovered in the terreiros will drive a new way of being in the world, a new way to fight for the justice of the Kingdom. A blackened faith is born and with it, consequently, new pastoral, ecclesiological, and theological implications. The need to investigate further this blackened faith raises, among the BPAs, theological reflections also in light of the processes of blackness. The realization that the God of life is not only the God of the poor, but also the God of the black, awakens us to the prophetic dimension of our presence in the world.

Final considerations

Since we started with a song, we will finish now with another song. "We are coming, we are singing, with rebellious samba, we are human, I heard the cry, of this black people, crying and fighting for right and justice, a cry for justice is in the air."[2] This cry for justice involves the dynamics of action of BPAs from the perspective of promoting racial equality. Being a Black Pastoral Agent in Latin America and particularly in Brazil is, above anything else, to be focused in the dramas lived by the black community, and to seek incessantly alternative humane practices.

It appears that in society, black women, although the majority, continue to be victims of sexism, as well as patriarchy and Eurocentric racism; black youth live in absolute vulnerability, being the biggest victim of the processes of extermination and social exclusion; the religious communities of African origin experience dilemmas as a result of religious intolerance against themselves and their religious practices, and all the ills secularly imposed by poverty. In this scenario, a BPA makes every day a covenant with the law of the Kingdom. A cry for justice is in the air! And the certainty that God hears the cries of his oppressed people, feeds the fight, engenders hope, and guarantees victory.

Notes
1. Walking song of the Black Pastoral Agents.
2. Song of the black groups written for the 1988 Fraternity Campaign that had the Black as theme, the same year in which the centenary of the law abolishing slavery in Brazil was celebrated.

Works Cited

Ardunini, Juvenal, 2002, Antropologia, ousar para reinventar a humanidade, São Paulo: Paulus.

Hoonaert, Eduardo, 1978, Formação do Catolicismo Brasileiro 1500/1800, Petrópolis: Vozes.

Hoonaert, Eduardo, ed., 1983, História da Igreja no Brasil, Primeira época, Tomo II, 3rd edition, Petrópolis: Vozes.

Rocha, Jose Geraldo, 1998, Teologia e Negritude: um estudo sobre os Agentes de Pastoral Negros, Santa Maria: Editora Pallotti.

CROSSCURRENTS

BLACK PASTORAL AGENTS AND THE BIBLE IN THE AFRO CONTEXT
A Hermeneutic of Years of Enchantment

Obertal Xavier Ribeiro

Introduction

In order to reflect on the 32 years of presence and action of the Black Pastoral Agents, it is necessary to consider the articulation between the Word and life. Amidst so much suffering, an enchantment remains: the certainty of our faith in a liberating God, who walked with our ancestors and walks with us. He reveals Himself through various and different manifestations existing in the black community, in religions and cultures, manifestations that create the need for dialogue and encounters. This revelation has shaped the way we celebrate and remember of the role of black people in these years of history and experience, in the places and spaces we occupy, in our origins, in the present and the future.

Interpreting these years indicates a path, a feeling of appreciation for the steps already taken, steps that were not taken by us, but that we continue to remember firmly today; we sing them, dance them, celebrate them, and finally live them.

From living to chanting

Part of this text was created and, one could also argue, lived from the daily commute to work on the train from Central, the mass transportation system that serves the Baixada Fluminense, and is part of the daily life of many black men and women of Nova Iguaçu. We first asked ourselves: Is this the place of the black and the poor? These comings and goings, of course, reminded us of slave ships. This inhuman type of transportation that once brought our black people from Africa is somewhat similar to the one that now, using railroads, takes people from the suburbs to downtown Rio de Janeiro to produce wealth for someone else.

We think of theology at this place in particular, taking the Baixada Fluminense as our reference. It is a place where many who came from other parts of Brazil live, people who profoundly experienced the Exodus and the scars of slavery; they move along, swung not by waves of the ocean but by the sway of the trains, dreaming about liberation on the quilombos (TN: hinterland settlement founded by slaves that fled from the plantations in Brazil).

It's worth remembering a poem by Solano Trindade[1]:

The filthy Leopoldina train running, running
seems to say there are hungry people
there are hungry people, there are hungry people...
Choo-choooooooooo!

Caxias station once again, to say it again, running,
there are hungry people, there are hungry people, there are hungry people

Vigário Geral, Lucas, Cordovil, Brás de Pina, Penha shuttle
Penha Station, Olaria, Ramos, Bonsucesso, Carlos Chagas
Triagem, Mauá, filthy Leopoldina train running, running
seems to say there are hungry people, there are hungry people, there are hungry people

So many sad faces, wanting to reach some destination, somewhere
The filthy Leopoldina train running, running
seems to say there are hungry people, there are hungry people, there are hungry people

Only in the stations while slowly stopping, it starts to say
if there are hungry people, feed them; if there are hungry people, feed them
if there are hungry people, feed them

But the air brake, authoritarian, tells the train to shut up, Pssssssssst!

This leads us to think and recall a very common song among Black Pastoral Agents when we were organizing ourselves to prepare our formation and our celebrations in the communities. We sung it many times in our meetings throughout Brazil: "Eu sou lá da África" ("I am from Africa"). It is worth revisiting the lyrics, so simple and meaningful to our experience:

>I'm from there! From Africa!
>If I'm not from there, my parents are, from Africa.
>I'm from there! From Africa!
>If I'm not from there, my grandparents are, from Africa.
>I'm from there! From Africa!
>If I'm not from there, my ancestors are, from Africa.
>Because of my color, because of my smile!
>Because of my walking, because of my Samba!
>I'm from there! From Africa!
>If I'm not from there, my parents are, from Africa.
>I'm from there! From Africa!
>If I'm not from there, my grandparents are, from Africa.
>I'm from there! From Africa!
>If I'm not from there, my ancestors are, from Africa.

It is a common song and memory among Black Pastoral Agents reminding us about what enchants us, and helping us recognize our origins and our place on the Earth, and consequently in the Bible.

From singing to enchanting

It wasn't just singing: More than that, our organization had a common interest, which was reading the Word of God. The Black Pastoral Agents discovered in these meetings and in the Holy Bible that people have a mission. This is the beauty of our work and our insertion in the Base Ecclesial Communities, reaching Santa Maria on the state of Rio Grande do Sul. With the accomplishment of having black people as the main theme of the national Fraternity Campaign in 1988 (The Fraternity and the Black: "Black, an Outcry for Justice!"), we sang and marked place and time—"Blacks, women, Indians. At the Church of Santa Maria, the oppressed cultures are coming up."

Their arrival "from there, Africa," was not without reason. They were exploited, but also identified as the people of God who escaped from Egypt, which is located in Africa. Examining both stories as a true encounter with the God of Life and Liberation, we discover the need to participate not only within Christian churches, but further, going toward religions of African origin, the traditions of our parents, our ancestors, in the terreiros (meeting places) for Umbanda and Candomble and in the traditions of the resistance like capoeira, maculelê, samba, pagode, and other expressions that delight the lives of our people. These new places have become references for a testimony of liberation and resistance, which was not exclusive to Catholic communities or the profession of Christian faith. It springs from the encounter and is a true witness of the presence of the God, who walks in other spaces. It resulted in a great place to make theology.

From enchanting to moving beyond the chant
Charmed with the assurance of God's presence in our lives and throughout our history, we moved on to read and interpret this presence and to construct the meaning of our own identity as black theologians. We also started thinking about our reality, and the possibility of a Black Feminist theology, which is how the women's group of the Black Pastoral Agents emerged. This theology surely comes from the poor in an ecumenical and pluralist manner, but it is beyond ecumenism; it addresses the need for an inter-religious dialogue, because religious leaders of African religions are not recognized in the process and ecumenical space. Considering this historical condition, we know of the non-recognition of the Pais and Mães-de-Santo (priests of Afro-Brazilian religions) for their religiosity, and we also know how much they suffer from harassment and marginalization, yet they are resilient and victorious.

Identification came from the Word of God itself in the book of Exodus:

> Yahweh then said, 'I have indeed seen the misery of my people in Egypt. I have heard them crying for help on account of their masters. So, I went down to release them from the hands of the Egyptians and to bring them to a good and broad land, a land flowing with milk and honey, the place of the Canaanites, the Hittites, the Amorites, the Perizzites, Hivites, and Jebusites. Now the cry of Israel came to me, and I also see the oppression with which the Egyptians are oppressing. Go, I will send you to the Pharaoh to bring out my people, the Israelites.

As we remember and recover these stories, the certainty of the loving presence of God, the God of the Exodus on this path of liberation, grows in our hearts and memories. It is important and good, even today, to reaffirm our faith in the Liberating God who sees the misery of His people, hears their clamor, and comes down to free them. In this liberating tradition, black women rescue the figure of Hagar. "Hagar gave a name to Yahweh who had spoken to her, 'You are El Roi,' by which she meant, 'Have I also here looked after him that sees me?'" The matriarch, the mother of her people, knows that God sees her and affirms her feminine vision of God, knows her situation, and determines her place and the place of encounter with her God.

The African slave, who also had numerous descendants, is both the unsubmissive and the submissive who seeks His rights, the one to whom God revealed Himself, the liberating mother who helps us to believe "in Him who lives and sees me." Created in the image and likeness of God, we recognize that the liberating action of God leads people to search for life within a community and with dignity. Looking at the first chapters of Genesis, we find ourselves with a God who created human beings in His own image and likeness. How often have we heard this text and reflected on it?

We heard these words with our collective ear and soul, as black men and women who have their faces and bodies discriminated against, exploited by an ideology that asserts their inferiority. We are created in the image and likeness of God, created from the earth, with the colors and the smell of earth; we take after the face of our Father-Mother. Our faces resemble the deity, who created us. This makes us raise our heads, recognize our dignity, strengthen our self-esteem, and walk in search of liberation, an exodus then, in search of new places, year after year.

It's God who occupies the spaces, steps out of His corner and takes a posture of love for His people. He creates and recreates continuously. He sees, hears, knows, comes down, and delivers. He shows Himself and lets Himself be seen. These should also be the steps of African-Brazilian theology, which would lead us to walk throughout time, a time of religious freedom. Being conscious of the need to walk toward religious freedom and to proclaim with others "I've got faith" has marked our journey. After seven years in the movement, the presence and participation in the fight for religious freedom is an expression of the place we want to occupy theologically. Together with other religious leaders, who dialogue as well with other various religious expressions, we are placed in a social sphere, in a position of building freedom and democracy.

We gradually discovered the great wisdom of meeting each other, a wisdom that enables us to receive and integrate the presence of the Living God in these new spaces, to assimilate and cultivate the possibility of exchange, giving and receiving. This allows us to rescue and receive the transmission of that ancient content present in the oral tradition of "our elders," which enables and ensures the spiritual state of listening to God, necessarily by listening to others in our time. This text then became a key reference; as we return to the origins of liberation, we are provided with a direction, in this context, a return to the origins of our people.

Back to the origins

It is necessary to affirm that African religion and culture left an important legacy, which is essential to understand the values of the black people who came from Africa and built their history on this part of the earth. With a particular method and entirely original elements, resisting all cultural and religious impositions, prejudice and racism, men and women of the terreiros (religious communities), the Babalorixas and Yalorixas have formed a religious tradition and cultivated spaces of faith, worship, preservation, resistance, and stubbornness since the days of slavery. It is this persistence and creativity, this authenticity and identity, these fundamental values that have crafted the cultural formation of the Brazilian people.

They offer us a way to worship God and to relate with nature—and they should be seen as makers of a transforming and revolutionary social and religious consciousness, enabling a mystical encounter with the creation and the Creator, surpassing religious spaces, reaching the sacred. As with capoeira, samba and carnival, this cosmovision has an importance and a meaning in which life and existence are united with the divine, as it is well expressed in a samba enredo from Rio de Janeiro: "Oh, what a beautiful thing, oh what a beautiful thing, God the Father, Creator, creates the black color, oh what a beautiful thing!"—a Samba Enredo, Third Prize for the Samba School Beija-Flor de Nilópolis, 1978.

> Danced in the air
> The echo of a joyful song
> Three African princesses

In sacred Bahia
Iyá Kalá, Iyá Detá, Iyá Nassô
Sang like this the Nago tradition
(Olorun)
Olurun! Lord of the infinite!
Order that Obatalá
Make the creation of the world
He left, ignoring Bará
And slept along the way and got lost
Odudua
The divine lady arrived
And adorned with great offering
Was transfigured
Five guinea fowls and the earth was made
White pigeons created the air
A golden chameleon
Was made into fire
And snails of the sea
She went down, in a silver chain
In an enlightened journey
Waiting for Obatalá
She is queen
He is king and comes to fight
(Ierê)
Iererê, ierê, ierê, ô ô ô ô
They fought a duel of love
And life appears with its glory[2]

Through this form of worship, we gain awareness as a possibility of construction for universal knowledge, providing a differentiated quality of life that rescues the human being, male and female, close to the divine, queen and king. These are references in the struggle for the planet's survival, and the search for better relations between individuals, groups, and society. A construction of values emerging from the history and culture of black people, in the beautiful and charming way of singing and telling. This provides us with some indications on how to think about this pooled experience throughout all these years.

New forms of the experience of God

We believe there is more than just one way to experience God. In our practice of faith, in the various religious and cultural manifestations, in our everyday life, in the face of an exclusionary society, there are also other places to experience God. A God who not only reveals Himself as a father, but also as a mother, as the earth, as a sister and a brother, as a friend. A God who eats and makes Himself food, dances, celebrates life and fights, manifests Himself in nature and in the symbolic life. It is a God who is also a black woman, a child, corporeal.

This manner of living and expressing our experiences with God, simultaneously rich and simple, teaches us not to absolutize the Christian experience as the only experience with God. Moreover, it pushes us to reflect beyond some indicatives based on certain elements that systematize the experience of life to a hermeneutics that needs to be updated after all these years.

Indicators for a black hermeneutics

The progress made in these 32 years offers us some direction. To outline a black hermeneutics is not an easy task, but we are certain that taking the path will teach us along the way. Thus, what we present here are some premises that arose from our experiences in biblical rereadings and from working with black communities. A biblical hermeneutics from the reality of black people requires a confrontation with traditional ecclesiologies, in pursuit of new ways of becoming a church with a Christology that has been historically built from a white, male ideology. Indeed, this model of Christology is problematic, where the person of Jesus Christ is the only basis of the revelation, with a liturgy which does not take into account the religious manifestations of black people and ignores their body language, their mystique, and their mystical traditions, while perceiving the Western and European assumptions as the sole starting points for celebrations.

The reading of the Bible from a black perspective demands a certain political position. One does not need to be black to read the Bible from a black perspective. A black hermeneutics cannot be regarded as a skin color issue, but as a political one. To embrace the cause of black people is to embrace a liberation process that implies a radical social transformation, where all of us can take part, with our cultural specificities and fundamental contributions to a society, which does not discriminate nor marginalize people on the basis of gender, age, race, or sexual orientation. Such a position necessarily clashes with colonial theology and forces us to search for new paths.

Postcolonial theology

From the colonial period to our present days, the resistance of black people has been a key element, guaranteed by the orality and practices of our ancestors. The orality and the transmission of knowledge within the religious spaces of African matrices, as well as the cultural traditions, ensured a very important legacy. It is in such context that we reflect on the African-Brazilian theology, taking into account the African religious and cultural expressions. Today, this is already discussed within academic circles, and the rich historical and cultural legacy is recognized for its contribution in the social and religious formation of the Brazilian people. However, it is important to stress how this formation was grounded on life and practice, in a context in which the Black Pastoral Agents are embedded.

We understand today the possibility of theological thinking and of considering the black issue in light of a postcolonial questioning of the African and Latin American context, in particular the Afro-Brazilian cultural, social, ideological and religious aspects. A fundamental question arises from the kind of thinking that favors the need to live and to create a theology, and a hermeneutics acknowledging personal, religious and community values, a way of being and thinking in an African place, or in our case, an Afro-Brazilian place. The initial question we asked ourselves is whether European theology is theology?

African theology needs to be approached from its origin, conception and mentality. In the same way we affirm the relationship between philosophy and theology, we find a relevant line of questioning between the European mind and its conception contrasted with the African mind we inherited.

> One of the main ones was Leopoldo Senghor's negritude project, which sought to reveal African identity by distinguishing the mental characteristics of Europeans and Africans. According to Senghor,

the European mind distances itself from its object and regards it without passion, using an ordained given system with preset laws that make the system intelligible to a neutral observer. On the other hand, Senghor states that the African mind does not dissociates itself from the world, but rather develops its knowledge of things by becoming at the same time subject and object, sensing matters passionately via participation.[3]

Therefore, we have not only another place from where we can reflect about theology, but also another passionate way to do it, in a closer, more engaging and participatory way. This is evident in the practice of making circles, where each person has an equal position. Basing ourselves on this argument we can agree with Bruce Janz that it is important to understand not what tradition means in the abstract, but what actually the African thought is, and how a local understanding and announcement by tradition enables Africans and Afro-Brazilians a better understanding of their own African lives, their own selves and the other, reality and the universe. Tradition is not an object of thought, but a way of thinking. It is a pointer in our world-life. The thought of Bruce Janz, when dealing with the situation of African philosophy—one of the themes of contemporary philosophy in action—contributes to this understanding of theology.

> [...] "What does it mean to make philosophy in this [African] place?" This is a phenomenological and hermeneutical question, rather than an existential one. It assumes that there is already a meaning contained in a lifeworld, rather than supposing that meaning has to be created or justified. This does not mean that African philosophy should ignore tradition, reason, language, culture and practicality as key concepts—quite the contrary. But each one of these concepts behaves like all other concepts as traces of a previously traveled territory of an inhabited landscape.[4]

Tradition points to what matters most, and to how it matters
Afro-Brazilian theology has to tend to its creative conceptual potential, which has its own roots. We must become part of the culture, of its ideas, not as concepts of tradition, but as the very tradition and religiosity. The question at stake here is: "what is the African and Afro-Brazilian

theology?" Understanding becomes possible when it is "geared towards the place." And it leads us to ask some question, among many other questions, throughout these years and in the future:

Where do theologies come from?

What is their relevance in life and in history?

Where is the place for these people?

A combination of ethnic and racial, national and even international, cultural and religious, political and ideological commitments of theologians affect the way theology is made. Theological thought is affected by the place where it is practiced and by the location in time when it is developed. Since the formation of the Black Pastoral Agents, 32 years ago, much has changed, even our place in churches, in society and in academy. The hermeneutical question that will allow us to interpret the next years is not purely theoretical hermeneutics, but rather the place of life—"lifeworld"—of history, of sensitivity, of the religious, the body, poetry, music, dance, the natural environment, the cosmovision, and so on.

Bringing black life to theology and reflecting on it, creating new territories and extending the scope of life will help us rebuild and project us in our path in the coming years. Here in this place, or wherever history may place us, we recognize the present, we look at the past, and we plan our future. It is necessary to reflect on a critical hermeneutical stance that takes into account its own origin, where and how it appeared, how it expresses itself, its own purpose and direction.

It's important to understand not what tradition means abstractedly, but what tradition is in African thought and how a local understanding will enable African and African-Brazilian people a better understanding of themselves and other people, the African life, reality and the world. Tradition is not an object of thought, but a way of thinking and interpreting. It is a guiding sign of the "lifeworld" or place which the Black Pastoral Agents had already built.

Final considerations

In order to consider the liberating action of God in the history of men and women, referencing the long history and struggle of black people in Brazil and Africa, and in the Bible as well, we must refer to a saving history built year after year. The last 32 years of the Black Pastoral Agents has been a search of identities, of encounters and of understanding the action of God along the paths, seas, roads, and trails that our parents and our ancestors have crossed, leaving us a huge legacy to follow and a path to travel. This leads us to a new attitude toward the continuity of traditions and expressions present in the history and culture of the Afro-Brazilian people. It is essential to consider the need to give a new meaning to the Bible, in the face of new questions, new interpretative spaces, and new subjects.

These are just some representations, among many others, indicating possibilities for reading, rereading, and living the historical experience, where the life of Afro-descendant people takes place, as they encounter theologians, poets, samba dancers, and experienced and wise people. Africa is in the Bible and in the life of Afro-Brazilian people, who went through and are going through an Exodus, which creates and recreates existence, while celebrating another year.

Notes

1. Solano Trindade denounced the inequality and the injustice in Brazilian society. He was a precursor of the debate about race in Brazil. Throughout His life, Trindade worked with poetry, arts, theater, and folklore, but he was above all the poet of the simple people. For His song cited here, he was arrested and had His book confiscated. In addition, in 1964, one of His four children, Francisco Solano, died in a prison of the military government. Trindade was instrumental in spreading art and craftsmanship that transformed the city that now is now as Embu das Artes (Embu of the Arts).
2. The creation of the world in the Nago tradition, by Neguinho da Beija-Flor, Mazinho, and Gilson.
3. Carel, H., D. Games, *Filosofia contemporânea em ação* (Porto Alegre: Artmed, 2008), p. 111.
4. Jans, Bruce, "A filosofia como se o lugar importasse: a situação da filosofia africana," in *Filosofia contemporânea em ação*, eds. H. Carel, D. Games (Porto Alegre: Artmed, 2008), p. 111.

CROSSCURRENTS

AFRICAN INDIGENOUS JUREMA
The Greatest Common Divisor of the Brazilian Minimum Religion[1]

Nancy Cardoso and Cláudio Carvalhaes

> To Afonso Maria Ligório Soares who taught us to do theology as pilgrims, from tent to tent, in transitory ways, but animated, since our pilgrim bodies are always the home of the Spirit.

Over the course of the last few decades, questions surrounding what encompasses a minimally Brazilian religion (MBR) have been discussed and debated in conjunction with the consolidation of the religious studies field. One of the most significant attempts to address the issue was articulated by Andre Droogers, who gathered contributions made during the 1970s and the 1980s in the Revista Religião e Sociedade (1987). Brazil is a country that has had to overcome its own self-understanding as a Catholic Christian country and to acknowledge its religious polyphony over and above any attempt by the Church to establish cultural consensus. This process of acknowledgment remains an important task today, as this process is still incomplete and the religious field has only become increasingly complex.

Carlos Brandão identifies "a great symbolic matrix of common use, onto which each group edits and adds its own repertoire of beliefs," and Pedro Ribeiro de Oliveira considers that "...there should be more than one set of religious elements available to different religions," suggesting that a possible MBR would stem primarily from popular Catholicism. Rubem Cesar Fernandes prefers to talk about a "common substrata capable of reaching an agreement among the many traditions" or "elements of general knowledge" that are shared by several religions with certain variations on the "relationship among each of the parties" (God, nature, human beings, deceased souls, and both positive and negative deities). He particularly debates the role and function of the "clergy" as a "translator" in relation to the religious mass seen as "polyglot," yet unable to translate its contents on its own. Drooger, however, believes that the MBR is not dependent on intermediaries (translator priests), nor does it need recognition from so-called institutionalized religions.[2]

Based upon this debate, Droogers proposes the following concept for MBR:

> It is a religiosity that is publicly manifested in secular contexts, that is conveyed by mass media, but also by ordinary language. It is part of Brazilian culture. It exists on a national level and can even serve nationalistic purposes.[3]

Since its inception, this debate has developed in many ways and has continued to inquire about Brazilian culture and what might be unique to it in terms of its relevance to the religious question. This process of actualization has taken two discernible paths: a descriptive research method based on science and methodologies used in anthropology, sociology, history, etc., and research centered upon particular subjects' (women, black people, gays, etc.) modes of belief. While the first path has solidified the intuitions present among the "patriarchs" of religious studies, the second has acknowledged the divergence in dealing with religious power and its representations (class, gender, ethnic, etc.).

Two important examples of this second research trajectory deserve to be mentioned here: Brazilian feminist and black theologies.

Ivone Gebara highlights the experience of poor, black, native women in Latin America: prostitutes, women who were abandoned by their husbands, etc., and gives priority to women making choices for themselves as the first step toward determining the role and function religion serves for them. In this sense, a real "minimum" does not exist, but we should still ask what the "minimum" for women is. Gebara relativizes all efforts at a so-called women's "popular reading of the Bible" and identifies a potentially more meaningful set of realities and power relations.[4]

Similarly, Afonso Maria Ligorio deconstructs the debate on syncretism and religious enculturation, asserting that most efforts to establish a viable "minimum" end up reinforcing the "maximum" religion and its capacity of annexation. To Ligorio, displacing the issue of enculturation as a means of correcting a decayed and flawed syncretism fails to deal with the power issues present in the religious sphere.

> Was it African and indigenous people who corrupted Portuguese Catholicism, or it was the latter who violated the ancient traditions of the former?[5]

This question highlights an ambiguous relationship, but loses its paradox to the extent to which the maximum religion occupies public space and defines the acceptable modes of belief through its visibility and ability to occupy mediums. This occupation confuses and/or erases the existing complex relations of power from view in the public space, and as a result, almost always lends support to hegemonic pretensions of power and knowledge—the very same ones that are laid down by the maximum religion.

Within this logic, creating a supposed single minimum not only loses sight of the existing and resilient elementary/minimum forms, it also loses sight of the disputes, conflicts, and modes of belief that are involved in broader class struggles—modes that create a place of their own, grant access to public space, and give a name to things and places that are both invisible or visible.

The descriptive and analytic efforts that identify an MBR through the use of public spaces end up strengthening the voices that intend to be "maximized" or "maximizing," particularly in theology. Three steps can be identified in this process of controlling the "minimum" religiosity:

1 Subordination of "minimum" expressions to the "maximized" religions so that the latter may appear to tolerate localized practices not likely to gain influence;
2 Usurpation and co-optation of certain ritual elements, languages, and objects that break with functional autonomies, as well as the theological displacement of experiences that are not easily tolerated or might gain influence;
3 Prohibition of and the fight against religious practices/beliefs with the potential to gain influence and maintain their functional autonomy.

The relationships between formal and informal religious systems are not limited to the (occasionally ineffective) attempts by certain institutionalized systems to subordinate, co-opt, or abominate, but are marked by an ambivalence between accommodation and resistance on the part of certain popular religiosities, an ambivalence that creates this apparent minimum consensus, or an equivocal/uncertain symbolic residue that will be accommodated as an MBR.

In this sense, the pursuit of common, shared, or displaced elements from diverse religious registries cannot be "minimized" by using descriptive and analytic logic. These elements do not fit within a pocket-sized ecumenism that, intending to maintain a public space for religion (theology), also constrains diverse and divergent expressions. Religion, like culture, is full of conflict, disputes, and violent power relations that legitimize subordination. Any expectation of an elegant appeasement of these rough edges is merely a restatement of the "maximum" modes of the Christian religion and its desire to maintain power in the public space. Public space does not appease the forms of colonization, slavery, and domination that persist among us. Only a particular way of thinking that proclaims itself as universal, normative, and superior (because it has been appeased!) can expect to look at such conflicts and identify the "minimum" of the others who are not as smart as they are.

If we must talk about "minimum" things, let us ignore the sanitized residues controlled by the patriarchal, white, and colonized voice of science and technology.

> Two elements help us understand a position that radically rejects a syncretic process in the Christian system. The first one is the self-understanding of Christianity as a religion that holds the only and true revelation from God. At the core of such pretension would be a concept of static (ahistorical) revelation that, based since its inception on facts of faith, would immunize this tradition against the several levels of syncretism that constitute any and every religious group along its historical development. Such a stance inevitably leads to an artificial conflict (ideological, ahistorical and idealistic): the kerygma revealed (by God himself) to the Christian community versus other religions that were subordinated to the laws of sociology.[6]

This discomfort is particularly important in helping Latin American feminist liberation theology to resist co-optation and falling into an easy "I-want-to-be public" theology. The ever-present challenge of dramatic social inequality and structural racism does not allow for any form of reduction.

Following the suggestion of a "minimum religion," we might also ask what a maximum Brazilian religion would be look like—perhaps a fact that comes before any interpretation, with a pretension to plenitude, purity, and authenticity, and to being tasked with organizing the world as democratic and universally representative. In contrast, the minimum religion would be viewed (because it would be interpreted as such) as partial, unofficial, deconstructive, dangerous, destabilizing, and unrepresentative except for in a few sectors of society.

Jurema's multisensory polyphonies

The women of the Agro Ecologic Web of the People of Bahia[7] gather to play ancient songs and produce dances and rhythms that continue to enchant the southern part of Bahia. "Enchanting" here involves being taken over by memory, by ancestors who were not defeated by death, invasion, or oblivion. All of southern Bahia is inhabited by enchanted men and women, orixás, and caboclas. There on the coast of Brazil, in between the forest and the seas, the first native communities met with invaders 515 years ago. The excessive conquering of the land, tearing down the forest, and enslaving the people served to de-evangelize the local people forever, making their gods and goddesses more beautiful and necessary. Bahia's history demonstrates the radical resilience of people and of their modes of belief as they fight for their land and territory.

The women first gathered two months before the event and anticipated their fourth full organizational gathering in December of 2015. It was an opportunity for 60 women to live together and talk to each other. The Agro Ecologic Web of the People of Bahia believe in

> the need to articulate our struggles against racism, religious violence and other colonizing and euro-centric practices that came with the ships of discovery and are still repeated, day after day, as if there weren't another way, as if we were beyond repair... it is time to cultivate a land where alliances are forged and we UNITE ourselves in wisdom and joy to defend our cultures, cosmo-visions and territories.[8]

What brought the women together for this meeting were questions of practices and debates on agro-ecology in a difficult and contentious political scene, as well as within a context of increased artificial planting of eucalyptus, pasturage set aside for cattle, and the growth of touristic enterprises. The Cabruca designates the forestation and way of life of traditional peoples of southern Bahia. The Cabruca includes both the preservation of large old trees and new ways of planting, interspersing cocoa among the fruits and trees of what remains of the Atlantic Forest. It is both from and in the Cabruca that the people of the forest draw their sustenance, maintain their pleasures and flavors, and delight in life.[9]

The articulation of traditional peoples' struggles for land and territory in the region joined together with the materiality of both the Atlantic Forest and of the Jurema and their rituals. In between conversations on agro-ecology, we met under the shade of Jurema and African indigenous pluralities.

Alternating between black and indigenous beats, smoke bathed the women and invited them to the circle. Inside the circle, we wove a web through the necessary, urgent, and extremely beautiful articulation of people fighting for their land. Jurema created for us and in us the opportunity and means of doing so. Each one danced in her own learned rhythm, but we let go, and an overwhelming sense of joy took over the space.[10] In between conversations, I asked the other women: What is Jurema? How does it work? The answers came mixed with stories and examples that spoke of individual and social bodies and territories: Jurema opens the body, opens paths, gives joy to festivities and rituals; Jurema closes the body and protects it from diseases and hazards; it prepares and strengthens the body for work and sustains it in struggle and hardship.

The meeting of a rural social pastorate: a theology of good living and Jurema
At the 2015 national meeting of the Rural Pastoral Commission[11], the experience of sumakkawsay (good living) was discussed. More than a concept or a phrase, sumakkawsay is an experience of the ancestry of native Andean communities that is reflected in projects advocating for life, and even in the constitutions of Bolivia and Ecuador. The question that was posed was whether the traditional peoples in Brazil also understood "good living" as an ancestry that projects itself as the uniting element in their struggles. Someone commented, "Sumakkawsay—would that be the

same as our understanding of an earth without evil?" Then, someone from the northeast of Brazil said, "We have Jurema!"

Each one then shared what he or she knew about Jurema and what it meant to the traditional peoples in the Brazilian northeast. Long-standing questions and intuitions were awakened: remedy, ritual element, medicinal plaster, beverage, multiple uses of plants that make up the imagination and daily life of many groups in the country and in the cities. It is both indigenous and bears African roots. It is a relationship with nature, with place, with ancestors.

> Jurema is a typical religious expression of northeastern Brazil. It is both a rural and urban religion, but scholars have only recently become interested in the urban Jurema that involves the confluence of other religious expressions such as umbanda, Catholicism, candomblé and voodoo from Maranhão. Its name, of Tupi origin, is linked to some species of trees found in the dry region of the northeast: Mimosa hostilis (recently reclassified as Mimosa tenuiflora), Mimosa verrucosa and Vitexagnus-castus, respectively known as black, gentle, and white juremas. The black jurema is used to make the beverage that gives the name to this religious world. It probably originated in pajelança and toré, religious systems that are at the base of indigenous sacred understanding.[12]

Jurema as a smoking hybridization

At this gathering of women, the paradigm of cultural and religious pluralism was essential to create unity among peasant, indigenous, and quilombola women, as well as among students and representatives of environmental organizations.

The economic models in place in southern Bahia have always favored large cacao, cattle, and, more recently, artificial eucalyptus farms, creating an environment where people and other living beings have been exploited and exterminated for the last 500 years.

The arrival of men and women from various parts of Africa reinforced in the territory the despair of not belonging. With no knowledge of language or place, these sequestered and enslaved people, through songs, prayers, and memory, maintained a sense of origin that was incredibly resilient. Demonized and silenced by their owners' faith, they quickly had to become familiar with the land, and they used names that they brought with them to designate rivers, rocks, and trees. De-evangelized by the love of the Word and the litanies imposed on them in an attempt to mirror European beliefs (in which they were unable to see their own reflections), black people opened their ears of resistance and learned how to listen for the singing of torés and how to recognize who they were without losing themselves or disappearing. In the eyes of the indigenous people, they saw windows of reconciliation with this place.

Nobody knows the exact moment when Jurema's smoke left the toré to beautifully envelop the powerful rhythm of African religion reinvented in Brazil. It may be that in the ancient quilombos, the common fate of natives and Africans created a spark of conviviality between the circles of the two and, at some point, Jurema's actions and infinite manifestations in the forest began to be shared by <u>torés</u> and *catimbós*. And thus, Brazil was created... even if only in its potential one day simply to be.

Political practices and daily struggles also accompany an articulation of the culture and religions of the local people. In one of the first Portuguese colonization attempts, native peoples of southern Bahia were quickly evicted and suffered a lengthy process of annihilation, assimilation, and alienation from the land. There were also black slaves, who were an important piece of many economic cycles, working on the land but remaining alienated from it. The landless were farm workers imprisoned by the coronels, whose stories reach far beyond the tales found in Jorge Amado's novels[13] and continue to permeate power dynamics in the region.

For years, each group resisted and fought these powers in its own way. However, with various successes in regaining the land and fighting repression, these movements began to grow closer and work together. At this particular gathering of women, we celebrated this trend of approximation and mutual recognition. Beyond objective goals of organization and creating a deeper political understanding, means of resistance and struggle reflect the wisdom and embrace of the mystical that spring forth and integrate profound discoveries and intuitions that serve us on our path to theology and spirituality. This is an uneven path, marked by many forms of violence, including the violence of strategic invisibilities that left deep scars still open in Brazilian religious history.

> At this point, we wish to point out that most likely the reasons for the invisibility reside in magic/religion dichotomy as value judgments. The persecution of terreiros, especially during the years of the Estado Novo (New State), occurred under police control as they considered terreiros under the term Charlatanism. In 1933, the Mental Health Service was created in Pernambuco, led by Ulysses Pernambucano and other intellectuals such as Gilberto Freyre, Gonçalves Fernandes, and René Ribeiro. Quite simply, the SHM was an attempt to raise Candomblé to the category of religion, considering it a component of the formation of Brazil, thus removing terreiros from police jurisdiction. However, that shift didn't happen to Jurema, which continued to be recognized as charlatanry and primarily accused of using false medicine for healing work. This attitude towards Jurema made Jurema's religious altars to be hidden within terreiros.[14]

This unfortunately did not happen to Jurema and its healing rituals, which continued to be understood as magic and not a formal religion, and which are constantly accused of charlatanism and the practice of false medicine. The fear of constant attacks caused Jurema to place its altars within terreiros, a movement apropos of ecumenism or religious pluralism. A deep solidarity based in shared strategies of survival connected Jurema with the terreiros, one sustaining the other, each protecting, honoring, guarding, and expanding the other. At the core of Jurema is an influx of religious energies, all joined to protect and empower the lives of its people.

The role of mystique

Jurema is like an old conversation between black and indigenous people that lingers in Brazilian history. It is a liturgical gathering in response to oppression. The mystique is created by and comes in the wake of the struggle, thus becoming and continuously transforming itself into the plural identity of indigenous and black peoples. The mystique, the spirituality of the people and their possible theological progress, comes from the continuous fight for life and survival.

> In brief, instead of providing a representation "of its own," Jurema multiplies the representations. It is not a single plant, but encompasses the (polysemy of the) whole forest. Its feet are cities. It resembles a woman, cabocla, a beautiful indigenous dark-skinned woman...

Powerful, heir of an oral culture, she roots herself in words: "its" natives sometimes manifest themselves as spiritual beings similar to romantic literary constructions or to images from civic celebrations (Santos, 1995); sometimes, when they effectively resemble people and indigenous communities, at least in part, they receive such an identity from concepts taken from literary anthropology.[15]

The memory of violence that lacerated (lacerates) the flesh of native and black people in Brazil creates trenches, prayers, movements, visitations, and healing. A shared solidarity and mystique capable of recreating known and unknown worlds, categories of thinking, and sacred movements ignored by the oppressor was maintained and continuously revived in the forest and in the encounters needed to live, however, big or small. The spiritual promiscuity between indigenous people and spirits, black people and enchanted ones, as well as their oral nature, reflects its maximized mystique, exhausted by the immediacy of the full life that is necessary to strengthen a celebrating people. With that, it confuses, deafens, and makes a mess of the metaphysically barbed Christian canon.

Mystique does not happen within forced doctrine or confessions of faith, but emerges out of a materiality of the dances and smoke that traverse unauthorized spaces and mystify people united against the violence of the law. Mystified, they live and survive; they rearrange their spaces and symbols. The mystique softens identities, skin colors, histories, legacies, traditions, and whatever else is needed. The enchanted ones and the spirits mobilize themselves to ensure the survival of the people. What once was distinct is now common; what was once separated now lives in and through relationship; what asserted itself as autonomous now participates in the dance of intersectionalities, in a continuous rediscovery that recreates worlds of life and ancient wisdoms.

When the people say, "We have Jurema," they are saying, "We have a measuring rod and compass, and we do not need your precision." In the fight for the lands that were taken, for the lives cut short, for the rights that were stripped away, decolonized bodies live their life-and-death struggle, trying to return to what was once theirs: their home.[16]

Possessed by enchantment

In contrast to the obsessive controls of Christianity, the indigenous and African-based religions are directed by the orixás and the enchanted.

Control is lost, and all is subjected to the directions and charms of the enchanted ones and the orixás. This possession defines what was and what will come to be, transfiguring identities and states of mind. It is a power that takes over, directing and organizing everything. The possession of these wonders goes beyond the formal analysis of a descriptive and defining theology that comes before living. Instead, they are concerned with the composition of energies and synergies, with the compensation of good for evil, the preservation of the good, and caution in the face of evil, without the particular polarities found in Christianity. The meeting space is always sacred, and it is in the trance, in the body, that the communication between distinct realities takes place.

Jurema and space

Jurema's mystique is not timeless, but keeps track of time through the space and the ground that provide life and harvest. Jurema is both a tree and a beverage with religious and medicinal properties to care for the people who gather; it is an entity, a place of worship and ritual, a metaphysical indigenous woman, a long line of enchanted people and caboclas, men and women from the desert and the water's edge, an object, a forest, a tree trunk. Many orixás landed here with the Africans, escorting their sons and daughters, and partnered with the local entities, because African religions leave a space open for gathering and adding various religious expressions. In the wake of those developments, Jurema expanded the African pantheon, and the orixás expanded themselves by living together with Jurema and the enchanted ones. In this deep solidarity and highly particular confluence, the space of mystique establishes itself in the communion of indigenous peoples, blacks, and caboclos.[17] Jurema is found in settlements. With the alienation of indigenous and black peoples from the land, their livelihood moved from the forest to the spaces of Umbanda. It lives in the interchange with the Umbanda rituals. But the notion of settlement links itself with the settlement of excluded people in lands that were stolen from the natives. Blacks were settled in this land, and now, they need to assert their rights to it. Uprooted, Jurema's roots in the settlement create a notion of belonging, even though a deadly melancholy remains its most primal song. Cosmogonies became intertwined and transformed. Settled in this land life, Jurema reconfigures the dimensions of public space and determines anew to what and to whom it belongs. This reconfiguration happens in the mixed reordering of indigenous and black cosmologies. African indigenous entities live off their deep relationship with nature. Thus, the struggle of the women from the Ecologic Web of the People of Bahia is this symbiosis between spirits and nature, tribes and quilombos.

Jurema as one who redefines class

The welcome of Jurema within the diversity of oppressed people recreates class structures. The expansion of the concept of and access to the sacred is plural and is detached from monetary value. Quite to the contrary, it breaks and balances out diversities, thus redefining class systems. Everyone sits at the Jurema table, and its table extends itself throughout the entire forest.

Parallels and disconnects with christianity

In the complex Brazilian religiosity, Jurema is a minimum–maximum religion, a non-religion that unsettles Western thinking. The very notion of religion is put to the test, since the concept of religion is a Christian invention that symbolizes the *religare* of the creation removed by sin from the God that created it. Jurema does not fit into this or any other notion of religion, but is rather a set of understandings, practices, and wisdom that arises from the ground and ingrains itself in the daily lives of peoples in all its forms, colors, and challenges. Jurema does not claim nor does it desire a status, be it minimum or maximum. On the contrary, it is the remaking of life, the sacred without dichotomy, immersed in life and things. It does not organize or accomplish anything by holding a view of the secular as being opposed to or different from the sacred. For indigenous and African peoples, everything is sacred, a dwelling of the spirits. Thus, the body, also sacred, gives itself to life lived with enchantment, the life of the body in all its fullness, without denial or guilt. The body is elevated when it is in a trance and meets the spirits, in contrast to Christianity, which denies the ability of the body to act as a sacred proxy. Spirituality/mystique happens through the materiality of dances, the rhythm of instruments and congas, and smoke. All covered in a haze, perhaps like the mysterious God *absconditus* of negative Christian theology. As a set of understandings and practices, the label of minimum–maximum does not fit Jurema, because it is at the same time both minimum and maximum, escaping pseudo-Christian definitions.

Jurema's crossbred liturgy

Jurema is a shared table of conviviality, relationships, and interchanges of power, a place of celebration, the enchanted world manifesting its charms and creating a hybrid, mestizo, "Brazilian" spirituality that is both disliked and feared by the minimum and maximum religions that breed through authentications completely foreign to Jurema's movement. Jurema is marked by its singularity and multiplicity: A place of multiple representations, it welcomes, expands, and reconfigures the needs of the oppressed—people shared by distinct gods who became common to all, for their well-being and survival. Jurema, a tree–root–trunk that through daily experiences lived with the people, becomes the potential of oppressed peoples', natives', and blacks' survival.[18] Jurema's crossbreeding comes from its originality and capacity for mutation and mutual involvement. In this sense, it is cannibalistic and symbiotic, becoming, from its originality, something else, beyond itself and because of itself. The very plurality of Jurema and its multiple forms are made not only of spirits but also of things and places, a materiality of the enchanted and charmers.[19] Thus, it confounds and defies the trinity that intends to unify Christianity. Jurema is much more than three persons. Its representations more closely resemble the multiple sacramental understanding that comes from Orthodox Christian theology than the Western Catholic–Protestant understanding of sacraments built on anywhere between two and seven sacraments. Reality and representation are mixed in several spiritual, mental, bodily, or even natural realities that are sometimes not embodied. Jurema can be drunk, the bark from its roots or trunk made into a beverage like the God that offers itself in the bread and wine. But Jurema may be mind-altering, while in the Eucharist, there is still total control of God through the forms of the ritual and possibilities of meaning.

Contributions to a Brazilian black liberation theology

Understanding black theology in Brazil requires a broader perspective, since liberation is found not only in blackness, but also in the composite colors of theology. No theology that feeds on itself can be upheld in the face of the white colonizer's power. The crushing of identities in the theological quehacer (the doing of theology) seems to be one more way to provide an ideology of conquest rather than an autonomous or self-determining mode of thinking. We propose a black theology based on its deepest shades, in the idea of a Latin American pan-Africanism and its stories in relation to indigenous hues. This co-relation, based on a profound religious pluralism, seems to us deeper, more congenial, and capable of offering not only anticolonial resistance but also new ways to live and reproduce life.

Diego Irarrázaval gives us four points to consider in the dialogue of Christianity with African religions: (1) celebrate and think in accordance with African ways about a recreation of the world; (2) identify ourselves and our continent as Afro-American; (3) celebrate the mystery of an African form where the body has a fundamental place in both revelation and the sacred; (4) engage with syncretism and with the particular wisdoms and sources we bring.[20] What is missing here is what Gebara reminds us of: the well-being that is the life of the earth and of the entire ecosystem.[21] The very life of the native and African nations is fully embodied in the movement of biodiversity. Similarly, we need to celebrate and think about indigenous forms of recreating the world. We must identify ourselves as the indigenous and consider our continent as being originally owned by the native peoples who were here first. We must understand the body, community, and environment as sacred places and engage with syncretism.

Thus, the reconstitution of a Latin American black theology would rescue a pluralistic, cultural, religious, and class paradigm that aims to liberate native and excluded people, and sees life on the planet as a fundamentally plural place full of meaning.

No black theology in Latin America can or should exclusively uphold Christianity. To base a black theology solely on Christian grounds would constitute the disempowerment of Latin American black plurality. Consequently, a black theology is only possible if it is deeply intertwined with all religions of African, indigenous, and Christian hues. For this reason, the inter-religious movement is essential, and Jurema can be a concrete space where this sharing happens.

In brief, we propose that any black liberation theology in Latin America: (1) needs to be constructed out of the relationship with indigenous peoples; (2) has to be mestizo and hybrid, and include women, gays, and oppressed people, because all black theology is composed of mixtures and intersections where oppressed people gather to discuss plans of resistance and transformation; (3) should always be a theology of settlement and class struggle: a theology of invasion, of reclamation of ownership, and of conquering by force, using all the resources of mystical symbols and the spirituality of oppressed peoples; (4) should start from the earth, the despised biodiversity stolen from excluded peoples; (5) should employ whatever resources it wishes, mixing or not whatever it wants with whomever it desires. There will no longer be a search for minimum–maximum religions.

Notes

1. "Brazilian minimum religion" can be somewhat related to the phrase "least common denominator" in English.
2. DROOGERS, André."A Religiosidade Mínima Brasileira." In Religião e Sociedade, Rio de Janeiro, 14/2, 1987, pp. 62-86
3. Ibid., 65.
4. Ivone GebaraGEBARA, Ivone. "Que Escrituras são autoridade sagrada? Ambigüidades da Bíblia na vida das mulheres na América Latina." In Concilium.Revista Internacional de Teologia, Petrópolis, n° 276, 1998/3, p. 10-25.
5. SOARES, Afonso Maria Ligorio. Impasses da teologia católica diante do sincretismo religioso afro-brasileiro. In: http://ciberteologia.paulinas.org.br/ciberteologia/wp-content/uploads/2009/05/impassesdateologiacatolica.pdf (access 15/12/2015)
6. SOARES, op.cit.,
7. The Agro Ecologic Web of the Peoples was created from the dialogues initiated at the I Bahia Conference of Agro-Ecology at the Terra Vista settlement in 2012. It is in charge of creating the annual agenda to support the development, empowerment, and emancipation of communities and their connections. Quilombolas, native people, masters of oral tradition, peasants, students, scholars, educators, children, urban, and countryside youth participate in and build the Web. In: http://jornadadeagroecologiadabahia.blogspot.com.br/p/blog-page_11.html
8. VIII Afro-EcumenicalMeeting of the Caxuté Community. In: http://jornadadeagroecoloigiadabahia.blogspot.com.br/. Accessed 20 December 2015.
9. Cabruca is a traditional agroforestry system in the region, which understands cultures within the shade of the Atlantic Forest's native trees. Cabruca incorporates and enjoys the arboreal remnants of the great original forest, which is preserved. This creates much confusion in the process of classification or any attempt to differentiate Cabruca from the Rain Forest, because the cacao crops ended up inheriting spectral characteristics of the Rain Forest. In this logic, the forest needs to remain standing and be preserved, because other plants such as cocoa, coffee depend on the shade of old trees to create an intricate system of

permanence and newness. Cabruca, Planeta Orgânico, in: http://planetaorganico.com.br/site/index.php/cabruca/

10. Articulação Pastorais do Campo, 2015, http://www.cptnacional.org.br/index.php/publicacoes/noticias/acoes-dos-movimentos/2482-articulacao-das-pastorais-do-campo-realiza-encontro-sobre-desafios-pastorais-no-campo

11. Articulação Pastorais do Campo, 2015, www.cptnacional.org.br/.../2482-articulacao-das-pastorais-do-campo-rea...

12. RODRIGUES, Michelle Gonçalves; CAMPOS, Roberta Bivar Carneiro. Caminhos da visibilidade: a ascensão do culto a jurema no campo religioso de Recife. Afro-Ásia, Salvador, n.47, p. 269–91, 2013. https://doi.org/10.1590/s0002-05912013000100008.

13. COELHO, Alexandra. O culto de índios e negros que chegou a Portugal. In: http://www.publico.pt/sociedade/noticia/o-culto-de-indios-e-negros-que-chegou-a-portugal-1665703 (acesso 20/11/2015)

14. RODRIGUES, Michelle Gonçalves; CAMPOS, Roberta Bivar Carneiro. Caminhos da visibilidade: a ascensão do culto a jurema no campo religioso de Recife.Op.Cit.

15. BAIRRAO, José Francisco Miguel Henriques. Raízes da Jurema. Psicol. USP, São Paulo, v. 14, n. 1, p. 157-184, 2003 . Available from http://www.scielo.br/scielo.php?script=sci_arttext&pid=S0103-65642003000100009&lng=en&nrm=iso>. access on 31 Dec. 2015. https://doi.org/10.1590/s0103-65642003000100009.

16. Here in this house/Nobody wants your good manners / When there is food / We eat with our hands / And when the police, the disease, the distance / Or some quarrel do us part / We feel it never stops / To fill with pain our heart / But we don't cry for nothing/ Here in this tribe / Nobody wants your catechization / We may speak your language / But we can't understand your sermon / We laugh out loud, we drink and we curse / But we don't smile for nothing / Here in this boat / Nobody wants your direction / We have no prospects / But the wind guides us through / The life that drifts / Is what takes us too / But we don't follow for nothing / Go back to your home / Go back there. Arnaldo Antunes, "Volte Para o Lar," Álbum Um Som, BMG Brasil Ltda, 1998.

17. "Jurema is a religious celebration (practiced differently by natives or caboclos) where the Jurema beverage is shared. Sometimes recognized as a specific religion in the complex scenario of Brazilian spirituality, the Jurema cult is diffused among religious practices where the beverage can have a more or less central role: pajelança, toré, catimbó, Umbanda, Candomblé de caboclo, etc. (Anthony, 2001)." Anthony, M., Des plantes etdesdieuxdans lés cultes afro-brésiliens: Essai d'éthnobotaniquecomparativeAfrique-Brésil. Paris, apud.: BAIRRAO, op.cit., (acessoem 20/12/2015)

18. "Sacred Jurema is what remains from the religious tradition of the natives that inhabited the shores of Paraíba, North Rio Grande and Pernambuco, and their pajés, experts in the mysteries of the hereafter, plants, and animals. When fleeing from the sugar cane plantations, enslaved Africans could find shelter with the indigenous tribes, where they exchanged religious knowledge with the natives. That is why, to this day, the greatest Jurema masters always have mixed native and black blood. Africans brought their knowledge about the egun worship of the dead and the divinities of nature, the orixás, voodoos and inkices. The natives contributed with their methods of invocation of spirits from ancient pajés and work with the enchanted ones from the forests and rivers. That is why the Jurema

is formed by two major lines." In "Jurema masters and the enchanted ones," *Jurema Medicina Sagradas, Aldeia de Shiva*, access on 06/01/2016. http://www.aldeiadeshiva.org/medicinas/jurema.html

19. For more information about the Jurema rituals, see Michelle Gonçalves RodriguesI and Roberta Bivar Carneiro Campos, Caminhos da visibilidade: a ascensão do culto a jurema no campo religioso de Recife. https://doi.org/10.1590/s0002-05912013000100008

20. IRARRÁZAVAL, Diego, "Salvação Indígena and Afro-Americana," in Teologia Pluralista Libertadora Intercontinental, Vigil, José M., Tomita, Luiza E., Barros, Marcelo (Orgs.), ASETT, EATWOT (São Paulo: Paulinas, 2008), 69.

21. GEBARA, Ivone, "Pluralismo Religioso, Uma Perspectiva Feminista" in Teologia Latino-Americana Pluralista da Libertação, op. cit. 298.

Works Cited

Alves, Antônio Marques Jr, Tambores para a Rainha da Floresta, a inserção da Umbanda no Santo Daime, master dissertation, PUC São Paulo, 2007, http://www.sapientia.pucsp.br/tde_busca/arquivo.php?codArquivo=5712

Amado, W., Bertazzo J., Aldighieri M., and Lopes S., 1989, A Religião E O Negro No Brasil, São Paulo: Loyola.

ATABAQUE-ASETT,1997, Teologia afro-americana: II Consulta Ecumênica de Teologia e Culturas Afro-Americana e Caribenha. São Paulo: Paulinas.

Bairrão, José Francisco Miguel Henriques, 2003, Raízes da Jurema, Psicol. São Paulo: USP, v. 14, n. 1, pp. 157–84, in: http://www.scielo.br/scielo.php?script=sci_arttext&pid=S0103-65642003000100009&lng=en&nrm=iso

Brandão, Carlos Rodrigues, 2004, da Fronteira da fé – Alguns sistemas de sentido, crenças e religiões no Brasil de hoje, Estudos Avançados 18 (52), USP In: http://www.revistas.usp.br/eav/article/download/10035/11607.

Coelho, Alexandra, O culto de índios e negros que chegou a Portugal, In: http://www.publico.pt/sociedade/noticia/o-culto-de-indios-e-negros-que-chegou-a-portugal-1665703

Camargo, M.T.L. Arruda, Contribuição ao estudo Etnofarmacobotânico da bebida ritual de religiões afrobrasileiras denominada "vinho da Jurema" e seus aditivos psicoativos, Revista Nures, Ano X, Número 26, janeiro-abril de 2014 http://revistas.pucsp.br/index.php/nures/article/download/24694/17574

Droogers, André, 1987, "A Religiosidade Mínima Brasileira." In Rio de Janeiro: Religião e Sociedade 14/2,

Estermann, J., 2013, Cruz y Coca - hacialadescolonización de larelígión y la teologia, LibreríaArmonía, Instituto Superior Ecumênico Andino de Teología (ISEAT).

Frisotti, H., 1996, Passos no diálogo: igreja católica e religiões afro-brasileiras, SP, Paulus.

Gebara, Ivone, 1998/3, "Que Escrituras são autoridade sagrada? Ambigüidades da Bíblia na vida das mulheres na América Latina." In Concilium. Revista Internacional de Teologia, Petrópolis, n° 276, pp. 10–25.

Grunewald, De Rodrigo Azeredo, 2008, Toré e Jurema: Emblemas Indígenas no Nordeste do Brasil, Cienc. Cult. vol. 60 no.4 São Paulo, In: http://cienciaecultura.bvs.br/scielo.php?script=sci_arttext&pid=S0009-67252008000400018

Irarrázavl, Diego, 2008, "Salvação Indígena and Afro-Americana," in Vigil José M., Tomita Luiza E. and Barros Marcelo, (Organizadores), Teologia Pluralista Libertadora Intercontinental, ASETT, EATWOT, São Paulo: Paulinas.

Mota, Clarice Novaes, BARROS, and José Flávio Pessoa, 2002, "O complexo da Jurema: representações e drama social negro-indígena," in Clarice Novaes da Mota, and de Paulino Albuquerque Ulysses (orgs.), As muitas faces da Jurema: de espécie botânica a divindade afro-indígena, Recife: Bagaço.

Mota, Clarice Novaes, 2008, Considerações sobre o processo visionário através do uso da jurema indígena Anais. In: http://www.abant.org.br/conteudo/ANAIS/CD_Virtual_26_RBA/grupos_de_trabalho/trabalhos/GT%2006/clarice%20novaes%20da%20mota.pdf

Oliveira, Marco Davi, 2004, A religião mais negra do Brasil. São Paulo: Mundo Cristão.

Pádua, Jorge Hage, 1991, Teologia negra da libertação - Expressão teológica dos oprimidos na América Latina, Estudos Teológicos, v. 39, n. 2, pp. 143–166, In: periodicos.est.edu.br/index.php/estudos_teologicos/article/.../715/650

Rodrigues, Michelle Gonçalves; CAMPOS, Roberta Bivar Carneiro, 2013, Caminhos da visibilidade: a ascensão do culto a jurema no campo religioso de Recife. Afro-Ásia, Salvador, n. 47. In: http://www.scielo.br/scielo.php?script=sci_arttext&pid=S0002-05912013000100008

Santos, Jocélio, 2005, O poder da cultura e a cultura no poder - a disputa simbólica da herança cultural negra no Brasil, Salvador: EDUFBA, In: http://static.scielo.org/scielobooks/hqhrv/pdf/santos-9788523208950.pdf

Sena, José Roberto Feitosa, 2009, Maracatu rural: uma herança religiosa afro-indigena na capital pernambucana, SOTER, Anais 22 Congresso, volume 3, In: http://www.soter.org.br/documentos/documento-t1xF1HqaxcboGYi.pdf

Silva, Silvia Regina de Lima, 2010, AbriendoCaminos, Teología Feminista y Teología Negra Feminista Latinoamericana, Revista Magistro, UNIGRANRIO, vol.1, num.1 In: http://publicacoes.unigranrio.edu.br/index.php/magistro/article/viewFile/1055/618

Silva, Wagner Gonçalves, 2011, Religião e identidade cultural negra: católicos, afro-brasileiros e neopentecostais, cadernos de campo, São Paulo, n. 20, In: http://www.revistas.usp.br/cadernosdecampo/article/viewFile/36804/39526

Soares, Afonso Maria Ligório, Impasses da teologia católica diante do sincretismo religioso afro-brasileiro, In: http://ciberteologia.paulinas.org.br/ciberteologia/wp-content/uploads/2009/05/impassesdateologiacatolica.pdf

Soares, Afonso Maria Ligório, 2002, Sincretismo afro-católico no Brasil: lições de um povo em exílio, Revista de Estudos da Religião – REVER, PUC SP, In: http://www.pucsp.br/rever/rv3_2002/t_soares.htm

Tromboni, Marcos, 2012, Índios e caboclos na formação da nação brasileira - A Jurema das ramas até o tronco: ensaio sobre algumas categorias de classificação religiosa, in Carvalho M.R. and Carvalho A.M., org. Índios e caboclos: a história recontada [online]. Salvador: EDUFBA, In: https://books.google.com.br/books?isbn=8523212086

Webpages

VIII Encontro Afro-Ecumênico da Comunidade de Caxuté, In: http://jornadadeagroecologiadabahia.blogspot.com.br/

Teia Agroecológica do Sul da Bahia, http://jornadadeagroecologiadabahia.blogspot.com.br/p/blog-page_11.html

Articulação das Pastorais do Campo, 2015, http://www.cptnacional.org.br/index.php/publicacoes/noticias/acoes-dos-movimentos/2482-articulacao-das-pastorais-do-campo-realiza-encontro-sobre-desafios-pastorais-no-campo

CENTRO ATABAQUE DE CULTURA NEGRA E TEOLOGIA, In: http://atabaque-cultura-negra-e-teologia.blogspot.com.br/

Cabruca, Planeta Orgânico, In: http://planetaorganico.com.br/site/index.php/cabruca/

Jurema Medicina Sagradas, Aldeia de Shiva, http://www.aldeiadeshiva.org/medicinas/jurema.html

CHRISTIANS AND YORUBÁ PEOPLE EATING TOGETHER
Eucharist and Food Offerings[1]

Cláudio Carvalhaes

> We only live by doing. Without doing, we are just existing.
>
> Padre Vieira

> I am only interested in what is not mine.
>
> Oswald de Andrade

> Religions and religious differences are an active and inseparable element of the cultural and political dynamics that are transforming the meaning of social and political connections in our time, when expressed from below, as emancipatory.
>
> Joanildo Burity

> I would say that there can't be dialogue between Christians and Muslims if there isn't a common practice. Any other dialogue outside of a common practice is just discussion. Byzantine nonsense.
>
> Frei Betto

This chapter presents the possibility of a broader form of Eucharistic hospitality which builds on early church practices and is consonant with the ongoing work of our spiritual/faithful *reformata semper reformanda* "reformed and always reforming." By exploring a possible relation between two religions in Brazil, Christianity (the Reformed branch) and Candomblé (an African Brazilian religion), I am trying to expand the inter-religious, racial, and global vocabulary, practices and notions of Eucharistic hospitable prayers. The issues at stake in Brazil's reality and the format of praxis proposed here can perhaps illustrate the growing need for churches everywhere to engage with strangers through new forms of theological dialogue and liturgical practices that can in some ways provide dialogue, justice, peace, and hospitality. Moreover, our globalized world continues to spread many forms of religions everywhere and Christians need to learn how to relate, dialogue, and live together with different forms of people's beliefs, practices, and worldviews.

Candomblé is such a religion that is apt to live in a globalized world with a strong and malleable capacity to adapt and adjust to new places and situations. Candomblé's gods travel with its people and welcome local gods where Candomblé people are received. Traveling from Africa, Candomblé changed and took on a new configuration in Brazil. Rachel E. Harding defines Candomblé this way:

> Candomblé is a rich and complex portico of ritual actions, cosmology, and meaning with deep and obvious roots in several religious traditions of West and West Central Africa—especially Yoruba, Aja-Fon, and Bantu. It is a (re)creation of these traditions, and others, from within the matrix of slavery, colonialism, and mercantilism which characterized Brazil and other new societies of the western hemisphere from the sixteenth through the nineteenth centuries.[2]

I am choosing Candomblé for what I am calling an inter-religious dialogical praxis for three reasons: (1) Candomblé is not the type of religion, like Hinduism or Islam, which other scholars normally pick for considering inter-religious dialogue or praxis and thus may offer new insights into the inter-religious work we need to do; (2) it is a religion, somewhat like Christianity, in which food and eating together play a central role in worship and thus provides an excellent inter-faith case study for reflecting upon boundaries in Eucharistic practice; (3) Candomblé has been a religion of which Christians have long been highly suspicious and have attacked throughout Brazil's history. It has become a radical other, especially for Protestant Christians, and my own faith has been deeply defined by the negation and condemnation of Candomblé people and their religious activities. Let me explain:

Candomblé is not found in the textbooks on the so-called world religions. It has no founder, no sacred texts, no normative traditions like Hinduism, Buddhism, or Islam to which most Christians interested in inter-religious dialogue normally turn. Like Christianity and the aforementioned world religions, it is also a religion firstly grounded in oral history and practices formed in local communities that reads the universe from their own social structure. However, Candomblé did not take the next step of forming sacred texts. Instead, it continued its movement and continuous formation through the passing of its own secret (*awó*) by oral history to those who belong to the group. As for its various traditions, they are not defined primarily by dogmas, religious, or theological ideas but rather by their practices defined by social groups (tribes in Africa) that move, transform, and give structure to their world. That is why it only makes sense for us, Christians, to establish a dialogical–practical relation with Candomblé people. In addition, Candomblé happens to be a religion, somewhat like Christianity, in which food and eating together play a central role in worship and thus provides an excellent inter-faith case study for reflecting upon boundaries in Eucharistic practice.

In Brazilian history, both Roman and Protestant Christianity fought fiercely against African religions. In general, Christians considered them to be lesser forms of civilization and their believers less human, engaged in superstitious and magical religious practices that belong to the Devil. Thus, Candomblé and other African religions seen as a threat to the Christian culture and well-being of the "free" religious life of Brazil. Moreover, since most of the members of these religions were black, one cannot disassociate this low view of African religiosities from a heavily marked system of racism underlying Christian views, concepts, and perceptions.

The widespread fear, anger, and suspicion of African religions in Brazilian culture have made African religions a mission field for Christians to conquer. Lately, this fear, anger, and suspicion have even taken more violent forms. To cite just one example, Yalorixá Dulce left the Assembly of God to become a mother of saint (a spiritual leader, a kind of pastor) in Candomblé. She told me that Christians came to her house, where her terreiro (worship space) is located, sang Christians songs loudly and even threw stones to interrupt and destroy the Candomblé worship celebration. This attack, I might add, was not out of step with Brazil's history of racism and Christian theological reasoning.[3]

Finally, Candomblé has become a radical religious other hovering around the Christian faith in Brazil. Once Prof. John Makransky asked the following question to a group of scholars who were doing inter-religious dialogue: "What is your (personal) fundamental motivation for doing this work and how does that influence your theology? Is it related to your predilections or is it something else deeper in you?"[4] My faith can only be understood when I look back and see that most of what I affirmed was grounded in a negation and denial of other people and other beliefs, including African religions. At school, church, and on the streets of São Paulo, I learned that Candomblé was a religion dominated by demons and controlled by the Devil. I could not cross the front door of a terreiro, a Candomblé worship place lest taken captive by those demons. Very early in life I became a fervent evangelist and my mission was to convert these demonized people who were made captives by the Devil and were going to hell.

It was much later that I started to learn that Candomblé people were not people of the Devil but my brothers and sisters. The movement away from fear and into a space of trust and admiration was neither quick nor easy. I had to meet them, I had to visit their own worship spaces, I had to invest myself, I had to see their rituals, I had to eat their food, and I had to invite them to be part of my own life. Thus, engaging new forms of relation here, I want to find and foster a somewhat safe space where Christians can connect with Candomblé people and, through practical movements, create a process of restitution for Candomblé people and a space of shared joy, care, respect, and hospitality.

This chapter holds the belief that by searching for sacramental possibilities through inter-religious dialogue/praxis and by exploring the relationship between Christianity and Candomblé, we can find a space for dialogue, reconciliation, connection, dismantling of racism, healing peace, and hospitality. Thus, my initial questions are as follows: Given the Brazilian history of slavery and racism, can we provide a space of reconciliation and hospitality through common rituals of eating, praying, and dancing? Can we offer sacred food to each other and can we eat together? Can the Eucharistic table carry food offered to Orixás (gods of the Candomblé)? Can the Orixás allow Christians to eat their food? How can do such things while respecting our own limits and expanding our possibilities?

One might ask why we must bring the history of colonization and slavery to the Eucharistic table? As we have also seen, the Eucharistic table establishes not only theological, liturgical, and ecclesiastical boundaries but also social/economic /political borders which delimit the ways in which a community defines itself, engages issues of power, and determines the norms and standards of its own identity and worth. In one word, the Eucharistic table offers a certain understanding of humanness. By taping into the ways in which Christianity in Brazil dealt with black people and their religion, the question of what it means to be human is open again. We, who are at the table, are also responsible not only for ourselves but also for those who are not there and for what is going on in our society.

Slavery and Candomblé in Brazil

The history of Brazil is the history of Indians, Europeans, Africans, and their religions. It is around these encounters that Brazilian cultures and identities were formed. The African people have been fundamental to this cultural, religious, and identity polydoxy. Africans enriched Brazil's ways of thinking, literature, music, food, religions, and ways of relating. Nonetheless, Brazil's history is deeply tainted by almost 400 years of slavery perpetrated by Portugal. The Portuguese, unhappy with the work of the native people, imported African people from their colonies in Africa. In 1590, there were as many as 36,000 slaves in Brazil; by 1817, there were 1.9 million, and by 1850, there were 3.5 million slaves. "In total," says Luiz Felipe de Alencastro, a Brazilian historian,

> more than 4 million Africans were deported to Brazil between 1550 and 1850, making Brazil the American country that received the largest amount of slaves arriving in the New World. If compared to United States in the same period mentioned above, Brazil received 43% of Africans, while the United States, from 1650 to 1808 received 5.5% of Africans brought to the Americas.[5]

In 1888, Brazil became the last major country in the world to enact a law ending slavery. However, slavery continued in many different ways, deeply affecting the people and religions of African descent. The impact of 400 years of slavery is still very much alive in Brazil today, but is made nicer by the Brazilian cultural apparatus. Brazil's racism is not an "in your face" movement with public signposts saying "blacks are not welcome here"; it is subtle and "nice," making people think that they live "in harmony" while it keeps black people at the bottom of society. This so called "cordial racism" shows the ideological myth of racial democracy in Brazil. Its niceness is so pervasive that it makes fighting against it way more difficult.[6]

This does not mean that there was no African resistance to it. One of the most significant was Quilombo dos Palmares[7] in the 17th century. Slaves fled from their owners and created these free cities in remote areas and were joined by the disfranchised. More than 20,000 former slaves and other socially rejected people, including Europeans and indigenous people, lived in freedom in their own sovereign place.

Brazil is slowly starting to delve more deeply into these differences and into the acculturation of Afro-descent peoples. As Africans arrived in Brazil, they brought their religions with them. However, slaves were forbidden to practice their religion and were forced to learn the Christian faith. Especially during the nineteenth century, the Portuguese made clear attempts to destroy the religious practices of Africans and Criolos (blacks born in Brazil). Candomblé beliefs and practices considered to be a sign of an uncivilized culture, featuring magic and pre-modern elements of religion that were not part of the modern civilized European Christian project for Brazil. Forceful attacks on Yorubá and other African religions continued in different forms until the end of the twentieth century.

Nonetheless, Candomblé and its people were able to survive in spite of continuous persecution by the Brazilian government and systematic repression by the police force until 1975 when a federal law was finally issued to protect *terreiros de candomblés* (worship places) from invasion, abuse, and destruction. From that time until now, it has been a continuous struggle for the Candomblé people, called "people of the saint," to survive and live freely in this nice and cordial racist South American country called Brazil.

Candomblé[8]

Candomblé is grounded in the mistery of *awô*, the secret that is transmitted orally to new generations of believers over time. Candomblé is passed on by the initiated as they live its religious precepts together. It has a non-structured orality at its core and only recently have efforts to write about African religions been made. In Candomblé, the tradition is sung and danced. The synthesis of the whole process, says Alessandra Osuna, would be

> the search for an energetic equilibrium between the inhabitants of the material world and the energy of those beings who inhabit the orum, a space dimension that could be called heaven, the interior of the earth or a place beyond anything that is known, according to different understandings of tribes, peoples and traditions. Each human being has an Orixá who protects him/her and that person will only know if s/he gets in touch with the Orixá through a ritual. By fulfilling the obligations ascribed by the Orixá, the person receives a reserve of energy and will gain more equilibrium.[9]

The same way that we cannot talk about Christianity but Christianities, we also need to talk about Candomblés, in the plural. Candomblé varies according to its various traditions: congo, jejê, nagô, queto, ijexá, angola. Roger Bastide says that "It is possible to distinguish each of these 'nations' from the way each nation plays the drums (with sticks or hands), their music, the idiom spoken, songs, liturgical vests, names of divinities and for certain aspects of the ritual."[10] Moreover, "'each house of Candomblé is a sentence', that is, each house of worship finds notions of right or wrong, its theologies and religious understandings of their histories and antecessors."[11]

Gisele Omindarewá Cossard, a very well-respected Yalorixás, engages three essential African traditions in the Yoruba line: "the Yoruba aspect of the houses of Ketu tradition, the Fon aspect in the houses of Jeje tradition and the Bantu aspect of the houses of tradition Congo/Angola.... The world of Candomblé is multifaceted."[12] However, the differences in the African traditions do not mean that the Africans are polytheists. Olorum, Olodumarê, and Zaniapombo are names for the same God creator of all. According to Vilson Junior, "Candomble is grounded on three pillars: (1) Secret—Religion or orality; (2) Respect—hierarchy; (3) Precept—liturgy."[13]

Pierre Verger, a French scholar who went to Brazil to study Candomblé and became a father of saint, a Babalorixá, defines Candomblé this way:

> Candomblé is for me very interesting because it is a religion of the exaltation to the personality of people. Where one can be what one

is and not what society makes you be. For people who have things to express through the unconcious, transe is a possibility for the unconscious to show itself.[14]

Candomblé carries a powerful view of the world, known and unknown, including myths of creation and offering ways that people can realize the potentiality and the fullness of their lives. Candomblé is a way of balancing the energy of the individual, the community, and the world. The movement between the visible and the invisible worlds, the connections with gods and entities (thus with oneself, communities, past, present, and future), the ways one can find healing and protection, the ways one is charged to live a just life are all part of the private sessions/rituals and public festivities. Everything happens ritually and the connection and responses to the Orixás conveyed through the rituals. The composition and demands of this very difficult and committed religion is a fascinating way to understand humanity in all its complexities.

Let us consider some of the main known elements in Candomblé:

Hierarchy and structure

The respect of hierarchy is based on the religious structure that has Olodumarê as the main God creator, Orumilá who holds all the wisdom, and the Orixás, voduns, and inquices who live in between the natural and the supernatural world. Within the social organization of Candomblé, there is a strong hierarchical structure where the Babalaôs and Yalawôs are the main leaders of the Candomblés, something like pastors/priests in Christian churches, and the iawôs, the initiated people, and then those who participate in one way or another way but are not necessarily members. The hierarchy is grounded in the line of ancestors of the African people and is the result of the ways in which the ethnic, sociocultural system with kings and queens of different nations on the one hand, and the religious system with Iorubás and Nagôs on the other were established in Africa. Kings and Queens were responsible for the well-being of peoples and communities and controlled the powers of nature. They were treated like gods. When they died, their reign was spiritualized and they became part of the history, memory, and strength of a community who made them sacred. They then become their guides and Orixás.

Worship

Candomblé is worship; it is service. Only those who are initiated know the secret and continue to grow into the knowledge of this secret. Candomblé is a religion that connects the material and imaterial world, giving space for the unconscious to reveal itself as part of the totality of the sacred. A religion that balances out the energies of these worlds and struggles with the imbalance of our attitudes and the balance of the world provided by Olodumarê, the main God creator, Orumilá. Candomblé is a service to the Orixás, gods that come from all forces of nature: earth, fire, water, and air. Babalorixá Aragão describes Candomblé as a monastery where people are in the world and the function of Candomblé and its priests/ess (Yalorixás /Babalorixá) is to take care of the initiated and the entities. Service is an exchange in Candomblé. The omniscient, omnipresent, omnipotent God (Olorum) does not need worship. The Orixás need worship! Most of the festivities are centered around singing, dancing, and eating.

Worship spaces: terreiros

Candomblé is an extension of the house, of the family. That is why the terreiros are always at the back or around of the house of the Yalorixás / Babalorixá. Terreiros/worship places are often located at the house of the mother or father of the saint. The terreiro has to be close to trees and gardens and plants since Candomblé is fundamentally related to nature where its sources come from. At each terreiro, often one main Orixá is the head of the worship place but all of the Orixás are welcomed and worshiped. It is their choice to appear or not. During festivities and specific works, the terreiros are the place where people stay, sleep, dance, eat, and live. The terreiros are the sacred places where "Orixás, voduns and inquices dance; the font where the iawôs (initiated) bathe, the sacred trees where Iroco and Tempo live; the little houses for Exú and eguns."[15] Grounded in African societies, Candomblé has complex social, cultural, religious structures, and its practices and beliefs are multiple, varying according to each terreiro. Terreiros became spaces for resistance and wrestling with old and new worldviews. At these spaces, thin and thick movements of memory, resistance, engagement, and solidarity were at work against oppression and death. As Harding puts it, these spaces refer "to socio-political, cultural, psychic, and ritual-religious locations within Afro-Brazilian experience... locations contain the implication of both boundary and movement."[16] These religious spaces kept by the African people were places that would contrast and offer alternatives to the streets (where poor, "worthless," abandoned people lived), and the senzalas (plantation slave quarters), destitute of dignity, value or pride, social locations imposed by a racist and slavocratic society. Terreiros, also called axé, the vital energy, were locations that helped Africans and African Brazilians to reposition themselves in relation to the new world of slavery, destruction and death. Harding establishes the relation of Candomblé to the African and African descent people.

> for these people and their descendants, Candomblé was an important means for the engagement of trauma. It represented an integrative process—pulling together and (re) organizing that which had been rendered asunder: family, identity and psyche.... Candomblé provided a means of re-membering and re-creating an identity of value and connectedness—to Spirit, to a pre-slavery past, to ancestors, to community. It also provided, cultivating African material and cultural elements in its rituals, an alternate meaning of Africanness, an alternate identity of blackness. And where the myriad of ignominies of life in Brazil created crises in psychic integrity, Candomblé offered transformative music and dance, community, and magico-pharmacopoeic healing. In the mutual embrace of humanity and spirit in Candomblé emerged intimations of wholeness-representations of the reciprocity of devotion and responsibility, the sharing of burdens and joys.[17]

Candomblé's terreiros were places where people participated fully, and this way of participating gave them a certain assurance of identity and self-worth, conditions to resist, restoring their strength, and living their lives under the crushing power of slavery.

Priest/ess

Father of saint, Babalorixá, is connected to Knowledge while the Mother of saint, Yalorixás, is connected to Wisdom. Long before, Babalorixás and Yalorixás were called servants. They are the ones who took care of the Orixás. The priest/ess (Babalorixás and Yalorixás) organize the worship event and make sure everything is done appropriately. They are the ones who hold the secrets of the religion and to whom the initiated owe respect and obedience. Also, they are the ones who receive and give the messages to the Orixás (entities/gods) and they decide what the worship acts, offerings, and work are to be made for the enjoyment of the Orixás and for the safety, blessing, and protection of the initiated. Rituals are corporeal and the priest/ess' (Babalorixá/Yalorixás) speaking generates energy.

Orixás

Orixás are bodiless, energetic forces that feel and think and experience things like us humans. The African understanding of the world divides neither the sacred and secular nor the human and godly behaviors of the Orixás. Orixás manifest themselves to human beings by possessing their bodies during worship at terreiros. A person chosen by the Orixá is an elegum, who has the privilege to be mounted by the Orixá. Anyone can ask and know and engage their Orixás without having to do the ritual of initiation. However, if a person is chosen by the Orixás, he/she will be asked to do the Orí, the making of the head, which is the ritual of initiation. Those who invoke the Orixás have to offer greetings, do liturgies, perform gestures and movements, sing, dance, and drum, cook, dress up with their proper colors, and follow the demands ordained by the Orixás. They have to offer food desired and spread it around the city but mostly within forests, as ways of fulfilling the Orixás desires. In everything, the believer has to obey the Orixá who in turn will offer miracles, healing, and a balanced life to the person. Orixás cannot be irritated. If they demand a work and it is not done, the believer will suffer the consequences.

Feasts, sacrifice, food, and offering

Festivities in Candomblé are powerful events with many people participating. However, as Roger Bastide said, "the public festivity constitutes only a small portion of the life of the Candomblé. The private rituals are more important than the public ceremonial. African religions will color and control every part of the life of its members, and (by ways of living its religion) the black person feels more African and end up belonging to a different mental word..."[18]

Kitchens are fundamental parts of the worship inside of the terreiros. As Edson Carneiro puts it:

> The kitchen ritual, filled with clay pans and stones to trite, with its novices and iabassês (kitchen chefs) is a fundamental point of any terreiro of any Candomblé nation... where the cook prepares the obligations, the food offerings and the drinks to the black gods. Everything is spotless. These kitchens used to be different from people's daily kitchen but now they look alike. But then and now, these kitchens hold secrets only those inside know. The way of preparation and to serve must follow some precepts.[15]

Kitchens have all the proper tools and ingredients for the cooking and preparation of the food. There is a high office, so to speak, in the work of the kitchen and a person, called Iabassê or Adagam, designated by the Orixá of the house, prepares the special food. Babalorixá Luis de Logun Edé says that "Nobody is asked if one is formally educated or not. The gift is perceived by the Babalorixá/Yalorixás and chosen by the Orixá to occupy the office. Often the person is born with this gift. Then she/he is trained so she learns how to do the many offerings for each Orixá."[19]

After it is prepared by people specially trained for it, the food/offering is (1) offered at specific sites in a procession at the sound of songs; (2) then brought to the forests or nature where the Orixá live; and (3) offered during the festivity of the whole terreiro and ate by the participants. Moreover, the offering of food to the Orixás is usually done in the evening since Orixás do not eat when the sun is up. Often Candomblé feasts end very late and with food. Gisele Cossard describes the end of a ceremony:

> It is usually too late for people to go back home... some of the yawôs (the initiated ones) go help serve the meal that is offered to the people present. This food is a generous offering of the terreiro to the whole community who came to the feast. However, according to the ancient people of the Candomblé, there is another meaning for this offering: the Orixás like plenty and they desire that all present leave with their belly full.[20]

However, there is way more to the meaning of food to the African religions. In fact, it was the women of the Candomblé who preserved and made known the African religions by ways of their ability with the preparation of the food and the making of their artcrafts: necklaces, wristbands, sewing, embedded cloth work, etc.[21] Rituals in Candomblé involve offerings of mineral, vegetable and animal kingdoms, healing, dancing, and percussion. The sacrifice of animals is a very important part of the religion. Only those who are part of the terreiro/axé can see it. Mostly, the fear is that non-believers will see it as uncivilized or barbaric. Each animal relates to a different Orixá. In each festivity, if the terreiro has the means, one two-legged animal should be sacrificed for Exú and a four-legged animal to the appointed Orixá of the house. The sex of the animal has to follow the sex of the Orixá. The Oxogum is the one who makes the sacrifice. Then, the sacrificed animal goes to the person in charge of the kitchen who prepares the food and makes it ready to be offered. After the food is offered to the Orixá in a separate room by the Babalorixá/Yalorixás, the food will be consumed by the faithful and also given to guests.[22] Every food offered to the Orixá has the power to change people's lives. Everyone can receive a blessing from the food. The food not eaten is kept for three days and after that thrown away. It was the African kitchen preserved in the African rituals that ended up going to the table of every person.

Vilson Caetano de Souza Junior says that "during the festivity, food is shared among people and means commensality. People share, live and memorize it. Food is memory and provokes emotions. Food in Candomblé has to do with the rescue of the memory of the people. The food during the service is to energize the Orixá, people and the place."[23]

The Babalorixá Luis de Logun Edé says that "Orixás eat the food that humans eat. However every offering has its own wisdom and ways of being prepared that include: enchanted words *(fó)*, prayers *(àdúrà)*, evocations *(oriki)* e songs *(orin)* connected to sacred stories *(itan)*, essential elements that are vital to the transmission of the axé. Life, power and creativity is what we use to do good."[18]

The structure of the food ritual is described by Bastide as follows: "In the morning, the sacrifice is done; the culinary preparation and the offering to the divinities happen in the afternoon; the public ceremony properly done is done when sun goes down and enter deep into the evening."[24] The eating together is a fundamental part of the festivity. Below Roger Bastide describes an experience of eating together at the end of the ceremonies. He says

> ... and before we all break up, a fellowship meal will allow the gathering of deities, members of the fraternity and the spectators who still remain in the worship room. The daughters of saint bring in dishes from the color of their Orixás, a little food, some of which had been placed in peji: white for Oxalá, blue for Yemanja, violet for Nanã... They sit around a towel placed on the same ground on which they deposited the sacred food. Each person takes a bit of the food from their god's plate, with both hands cupped, then the person scoops the food in his/her hand and raise it to their mouth. After that, it is offered a bit of each dish to the sons of other Orixás in order to cement the solidarity of the group through the sharing of the food. The leftovers are placed on banana leaves, are offered to the spectators who are standing near the daughters of saint who are seated- the various food offering from the multiple Orixás fraternally mixed in a kind of fraternal mixed vegetable tray; it is mandatory to eat with your hand. One should not confuse this repast, which is a communion, with the collation sometimes served to important guests between a calling dance and the dance to the gods. This is something very different, a kind of triple solidarity to happen before returning to the mundane world: first, between the divine and human, then the fellowship among the members who belong to different deities, and sometimes even rivals; and finally among the fellowship of the uninitiated so that a little bit of Africa that was lost can be found again and penetrate into their lives. The group of the faithful go beyond the fellowship of the sons and daughters of the saint. Entering a Candomblé is done gradually and there are many degrees of inclusion ...[25]

The food/offerings is an essential part of the life of the religion and the community, a way of re-enacting a relation with nature, commensality, memory, resistance, offering, joy, and celebration between the deities, inner, and outer community. Once we have gained a brief knowledge of Candomblé, how do we frame this dialogical praxis? What is at stake here?

Inter-religious dialogical praxis

In Latin America, there has been a great movement of theologians working on "Intercontinental Plural Liberation Theologies."[26] These theologians are aware of the need to expand the dialogue and create opportunities for theological conversation and sharing life together. As a result, they are trying to expand the discourse of liberation theology into the field of religious pluralism and engage indigenous and Afro-descent religions, spiritualities, and worldviews. This new way of engaging theology has been called "new and positive look," "pluralism as principle," "new compassion," and "macro-ecumenism, a new word to replicate a new reality and a new consciousness."[27] This liberation inter-religious dialogue is challenging us to engage ecology issues affecting the life and beliefs of the poor and to include women.[28] At the core of this Christian work, says Teixeira, "there is a convocation to hospitality, to courtesy and acceptance to alterity."[29] As we all engage into this project, Marcelo Barros calls our attention to an important aspect of its methodology.

> "Why, all of sudden theologians and anthropologists start to see positively what was called syncretism that historically, authorities and intellectuals always saw as negative what once was so negative? The only explanation we have is that such an opening happens when we are able to look at this question not with confessional eyes or from the perspective of the institution, but rather, with an eye of love towards the people, worrying about their life and liberation."[30]

This call is very important since intellectual thinking without emotions and feelings and the body being involved, as obvious as it might be, cannot entail a full inter-religious dialogue. Love is a fundamental presupposition for Christians, and worrying about people's life conditions and possibilities of liberation is more important than any methodological tool we choose to work with.

This present project hopes to contribute to this field by expanding what liberation theologians have been thinking about inter-religious dialogue in Latin America by bringing into the heart of this dialogue the need of radical hospitality described in previous chapters. In so doing, the relation between Christians and Candomblé people becomes grounded in practical ways to welcome each other. Starting from the gospel's love commandment as requiring radical hospitality to one another, this way of understanding inter-religious relationships hopes to move beyond detached dialogues to provide down-to-earth tools that can possibly, give practical shapes and forms to the notions of multiplicity, plurality, and infinite love as envisioned by Gebara, Barros, and many other inter-religious thinkers.

Theologies of religious pluralism and comparative theologies are based on reflection and practice. From a Latin American perspective, we must return to Antonio Gramsci's notion of the "organic intellectual."[31] Liberation theologians in Latin America have viewed the notion of the "organic intellectual" as a facilitator, one who gathers information hidden by ideologies, connecting it with the formal knowledge that can serve as critical tools, and engaging the pulsing reality and wisdom of the poor in order to create a different praxis that will transform the social situation and bring about liberation.[32]

The organic theologian assumes the need to change Brazil's social threads, especially those of Christian hatred that endanger the living and the religious reliefs of Yorubá people. Thus, starting from our "religious–inter-religious" perspective, we must assume that the organic theologian must take a step ahead and enter other's religious communities in order help facilitate the dialogue and the sharing of life together. In addition to the organic theologian, the organic liturgical theologian in particular must take steps as he/she is the one who considers rituals and performances, gestures, body postures, prayers, voice, hearing, vision, touch, taste, dancing, and songs as key "texts" for inter-religious dialogue.

Since Yorubá religions do not have a sacred text but is grounded in non-structured orality, the organic liturgical theologian must learn how to best engage this dialogue through religious and non-religious practices. Thus, ritual theories, liturgical reasoning, performance studies, everyday life theories, affect theories, constructive inter-religious theologies, and so on can and must engage dance, songs, bodily movements in order to help frame this inter-religious dialogue. In Christianity, the law of prayer/ *lex orandi* is what helps the law of belief/theology-*lex credendi*. In this dialogue, the law of dancing, drumming, dancing, and eating in the Axé along with the law of prayer and singing and eating in the Christian services is the *lex-agendi*, that is, the laws of respectful ethical living. As a result, a *lex-vivendi* is constantly reformed, a life where spaces of generosity, commitment, love, and care are fully lived.

It is the doing of religion that is at stake here. As J. Edgar Bruns puts it theologically, "God is the doing of something."[33] How can we understand each other from our religious practices, or, our very doing of God? What methodology, what journey, path, or road, is the organic liturgical theologian to take here?[34]

Gebara suggests what the articulating point might be: "the recognition of the pluralistic founding principles of our existence and life itself, invite us not only to understand ourselves, again, as human beings, but also, to create politics of dialogue that will help us get once again, to that which we call common good."[35] Moreover, according to Diego Irarrázaval, this process includes the ability to be open to and to appreciate the symbols of salvation that are present in other's religious search. From a Christian point of view, this process involves a recognition of the sacramentality of somebody else's religion and how the sense of the sacred is fluid and permeable in our living together.

> Sacramentality (according to the Catholic perspective) runs through the veins of the Latin American population. However, it does not limit itself to this or that church. So much of Latin American ritualism shows the importance of symbols that configures the spirituality and praxis of the daily life of people. God is loved in the everyday life and concrete realities that always carry symbolic value.[36]

Ararrázaval sees the notion of symbiosis as a perspective to approach the systems of symbols of black people, which engage "different elements that conjugated, make space for a bigger life."[37] It is through a symbiotic process of dealing with opposing forces without dichotomy or contradictions that Africans and their beliefs and practices have engaged the new land, Brazil. Christians could learn from this symbiotic movement.[38] We don't start with orthodoxy but with orthopraxis. Everyday life is the criterion of religious truth, and in that regard every religion might carry the possibility of holding a sacrament, that which is vital, important, and necessary for the living of one's life. Thus, while Candomblé has its own set of beliefs and sacraments, it does not need to undo some other faith structure, or sacrament, in order to relate or engage in dialogue; it respects and engages somebody else's sacrament for everything belongs to everybody.

Irarrázaval ends his work by offering four main points of dialogue in the Christian-African religions:[39] (1) to celebrate and to think, meaning that the celebratory way of the African religions are ways of thinking, of constructing their lives, and recreating the world; (2) to identify ourselves and our continent as African American, calling ourselves Africans so as to help us embrace the life, history and the religious elements of the African religion as common to us all; (3) to celebrate the mystery of the African way, which is the celebration of the sacred in our bodies, and to realize that the body is a privileged foci for the revelation of the sacred; and (4) wrestle with syncretism and belongings. While Irarrázaval does not explicate what belonging means, he quotes Maria Cristian Ventura to say that Afro religiosity has the power to recreate their worlds from the available religions that they have at hand. Thus, a disposition to this form of syncretism, of recreating our worlds from each other religious wisdom and tools, is a way of relating with the African religions in Latin America.

One point not mentioned by Irarrázaval but fundamental in this process is the connection with the earth. Ecology is a central aspect of this dialogue since the African religious practices are markedly steeped in elements of the earth. Every Orixá has a connection to some aspect of the mineral, vegetal, and animal world, and every terreiro is always around earth, trees, and plants. Without the eco-system, Africans would not be able to live their religions. (Neither would Christians for that matter.) For a pluralistic theology of liberation to happen in Latin America between Christians and Yourubá religions, the commitment to peace and justice must accompany the commitment to the defense of the environment. "This is the ground from which we try to build a true communion between different religious communities with their own doctrinal, ethnic, linguistic and ideological elements."[40]

She was a Methodist pastor, a faithful one to her church. However, for some reasons unknown to her, her heart was very much attuned to the drumbeats of the terreiros. So much so that she decided to study Quilombo Zeferina and the presence of powerful women in that community. A great solid academic work. However, this work got her body closer to her heart and she started to participate in the Candomblé festivities. So much so that she was called to do the initiation process. She then said no because she was faithful to her Methodist tradition. Then one morning, While she was preaching about the Holy Spirit, She was taken by her Orixá and started to move the way she did at the terreiro one night. The people of her congregation thought it was very strange but she said it was the Holy Spirit and whole people had their concerns, they believed God had manifested Godself in her. She was fine to move in between these two religions but at that day she said: " I can't do that." I must honor my Orixá and must leave the church. I will always love the church and Jesus Christ but my work is at the terreiro now.

Christianity-candomblé: movements and challenges
The opening to another in Christianity is neither a new thing nor a choice. Rather, it is a demand built into the core of the gospels and grounded in love. As Sharon V. Betcher says, using Jean Luc Nancy, Christianity has "an obligation 'the great open.'"[41] As part of this obligation to the "great open," which is an unknown, unforeseen space, Christians must always learn again the ability to offer a radical hospitality, and eating together with strangers and expanding the table of Jesus Christ must be a common practice. Again, this "great open" does not mean doing away with Christian beliefs, for the Eucharist must always carry the powerful message of the revolutionary memory/anamnesis of Jesus Christ given, broken, and shed for all, food for the world. For Candomblé people in Brazil, these theological claims are not foreign. They have been listening to it throughout their history in Brazil, and will not taken offensive at them. On the other hand, Christians could learn the claims Candomblé people make and honor their faith. At this crossroads, Christians will have the opportunity to live the gospel as a culture of hospitality, embrace, and healing. How we deal with each other's theological claims will be decided along the way. The only demand is that we must be near each other, preferentially at the Eucharist/food offering table(s). What then should we consider for a possible dialogical praxis?

Holy spirit
Every beginning depends upon the Spirit, both for Candomblé and for Protestants. For Christian Reformed people, we cannot start anything if not first deeply moved by the Holy Spirit. Our acts of praise and work to God are always a response to God's love, generosity, and demand. For Candomblé, the Orixás and entities move the energies and make us respond to their calls and demands.

For Reformed people, the emphasis on the Eucharist is not the table or the elements but rather the Christian assembly called by the Holy

Spirit. At the table, there is common food/common good and under the power of the Holy Spirit, we gather as strangers and become a family. At table, we engage God's sources of power and healing that invite mutual conversation and transformation. Reformed people are able to say boldly that "Through 'eating Christ' in the meal, this community is strengthened and preserved in its task to be the body of Christ in and for the world. With these meanings foregrounded, the meal becomes a central symbol for this new community. "[42]

A radical trust in the work of the Holy Spirit is issued so that the table of Jesus Christ becomes open, breaking down walls of self-enclosed religious membership and sameness. The presence of the Spirit at the table calls us to live radically in an egalitarian manner, sharing food, wisdom, resources, love, and care for the world. The table of Jesus Christ empowered by the presence of the Holy Spirit, offers forgiveness, healing, and reconciliation, even if continuously interrupted by fear, hatred, anxiety, injustice, death, and the perils and conflicts of the world.

Since God is the one who manifests Godself where God wants, and makes a covenant with whomever God wants, we are the ones, inspired by the Holy Spirit, to create channels for God's grace to be experienced in ways that we may not yet have been able to experience. Here we are trying to find ways in which the covenant of God can be expanded and offer hospitality to people of other faiths. We are the ones who become channels of God's incarnation.

Around the table, Christians have their Bibles, their food, their songs and their prayers praying "Come Spirit Come." However, in this dangerous prayer, the coming of the Spirit can become the coming of a stranger, a guest, one whom we were not expecting or even desiring. Once we pray "Come Spirit Come," the move of the Spirit cannot be controlled any longer. Perhaps, after our prayer we might have to welcome Candomblé people dressed in their white dresses, dancing and singing, asking for the Orixás to come and move energies through the primal energy Axé.[43] Once the Holy Spirit takes over, we must follow. At the table, we share food and struggle together to find balance in the life of individuals, of our communities, and of the world.

The Holy Spirit and the Axé are the moving forces that establish, shift, and balance the world and all of our respective universes. The Holy Spirit and Axé can transform whatever they want and are the very source of life. Christians and Yourubá people are totally dependent on their movement, and they are the sources we tap into so that we can engage each other around the table and become able to expand our religious horizons.

The engagement with Axé and Holy Spirit can become a vital theological response to the globalized world we live in. The increasing sense of dislocation marked by the growing flow of people around the globe, the hybridity of immigration, the accumulation of capital in the hands of less than 500 people around the world, the trafficking of people, the brutality against women, the shifting markets of labor and the growing new diverse local neighborhoods are just some of the signs that demand our theologies and communities to deal with the constant flow of identities and "mobile personalities."[44] The force, potency and agency of the Holy Spirit/Axé can help us engage challenges and dismantle deadly world realities.

The Holy Spirit/Axé can also help us find plural identities not in the de-ritualizing of our religious rituals but rather, in the renewing processes of the ritualization (the expansion of our rituals) of our beliefs as we encounter others along the way. In a lecture given at Union Theological Seminary after the beginning of the Iraq war, Professor Janet R. Walton asked us: "Would your service be the same if a person from Iraq enters our churches?" For some people, this question must be answered immediately with a "no," since what we do is who we are and we cannot change who we are. Nonetheless, if we could entertain the possibility of a "yes," we would need to change our worship. We can become better with the presence of another who talks about his/her own experiences and we can start attending to the words and gestures we use in our communities. If a person from Iraq is with us, we can learn about ourselves and wrestle with ways to live out our faith in more expansive, powerful, and welcoming ways. This attention to someone else does not mean to silence ourselves to shy away from who we are or what we believe, but rather the presence of another can be an opportunity to expand who we are. The Scottish Council of Churches said: "We become human through our relationships—with ourselves, others, creation, and God. Reformed spirituality is first and foremost about being grounded in what holds us in common with one another and grounded in what it means to be human." While concerned with Christian unity, this message can be help us to broad our own liturgies and theologies as well as help us embrace those who differ from us in large or small ways.

The Spirit of God shows itself through movements of unfolding openness and alterity, movements marked by dis/placements of generosities. The Spirit of God must be seen in my responsibility to myself, but always in relation to somebody else, even if this somebody else throws me at an abyss of inescapable inner and outer workings and challenges. The presence of somebody else at the table of Jesus Christ connects me to unexpected obligations toward this other and that person's people, a people that I might not have paid attention to until that moment. Thus, the movement of the Spirit in us can be a call to us to pay attention to somebody else.

From this place of unexpected openness given by the Spirit, Christians can find a common ground to welcome Candomblé people. There are common elements for a theology of the Spirit in Christianity and Candomblé. Some of them are (1) the Holy Spirit/Axé have a deep connection with the body and without our bodies there is no community. In both religions the Spirit/Orixás can possess bodies. (2) The Holy Spirit and the Axé/Orixás help us not only deal with our daily life, our struggles, our wounds, but also give us strength, wisdom, and vision to go through life. (3) The Holy Spirit/Axé always make us engage with a guest or visitor; (4) the Holy Spirit/Axé are deeply connected with creation; (5) it is the Holy Spirit/Axé who create and sustain the gathered communities; and (6) the manifestation of the presence of the Spirit/Axé is both worship and work.

In Candomblé, the relation between the Spirit and human bodies is seen in the possessions that occur during the public and private festivities, when the Orixás choose some of the initiated people in order to "ride" on their bodies as if the Orixás were mounting on horses. Believers become horses of the entities. In Christian communities, prayer for the Holy Spirit to come and take our bodies, and control our minds, mouth, and gestures are common. The surrendering to the Holy Spirit is something that Christians search for while worshiping God. In Pentecostal churches, bodies are literally taken and they shake, dance, move, and are at the mercy of the leading of the Holy Spirit. The possession of the bodies seen in both Pentecostal Christian and Yorubá gatherings have almost the same body postures, gesturing, and general movements.

Christianity spiritualizes the body in order to get to a place of acceptance with God. Based on guilt, the body needs to be sanctified, and for that it has to engage in sacrifices, like fasting, sexual abstinence, and penance, so the body can mortify the flesh and become finally spiritual, through an asceticism toward God.

Within Afro-religions, including Candomblé, black, and womanist traditions, there is an opposite movement, toward the embodiment of the Spirit. Without dichotomy or guilt, the body is desired by the Spirits, the Orixas, who come to the body freely without sanctification, to communicate with his/her own people. The body is thus the place of interlocution, of connection, of communion. Possessed by the marvelous, the body dwells in transcendence!

Candomblé and Christian believers pray for the Holy Spirit and entities for guidance and wisdom in their daily lives. They bless the Spirit, and they walk in their daily life in ways pleasing to the Holy Spirit/Entities. Both religions have a deep commitment to the transformation of society through their beliefs and practices. For both religions, God is always doing something through us. Or, using J. Edgar Bruns words, "God is the doing of something"[45] in our religions.

It is in, under, through and around the Spirit/entities in our diverse bodies and rituals that we can recreate our daily and common life within and among ourselves. In both religions, God/Orixás are doing something in and through us and we are also doing something in and through our liturgies/worship recreating the world, recreating life. As Maraschin says, "It is in the body that we are spirit especially when our bodies are ready to recreate life. Let us, then, make of our bodies our main instrument of worship."[46] Open to the unknown movements of the Spirit and the Axé, we move along together.

Being at the table

The gathering of Candomblé and Christian people around the Eucharistic table can issue a powerful call to that part of Brazilian culture which hates and fears Candomblé, which continues to demonize them as a "Godly" way to destroy them. Gathering together and sharing each other's food is a way of offering a version of the Christian gospel that is committed to keeping each other alive, in love and care, with the right to live and share faith fully. This is a gospel that continues to require us to love, day, and night, God and our neighbors, no matter what faith these neighbors profess and live.

Each community will be open to the Spirit and to the calls both going around the table and inside their minds and hearts. Baptism will always be a call to the Candomblé people to engage more fully in the Christian faith. And the Orixás will also invite Christians to "make their head," which is the initiation ritual to become a Candomblé believer. These calls should never be understood as threats but as loving offerings of our best to our friends, as circular movements of the Spirit/Orixás to each other to expand our hearts and minds. And each one of us will decide what to do. Then, the words of institution or Christian prayers and songs will be carefully and powerfully said/sung as well as the sacred words and songs of Candomblé spoken by the Babalorixás and Yalorixás.

For the Candomblé people, the ability to make their own theological claims freely at such a central Christian event can represent a Christian request for forgiveness, a historical restitution of the Candomblé's own worthiness, as well as the undoing of the historical stereotype of Candomblé people as the Devil's presence in Brazil. For Christians, the Devil has no place at the table of God, and it is always undone there by claims of truth, life, justice, and hope. By being at Jesus' table offering gifts to the Orixás, Candomblé people and Candomblé theological beliefs gain a new and privileged place, both religiously and culturally, expelling a complex misunderstanding and demonization of their faith within the Christian circles and the larger culture, because at the Jesus table, they are deeply honored by those who worship the God of Christianity.

Eucharist and food offerings

Part of this mutual knowledge has to do with our respective understandings of food and of how we should engage each other through our sacred food. Most religious discourses around food have to do with the delimitations of others and ourselves. Food establishes the distinctiveness of our faith and creates boundaries that can present mixture and impurity or, in other words, to impede some relationships from occurring. Notions of foreignness and otherness are very explicit in the inner definitions of sacred food and we must pay attention to it.[47] In 1 Corinthians 8:1–13, the apostle Paul discussed eating food sacrificed to idols. He argued that the freedom we receive from God does not prevent us from eating that kind of food. As we grow into knowledge of God's freedom, we slowly lose our fear to face the difficulties involved in accepting food that is marked as beyond our customs or religious regulations. Thus, we must be careful with those in both Christian and other communities, who cannot understand this freedom and prefer the freedom of sticking to their norms. Each community should discuss these regulations and delve into the reasons of their own and other's belief system's regarding food and identity. As Paul said, "food will not bring us close to God,"[48] but certainly, it can bring us closer to each other. God's call to us comes before our gathering, laying down the very ground for our gathering and demanding that we figure out how this love should be lived, out of practice. Once we have welcomed each other to our common tables/ground, we can start to lose the fear that the other represents to us.

As the apostle Peter received God's command to eat everything he saw, we are also commanded to be open to attend to our neighbor's food through and beyond our regulations: "The voice said to Peter again, a second time, 'What God has made clean, you must not call profane.'"[49] If Paul tells us to be open, Peter's dreams show God demanding him to eat. How can we move around Paul to Peter as we ponder about the precious food of Candomblé? An honest conversation between these two communities will help us dispel the notion that Candomblé people eat food prepared for the devil. To be religious–inter-religious is not only to deal with intellectual religious differences but also, to eat one another's food. The aphorism "we are what we eat" is especially true with regard to religion and to be religious–inter-religious life. Moreover, we become what we eat and it is precisely because of that possibility of becoming that people of saint and Christians need to eat together to establish connections of love and care, to dispel hatred, to recreate Brazil into a more welcoming religiously diverse country. At the end, as Paul again said, "love builds up."[50]

Eating together has to do with creating love, building community, sharing memories, and acceptance of the other's as God's gift to me. As we gather together we start to see the theological as well as the social, political, and cultural possibilities that this gathering, this eating together, can create among our people. I believe that a whole new chapter in Brazil's history would be inaugurated. Forgiveness and reconciliation would be worked out not by state authority as in South Africa, but by two religious groups showing themselves to each other, finding ways of mutual reconciliation, asking for ongoing forgiveness, engaging our cordial racism, and learning to honor each other's faith.

Since the central questions of this book asks how the borders of the eucharist might be negotiated so that other people who are not used to being part of it can participate, we believe that occasions of generosity are possible for these different peoples of faith. When we start the conversation, Babalorixá Aragão tells me that we need to return to the original Eucharist which was a meal, a whole meal. As a former Roman Catholic seminarian he knows well what he is talking about. Christian meals at the beginning were not about the blood and flesh of Christ but about memory. He says: "God makes Godself food, food for the community. It is not the mythic element that counts at the beginning of the meal, but the way that Christ chooses to be remembered. From all of the possible ways that the disciples can use to remember Jesus, they choose the sharing of the bread. The most divine part of Jesus, the most powerful moment that Jesus manifested as a Messiah, as a divine being was his sharing and his sharing of a meal. Later on, it was around a meal that they remembered Jesus stories. The most original Christianity, the most charismatic, the most Pentecostal is exactly it: the sharing of bread and life."

In Candomblé however, there is not the same type of remembrance of that Christians have of Jesus Christ, since the entity is there, present at the service. For Candomblé, the presence of the entities does not point back to a primal event, as Christians do with the Last Supper in the Upper Room. However, the possibility of the presence of the entities and the presence of Christ in a worship service where there is sharing of food is a common theological aspect for both religions.

The blood and sacrifice in Candomblé, the slaughter of the animals has to do with the scapegoat, can be compared to the Jewish Day of Atonement, when a goat was offered to cover people' sins. In Candomblé, the animal is offered for the sake of the community and in this process, the animal has to want to offer itself to the community. If the animal doesn't eat the leaves it is given, it is not ready to offer itself and the celebration can only happen when the animal offers itself to bless the community. This ritual is important because it keeps the energy flowing and moving, and it continues the encircling of the relations humans and animals and entities have. Animals are messengers to the entities, and they serve as connections.

Babalorixá Aragão reminds me that Africans do not have problems with blood. It is not dirty or impure as some of us believe. Everything is sacred in the African worldview. Blood is food and a precious food, the best offering we have. When the animal dies, he transfers the energy of the blood to the stones and reinforces the connection between the entities. Blood is a channel for deep communion, energy that gives life to the relation between animal-entities-community. In this process, the interconnectedness of life is assumed, the inter-related participation deeply connected with honor and respect. Each sacrifice is done with care, devotion, libations, ritual objects properly consecrated, an follows a ritual order.

Each entity has some kind of food prohibition. There are two types of food: dry (grains) and wet (blood) food. Food offerings are offered to the Orixás and are eaten by the initiated. The food that is offered and is not eaten is given to nature: to the river, sea, or earth, where the entities live, encircling the movement of life. We can offer our simple food and the Orixá will receive it. The places prepared for Orixás at terreros called assentamentos and these places have a heightened sense of the sacred. We could say that these assentamentos do not symbolize the Orixás but instead, they are the Orixás. In the same way, the bread and blood in the Eucharist for Catholics do not symbolize the Eucharist but are the Eucharist. The Christian God is present in the bread and the wine, and in the Candomblé, the stone, the house, the place prepared for the Orixás are assentamento, are the Orixás. For instance, the bowl and the food that are offered to the Orixá are not containers of the Orixá but are the Orixás themselves.

Expanding each other's faith, practices, and theologies through commensality

Food and drink are precious liturgical-theological elements in the life of these two communities. Both celebrate God's creation and providence. The entire cosmogony of Candomblé is grounded on the meaning and importance of earth. God's and Orixás are deeply related to the earth and herbs, plants, food, drink, etc, all things from the earth, do the connections between this and the outer world. Moreover, the elements that mark the liturgical objects and worship in Candomblé all come from nature. Both rituals need food and they have deep connections with creation, ecology and can only be sustainable if understood as part of a larger ecosystem where life is lived at the table and on the floor, in gatherings and in rivers and forests, in the air and in every part of God's creation. Together, we can fight for our common good, the ecosystems, and the biodiversity which is a powerful way of working for peace.

The sacredness of these worshiping events is a common mark in both religions. Through this food, God is manifested through Jesus/Holy Spirit, and Olodumarê through the many Orixás and other entities. The doing of the sacrament of Eucharist is a way of worshiping God by obeying God's command to do this in memory of Jesus Christ. As for Candomblé, food offerings are carrying out promises and works of praise to please the Orixás so they will continue to bless the lives of the community.

It is interesting to see how women are at the center of the preparation of these sacred foods. The worship can happen only if the food is properly prepared. I remember my mother preparing herself in order to prepare the food for the Eucharistic table. Jan Rudolph, s student of mine at Louisville Seminary once mentioned in class how her African American grandmother used to literally iron all of the breads the day before Communion Sunday. In Bahia, I participated in a ceremony to the Orixá Ogum and the women carefully prepared the food many days before. Good and well prepared food and drinks are key to make the festivities efficacious.

Both the Eucharist and the Candomblé worship are rites of passage and political acts. Historically, while in Brazil we can say that the Eucharist, since it was attached to the powers that be, it was more attuned to a rite of imperial reinforcement, in Candomblé, the food offerings were liturgical acts of resistance and resilience. In any circumstance, both rituals enact ongoing passages in the life of the individual, larger community, and the country.

Christian Eucharist is grounded in the ecclesial understanding of a cloud of witness that surrounds this community of faith. The presence of the ancestors can also be related to the presence of Christ in history. As for Candomblé, the belief in the ancestry offers the assurance that this community of believers is continuously empowered by the presence of the ancestors who have prepared the way for them. Both religions can share these commonalities of their cloud of witness and ancestry.

Eucharist is celebrated around the table, and food offerings are done around a table or on the floor. For Christians from Reformed traditions, the table reminds them of the place that Jesus had the last supper with his disciples. For Candomblé people food on the ground emphasizes the deep relation of the food with the earth, and to those places of nature that are related to each Orixá. The sharing of each one's food around the table and on the floor can be a powerful way to engage each other rituals and experience the differences and commonalities between their rituals.

At the common table/floor Christians will have their sacred book, the Bible, and the Yoruba people will have their oral culture. Each group can share their stories of faith and transformation in different ways.

Candomblé has way more theological connections with the Eucharist where the Eucharist is understood as a sacrifice, as the Roman Catholic Church. The shedding of blood and the expiatory event of Jesus can be related to the animals sacrificed in Candomblé. If the Christian sacrifice brings forgiveness, the Candomblé sacrifice brings protection. Some Protestant understandings of Jesus death as a ransom can also relate to the animal slaughter and food offerings that honor/pay/negotiate with the Orixás.

Perhaps, Candomblé people can teach Christians how to engage more deeply with the cooking and the relation between food, preparation and the sources of its food. For Reformed people, the Eucharist is not often thought of as an open table with enough real food for all. Instead, it is a reminder of a full meal, a memory of a feast and not necessarily a joyful celebration. People don't actually eat the food from the Eucharistic table but join in sharing a meager piece of bread and a tiny sip of wine/grape juice. Candomblé people can also help Christians to have a sense of commensality around sacred foods. The food offerings are always plentiful in worship services and are offered not only to the Orixás but also to the community. For Reformed people, the Eucharist is not often thought of as an open table with enough real food for all. Instead, it is a reminder of a full meal, a memory of a feast and not necessarily a joyful celebration. People don't actually eat the food from the Eucharistic table but join in sharing a meager piece of bread and a tiny sip of wine/grape juice. Perhaps Candomblé people could learn with Reformed people about the Protestant principle that confronts power, hierarchical unbalanced religious structures and works for social change.

At the end of our conversation, I blatantly asked Babalorixá Aragão if it is possible to place food for the Orixá at the Eucharistic table/altar?

And he answered with a loud "yes!" and continued: "We gather the food of our extended family and everything belong to God. Or better said, is it not everything God?" Aragão's answer affirms the conditions of the possibilities for this dialogue, connections, and relationships.

Learning with Christian ancestors—Holy kiss as a liturgical practice to be engaged in inter-religious praxis

In this rehearsal for a possible future for our societies and religions, I call upon the early Christians and their liturgical gesture of Holy kissing to help us engage into this relationship-dialogical praxis. Kissing is a common practice in many religions and I am not claiming that Christians invented the Holy kiss. Instead, the idea here is to learn about the liturgical kissing from the early Christian practices and how it can enhance our own religious communal living. The Holy kiss from the early Christian churches is one that combined the liturgical gesture of getting close to each other, the sharing of the breath/presence of the Spirit and the eating together and the negotiation of social structures. The Holy kiss was a practice that wove together several layers of life. Paul and Peter will write to different communities to kiss with a Holy kiss and a kiss of love. (Romans 16:16 and I Peter 5:14).

Early Christian scholar Michael Penn says that in this gesturing, "Family, spirit, reconciliation—seemingly abstract concepts—the kiss transformed these into embodied actions." For the Greco-Roman world, any gesture in public space was an "exercise of power... the exchange of the ritual kiss (should be viewed) as praxis—the combination of interpretation and action... the kiss was not just an object of discussion, but also a physical action."[51] This liturgical embodied gesture can help us go from the secure mode of inter-religious dialogue to the more scary space of praxis.

More than that, the ritual kiss became a way of life, a connection between faith and familial kinship, a social bond. For a brief moment, the ritual of kissing each other would break the class boundaries and social status, the insurmountable divisions that were existent in that society. Michael Penn writes about the ritual of kiss as social bound and community building that has similarities with our inter-religious dialogical praxis. While he is writing about the Christian communities, one can say that the blurring of boundaries during that time can be correlated with the blurring of social and religious boundaries of our time. He says:

First, the familial connotations of the Greco-Roman kiss help portray the Christian community as family. Second, its connections with spiritual exchange emphasizes community member's pneumatological bond to each other. Third, especially as the kiss moved from a seal of prayer to part of the Eucharist service, Christian leaders attempted to decrease internal tensions by fashioning the kiss into a reconciliation ritual. Finally, the kiss as a physical action uniting two individuals was correlated with the creation of a unified body.[52]

Expanding on these reasons, we could say that liturgical kiss can enable us to expand the idea of family beyond the boundaries of Christians beliefs. As Philip Penn notes, "the parameters of kissing could be expanded regularly to include nonfamily members, or those whom one kissed during Christian rituals could be redefined as family."[53]

Second, since the kiss emphasizes the connectivity through the breath, the belief that one would share one's very soul to another through the kissing, we can also say that the pneumatological presence of the Holy Spirit/Axé can be our common sharing, the offering of our best gifts. In this offering to each other what we have as the most precious, we can engage our bonds of affection and belonging to each other through the exchange of our kisses. To kiss is to draw one's heart into somebody else's, it is to receive his/her breath, his/her very life into my body. To kiss somebody is to establish a bond of peace and I cannot withdraw my body and myself from this person anymore. I am bonded to this person now. That is why a kiss might be a scary gesture, especially when we are trying not to interfere in each other's lives and being civilized and respectful in this a individualistic culture. The "spirit" of our culture is a spirit that does not want to share, to exchange, to live together. The promise and hope of the exchange of the Spirit is what these religions can offer to the Brazilian culture and to the world. The Holy kiss is a collective practice that goes against the tide, one that perhaps can challenge this narcissistic culture that pushes people into withdrawing from one another.

Third, the Holy kiss as a bond, a gesture of deep commitment, of forgiveness, a familiar gesture of affection, an affirmation of belonging, an act of love, social, and communal love. That is why it was done first during the Eucharist. Penn reminds us "the ritual kiss can unite the participant's souls and cause individuals to forgive any wrongs." There is a powerful event happening when we kiss each other. John Chrysostom wrote: "The kiss is given so that it may be the fuel of love, so that we may kindle the disposition, so that we may love each other as brothers [love] brothers, as children [love] parents, as parents [love] children. But also far greater, because those are by nature, these by grace. Thus our souls are bound to each other."[54]

Finally, The Holy kiss is a liturgical gesture that connects individual bodies to a larger body, the social body that we might call the body of God. Michael Penn says that "several early Christian writers connected the kiss, spiritual exchange and group cohesion."[55] When I kiss somebody, I give this person a part of myself that only this person will know. Moreover, I offer to this person my social group, I open the entrance door for the other to be part of my family and life. Thus, through the participation of several groups of affection and social connections, we become responsible for each other. When we do it in an inter-religious dynamics, the radical other changes its status: from a threat, the Candomblé people become a blessing to me, a help for my Christian living in society, an assurance of larger double belonging, an expansion of my soul, a respectful touch in my body, a gift to my faith and vice versa.

Reformed/Candomblé people eating together: a practical itinerary
If Christianity works around the spiritualization of the body through acts of sanctity such as Eucharist, penitence, fasting, privation, etc; Afro-religions works around is the embodiment of the spirit through the coming of the entities that possess the bodies and dance, eat, celebrate, talk, laugh, etc. These different forms of movement around the sacred are both a challenge and a blessing and must be considered as we plan this dialogical praxis.

Both religions have embraced foreign elements into their structures of faith and practices, adapting themselves to their surroundings through different processes. Neither Christianity nor Candomblé are pure, autonomous, culture-free, and homogeneous religions. Moreover, it was the presence of each other that ended up defining their ways of being in Brazil. After living together for almost 500 years, offering an open table to share the Eucharistic food with Candomblé brothers and sisters and having

Christians eat at a Candomblé festivity should not be a strange move or an act of infidelity form both parts but instead, a mutual offering of a blessing and a gift.

This movement of mutually going after each other must be carefully crafted and created according to the conditions of possibilities that this impossible gathering might be. The itinerary has to be done by the two communities once they have established a bond of trust and accept that this dialogue/engagement entails a great amount of vulnerability. Christians should be reminded by what Paul Knitter said: "to be loyal to Christ, one must be vulnerable to others."[56]

As we ponder about possibilities of dialogue and life together, we must consider strategies that come up from practice through and across the folding of differences. Starting points, movements of the sacred, and end results are completely different. What can we learn from each other? Around the relation spirit/body body/spirit, we can expand the possibilities and understandings and practices of faith.

In order for this dialogue to happen, a lot of misunderstanding will happen. Our theological work is to help each other undo, as much as we can, these misunderstandings, knowing however, that the incommensurability of each religion will always remind us of this impossible dialogue.

From the Reformed traditions perspectives, this impossible dialogue must carry that aspect of the Protestant principle which is to call into question any and every aspect of the Christian faith so it does not run the risk of becoming an idolatrous worshiping community and continue the perpetual movement "to be" reformed: *ecclesia reformata semper reformanda*.

This itinerary imagines God coming after,[57] as after us helping us to get together, but coming after as showing up later, after we have gone through the hardships of a possible dialogue and engagement. Concrete steps might attend to the following: first, we visit each other's sacred spaces to see each other in our own worship services. Then, we gather to eat a common non-religious meal together and bring about questions on our practices thus initiating the conversation. For this gathering we start by greeting each other and kissing each other's cheeks. Then, when we eat together again. Before we eat, the Yoruba people explain why and how they do what they do, especially their food offerings. Then Christians explain why they do what they do and explain the Eucharist. Both show each other what is at stake in their celebrations and the living of their faith. Then we decide what we can or cannot do/eat together for now and try to formulate possibilities within these fundamentally different rituals. Then, we go back again to each other's worship services and try to participate as we are allowed. Songs, prayers and passing of the loving kiss of peace are shared. Then, we eat again and we bring the elements of our celebrations to show people how we do it. Then we allow those who want to take a step further to participate at each other's tables. We start with the hospitality of the Eucharistic table, writing a Eucharistic prayer that welcomes our brothers and sisters from Candomblé and evoke Axé and the powerful history of Candomblé in Brazil to make who we are. As we continue, the next time at an Eucharistic table, Candomblé people are invited to talk and bring foods offered to the Orixás. Every time we celebrate the Eucharist we eat a whole meal at the table.

Within this process asking questions is fundamental: Besides the questions about practices we, as Christians, must engage questions regarding our own involvement and mutual knowledge: (1) If we are to eat together, how should we to do it? (2) If I participate in the Yoruba meal, what and how will this participation change in my own view and practice of the Christian Eucharist? (3) What might the Yoruba meal change in my own understanding of community, resistance, memory, ancestry, commensality, thanksgiving, possession of the Spirit? (4) Can we share prayers and songs together? (5) What is community for me as a Christian after that experience? (6) What is the memory process here and how does it affect my own understanding of memory here? (7) As a Christian, if I participate in the Yoruba meal, what does this participation change in the Christian Eucharist? (8) What does the Yoruba meal/food offering change in my own understanding of memory, of resistance, of community? (9) What is the sharing of the meal invested with? (10) What are the theological aspects of it? Learning form religious others engages our total being. Emotions, feelings, body, mind, and spirit are all intertwined in this process. How can we be informed and reformed in this bodily engagement?

In this process, we might educate each other by teaching each other about the history of our faith and practices. Both communities could search the history of Christianity/African Religions in Brazil, face the "cordial racism" in the Brazilian culture, and find places where connections between Christianity and Candomblé were not only about destruction but also about help, protection, and mutual care. In other words, look for ways in which reality supplanted what the official rhetoric proposed and how Africans, Europeans, and indigenous people constructed small harmonies and communal experiences. Zumbi dos Palmares can be a beginning. What were the accommodations made between Christianity and Candomblé? Find where the connections, symmetries, commonalities, and sound parallels were and are. As a theological process, a more socially and historically oriented research could be done to foment a solid theological ground.

We are feeding each other here not only because we are morally obligated to do so. We are gathering together and feeding each other because we must create not only a possible new world but a necessary one, one that will expand our possibilities and make our lives and our country bigger and better for us and for the future generations. We are feeding each other because we must heal the wounds of our common history, and turn to each other in respect and honor. We are learning and practicing and gathering because it is God's demand that we love and care for each other. We are eating together around our tables/floors because we are offering a radical hospitality to each other and this hospitality can only come if we are bounded by the Spirit.

Conclusion

It is impossible to offer a lucid and honest introduction to Candomblé in these pages. However, the idea here is for us to have a glimpse of this religion so we can honor the people of the Candomblé and start to think why such inter-religious dialogical praxis is not only possible but truly necessary.

Symbiosis and Phagocytosis can be key theological elements to be developed in this dialogue. Also the notion of ritualizing/ritualization as proposed by Catherine Bell and Ronald Grimmes and explained in the next chapter is also an important element of this dialogue as we welcome each other into our rituals and invent other common rituals to enhance our dialogue and mutual care. We have also learned from ritual theorist Jonathan Z. Smith that rituals are also forms of engagement with that which we hope to see happening. When we create our rituals, we are struggling between the reality we live and the reality we strive for, the reality we want to see happening. In this inter-religious dialogical liturgical praxis, we also struggle between a reality that puts these two religious groups at odds and a reality that see them eating, drinking, praying, and dancing together.[58]

As we are able to explore some of the history of slavery and Yorubá religion and raise new challenges related to the so-called Brazilian religious diversity and its "cordial racism," also engage the hospitality of the Eucharistic table and the sharing of a Holy kiss, we can find a common space to transform this history and break down historical alienation and religious hatred. The hope continues as we try to foster dialogue and rituals between Candomblé and Christianity as a way to stop violence, engage in deep appreciation of each other's religious choices and enable each other to be fully humans in and through our deepest religious callings.

At the end, we must remember that our commitment is grounded in love. Marcelo Barros reminds us once again:

> "Evidently, every spiritual path is an itinerary of love and cannot be explained intellectually. It is a mystagogy. It is a mystery that can only be explained through an intimate relation of life... We can be lovers that offer ourselves to serve. From what is divine, there is title of property. Access is free to all to search what makes our hearts alive. No mortal can tame the wild wind. Mystery, is our peace and the religious paths, our parables of love."[59]

And as Ivone Gebara says,

> the question of pluralism invites us, again, to the thinking, to the proximity to wisdom, to the friendship with the different, with those who are close by and afar as expressions of this amazing complexity of life. And that is the same for our theologies, because, at the end, its certainties have to do with the weak, uncertain, plural and always renewable trust in this love that sustains us: "Where there is love, Go will be there..."[60]

So this love lived around food and communities. Christians and Candomblé people creating a space of care and love and welcome that there isn't one yet in society. A place where people is what they hope to be, where their identities are forged, developed, transformed. Like the early Christian churches or the Quilombo dos Palmares. A place to be not what society wants us to be necessarily but place for free exploration of one's hopes, beliefs, and dreams. Spaces where respect and protection are intrinsic to it and where we re-imagine our lives and our world. A space to dance samba and sing hymns and Yorubá songs. A rather impossible space for sure. However, we will never know if that is possible or not if we don't try, practically, moving near each other.

Notes

1. This article was published in *Sacraments and Globalization: Redrawing the Borders of Eucharistic Hospitality* (Eugene, OR: Wipf and Stock, Pickwick Publications, 2013), pp. 203–241.
2. Harding, Rachel E., A Refuge In Thunder. *Candomblé and Alternative Spaces of Blackness* (Indiana: Indiana University Press, 2000), p. xiii.
3. Some Christian friends tell me that several churches have as their mission goal to close down a number of terreiros every year.
4. This question was asked in a plenary of the Cohort II of the Luce Seminar on Theologies of Religious Pluralism and Comparative Theology, developed by American Academy of Religion. Chicago, May 2011.
5. De Alencastro, Luiz Felipe, As Populações Africanas no Brasil, http://www.casadasafricas.org.br/site/img/upload/680108.pdf
6. "Cordial man" is an expression created by historian Sérgio Buarque de Holanda to describe the ways Brazilians live. See Sérgio Buarque Holanda. *Raízes do Brasil*, (São Paulo: Companhia das Letras), 1997. The book was first published in 1936. However, "cordial racism" was an expression created later to capture the kind of racism in Brazil that is constantly denied. Marcelo Coelho says: "Perhaps, one of the horrors of the 'cordial racism' is that prejudice expresses itself when somebody says 'I don't have prejudice.' To say that 'in there is no racism is true to a certain extant (there are no benches on public square dividing whites and blacks as it was in the United States) but this is misleading in a deeper analysis." Marcelo Coelho, "Estranhamento conduz 'racismo cordial'," (Folha de São Paulo, 28 de junho de 1995). http://www.cefetsp.br/edu/eso/comportamento/racismocordial.html
7. Quilombos. These places still feed the memory of black people in Brazil in their struggles today. As new Quilombos continue to exist, African religions are still powerful strongholds of resistance, empowerment and transformation even though mostly forgotten by the government. For more information about Quilombo dos Palmares see: Carneiro, Edson. *O Quilombo dos Palmares* (São Paulo: WMF, Martins Fontes), 2011. Flávio.Gomes, Palmares (São Paulo: Contexto), 2005.
8. I ask for Agô (permission) to the Orixás, to the Candomblés of Brazil and people of saint to delve into a little their beliefs and practices.
9. Alessandra Osuna: http://ebomealessandraosun.blogspot.com/2008/04/significado-do-candomble.html
10. Bastide, Roger, O Candomblé da Bahia, (São Paulo: Companhia das Letras), 2009, p. 29. This book is a great resource for understanding the structure, meaning and movement of the ritual services of the Candomblé in general, but most properly of the services done in Bahia.

11. Oliveira, Rafael Soares de, (Org) *Diálogos Fraternos Contra a Intolerência Religiosa* (Rio de Janeiro: DP&A Editora & Koinonia), 2003, p. 14.
12. Gisele Omindarewá Cossard, Awó, O Mistério dos Orixás, (Rio de Janeiro: Pallas), 2006, p. 12 (my work will rely heavily on this work.
13. Vilson Caetano de Souza Junior, http://www.youtube.com/watch?v=VuGlStsTVBc&NR=1
14. Pierre Verger commenting on Candomblé, at Pierre Verger Foundation: http://pierreverger.org/fpv/index.php?option=com_content&task=view&id=14&Itemid=41&limit=1&limitstart=2&Itemid=155
15. Edison Carneiro, op. cit., 20–21.
16. Harding, Rachel E., A Refuge In Thunder. Op. Cit., xvi.
17. Ibid.
18. Roger Bastide, O Candomblé da Bahia, op. cit., 27.
19. Babalorixá Luis de Logun Edé, A Relação da Comida no Candomblé: 25 Anos de Logun Edé." http://www.youtube.com/watch?v=8IxS7vQUQNg.
20. Ibid., 123.
21. Maria Helena Farelli describes the essentials in the Candomblés terreiros founded in Bahia: "Black princesses with ivory smiles conducted their god to the dirty streets of the cities and the moonlight of the countryside. And for their divine lords they prepared the best spicy food, cooked with wood in within their mysteries. Were it not for them, queens and African priestess, brought as slaves from Benin and Angola, how would their gods come live in Brazil? ... Foods for the saints are traditional, necessary, and they make the beauty of the religious festivities... Around the terreiros people live in order to adore their gods and ancestors and to them they prepare drinks and food that constitute one of the links between aiê (earth) and orum (heavean) through the axé (the magical force). All of the African-Brazilian supernatural world like food. They must be fed. Blood, dendê (palm oil) and ataré are part of the menu. If you haven't eaten the delicious food and the nectar drinks you should experience. If you follow the precepts, the food will be done so well that all of the gods will come from Africa and Haiti. Let us salute our Orixá, the owner of our ori (head) and live without the notion of sin, which brought so many bad things to the African who didn't know what sin was. Axé to my ancestors white, black and indigenous, for it is time for the delicious food form Bahia." Maria Helena Farelli, Op. Cit., p.12.
22. Roger Bastide, Op. Cit., 31. This is a practice in most terreiros/axé but some babalorixás like Luis de Logun Edé do not like to offer the food.
23. Vilson Caetano de Souza Junior, "A Relação da Comida no Candomblé: 25 Anos de Logun Edé. Part II" http://www.youtube.com/watch?v=VuGlStsTVBc&NR=1.
24. Bastide, Op. Cit, p. 34.
25. Ibid., p. 40.
26. Vigil, José M., Tomita, Luiza E., Barros, Marcelo, (Organizers) *Teologia Pluralista Libertadora Intercontinental. ASETT, EATWOT* (São Paulo: Paulinas, 2008).
27. Faustino Teixeira, A Teologia do Pluralismo Religioso na América Latina, in Teologia Pluralista Libertadora Intercontinental, op. cit., 31.
28. Ivone Gebara calls this study to include women since the "principle that structures it cannot be only male. Its expression has to be multiple, plural, infinite." Quoted in Faustino Teixeira, A Teologia do Pluralismo Religioso na América Latina.

29. Faustino Teixeira, A Teologia do Pluralismo Religioso na América Latina, in Teologia Pluralista Libertadora Intercontinental, op. cit., 39.
30. Barros, Marcelo, Multipla Pertença, o Pluralismo Religioso, in Teologia Pluralista Libertadora Intercontinental, op. cit., 54.
31. "Every social group, coming into existence on the original terrain of an essential function in the world of economic production, creates organically, together with itself, one or more strata of intellectuals which give it homogeneity and an awareness of its own function not only in the economic but also in the social and political fields." by Gramsci, Antonio, "The Intellectuals: The Formation of the Intellectuals," in Selections From The Prison Notebooks Of Antonio Gramsci. [by] Antonio Gramsci. (New York, NY: International Publishers, 1971). p. 5.
32. Priests, pastors, professors, such as Carlos Mesters, Ivone Gebara, Leonardo Boff, Milton Schwantes, Richard Shall, Nancy Cardoso, Pedro Casaldáliga, Don Elder Camera, Don Paulo Evaristo Arns, just to name a few, have deeply engaged the life of the poor and with them, organized local and national movements of liberation in Brazil (Pastoral of the Land Commission, Landless Movement, Romaria da Terra, workers' rights, violence against women, etc.), as well as created discourses that were marked both by the intellectual academy and the concerns and needs and wisdom of the poor.
33. J. Edgar Bruns quoted by Sharon V. Betcher, "Take my Yoga upon you: a spiritual pli for the global city" in Catherine Keller & Laurel Schneider, eds., *Polydoxy: Theology of Multiplicity and Relation* (New York, London: Routledge, 2010). p. 72.
34. José Maria Vigil renews Latin American liberation theology's methodology based on Paulo Freire's work: to see, to judge, and to act and frames it around theologies of religious pluralism as "a new way of living religion, a new practice." Vigil, José Maria, *Teologia do Pluralismo Religioso, para uma releitura pluralista do Cristianismo* (São Paulo: Paulus, 2006), p. 15
35. Gebara, Ivone, "Pluralismo Religioso, Uma Perspectiva Feminista" in Teologia Latino-Americana Pluralista da Libertação, da Libertação. Luiza E. Tomita, José M. Vigil, Marcelo Barros, eds, *ASETT, EATWOT* (São Paulo: Editora Paulus, 2006), p. 297.
36. Irarrázaval, Diego, "Salvação Indígena and Afro-Americana," in Teologia Pluralista Libertadora Intercontinental, op. cit., 69.
37. Ibid.
38. This notion can be also correlated to the notion of inclusivism. While Christian inclusivism sees value in other religions, it appropriates things to itself but retains only what it recognizes, turning what it appropriates into its own system, holding within itself notions of salvation, truth and revelation that are valid only within the Christian system. What it does not authenticate it demonizes/destroys and dismisses. What Aragão advocates in Candomblé as inclusivism is very different and pertains to symbiosis. Candomblé embraces other beliefs and practices and make it part of its own system without devaluing it into or making it turn into its own categories as a way to destroy other's alterity and relevance in its own way. Instead, this symbiotic process engages different realities to live together to fight a stronger adversary that might want to destroy the larger system. This way of relating to other religions allows Yoruba believers to live religious-inter-religiously since any religion can be of help for the struggles of daily life.
39. Ibid.

40. Barros, Marcelo, "Multipla Pertença, o Pluralismo Religioso," in Teologia Pluralista Libertadora Intercontinental, op. cit., 66.
41. Ibid., 67.
42. Invitation to Christ, PCUSA – http://www.pcusa.org/resource/invitation-christ/
43. "Axé is the primal force, life principle, sacred force of the Orixás... is power, is charisma, it is the root that comes from the ancestors; we can gain and lose Axé, axé is a gift from the gods...; it is above all, the very house of the Candomblé, the temple, the roça (place where you plant for your family) the whole tradition." Reginaldo Prandi, Os Candomblés de São Paulo (São Palo: Hucitec-EDUSP, 1991), pp.103–104.
44. Betcher, Sharon V., "Take my yoga upon you. A Spiritual Pli for the Global City," in Catherine Keller & Laurel Schneider, eds, Polydoxy: Theology of Multiplicity and Relation (New York: Routledge, 2010), p. 58.
45. Cited by Betcher, Sharon V., "Take my yoga upon you. A Spiritual Pli for the Global City," in Catherine Keller and Laurel Schneider, eds, Polydoxy: Theology of Multiplicity and Relation (New York: Routledge), 2010, p. 72.
46. Jaci Maraschin, The Transient Body: Sensibility and Spirituality, paper presented at the event "Liturgy and Body;" Union Theological Seminary, New York, October 20, 2003.
47. For a fascinating work on this topic see David M. Freidenreich, Foreigners and Their Food. Constructing Otherness in Jewish, Christian and Islamic Law (Berkeley: University of California Press, 2011).
48. 1 Corinthians 8:8 NSRV
49. Acts 10:15 NSRV
50. 1 Corinthians 8:1 NSRV.
51. Michael Philip Penn, Kissing Christians: Ritual and Community in the Late Ancient Church (Philadelphia: University of Pennsylvania Press, 2005), p. 15, 35, 50.
52. Ibidem., 8.
53. Ibidem., 36.
54. John Chrysostom, In epistulam II ad Corinthios 30.2 (PG 61, 607), in Michael Philip Penn, Kissing Christians, op. cit., 34.
55. Michael Philip Penn, Kissing Christians., 39.
56. Knitter, Paul, Introducing Theologies of Religions (Maryknoll, NY: Orbis Books, 2008), p, 209.
57. Taylor, Mark C., After God (Religion and Postmodernism) (Chicago: University Of Chicago Press, 2009).
58. "Ritual is a mean of performing the way things ought to be in conscious tension to the way things are." Jonathan Z. Smith, To Take Place: Toward Theory in Ritual (Chicago: University of Chicago Press, 1987), p. 43.
59. Barros, Marcelo, Multipla Pertença, o Pluralismo Religioso, in Teologia Pluralista Libertadora Intercontinental, op. cit., 60.
60. Gebara, Ivone, "Pluralismo Religioso, Uma Perspectiva Feminista" in Teologia Latino-Americana Pluralista da Libertação, op. cit. 298.

CROSSCURRENTS

THE IMPORTANCE OF THE INTERSECTIONALITY IN THE STUDIES OF GENDER AND RELIGION
A Short Analysis of the Ogum Omimkayê in Salvador, Brazil

Sílvia Barbosa

Initial considerations

In order to consider the articulations between the social categories of gender, race, class, and age/generation in the interior of the Candomblé Ilê Asé Ogum Omimkaye, it is necessary to understand the contemporary debates that created the uses of these categories and their intersections within the analysis of feminist theories and social sciences. To think about these categories, we need to understand them without creating a hierarchy, since the relevance of these categories is directly related to the socio-cultural context in which the subjects are living.

Candomblé is not the only context in which the distribution of power[1] is the result of the hierarchizing of physical space or religious action, but it does represent a space where the unbalanced distribution of power can be a result of disparities related to gender, race, class, and age/generation. In this sense, it is necessary to understand these social categories articulated within this religious universe, knowing that these sources compose the social life of Candomblé men and women.

The distribution of power in the Ilê Asé Ogum Omimkaye will be analyzed considering these categories—gender, race, class, and age/generation, as constitutive of the social–cultural process in which they are a part of and organize the lives of their religious subjects. Social groups are never homogeneous, and the Candomblé people have, like any other group, their heterogeneities and specificities.

In this context, discrimination by gender is not eclipsed by the exploration of class, but finds support in sexism and racial differences naturalized and perpetuated in society. Racism in the same way is grounded in inequalities also naturalized by racist ideologies that create hierarchies as ways of perpetuating these inequalities. Similarly, age/generation also marks spaces occupied by individuals in society. While all these dimensions have been naturalized and universalized with the intention to perpetuate social inequalities, they also constitute interconnected oppressions (Gonzalez 1984, Motta 1999).

To illustrate these intersections in the Ilê Asé Ogum Omimkaye, we have used theoretical frameworks from scholars such as Lélia Gonzalez (1984), Alda Brito da Motta (1999), Kimberlé Crenshaw (2002), and Avta Brah (2006). Other authors were used to give support to the study, namely the voices of those I interviewed, the Ogã[2] and Iya-Egbé,[3] of the house as well as the Iyalorixá[4] of the terreiro, all participants connected with the religious field of Candomblé Ketu in the Ilê Asé Ogum Omimkaye.

Ilê Asé Ogum Omimkaye: relations of power and intersectionalities

The Ilê Asé Ogum Omimkaye is located in the neighborhood Fazenda Grande III, Cajazeiras, Salvador-BA. It has Ketu origins, shows continuities, and discontinuities from Ketu tradition and has being in operation for more than 20 years, with traditional and modern characteristics. Having its own worship space, it functions in a large building with a few smaller buildings around it. In that space, during periods of festivity, 120 people are always present. Of the people present, 30 are associated with the Ilê and are involved in the various activities of the terreiro, such as administrative meetings and religious celebrations.

The leadership of this terreiro is largely feminine, organized by the Iyalorixá, the spiritual leader, by the ebomis, ekedes, and small mothers who hold a significant portion of the power that is expressed in the priestly function, preserving the cultural heritage and Afro-Brazilian identity, as well as the daily authority over the people involved in the ceremonies of the Candomblé.

It is important to say that the Ogãs, male associates, do have important offices in the religious hierarchy. Nonetheless, in the Candomblé of

Ketu, the major cultural and structural power is based on matrilineality, where the women (mothers in particular) are the focal points of this system of power.

In the Ilê Asé Ogum Omimkaye, the system of filiation occurs in the form of consanguinity and consideration. This filiation model is related to the idea of kinship proposed by Marcelin (1999), who argues that filiation, organized by consanguinity and consideration, goes beyond the American form of kinship. It comes from the supposition that "blood is thicker than water," the ethnocentric logic that privileges bonds of blood rather than affiliation.

Marcelin (1999) boldly presents the category of "consideration" as necessary and sufficient to identify those who are parents (without being necessarily of blood), since a parent can be also recognized as such by consideration. In the symbolic kinship of the families of saints, what prevails is the bond of consideration. Thus, to be a "mother of saint" is, before anything, to recognize that this son is her son, this daughter is her daughter, to honor the obligations that these relations require.

In the social sciences, socioeconomic analysis is overvalued. In religious spaces, the mystic-ritual universe is often claimed as the only and central place for identity formation and conflict, even though this religious space is crossed by multiple individual and social identities that compose the subjects who belong to this space. Nonetheless, there are more expansive conflicts of meanings that, while they interconnect with the religious, they also nuance the religious intersection. Scott (1994), p. 18) argues that:

> The groups' identities are an inevitable aspect of the social and political life, with these two dimensions interconnected, with the differences of groups being more visible, salient and problematic in more specific political contexts. In these moments, when exclusions are legitimated by differences of groups, when economic and social hierarchies favor some groups against other, when the set of biologic or religious or ethnic or cultural characteristics are valorized in detriment of others, that is when the tension between individuals and groups emerge.[5]

Even though identities are in perpetual motion and difficult to consolidate according to various historical times, some references are fundamental to each social group. We cannot understand them as fixed arrangements since these identities are built within social, cultural, political, and other contexts, and a variety of differentiated tensions emerge from those intersectional identities, as Scott mentions.

For instance, Avta Brah observes that the understanding of the term black acquires a variety of social and political meanings due to its differential contexts. Brah questions "what is in a name? "what is in a color?"[6] evoking multiple meanings for identities and ethnicities that form our constructed notions of race. Some social groups experience the construction of its racialization from conditions delineated by its whiteness, even if crossed by comprehensions of class and gender that can be moveable in various social structures. The binary white/not white has been connected, historically, to the process of racialization of individuals, even if, in differently actualized in different contexts.

We can infer from these considerations that even today Candomblé contexts are still understood as exclusive places for black people, or individuals who have some sort of Afro-descended ethnicity. These spaces were forged by the black identity that only later was racialized, even though these religious spaces are frequently marked, even if in small numbers, by other ethnic–racial groups. They were inscribed by specific political and identity crossings that built the experience of racialization in these places in various ways. Many of the political battles are grounded in the construction of Candomblé as spaces for religiosity and blackness. We need to study the presence of the "non-white," of "negritude," of "being black" within these religious spaces.

Hugo is a black, 40-year-old man who has been in Candomblé for nine years and is the Ogã of the house. When he speaks, we can sense a thin connection of "being black" in this religious space. When asked if it would be possible to develop one's spirituality by entering through the ethnic door, his answer was yes, it would be possible. However, it is not only the blackness of an individual that makes one a member of Candomblé, since spirituality threads through the individual and his/her Orixa. Hugo said that his "state in Candomblé" made him think that ethnicity is not the only vehicle into Afro-descent religions, "since one does not go to the Candomblé only because of an ethnic question, but it can indeed be the entering door. You get there and perceive that there are way more things at stake."[7] What can we stress form what Hugo says?

Our interviewee puts the religious and ethnic questions in hierarchical positions, understanding that, within the religious environment, the racial questions are subsumed by the religious questions and the presence of the Divinities—Orixas—as much as the mystical vocations directs each member. From these affirmations, we can see how interconnections between the hierarchical valorization of the religious powers and vocation call that come from the Orixa. The ethnic and racial relations are secondary, allowing the sensible and complex structures that form the ethnicity and create images of "being black" in the Candomblés to emerge. In other words, according to Hugo, to be black is not the most important thing to this religious organization, but rather, the call one receives to join Candomblé. This call, based on a religious vocation, or even a mystic necessity that cannot be explained rationally, may be a call coming directly from the Orixas.

Hugo's statement makes us think about the emblematic historical constructions of social, class, race/ethnicity, and religious circulation in the religious spaces of African religions. In the general statements made by Hugo, a member of this Candomblé, we see that Candomblés often are religious spaces made of subaltern order, religiously manifested by individuals of poor classes, blacks, and ethnic minorities.

Lucinha, a black woman, 52 years old, Iya-Egbé of the terreiro, reaffirms the pejorative connections many people make about Candomblé and the devil due to rituals of passage and spiritual trance.[8] The endless attacks and the violence received by the Candomblé religious spaces throughout the country are the consequence of racist religious thought built around these spaces that conflate the uncommon with the devil, dirtiness, and blackness. Even though several research works have undermined this racist sensibility, this image still undergirds the national fear of the unknown and regard of African rooted religions as belonging to the underworld of irrational beliefs, racial inferiority, and superstitions. Even if Hugo does not immediately associate the religious space of Candomblé as black religion, from these presuppositions that mark the race/ethnicity of the individual, these social markers are present and manifest their power when acts of violence hit Candomblé people all across Brazil.

Mother Dulce, black woman, 67 years old, Iyalorixá of the terreiro gives us an intriguing testimony. When asked about what might have changed her mind after the insertion of Candomblé, she boldly said:

[...] I change a lot, because before, in fact, I didn't have religious obligations, I lived that life of a Christian that... I didn't have much responsibility with my previous religion... However, after I began to have a history in this axé, I changed. I have responsibilities to fulfill my tasks, here you know you came from "senzala" and what you have in the senzala? Work, lots of work.[9]

In the words of the Iyalorixá, it is clear to see that her connections with the Afro-descended people comes from deeper roots, even from the "senzala," the place where slaves, her ancestors were placed to live and work. This connectivity defines the understanding of what her "I" means in black identity.

As Geertz says,[10] we can't get "under people's skin," but we can try to understand "with what," or "through what" or "by means of what," people comprehend the world in which they live. In the case of Mother Dulce, we can see her values, her reading of reality, and fundamentally the construction of her own self, as crossed by ethnic and religious elements, all of them constituting the singularity of being black, from the senzala and from the context of her work as leader of this Candomblé.

For this Iyalorixá, her religious and social difference is marked by her ancestors, by the knowledge that she has of herself, and her condition as one descending from slaved Africans. Her affirmations are contrasted with Hugo since it gives us an entrance into the complex structures of identities of the subjects within the same religious unity. Mother Dulce, Iyalorixá of the terreiro, and Hugo, an Ogã of the terreiro, have different perspectives about the questions pertaining to race and possibly, what constitutes the individuals at the Ilê Asé Ogum Omimkaye.

For the Iyalorixá, Candomblé brings us almost immediately to a reality deeply marked by slavery, suffering, and work, that permeates her life and all of the people of black identity, within a structure of "heavy" responsibilities that she assumes when she comes inside of the religious space. When the Iyalorixá expresses her understanding about her insertion in this religious space, she also allows distinctive characteristics that come from her own trajectory and experience.

The experience of this Iyalorixá through Candomblé gave her perspectives that she didn't gain in any other religion she participated in before coming to Candomblé. It was from her religious attributions and responsibilities in Candomblé that she gained religious maturity that helped her have a stretched understanding of an amplified sense of society. Mother Dulce's words allow us to observe that her experience within this religious field helped her codify a world marked by ethnicity and class rules, but also by an attachment to the African descended people through her connections with Candomblé.[11]

To debate these intersectionalities allows us to perceive the "coexistence of diverse approaches"; different perspectives that trace diverse thoughts on "difference and power," reflecting the margins of agency given to subjects in their real possibilities for action through their social and cultural borders. According to Kimberlé Crenshaw:

> The same way that it is true that women are somehow subjected to the weight of the oppression of gender, it is also true that other factors related to social identities, such as class, caste, race, color, ethnicity, religion, national origin and sexual orientation are also differences that can discriminate various groups of women. Such differential elements can create problems and vulnerabilities exclusive to specific subgroups of women, or that can affect disproportionally only some women.[12]

What Crenshaw (2002) signals is becoming, academically, a growing challenge to gender studies. She alerts us to the existing differences of forms of living, discrimination, vulnerability; women having different perspectives that diverge and converge within specific social groups that create diverse general conditions that orient social oppression and discrimination within groups as they build their social self.

What configurations of power can we learn from these interviews? The power of the mother of the saint is nurtured from her work and the diverse religious responsibilities within that religious place, in the administration of the terreiro and in the distribution of the multiple tasks within the house, constantly re/configuring the power that was given to her by the Orixas and the community.

Buying, cleaning, sewing, caring, and the "watching over of the saint" are determined tasks on specific days for the saint's realization where all the community of the terreiro have specific attributions. They are determined in two planes: the spiritual and the material needs, both converging toward the maintenance of the terreiro and the protection of the mystical knowledge that can be preserved and passed on. The organization of the religious work also reflects the different attributions of gender, vocations, and the possibilities of insertion within this religious space, causing us to reflect on the connections between gender/work/generation, three axes that order diverse social communities and their own sense of organization.

Lucinha offers an interesting perspective about the division of work within Candomblé, stressing that men and women have different offices with specific functions that follow hierarchies that need to be respected. According to her:

> I think, [...] each one should stay in their offices, their own designated places and assume what is their own right. [...] Since the African arrival in Brazil... By slaves... Men and women should work together, knowing that there are different functions that are attributed exclusively for women; which does not mean that men are excluded, for men are fundamental in Candomblé, especially to play the drums, in Candomblé nothing can be done alone, we work with the two genders, and both must work together, so they can add together, so they can grow and end this discrimination that says here one cannot be because one is man, or there one cannot be because one is a woman.[13]

From the specificity of gender, we can see that men and women are invited to work, actively, in the religious space of Candomblé; however, these works are defined according to the sex of each member, their age, and their belonging in the religious space. For example, Lucinha, herself a Iya-Egbé, a position of extreme importance that places her as the second in the house, only below the Iyalorixá, says that both genders, men and women, need to work together, while the function of playing the drums is an exclusive function of men. Another exclusive function of men is Ogã, responsible for all kinds of services within the terreiro, including playing the songs attributed to the Orixás. Under the office of Ogã, Hugo, the Ogã of the house, says that among his functions, he is to...

> [...] fix the house of the Orixá when needed, lift the saint when needed, clean the house of the santo, make the sacrifices for the obligations of the saint and, if needed, care for the house in the

moments of the festivities, welcoming people for this moment [...].[7]

The specificities of the work of the Ogã, described by Hugo, help clarify the nature of the work of the women at this terreiro. For example, the women Ekedes are responsible by the Orixas more directly, to "care for the saint, to dry off the saint, to dress up the saint and guide the sons of the saint" when any of the sons are incorporated by his Orixá.[13] The functions of the Ekede remind us of the act of caring, remembering that within the larger social organizations, the act of caring in itself has always been a female attribution. From these observations, we can trace a parallel between the specific religious functions, Ogãs/males, and Ekedes/females, within the terreiro. The Ekedes are closely related to the functions of caring, which is connected to care of the subjects of the Orixas, and of the sons of the saint. As for the Ogãs, their functions are closely related to a kind of structural care for the well-being of the house, things related to musical instruments, cleanliness, and maintenance of the spaces for the saints and the sacrifices.

The gender perspectives become more important when we explain the social trajectories of women and men. Their diverse trajectories allow for the diverse formation of their social identities, living distinct forms of systems and social relations regarding gender, class, race/ethnicity, and age/generation. It is exactly the ways in which these subjects comprehend these systems that integrate them into society as well as create social disparities.[14]

In this way, it is possible to infer that the relations between subjects within the religious fields are crossed by their own social classes, genders, races/ethnicities ages/generations, transforming their notions of sociability, comprehension, and reading of the religious space, all of it influencing their own insertion in the group. The insertion of an individual within this religious universe creates forms of readings of this space that are marked by experiences lived personally and collectively. Thus, each individual will use his/her various social perceptions to rebuild these spaces for sociability, alterity, faith, mystic, political disputes, power relations, etc.

Final considerations

This research served to highlight a small finding about the relations and intersectionalities that can be observed in a religious field. The statements of the interviewees, rich in symbolism, showed various textures where power is revealed in Candomblé through gender, race, and class as substantial sources for the social and religious organization of that space. We can observe that in the speech of the Iyalorixá, of the Ogã and the Iya-Egbé, that there are both defined connections within the religious collective, but also divergences, demonstrating that each subject comprehends and constructs its participation in the Candomblé in unique heterogeneous ways, with individual points of views about their own activities, responsibilities, and insertion in this religious field.

This analysis emerged from the comprehension of intersectionality as the central point for the theoretical approach and in its multidimensionality in the formation of the relations of power. The analysis helped us understand more complex connections and dynamics in the relations between individuals within their religious field, without fragmenting either their individuality or the religious collective. The connections pointed to the dynamics of gender, race/ethnicity, and age/generation and allowed us to see, in deeper ways, the individuals and their collective relations, demonstrating that the minutia of the individual's being, while drenched in its collectivity, presents forms of living and knowing that are inherently part of their personal experiences and subjectivities. This points to new social relations, new forms of interpretation of the world, and can model new forms of power.

Further research into other important connections within the intersections is necessary, but we can see, even in this short analysis, that the social arrangements and the relations of power are affected by the categories of gender, race/ethnicity, and age/generation in hierarchical structures. In order to contemplate individuals with roles and places that are specific within religious spaces, these intersections must be considered.

Notes

1. Based on the reading of Vivaldo da Costa Lima, "A Família de santo nos candomblés jeje-nagôs da Bahia," pp. 80–82, and as participants of these places/rituals, we can mention that the distribution of power in the terreiro (worship spaces) is structured as a hierarchy of power based on seniority and heritage within the traditions of Candomblé and Ketu. The circularity of power is effective between the Candomblé members from religious offices and functions in the terreiro. *Iyalorioxá/Babalorixá* are Mothers or Fathers of Saint. This is the higher position within the Afro-Brazilian tradition. *Alagbá*: a male office, chief of the Oyê. In some houses, he is also called as Ogã. They can do civil and religious tasks but they don't

get into a trance. *Mogbá:* male office specific to the Orixa Xangô. Minister of Xangô. *Tojú Obá:* Also, a male office specific to the service to Xangô. Eyes of a king. *Iya-Egbé/Babaegbé:* second person in the Axé/terreiro. Counselor, responsible for the maintenance of the order, tradition and hierarchy. Iyalaxé: woman, mother of the Axé, the one who distributes the axé and takes care of the ritual objects. *Iyakekerê:* woman, small mother, second priestess of the axé/community. Always ready to help and teach all who are initiating. Babakekerê: man, small father, second priest of the axé/community. Always ready to help and teach all who are initiating. *Ojubonã* or *Agibonã:* foster mother, supervises and helps in the initiation. Iyamorô: responsible for the *padê* of Exu. *Iyaefun* ou *Babaefun:* responsible for the white painting of the *Iaôs. Iyadagan* and *Ossidagã:* Help with the *Iyamorô. Axogun:* priest responsible for the sacrifice of the animals. Depending on the case, in the ritual of initiation, this priest can assume another office, since *axogun* is an *ogã. Aficobá:* responsible for the sacrifices of the animals of Xangô. Aficodé: responsible for the sacrifices of the animals of Oxossi. *Iyabassê:* woman, responsible for the preparing of the sacred food, food of the saints. *Iyarubá:* she carries the mat for the one initiating. *Iyatebexê* or *Babatebexê:* responsible for the singing of the public feasts of the Candomblé. *Aiyaba Ewe:* responsible in determined acts and obligations to "sing leafs." *Aiybá:* drum the *ejé* in the ritual obligations. *Ològun:* mostly a male office but sometimes a female too. S/he provides the *Ebós* of the obligations, preferentially for the sons of Ogun, and then Odé e Obaluwaiyê. *Oloya:* female office, she prepares the *Ebós* of the obligations when *Ologun* is missing. They are daughters of Oya. *Iyalabaké:* the guardian of *alá* of osaala. *Iyatojuomó:* responsible for the children of the axé. *Pejigan:* responsible for the axés of the house/terreiro. First Ogan in the hierarchy. *Alagbê:* responsible for the ritual drumming, food, conservation and preservation of the sacred music instruments. They don't get into trance. In the cycles of feasts they must wake up before dawn to prepare for the beginning of the day. If an authority of another axé arrives at a certain terreiro, the *Alagbê* must pay homage. In the Ketu Candomblé, the atabaque drums are called *Ilú.* There are other *Ogãs* like Runsó, Gaitó, Arrow, Arrontodé, etc. *Ogã:* drummers of the atabaques (they don't get into trance). *Ebômi:* people who have finished their 7 years of initiation (meaning: the older brother). *Ekedi:* server of the Orixa (they don't get in trance). Iaô: daughter/son of the saint who has been already initiated and get into trance with the Orixá of his/her head. *Abiã:* neophyte. Every *abiã* is a person that enters to the religion after they have passed the ritual of washing of the beads and the bori. It could be initiated or not, depending on the desire of the Orixá. *Sarapebê* is responsible for the communication of the Egbe (similar to public relations). *Otun* and *Osy Axogun* are helpers of *Axogun. Apokan* is responsible for the worship of Olwuaye e o Olugbajé.

2. *Ogã* with the office of *axogum.* Priest responsible for the sacrifice of animals.
3. *Iya-Egbé* is the second person of the axé. Mother and Counselor, responsible for the tradition ad hierarchy.
4. *Iyalorixá* is the mother of saint. It is the highest office in the Afro-Brazilian tradition.
5. Scott (1994).
6. Avta Brah 2006, p. 332–333.
7. Interview with Hugo, April 16, 2014.
8. Interview with Maria Lúcia, nicknamed Lucinha, on September 23, 2012.
9. Interview with Mãe Dulce, September, 11 2012.

10. Geertz 1997, p. 88.
11. Geertz 1997, p. 87–91.
12. Kimberlé Crenshaw 2002, p. 173.
13. Interview with Maria Lúcia, September 23, 2012.
14. Motta 1999, p. 193.

Works Cited

Brah, Avtar, 2006, "Diferença, Diversidade, Diferenciação," Cadernos Pagu [online] **26**, pp. 329–76.

Crenshaw, Kimberlé, 2002, "Documento Para o Encontro de Especialistas em Aspectos da Discriminação Racial Relativos ao Gênero," Estudos Feministas **1-2002**, pp. 171–89.

Geertz, Clifford. Do ponto de vista dos nativos. In: _____ O Saber Local: novos ensaios em antropologia interpretativa. Petrópolis: Vozes, 1997.

Gonzalez, Lélia. Racismo e sexismo na cultura brasileira. Revista Ciências Sociais Hoje. Anpocs, 1984.

Lima, Vivaldo da Costa, 2003, A Família de Santo Nos Candomblés jejes-Nagôs da Bahia: Um Estudo de Relações Intragrupais, 2 ed, Salvador: Corrupio.

Marcelin, Louis Herns, 1999, "A Linguagem da Casa Entre os Negros no Recôncavo Baiano," Mana [online] **5**(2), pp. 31–60.

Motta, Alda Brito da, 1999, "As Dimensões de Gênero e Classe Social na Análise do Envelhecimento," Cadernos Pagu **13**, pp. 191–221.

Scott, Joan W., 1994, Gênero: Uma Categoria Útil Para Análise Histórica. Educação e Realidade, Recife: SOS Corpo.

CROSSCURRENTS

LIBERATION THEOLOGY IN BRAZIL
Some History, Names and Themes

Cláudio Carvalhaes and Fábio Py

Liberation Theology is not just one theology among many others. No! Liberation Theology, as we understand it, is a matter of survival, of life and death. It is a place where faith, discourse of God, and real life meet in order to protect and expand the possibilities of life, in the eco-biodiversity of the planet and in the possibility of justice for the poor. We didn't choose Liberation Theology; we were chosen by it, and it is because of Liberation Theology that we are here today. To take away Liberation Theology is to mute our voices; we become tongue-tied, inarticulate, dumb.

We are among the third generation of liberation theologians in Latin America. We attended Protestant churches, had a more conservative upbringing, and through social resistance and seminary formation, we were introduced to Liberation Theology. Our beginning text was Gustavo Gutierrez, a Catholic theologian, and we struggled to understand the book. But it led to a time of discovery and excitement! Rubem Alves, Richard Shaul, Julio de Santana, Jaci Maraschin, Leonardo Boff, Milton Schwantes, among many others, influenced us during the height of Liberation Theology. Priests and pastors were giving rise to the movement through churches and Base Communities, gaining consciousness about their social situation and how God Was calling them to a new day! Many women engaged in theological work as well and were beginning to shift the map of the theological production. Great theological material was produced, Liberation Theology pulsed everywhere, and socio-political transformations spread all across Latin America.

It is not our task here to give a long historical account of the processes and movements of Liberation Theology in Latin America, but rather to highlight the work of a few Latin American liberation theologians, namely Rubem Alves, Ivone Gebara, Milton Schwantes and Nancy Cardoso. Liberation Theology concerned itself with the poor and in that way engaged the black people of Latin America. But we failed to include black theologians and Liberation Theology as a whole neglected race in their work.

We will begin by highlighting the ways in which liberation theologies started in Latin America with a few notes about its major tenets. Then, we will present a small part of the work of these four theologians mentioned above. We will finish with some words about what is left undone.

Liberation Theology was not the creation of one theologian. Gustavo Gutierrez did not begin the movement; it was the work of the people, through grassroots movements calling for justice, in collaboration with priests and theologians, that deeply shaped Liberation Theology in Latin America. Moreover, Liberation Theology is best understood not only by looking at published books, but also by looking at the movement of the church. In the 1950s and 1960s, Latin America experienced extensive influence and control by the United States. In the midst of McCarthyism, the United States was afraid that Russia would take over other countries besides Cuba. The CIA supported radical conservative groups seized power in many countries in Central and South America: Chile, Argentina, Brazil, El Salvador, Nicaragua, and so on. The School of the Americas was an ongoing colonizing institution that supported the CIA's desire to take over the Latin American continent. SOA trained local people to kill their own people and promised money and protection for those who cooperated. The massacre in El Salvador, the killing of Oscar Romero and the priests of Universidad Catolica, the military coup in Brazil and Argentina can be explained by the deadly power and influence of the United States in Latin American countries.

Liberation Theology came out of the struggle against external domination and socioeconomic oppression. To see the beginning of Liberation Theology in Latin America, we must go to the conferences of CELAM, the Latin America Episcopate Conference of Medellín in Colômbia, where in 1968 the cries of the people in Latin America began to be heard. This was the birth of a movement that, pushed by the Second Vatican Council, connected with the people through base communities. The church expanded into a new movement, with the help of the priests who gathered locally with the people.

The decade between the 1968 CELAM conference in Medellín and 1979 conference in Puebla, Mexico, was an active time for Latin America and Liberation Theology. The movement was strong and CELAM defined and expanded the concept of God's "preferential option for the poor." Theologians, Biblicists, ethicists, priests, educators, along with the people, all gave shape to the movement. During that time, academic thinking developed the "dependence theory" that criticized Latin America's heavy dependence on US colonization. Theologically, countries from the third world created the EATWOT: The Ecumenical Association of Third World Theologians which was an essential organization that engaged the social realities of poor countries and expanded the voices of poor people across the globe.

This massive movement created social and political structures all across Latin America that challenged the elite: the Workers Party in Brazil elected Lula, the first peasant to be elected a president in Latin America; the Landless Movement became the largest social movement in the world; the Zapatistas and Subcomandante Marcos in Mexico, the Sandinistas in Nicaragua, and even the recent global network called A New World is Possible, were all influenced, some more, some less, by the beliefs and organization that came out of base communities and liberation theologies.

It is only within this larger context of the whole church and society that we can understand the work of major theologians. Gustavo Gutierrez' book, "A Theology of Liberation: History, Politics, and Salvation," for instance, comes as the first major practical–theoretical reference from a long history of death and oppression in Latin America. Gutierrez shaped many of the practices and much of the thinking within grassroots movements.

Most of first generation of liberation theologians received a solid theological foundation in Europe, and they had the courage to recreate Latin American theology based on what the daily life of the people. The first generation included Juan Luis Segundo in Uruguay, Jon Sobrino and Ignacio Ellacuría en El Salvador, Gustavo Gutierrez in Peru, Elsa Tamez in Costa Rica, Enrique Dussell in Mexico, Pablo Richard in Chile, José Miguez Bonino in Argentina, the brothers Boff in Brazil and many, many others. Priests were fundamental to the process of remaking theology: Don Oscar Romero, Pedro Casaldaliga, Helder Camera, Paulo Arns and many others empowered the people and gave them hope to believe along with the faith they had received from God!

This historical account is insufficient, but it aspires to signal, in very broad strokes, the contours of Liberation Theology in Latin America.

Major themes in Liberation Theology

Method

Liberation Theology expands the sources of God's revelation. Along with the documents of the church and the Bible, the lives of the poor became not only sources for the discourse of God, but a hermeneutical axis from which faith and doxa would be understood. Praxis became a complex way of engaging life, theory, tradition, and theology.

Salvation

As a consequence, one of the major themes of Christian theology, namely salvation, gained new meaning. Salvation *from* this world became salvation *within* this world. Salvation became liberation from structural social sins, and the life found in Jesus Christ could now be realized in history! The hope for another world no longer precluded the fulfillment of the Kingdom of God in our world. Instead there was hope that the movement of the Spirit could help us live life in fullness here—in our moments of already here and not yet!

Preferential option for the poor

Liberation theologians read the Bible from the side of the poor and insisted that from the Exodus story to the prophets, from the incarnation of God in Jesus to the life, death, and resurrection of Jesus Christ, and from the life of the church through the salvific manifestations of God in History, God clearly shows a preferential option for the poor.

Class struggles

Through the struggles of the poor, we see that the world is marked by battles for wealth. The desire for money and accumulation of wealth creates a distinction of people and establishes class struggles. Economic disparity and hierarchical division of people into classes undergird state control of the people and the law. As we look into the concrete realities of our people, we look at the economic, the social, the political, and the cultural aspects of our lives and we see poor people eaten up by economic and political powers controlled by a very small elite. There is no way to read the Bible and understand God's love if not through the lenses of injustice and death caused by class struggles.

Consciousness

The preferential love of God for the poor not only lifts up the poor as receptacles of God's love but also as agents of God's love in the world. Jesus in the midst of the poor, naked, hungry, thirsty imprisoned points to where God dwells and where salvation comes from as we consider the presence of God in history. The gospel read within poor communities has the power to turn each person into the subject of his/her own history. Conscious of our call to determine history, we are the ones empowered by God to work with God to give rise to the utopia of the Kingdom of God in our midst.

Gramsci

Theologians become "organic intellectuals" (Gramsci), grounded in their academic work and living with the poor, who are well-versed in their own wisdom. Gramsci help people gain, in the words of Paulo Freire, conscientization of their power and the possibility of enacting transformation in this world as subjects of their own history!

Let us now take a glimpse at four main Brazilian theologians.

Rubem Alves

The first time Liberation Theology appeared in book form was in the work of a Protestant theologian and pastor called Rubem Alves.

Rubem Alves was a Brazilian theo-poet, educator and storyteller, and a former Presbyterian minister who has deeply shaped the history of Protestantism in Brazil, both by his own history in the last fifty years of the twentieth century and by his diverse writings. His book "Protestantism and Repression. A Brazilian Study Case," published in English by Orbis Books, is still a landmark in the analysis of Protestantism in Brazil.

In 1963, Alves studied at Union Theological Seminary in New York City. In 1964, when he went back to Brazil to be a pastor of a church in the countryside of his own state, Minas Gerais, Brazil, he was taken by the military dictatorship. Alves became an enemy of the government, mainly because his beloved church, the Presbyterian Church of Brazil, denounced him to the dictators as a dangerous thinker.

The church leaders at that time were aligned with the military and helped the government to get rid of dangerous minds. Nevertheless, helped by Presbyterians in North America, he came and lived in exile in the USA where he did his Ph.D. at Princeton Theological Seminary. His dissertation's title was named "Towards a Liberation Theology." He tells us in the preface of the Brazilian publication that this idea of liberation was totally unknown at that time and the dissertation committee asked him to rewrite it all in one more year. It was Richard Shaull, his mentor, who did not let it happen.

Later, a Roman Catholic editor was interested in his dissertation and wanted to publish it. His only condition was to change the title because nobody would understand the meaning of "Liberation Theology." Influenced by Moltmann's theology of hope, the book was then published with the following title: "A Theology of Human Hope," containing the seeds of the agenda of Liberation Theology.

Harvey Cox wrote the preface of his book, stating that theologians in the north should do theology *with* theologians in the south and not about them anymore. Alves' book was written prior to Gustavo Gutierrez's "Liberation Theology," and later Alves became good friends of professors James Cone and Walter Wink, forming, in professor Alves' own words, the "three musketeers" of Union. After he returned to Brazil, Alves actively worked with education, publishing several books including children stories.

Through his studies and writing, Alves came to believe that academic work would not actually change people. From that moment, he changed his language, his sources, and his ways of constructing knowledge, believing that transformation was possible only by speaking to the hearts of the people. He began to draw freely from the works of Nietzsche, Gabriel Garcia Marques, Albert Camus, Freud, M. C. Echer, Octavio Paz, Saint Augustine, Bonhoeffer, Feuerbach, Bachelard, Beethoven, and a broad collection of poets, movies, and Brazilian writers to weave the word made flesh and love through his poetry, politics, cooking, beauty, theology, alchemy, memories, and desires. Theology for Alves took the form of playing with words as an attempt to understand the mystery of God.

Alves' work falls at the border where theology and poetry meet, and he became a theo-poet, freeing theology from any attempt to be locked within the cages of hermetic theological dogmatic discourses. He opened up the horizons of theologians in a myriad of ways, offering us exciting and unexpected possibilities for curious dialogues and unpredictable results. From the hand and heart of one of the first and main Latin American liberation theologians, we receive always a passionate account of God and life, an account that still carries an utopian horizon for a new world of poetry, magic, beauty, and liberation.

Ivone Gebara

Philosopher and theologian Ivone Gebara is a nun from the Order of Our Lady of Conegas of Saint Augustine. She worked for more than thirty years with Don Elder Camera, Archbishop of Recife, including eighteen years at the Institute of Theology in Recifeshe, until the Vatican closed the Institute in 1989. In a small town called Camaragibe, near the capital of Recife in the Northeast part of Brazil, Gebara worked mostly with poor people and battered women in the Recife area. Her work as a theologian cannot be separated from her work with the people. Even her office, the place where she wrote her theology, was filled with children running around. She had a very old computer, and I remember she used to ask me not to sent big files because it took forever for her computer to open them. Gebara is now retired and but continues to write and give talks everywhere. I had the privilege to tutor two classes she taught at Union Theological Seminary in 2003 and two years ago I edited a book to honor her called "Dear Ivone."

Ivone Gebara is one of the most important theological voices in Latin America. In English language, we have two of her major works: "Longing for Running Water: Ecofeminism and Liberation," published in 1999 and "Out of Depths: Women's Experiences of Evil and Salvation," published in 2002. In 2012, she gave the plenary of the American Academy of Religion titled: "Knowing the Human, Knowing the Divine for the Human: Perspectives from Vulnerable Corners of Today's World."[1]

She also has a vast number of articles published in Portuguese, Spanish, English, and French. In 1997, she published "Teologia EcoFeminista" (São Paulo: Olho D'agua, 1997) and just two years ago, she published a new major book in Portuguese called "Urban Theology; Essays on Gender,

Ethics, Environment and the Human Condition." (São Paulo: Fonte Editorial, 2014). In 2014, Nancy Cardoso and I edited a book to celebrate her life and thought: "Dear Ivone, Love letters of theology and feminism." Prof Chris Tirres wrote one of the letters.

In 1989, she gave an interview to a major magazine in Brazil and "off the record" she talked about abortion amidst the women she worked with. When the magazine was published, that conversation was added; she was silenced by the Vatican and sent back to Belgium to be reeducated. During that time, she wrote the book "Out of the Depths: Women's Experience of Evil and Salvation." Gebara has lived her life for the church and the poor people of Brazil. Nonetheless, she was often harshly critical of the church and its male dominance.

Gebara has a different understanding of theology. For her, God is not a fixed being beyond creation and sufficient in itself, as male theologians insist so as to control both the knowledge of God and people. This understanding of God is used by the patriarchal leadership to claim that they alone hold the truth of God. This control and tutelage shuts down the voices of women, and those who do not operate with that understanding of God. Instead of considering God as an essence, a self-enclosed being to whom we go to find wisdom, she sees God as a mystery that permeates the lives of men and women and the whole creation.

In her short book "What Is Theology?", Gebara writes that theology is the cloth we wear on top of our experiences and deep feelings. The problem is that we wear only one piece of cloth and we never take that off. Instead, she says, we should take off our religious clothes often so we could discover our bodies, our feelings and then experiment with different cloths so we can learn other ways to talk about our experiences with God.

Theology is a process of knowing and patriarchy has forced us to think in univocal ways offering us only one piece of cloth to understand God and ourselves. For Gebara, religious experiences are born and lived in and through our bodies and it is in these bodies and bodies' relations that we can find the threads of what God might be in our midst. There is a tapestry of solidarity and connection that gives us, in different bodies and unique feelings, a sense of what and who God might be: a mystery that graces us in many forms and shapes. It is this mystery, lived in the plural ways of living that begs for different forms of knowledge to give different accounts of God, of ourselves and our lives together.

We are biology and logos, she says, life and word, and it is in the relation between the earth and our bodies that we create symbols and meaning. This meaning is fundamentally connected with our ability to listen to our bodies in connection with the body of the earth. From this deep interconnectivity, God comes to us not from above, from a formatted kind of knowledge, but from within our lived experiences. The less we can interrelate: bodies, feelings, experiences, and the movements of the earth, the further we get from God, the mystery who lives in the midst of our experiences.

Patriarchal thinking does not have this form of relationality since it is often detached from these sources: body, feelings, and the earth. The consequence of this unrelated form of thinking is the creation of a top down structure to define the logos so as to keep a homogeneous concept of God and power. Speaking as an eco-Latina theologian, she pushes for a diversity of voices, with women included in the officiality of the church, and for a more integrated sense-knowledge, with different ways of experience-knowing and constructing knowledge. Women's knowledge is able to deal with the complexity of this connectivity and with the real problems that pertain to the daily lives of people, including sexual and health issues, bridging the abyss between temporal and religious power exposed by dogmatic thinking.

The intellectual work of women has been able to reveal the patriarchal method of knowing which is associated with absolute power through the development of dogmas around perfection and purity mirroring the absolute representation of masculine power over all else that is not male. Thus, through history, God, Jesus, and the Holy Spirit have only received masculine representations. The presence of Mary for instance serves only to reify the masculine power of a patriarchal system of domination.

For Gebara one of the new challenges of theology is to go plural. She has been writing lately on Christological pluralisms and the need for Christian thinking to engage in plural dialogues and interreligious dialogue. Plural dialogues entail the need for a variety of voices. Women for instance have to fight the patriarchal system that has oppressed them as neither proper nor capable of theological thinking. Along with women, black people, indigenous people, and queer people have been relegated to a marginal space. They have resisted and are making the theological discourse more plural and more consistent with our societies and our ways of living; however, due to the historical hegemonic singular forms of thinking, these groups are still left in the margins. The plural conversation is more common outside of the official realm of the church.

What this singular way of theology also does is to avoid plural-common ways of thinking which robs us from plural ethical forms of assessing and negotiating life and respect in the bigger polis/city. Gebara says that the problem for our theologies is not pluralism but rather a lack of a *modus vivendi* that is grounded in generosity, affection and respectful of rights and aspirations. As for interreligious dialogue, Gebara says that again the women's perspective can deal with the real life of people in their daily struggles in much better ways, creating necessary bridges to create a world that is open to different affections, thinking, sexualities, and practices.

Gebara has seen the power of women in the creation and recreation of life even in the midst of ongoing patriarchal, economic, political, gender, sexual, and social oppression. It is within the lives of women and their experiences of evil and salvation that she finds God, this mystery that continues to move in and through the lives of poor women. Thus, it is through the work of women, ecological justice, equality of gender relations, and plural ethical relations that theology should be made, not only for the sake of theology, but for the sake of everyone's lives and the life of the planet.

Milton Schwantes
Milton Schwantes was born in 1946 in Tapera, Rio Grande do Sul (RS), in Southern Brazil. In 1966, he started his training at Faculty of Theology of the Evangelical Church of the Lutheran Confession in Brazil. He had access to different theologies, but he was most interested in Richard Shaull's "Theology of Revolution" that helped him to broaden his vision beyond Germanic studies and toward the revolutionary decade of 1960. Inspired by Shaull, he realized that social change can be unleashed by small revolutionary groups, as happened in Cuba. He completed his Ph.D. in 1974 at Heidelberg University, incorporating in his vision a refusal of the capitalist system by criticizing modernity based on an idealized past. There, Schwantes had access to the material of the Weber Circle, which included authors such as Georg Lukács and Ernst Bloch.[2] In his stay in Heidelberg, he was able to expand his exegetical work as a negation of modern civilization, which was key to the development of his Liberation Theology. His Ph.D. work focused on the poor in the Hebrew Bible, as a

continuation of his interest in the undercurrent of history and its disenfranchised people. Here is what he says about this work:

> The right to receive food and land from society. The right to receive from society support in the midst of a need and in crisis, amidst relatives and the community. I also wanted to know who exactly the poor are. The term "poor" in the Old Testament and in the Bible, is used differently from how we use it today. We understand the poor as those who are in need. The Bible understands the poor as those who have the right to reclaim social rights owned by them. In the biblical tradition, a poor person is not a beggar asking for things, but one who demands his share in society.[3]

Schwantes recognized the poor in antiquity as recipients of rights, updating the term for our current times when the poor are treated as subhumans. When he returned to Brazil, he became a pastor for the next four years at the Cunha Porã Parish, a rural area in the state of Santa Catarina where about 1,200 people lived. There, he developed along with the campesinos a pastoral theology that paid attention to small farmers abused by the military dictatorship.

In "Justice and Land" and "Small Farmers of West of Paraná," he wrote about the people of Cunha Porã based on the book of Micah, relating them to the poorest people in the rural areas of Judah to see how his people could organize themselves, originating the first movement settlements in southern Brazil.[4] During his time there, he gained a sharper awareness of how biblical reflection on social actions could help to develop Lutheran pastoral work in the field.

Between 1978 and 1988, he worked at the Lutheran Theological Seminary as a professor of Old Testament. There he lived in the favelas (the poorest areas in Brazil) of Sao Borja. From 1985 to 1986, he helped the settlements of Base Communities of Anonni, where the Landless Movement began.[5] Schwantes' writings cannot be separated from the context of his life with the small farmers in Brazil. His texts "God Makes A Tent With Us" and "God Speaks To The Campesinos" show the deep relation between his scholarship and his ground work.

Schwants also worked with CEDI, Center for the Popular Reading of the Bible, as an organizer of the campesino pastoral work. From this time, we see his important work called: "Prophecy and State: A proposal for a Prophetic Hermeneutics."[6] In his work he denounced the abuse of small farmers by agribusiness with the support of the military government. In response to that abuse, he articulated the situation of the poor in social rural movements:

> Another example: it becomes more comprehensible when Amos talks so mighty about the exploitation of the poor by the State, attributing to them the end of the oppressive monarchic State, while Hosea, living in the same state doesn't even mention the poor. That is because Amos came from the impoverished campesinos. His contestation to the dominant class and to the State is grounded in his local situation and his faith in a God who had the same care for those exploited in Jewish society. Wrapping up this attempt to understand Amos, I conclude that his message is not about the end of a people, but the end of those who are totalitarians, while he draws some hope, even in implicit ways, as a prophet who comes from the campesinos of his time. The specifics of the radical prophecy must be located in the antagonism with the State. The reign of kings is not his issue. His basic theme, when he talks about the ruins of the basic institutions of this state/reign is the end of temple/palace, of the city-capital and of the king. In this antagonism, we see the mirror of an opposition between city and rural people, and we must search for the roots of the prophetic movement in the countryside of Israel and Judah, in its small farmer workers. Thus, the conflict with the state doesn't come out of the priesthood. Neither does it comes from the question of the place of the State within the existent orders. I can imagine that for those who look at the State from this perspective, it will not be easy to find any antagonism. It is precisely in this perspective that the prophecy of the old testament can help us rediscover that the contestation to the oppression organized by the apparatus of the state is neither from the temple nor the social stability that comes with this. It has its origins precisely in the margins, or better: in the struggle of those who actually produce, of those who work in the land, if we think in terms of the Old Testament. That is why it is easy to understand when a church is not able to figure out the existent prophetic conflict suffered by the state, when this church does not live in this marginal space.[7]

In this fragment, Schwantes does not say that there is an "end for the people" but rather invokes the *modus totalitarius* of the States: oppression and exploitation of their supporters. Through the Biblical text, and shaped by the Brazilian reality, the young Schwantes placed his hope in the prophecy that "comes from the Campesino movements."[8] Resistance can only be made by a complete "antagonism against the state," which, since antiquity, is grounded in the urgency of the End of the Temple and the palace, of the capital city and the king. In this sense, the ground of his hermeneutics puts in check the military state in that moment, its relations to the Christian churches and its relations of exploitation between the city and rural areas. Schwantes differentiates priests and prophets. For him, the prophets are the ones who organize the resistance in the fields and small towns, while the priests are the ones who fail to offer any critique toward the State. He writes: "The priests never seem to consider the place of the State in the order of existing things."[9] From the Brazilian reality, he posits that the priesthood is not made by those who denounce injustice, but rather are those who are interested in the development of these institutions. The struggle comes from those who produce and work, not from the temple of sacred stability.[10]

For Schwantes, the most consistent message was to the church that was trying to silence the prophetic commitment. For him, it is the church and popular organizations that must declare their divergence from the State and assume their prophetic roles.[11] In his fundamental book, "Projects of Hope: meditations on Genesis 1-11," we find one of the most significant texts he wrote. Speaking to a gathering of Base Communities in Ecuador, he eliminated bibliographical notes in the book because for people citations wouldn't matter. One of his enduring themes is the importance of the class struggle: "the owners of power try to amputate the popular desires."[12] Inspired by Marx and from the life of the campesinos, he denounced the logic of capital in transforming everything in consumerism: "[the owners of power] try to substitute the images of the lives of the suffering ones with the images of consumerism, televised happiness, and surreal soap operas."[13]

When interpreting Genesis 4, Schwantes indicated how the presence of the divine is in the field, in Abel, killed by Cain, an arrogant urbanite. With his theological sensibility, he wrote that Cain only had a chance to survive when he became a farmer, as a provocation to the rampant capitalism in Brazilian cities. For him, the cities could only be a way out for humanity if they could be rebuilt using the forms of rural communities, meaning, by "ways of the campesino organization."[14] Schwantes does not believe in social transformation based on urbanistic techniques and machinery but instead in forms of organization that already existed before capitalism.

As a conclusion to this short introduction to the thought of Milton Schwantes, we return to one of his metaphors to explain the present time and with it, show how the Marxian utopia still moves him:

> [the owners of powers] repress and kill those who organize themselves to fight for a roof over their heads or a piece of land to plant. However, as much as the powerful destroy the flowers and smush the gardens, they will not impede the Spring.[15]

From the perspective of the oppressed of the South of Brazil by capitalist exploitation, he links the popular movement of the reading of the Bible with the pastoral work of the land, the paraphrased metaphor of Marx about imminent revolution and the impossibility of the powerful to shut down popular desires. The "Spring of the People" is a place like no other, dedicated to the equality of all human beings and where rich and poor would not exist anymore. In his work, issues of land, bread, and life are the most fundamental questions of humankind and these are the central frames of his book on Genesis 1-11.[16] When he talks about the powerful, Schwantes says that they foment domination and alienation, tying up popular communitarian projects of struggle for the common good. His hope, based on the work of land/campesinos pastoral agents and organizations, was that religion would be a place where the struggle for the dignity of humankind would oppose capitalism and its modern oligarchies.

Nancy Cardoso

One cannot talk about the Methodist pastor Nancy Cardoso without saying that her texts are to be read amidst sighs, transgression, and sweat. In fact, the reading of Nancy causes emotions, transgresses boundaries as we can see in some of her classic articles for RIBLA (Journal of Latin American Biblical Interpretation): "Ah! Love in its Delights—A Feminist Reading of the Song of Songs," or "Without Losing our Tenderness: Never! Men Badly Loved and Women Prisoners of Love" and "A Sword

Crossed In My Body: Painful Readings of Maternity." Cardoso Pereira has a vast portfolio and we decided to focus on her last writings. First, we mention an interview she gave about agribusiness, food sovereignty, fast food, and the theology of "Times of Creation." She carries a prophetic tone to denounce the inequality of production, distribution, and profit by the industries, and stress the class interests behind the discussions about the intentional production of hunger on the planet, justifying the production of food by the "idol of agribusiness"[17] and increasing the profits of fast-food businesses. She says:

> The world never before had so much capacity to produce food! However, hunger continues looming for 1 billion people. Big business continues devouring the earth, seeds and water, making fortunes for a minority on the planet. The productive processes of agribusiness are extremely destructive and do not meet the needs of all. We eat badly and we are deeply affected by the fast food logic of the "time for profit." The Time of Creation is a challenge to rethink the processes of feeding and retro-feeding within all beings and humanity.[18]

With the pastorals and the landless, she is concerned with food production and the exploitation of the land/nature by rural workers. Consequently, her criticism is direct at the agribusiness that inherited the vast monoculture lands in Brazil and employ advanced technology while creating precarious conditions for its land workers, echoing the time of slavery. Because agribusiness utilizes the land ownership structure created by European colonial capitalism, the revolutionary theologian whose feet are used to walking on the land points out that the "Time of Creation is what can help us to think about feeding people outside the mass-produced food of agribusiness."[19] She considers that the way out of this situation is the organization of the campesino forces to strengthen small-scale farmers.

Cardoso Pereira became more engaged with the land movements after 2013, when she started to work full time with the Pastoral Commission of the Land. Since then, she has focused on food production and the exploitation of land/nature and of rural workers. One of her texts[20] stresses how these issues are interrelated, using the brilliant image of "Mother Earth" that is so familiar to the natives of the American continent to denounce it: "the Great Mother tolerates it all and can continue to be milked by the male-humanity."[21]

The text problematizes the naturalization of the construction of the idea of "Mother Earth" by the modern male status quo that implicitly appeals to the popular imaginary by suggesting that "Mother Earth" can handle/tolerate it all, even the continuing devastation by the modus of Brazilian capitalism. She starts describing how the idea of the "Mother Earth" has been used in ways that would be primarily against the modern way of life:

> In the context of this framework of civilizational crisis, the uses of mother-earth work as an element of continuity and as a possibility of rupture and renovation, demanding an effort for understanding and critique. Particularly, critical thinking must denaturalize the uses of the mother-earth binary, identifying its vectors of meaning and, from a feminist political perspective, understand the potential and the limits of this imaginary.[22]

To Cardoso Pereira, only a feminist critique is capable of mobilizing anticapitalistic intelligences that would challenge the naturalization of this ancient (mythic) imaginary of the native peoples. She realizes that the "Mother Earth" metaphor is being used to justify the continuing exploitation of the planet, objectifying our relationship with nature.[23] Large businesses use this metaphor to say that we can keep milking the great "Mother Earth," since she tolerates it all.

Cardoso Pereira constructs her theological critique alongside practical theology, carnality, social reflections, and the movements that fight for rights and/or another world. She points out that the true construction of the "Mother Earth" metaphor must, above all, radicalize it in favor of the social movements of women victimized by male heteronormative capitalism:

> Even after much critique work and organization of women and feminist movements, the explanatory models based on binary oppositions such as male/female, culture/nature, positive/negative, reason/ intuition continue to operate in our culture. In the Planet Mother Earth metaphor, even though it is formatted by divergent economic and political contexts, the representation of maternity continues to be consistent and to interfere at different levels in the fights of

women, particularly regarding ecofeminist agendas. Women and nature share a common disdain by economic studies in general, as they are considered a "resource" to satisfy male needs in particular, or human needs in general with intrinsic auto regeneration capabilities, which also means that they can do without care.[24]

According to Cardoso Pereira, both women and nature are used in marketing campaigns despite the disdain of the current economic systems for them, as their role is solely the "satisfaction of male needs."[25] Bringing together the exploitation of Mother Earth and feminist and ecosocialist values, she suggests the gentle mother allows herself to be used or, in fact, exploited by her own children in the name of a love for their land. For the well-being of her children, the "Mother" (in the metaphor of the Earth) allows herself to be "used" by her offspring to sustain life, enacting the violence of utilization and exploitation before an unequal land. The perfect gentle mother land, as Cardoso Pereira writes:

> The cultural management of "motherhood" allows and requires this resolution based on ambiguity to dissimulate the discomfort of the relations of violence and subordination that found the "mother land" and its delimited "land." The discipline of the children is based on the gentleness of the "mother." The love for the "mother land" is the love for the "mother" who wishes to dissolve the real violence that founds the State, distributes the "land" unequally and establishes the imperatives of voluntary submission. Patriotically.[26]

In this sense, Cardoso Pereira is a representative of Feminist Liberation Theology. From the actions of the Pastoral Commission of the Land, she unites in an explosive way this theory in books, articles, and seminars, and in her practice with the social movements. Again, we assume that Liberation Theology would not only be a position (status) in life, but also a way of life that proposes a complete engagement with society. In this sense, we highlight this brilliant Methodist theologian and her antimodernity conspiracy to burn down male Brazilian capitalism anchored on large estates built on the genocide of black, native, and poor peoples. Cardoso Pereira's path of sighs, sweat, and transgression is the organization of economic and social victims as a concrete way to dismantle the heteronormative urban life of modernity.

Conclusion: on the Liberation Theology and the alternatives in Brazilian cities

Alongside these Liberation Theologians, there is also a companion line of black Liberation Theology in Brazil that expresses resistance and the organization of more vulnerable segments of society. We acknowledge that, theoretically, there are changes in the Brazilian humanities, to which the Liberation itself belongs, articulated to face the creation of the modern Brazil. Since the decades of 1950 and 1960, Brazil has undergone profound changes that go beyond political issues. These are transformations that arise from the urbanization that has sprawled to former rural areas.

This complex phenomenon is part of what Bonaventura de Souza Santos calls "globalizations that spread through the geographies of the Southern part of the World."[27] It started with the increasing industrialization of agriculture to adjust the Brazilian economy to substitute imported goods, a process that began during the Old Republic. In the decades of 1950-1960, Liberation Theology began to sprout, a mixture of (catholic) political theology and (Protestant) revolution theology. As indicated, Liberation Theology appears grounded on the foundation of Sociology, questioning Brazilian Christianity and its ties to capitalism.

From its original sociological base comes the notion of totality, the discourse on evolution and class struggles. These terms were all part of the lexicon of the progressive agenda at that time. In this context, Liberation Theology profited from the mentality of urban solidification of the first cities, as put by Ciro Flamarion Cardoso[28] who relates Brazilian geopolitics and the fixation of Marxism in Brazil. In addition, the totalizing discourse made sense because of the revolutionary fights/victory of the campesinos led by Fidel Castro and Ernesto Che Guevara and, on the other hand, unified the sense of fight against the civil-military dictatorship that ruled in Brazil at the time, an enemy also present for Liberation Theology.

Currently, because of the fall of the Berlin Wall, Ciro Flamarion Cardoso states that "Marxism [has lost] strength, as have the totalizing attempts of the knowledge of the humanities."[29] Diversity, the polyphony of voices and plurality expanded in Brazil during the decades of 1980 and 1990, following disillusion with Marxism and the expansion of globalizing neoliberalism. As Raquel Rolnik e Klin points out, the expansion of knowledge with many pluralities and the integration of urban networks in the metropolis created a "landscape of political and territorial restructurating and economic openness without technological and industrial compensatory policies, generating a dissociation of mentalities favoring pluralities."[30]

Thus, from 1980 onwards we observe an expansion of urban capitalism in Brazil, producing "privately, the 'city'."[31] Capitalism became more entrenched in Brazilian culture, silencing the voices denouncing exploitation and brutality, and reducing resistance. At the same time, capitalism demanded a precarious insertion of Brazil into modernity, with poor conditions in the cities particularly in vulnerable settlements. The people most exposed from this new urban neoliberalism in Brazil were black people, natives, women, and gays.

Most of these people had led a precarious existence since the formation of Brazil. In modern times, they were forced to migrate to the poorer neighborhoods and the favelas in the cities. They formed the Brazilian ghettos that, through different perceptions and thinking, began to express a new agenda of self-recognition in response to the expansion of capitalism. This process coincides with the process of disillusion with Liberation Theology, when the poor began to be identified with black people, natives, quilombolas, and LGBTQA communities.

During the expansion of Brazilian neoliberal capitalism, the face of the poor became apparent among the victims of the system, strengthening their identities[32] —a nexus of theological thought arising from the metropolis. Liberation Theology that elected to be close to the social revolution, developed an interest in resistance, identities and survival amidst capitalist exploitation. Theological training centers that used to be engaged with political Liberation Theology became spaces to experience different theological voices from different marginalized bodies.

This whole complex, urban-theological phenomenon was called "pluralist Liberation Theology"[33] —an explosion of theologies with few universalist pretensions that express certain commonalities regarding the refusal of capitalism and the defense of life against the process of human degradation by Faustino Teixeira. To him, Liberation Theology would be the horizon for the path of "pluralist Liberation Theology."[34] All these theologies—black, feminist, ecologic, native, gay, queer, and other theologies—would fight for justice for the peoples excluded by the meritocratic capitalism.

Moreover, challenged by the all-dominating global forms of neoliberalism, it will be necessary for these theologies of liberation and others that do not yet exist, to continue/begin to work with other discourses in new forms, sources, and movements of thought and practice, and to continue to engage with the communities of those suffering and speak from there, about the possibilities of economies of solidarity and against the economies of exclusion, speak about the dominion of economic empires, about public spaces and policies, education, communication theories and political memories, history, many psychoanalysis theories, liturgy, performance and theater, political theologies and the forms of the political left to rethink and offer a new world, about the expansive forms of sexuality, the plurality of negritude forms of living, interreligious dialogues, forms of disabilities, the empire of drugs, militarization, agrarian reform and housing, trafficking of persons and slavery, land grabbing by agribusiness and the genocide of our indigenous people. All of them under as forms of decolonizing thinking and practice, addressing the unjust realities of Latin America.

Regarding black theology, we must say that while black theology was developed in United States by the powerful work of James Cone, in Brazil it never fully developed due to explicit and implicit racism. The explicit racism in society never consider black thought or black theology proper thinking and within the circles of liberation theologies, it was most often done by white theologians who could not perceive the fundamental problem with its implicit racism. That lack of a developing black theology also attests to the fact that black liberation theologians hardly had any presence in theological institutions. Nonetheless, we can say that while some initiatives are now sprouting in Brazil, this theology has been present in an embryonic form since the decade of 1990. Three groups fostered the Afro-American thought in Brazil. There was the "Identity" group, formed at the School of Theology in Sao Leopoldo and led by the North American theologian Peter Nash. The other group, also beginning during the 1990s and shaped within the Catholic Church in Sao Paulo was the Atabaque Center of Black Culture and Theology.[35] The third group was created by the Methodists at the Ecumenical Center for Black Culture (Cecune) in Porto Alegre.[36]

Particularly, Peter Nash linked biblical labor with black sensibility, denouncing the pejorative terms used to refer to Blacks in Southern

Brazil. He developed an intense process to bring students to self-identify as Blacks and accept their own afro and Afro-Brazilian identity. In 2000, Peter Nash returned to the USA, and the Colombian Catholic biblicist Maribel Mena Lópes took his place for a short period.[37] Now, in addition to the Catholics, Lutherans, and Methodists, other paths are appearing in Brazil. Today, a significant number of Blacks that assume their own identity are from diverse Pentecostal denominations. Would they create new theologies?

The Atabaque group was made up of anthropologists, priests, and thinkers who extended black theological thinking beyond the limits of Christianity. Black theological thinking in Brazil wanted to transform the hermeneutical task from a (white) enterprise into a black oikos, a black house, a place where the various forms of black religions expressions from Africa and Brazil could be thought from a full sense of blackness, from different keys, forms, sources, and experiences and authentically made by black people. Reinaldo João de Oliveira asked: "Is there a hermeneutical thinking? If it exists, is it a thinking that was effectively Black/Afro? Moreover: is it contextually black, fundamentally Afro-Latin-American theological thought?"[38]

Black theology is being developed now in Brazil, particularly in (mostly Pentecostal) churches in popular neighborhoods, creating and shaping a new face for the Protestant/evangelical movements in Brazil. These are lay faces from local/popular communities. We are now in the plurality that provided Liberation Theology with readings and experiences that today condition the transformative potential of the poor and excluded peoples in Latin America. Not only those recognized by Liberation Theology as "poor," but the blackened crowd of victims with a plurality of languages and shapes that began to produce theology from their own experiences and resistances in face of meritocratic capitalism.

Nonetheless, the fight is intense and full of challenges. There are no religious educational institutions in Brazil, whether Christian seminaries or departments of religion, that deliberately support black theological thinking. These institutions are mostly made up of heterosexual white males. If the black man does not have space in the academic institutions the presence of the black woman is even worse. The struggle of black women to develop for their autonomous thinking is absolutely difficult. Racism coupled with patriarchy in Brazil has disastrous results, which means that women in general, queer people/LGBTQA, and people with disabilities are not even on the fringes of these educational institutions or academic production. Latin America still maintains a profoundly strong white patriarchal structure and the known Liberation Theology so far did very little to draw attention to these social disparities and injustices.

More than ever, Latin America needs liberation theologies that break with the present, conservative, and/or liberal theologies that serve only the middle or the dominant classes, with theologies in most cases isolated, self-fulling, autoimmune, and committed to the powers that be. Latin America needs new theologies of liberation that speak and live the God who (still) prefers to live among the poor, among women, children, immigrants, indigenous people, people with disabilities, peasants, blacks, and all those who live without minimum conditions of life and in so many forms of vulnerability.

Perhaps the next forty-five years of Liberation Theology will correct who spoke, what was not spoken or what was not done. Perhaps, using different sources, bibliographies, experiences, and relations, but always committed to those who are still placed on the crosses of suffering and exploitation in our beloved Pacha Mama.

Notes

1. https://www.youtube.com/watch?v=0u-w0k_tn50.
2. Dreher, Martin, 2006, "Milton Schwantes: Um Perfil Biográfico", em: Carlos Dreher e Isolde Dreher (org.), *Profecia e Esperança: Um Tributo a Milton Schwantes*, São Leopoldo: Oikos, p. 15.
3. Schwantes, Milton. A Teologia e o Direito Dos Pobres—Interview with Schwantes at Unisinos. Accessed at 10.03.2014. Available at: https://www.metodista.br/fateo/noticias/duas-entrevistas-com-o-professor-milton-schwantes.
4. Op. cit.
5. To know more about the Landless Movement in Brazil see http://www.mstbrazil.org/content/history-mst visited 12/10/16.
6. Schwantes, Milton, 1982, "Profecia e Estado: Uma Proposta Para a Hermenêutica Profética", *Estudos Teológicos* 22(2), pp. 5–48.
7. Op. cit., p. 69.
8. Py, Fábio, 2016, "The Lutheran Rebellion in the Brazilian Countryside," *Crosscurrents* 12, pp. 156–8.
9. Schwantes, Milton, 1982, "Profecia e Estado: Uma Proposta Para a Hermenêutica Profética", Estudos teológicos, São Leopoldo 22, p. 105–45,1982.
10. Op. cit.

11. Schwantes, Milton, 2011, *Projetos de Esperanças: Meditações Sobre Genesis 1-11*, São Paulo: Paulinas.
12. Op. cit., p. 9.
13. Op. cit., pp. 9–10.
14. Op. cit., pp. 84–5.
15. Op. cit., p. 10.
16. Op. cit., pp. 11–8.
17. Pereira, Nancy Cardoso, 2007, "Agronegócio & Religião: Pretensões & Profecias". EcoDebate, 19.10.2007. https://www.ecodebate.com.br/2007/10/19/agronegocio-e-religiao-pretensoes-profecias-por-nancy-cardoso-pereira/.
18. Op. cit.
19. Op. cit.
20. Pereira, Nancy Cardoso, 2013, "Dos Filhos Deste Solo Não Sou a Mãe Nem Gentil: Do Imaginário da Mae-Terra à Critica Eco-Feminista," *Caminhos* 11(2), pp. 123–38.
21. Op. cit.
22. Op. cit., p. 124.
23. Op. cit.
24. Op. cit., p. 125.
25. Op. cit.
26. Op. cit.
27. Souza Santos, Boaventura, 2002, *Os Processos da Globalização*, São Paulo: Cortez, p. 51.
28. Cardoso, Ciro Flamarion, 2001, "Tempo e História", pp. 9–21.
29. Op. cit., p. 13.
30. Rolnik, Raquel, and Jerome Kilnk, 2011, "Crescimento Econômico e Desenvolvimento Urbano," *Novos estudos* 89, pp. 89–109.
31. Op. cit.
32. Cardoso, Ciro Flamarion, 2001, "Tempo e historia", pp. 15–20.
33. Teixeira, Faustino, 2012, *O Pluralismo Religioso no Coração da Teologia*, São Bernardo do Campo: Nhanduti.
34. Op. cit.
35. http://atabaque-cultura-negra-e-teologia.blogspot.com/?m=1.
36. Leyva, Pedro Acosta, Ezequiel Souza, and Luis Carlos Mello, 2006, "Historia do Grupo Identidade: Uma Década de Vida e Contribuições!" *Identidade!* 9, pp. 21–41.
37. Op. cit.
38. de Oliveira, Reinaldo João, "Existe um pensar hermenêutico-teológico negro?" in http://periodicos.est.edu.br/index.php/identidade/article/view/2202/2099.

CONTRIBUTORS

Sílvia Barbosa has an undergraduate degree in Theology from the Methodist University of Sao Paulo, specialization in Theology and Latin American History from the EST University and PhD in interdisciplinary studies on women, gender, and feminism from the Federal University of Bahia. Published author of books on gender empowerment and race in the Urubu Quilombo, and on Ketu Candomble.

silreligare@hotmail.com

Nancy Cardoso, Methodist pastor, feminist theologian, agent of Land Pastoral Commission (CPT-Brazil), and member of the Palestine and Israel Ecumenical Forum (PIEF);

nancycpt@yahoo.com

Cláudio Carvalhaes, Presbyterian pastor, liberation theologian, liturgist and artist, associate professor of Worship, at Union Theological Seminary in New York City.

www.claudiocarvalhaes.com
ccarvalhaes@uts.columbia.edu

Maria Gabriela Hita, post-doctorate at the Manchester University and professor of the Graduate Program on Social Sciences and Interdisciplinary on Women, Gender and Feminism at the Federal University of Bahia.

mghita@ufba.br

Ronilso Pacheco comes from Sao Gonçalo, Rido de Janeiro, Brazil. Undergraduate student in Theology at the Pontifical Catholic University of Rio de Janeiro, social interlocutor at the Viva Rio organization, and advisor for several social movements working in the defense of human rights. Author of the book *Ocupar, resistir, subverter: igreja e teologia em tempos de violência, racismo e opressão*.

ronilsosilva@vivario.org.br

Fábio Py, PhD in Systematic Theology at the Catholic University of Rio de Janeiro, is a protestant theologian working on the relation between faith and politics. Guest Professor at the Political Social Programs at the State University of North of Fluminense (UENF). He is the author of "Critique to the Lower Ecology." (São Leopoldo & São Paulo: Cebi & Fonte Editorial, 2014). He is an Editorial board member of the Journal Plura, Studies of Religion from the Brazilian Association of History of Religions. ABHR – http://www.abhr.org.br/plura/ojs/index.php/plura). He is a columnist of the Magazine Caros Amigos under the theme of Religion and Human Rights. (http://www.carosamigos.com.br/).

pymurta@gmail.com

CONTRIBUTORS

Obertal Xavier Ribeiro is from Nova Iguaçu - Rio de Janeiro. He is currently an assistant professor of education at the Federation of Faculties Celso Lisboa in the area of Philosophy. Professor of Religious Education in the State. He holds a Doctorate in Theology with concentration in the area of Religion and Education at the Superior School of Theology, EST, RS. He is a Master in Literature and Human Sciences at UNIGRANRIO - University of Rio Grande. He specializes in Biblical Theology at the Superior School of Theology, EST, RS. He was in the priestly ministry for 12 years in the Diocese of Nova Iguaçu. He continues to advise the Diocese of Nova Iguaçu in the area of biblical formation. He works as a pedagogical advisor at CEAP - Center for Articulation of Marginalized Populations with remnant populations of quilombos and in the training of teachers of Elementary and Middle School in the area of History and Literature of Afro-descendants. He develops social projects for income generation and alternative work in the area of selective collection of non-perishable garbage since 2004. He holds a bachelor's degree in Theology from IFTPS - Paulo VI Diocesan Seminary - Nova Iguaçu - RJ and São Bernardo Methodist University - São Bernardo - SP. He holds a bachelor's degree in Philosophy from IFTPS - Paulo VI Diocesan Seminary - Nova Iguaçu and Santa Úrsula University - RJ. He holds a postgraduate degree in Philosophy from Universidade Cândido Mendes - RJ. Address to access this CV: http://lattes.cnpq.br/7800511322792289

ribeiro.obertal@gmail.com

José Geraldo da Rocha, PhD in Systematic Theology by the Pontifical Catholic University of Rio de Janeiro and professor at the Graduate Program in Humanity, Culture and Arts at Unigranrio. Research productivity scholar 1A Unigranrio/Funadesp. He is a black pastoral agent and lives in Duque de Caxias, Rio de Janeiro, Brazil.

rochageraldo@hotmail.com

Marcos Rodrigues da Silva has an undergraduate degree in Theology (1984) and a master degree in Dogmatic Theology (1997) from the Our Lady of Assumption Faculty of Theology. PhD in Religion Sciences by the Pontifical Catholic University of Sao Paulo (2014) and post-doctorate in Education. Member of the Atabaque Center and associate researcher of the Ecumenical Association of Third World Theologians.

marcosrit@gmail.com

Leontino Farias dos Santos, from Sao Paulo, Brazil, has an undergraduate degree in Theology, a master degree in Social and Religion Sciences and has a graduate degree in School Administration. He is a humanist clinical psychoanalyst and PhD candidate in Psychoanalysis at the Atlantic International University. Vice-Director of the Sao Paulo Faculty of Theology of the Independent Presbyterian Church of Brazil.

leontinofarias@hotmail.com

CONTRIBUTORS

Cristina da Conceição Silva lives in Rio de Janeiro and is a teacher in Nova Iguaçu. She is a PhD candidate at the Graduate Program in Humanities, Cultures and Arts of the Unigranrio.

cistinavento24@Yahoo.com.br

Marcos Palhano, photographer, researcher, social educator. He lives in São Paulo.

olhodobturador@gmail.com
http://marcospalhano.wix.com/fotografias

CROSSCURRENTS

INTRODUÇÃO
Religião Negras No Brasil

Introdução

Cláudio Carvalhaes

O Brasil nunca foi o paraíso onde as raças viveram em paz e harmonia. O mito do "homem cordial"[1] na sociedade brasileira, um conceito/arquétipo do cidadão brasileiro comum, dizia que mesmo que esse homem não fosse feito de bondade, era certamente feito de afeição. Essa afetividade que sem dúvida existe no brasileiro encobre como uma folha ideológica, a crueldade e a violência do racismo brasileiro. Assim, ao acreditarmos na afetividade brasileira, acabamos por viver a aparência de um país harmonioso e pacífico. Contudo, essa aparente forma de ser brasileiro é motivo de orgulho para uns e morte para outros. Muito embora presente em toda a história brasileira, o racismo e a luta de classes manifestou-se recentemente, lançando no abismo um conceito que persistiu enquanto a riqueza e o poder no Brasil não mudaram de mãos. O que vemos hoje no Brasil é um descaso sem filtro com os negros, indígenas e minorias desse país. Quanto ao racismo mais especificamente, o fato do Brasil nunca ter tido uma guerra pelos direitos civis para lidar com sua história racista, como se nunca tivesse existido racismos descarados na história brasileira para se dar conta, fez os brasileiros não atentarem para as formas profundas de racismo na cultura. Entretanto, a história colonizadora do Brasil pode ser contada em uma única palavra: racismo. O Brasil foi o ultimo país a assinar uma lei antiescravagista. Os brancos que vieram ao Brasil continuam a controlar o país. A mesma elite branca que controla a economia financeira do mercado, que controla a criação das leis e controla o poder político. Nas veias profundas na historia colonizadora do Brasil corre sangue do povo indígena e do povo negro.

Acredito que a descoberta da minha própria negritude e como ela me formou e deu forma serve como espelho para o que acontece no Brasil hoje de forma geral. A negação da negritude, o medo de tudo o que é negro, a eliminação intelectual, emocional e física de todas as raízes negras, a demonização das religiões negras e o privilégio de poder negar meu próprio racismo são algumas das formas pelas quais eu nunca tive de me envolver com minha própria negritude e pude me esconder atrás da simples aceitação de minha aparente e pura brancura. Eu posso facilmente passar por branco e não viver nada do que o povo negro tem que viver. Da mesma forma, as teologias da libertação ainda estão em débito com o povo negro. As teologias da libertação também poderiam passar como teologias brancas e heterossexuais debaixo dos trópicos sem precisar lidar com a violência do racismo.

Da mesma maneira, as teologias da libertação não conseguiram entender a força da opressão do racismo no Brasil. Enquanto a teologia da libertação aparece na América Latino nos anos 60, o trabalho da teologia negra aparece apenas nos anos 80. Esse dado isolado já seria o suficiente para mostrar como os teólogos da libertação nunca se envolveram com a questão do racismo como uma forma de opressão central no continente. Também não é possível para a as teologias da libertação dizerem que não sabiam dessa ausência em seu discurso. O teólogo negro James Cone, que começou com a teologia negra nos Estados Unidos, fez repetidas e duras críticas aos teólogos latino-americanos da teologia da libertação nas reuniões do EATWOT, chamando-os mesmo de racistas. Ainda hoje, as escolas de teologia e os departamentos de religião no Brasil são majoritariamente ocupados por homens brancos heterossexuais. A maior parte dos trabalhos produzidos por teólogos negros da libertação se deram em movimentos pequenos em diversas partes do país, mas sem nenhum apoio institucional aos pensadores e pensadoras negras/os. O resultado é que a produção teológica negra acaba por ser pequena, espalhada e ainda por ser desenvolvida.

Apesar de toda dificuldade, existe um bom trabalho produzido desde os anos 80. O cenário político e econômico é agora muito diferente. Uma nova ordem social, com novos desafios, novas religiões e novos atores sociais e religiosos, novas emoções, novas formas de socialização, novas tecnologias, novos formatos de comunicação, novas formas neoliberais da economia, novas parcerias transnacionais, novas sexualidades, novos desejos e novas necessidades materiais, assim como novos desenvolvimentos criaram novas demandas, novas formas de opressão, novos desafios e novas formas de violência. Estes são tempos difíceis que demandam novas formas de pensamento negro que ainda estão por serem imaginados.

Certamente o escopo desta revista é pequeno diante de tamanhos desafios do nosso tempo. O que esta publicação quer fazer é dar um pequeno relato da história da teologia da libertação no Brasil e do pequeno espaço que a teologia negra tem historicamente sido desenvolvido. Esta revista também quer dar uma idéia do que pode ser feito, o que precisa ser desenvolvido e o quais são as interseccionalidades religiosas do pensamento negro. A ideia era reunir o trabalho de vários autores negros que estão tentando achar formas de pensamento em meio a um ambiente hostil, especialmente para mulheres negras. Mesmo nesse coletivo de autores, temos três mulheres participando. Acredito ser essa a maior fraqueza desta edição. Entretanto, com esse problema sempre diante de nós, precisamos juntos criar espaços para outras vozes femininas, aqueles que queiram continuar esta conversa e este projeto teológico-cultural/social/gênero /sexual/político. O peso patriarcal na formação e desenvolvimento das teologias da libertação na América Latina tornou invisível as vozes de todas as mulheres! Vozes, movimentos e espaços feministas tem sido suprimidos e mantidos na invisibilidade. Eu convido assim aqueles que tem fortes críticas a entrar no diálogo que estes textos geram e a submeter trabalhos para edições futuros. Nós precisamos de mais gente para participar desse projeto, especialmente mulheres, o povo *queer* e indígenas, para poder começar uma nova revista, um novo tempo!

Há muito o que se fazer! Este projeto é simplesmente um veículo para algumas vozes, uma busca por parceiros e companhias que possam compartilhar de alguma maneira a possibilidade de uma nova plataforma de pensamento. Assim, esta revista se oferece como uma pequena voz e como um ponto de partida para essa velha-nova conversa, um convite para um estudo mais profundo e para uma reflexão mais abrangente. Esperamos que este seja somente um re-começo e que outras vozes continuem onde paramos, ou que comecem onde sequer pensamos que podíamos pensar. Vozes importantes estão se levantando e o futuro está prenho de mo(vi)mentos que estão buscando conhecer o que já se fez, e tentar expandir, rompendo e conectando com comunidades negras e saber o que estão fazendo de acordo com as necessidades e desejos deles.

Novas práxis, novas teorias e novas formas de libertação estão acontecendo. Nossos desafios são maiores agora. A teologia da libertação, mais necessária que nunca! Mas para isso, precisamos continuar com o enegrecimento de nossas teologias. Assim, com nossas teologias negras, a gente pode também enegrecer as lutas de classe ao trabalharmos na intersecção entre raça, classe, gênero, povos indígenas, sexualidades e ecologia, portadores de deficiências, e a ecologia.

Para fazer acontecer esta edição, os desafios da tradução dos textos foram enormes e praticamente impossíveis de se fazer e se auferir e conferir a cultura, o contexto e a língua de um outro povo em sua plenitude. Tradutores/as e editores/as capazes trabalharam nestes textos. Minha gratidão a Tiago Chivegatti, Alice da Cunha e Josefina Terrena pela tradução dos textos tanto para o inglês quato para o português; à Mércia Chivegatti pela correção do português, ao Tiago Chiavegatti pela formatação final e a Katie Mulligan que fez um trabalho maravilhoso de edição, tentando arrumar os trabalhos no idioma inglês. Entretanto ela também é limitada em sua compreensão linguística e sua habilidade de deixar a linguagem clara para o leitor de fala inglesa. Sou também muito grato pelo apoio e suporte do Seminário Teológico União em Nova Iorque. Sem o União, esse projeto não teria visto a luz do dia.

Eu sou muito grato a todos os autores que participaram dessa jornada. Todos imensamente capazes e brilhantes! Finalmente eu sou muitíssimo grato ao companheiro Dr. Marcos Silva, que é parte fundamental da história de um dos grupos mais importantes da teologia negra recente no Brasil, o Grupo Atabaque. Foi ele quem começou todo esse projeto e eu somente o segui. A ele minha mais profunda gratidão.

Gayraud S. Wilmore define assim a história dos negros norte-americanos da seguinte maneira: "Há três temas dominantes ou motivos fundantes na história da chegada dos africanos em Jamestown, Virgínia, em agosto de 1619 até o presente. São eles: sobrevivência, elevação e libertação."[2] Eu acredito que podemos contar a história dos Africanos todos no continente americano dessa maneira. Ao me envolver nesse projeto, eu quero fazer parte ativa dessa história, de entender, honrar e manifestar essas mesmas formas de sobrevivência, elevação e libertação. Acredito poder assim aprender a amar melhor um povo que eu chamo de meu!

Introdução

Marcos Rodrigues da Silva

A diversidade cultural e a formulação de uma epistemologia afro — reflexões teológicas desde o Brasil — constituem um campo de estudos desde a prática teológica e filosófica dificilmente delimitado devido às inúmeras e tênues fronteiras com outras áreas de conhecimento. Este é o exercício que pretendemos buscar e abrir uma reflexão a partir de movimentos históricos afros, na história de lutas e compromissos sociais e eclesiais, já constituídos por outras tradições de crenças e saberes. Não pretendemos neste momento, portanto, defender uma hipótese que seja delimitadora de conhecimentos e saberes.

Partimos da segunda metade do século XX, período em que ocorre o movimento teológico com ênfase nas realidades vividas pelos mais pobres na América Latina. O instrumental de análise e pensamento tinha uma base eurocêntrica.[3] Assim foi se estabelecendo uma proposta de instrumento balizador de interpretação dos atos e atitudes dos empobrecidos. Neste contexto nos deparamos tanto com as contribuições das crenças e saberes dos povos negros na diáspora afro-americana, quanto com os conhecimentos e a reflexão científico-tecnológica universal. Esses parâmetros oferecem, a seu modo, referenciais para a sobrevivência do planeta e qualidade nas relações entre sujeitos, grupos e sociedades.

Como pressupostos, propomos partir da noção de diversidade. Somos diversos. Essa verdade fundamental é sempre ameaçada por ações individuais e coletivas de intolerância. Somos diversos historicamente, etnicamente, linguisticamente e, da mesma forma, somos diversos religiosamente.

A diversidade religiosa é profunda. Ela existe entre ateus e religiosos, entre formas distintas de religião: cristãos e budistas, islâmicos e religiões tradicionais africanas, por exemplo. Entre ramos religiosos com pontos em comum, como judeus e muçulmanos, entre expressões internas de uma mesma religião, como católicos carismáticos e adeptos da Teologia da Libertação, nas tradições construídas dos valores da oralidade como os povos indígenas e afro-americanos e, mesmo entre expressões geográfico-históricas da mesma fé como católicos espanhóis e católicos norte-americanos.

Também na afirmação de Albert Memmi, "Se todo colonial está de imediato na condição de colonizador, nem todo colonizador está fatalmente destinado a tornar-se um colonialista. E os melhores se recusam a isso."[4] A constatação de Memmi entre ser colonizador e se afirmar como colonialista é uma relação dialética que envolve o ser e conviver do opressor e o oprimido. Nesse sentido, para Memmi existe uma vinculação entre esta noção de hierarquia racialmente fundamentada e o controle das mais diversas formas de produção material e simbólica nas regiões colonizadas.

No mesmo cenário Memmi faz um diagnóstico das consequências que atingem o ser-negro escravo colonizado, relata: "Esse entusiasmo pelos valores colonizadores não seria tão suspeito, contudo, se não comportasse seu avesso. O colonizado não procura apenas enriquecer-se com as virtudes do colonizador".[5]

E acentua Memmi que é a repressão é uma das formas de produção do conhecimento dos povos colonizados, com seus universos simbólicos e seus referenciais de sentido. O autor aponta igualmente que a destruição de um povo, de identidades e de histórias há uma luta pela autoafirmação, "O colonizado se aceita e se afirma, se reivindica com paixão". Mas quem é ele? Certamente não é o homem em geral, portador dos valores universais, comuns a todos os homens.[6]

Por fim, podemos constatar a imposição parcial da cultura dos dominadores, na medida em que isto era necessário ao controle e instrumentalização das culturas locais de acordo com a lógica do novo padrão de poder.

Contextualização do tema

Nosso objetivo é partir do estudo e reflexões elaborados por pesquisadores afro-brasileiros que refletem e facilitam um olhar de aproximação aos passos dados desde suas práticas e estudos. Pretendemos, nesta produção de textos, nos aproximar e sistematizar o que significa este exercício de elaboração no campo da teologia latino-americana. Tudo acontece desde uma prática comunitária, modeladas nas comunidades familiares, nos terreiros, nos santuários, com acréscimo de outras contidas nos estudos elaborados nas universidades. Juntaram-se fatores que colaboraram para que uma obra fosse elaborada, muitos elementos de uma epistemologia afro num tempo cronológico, desde a segunda metade do século XX até este começo do século XXI.

Ao ter este ponto de partida não o consideramos como limite, mas enfocaremos um amplo território que possibilita momentos de encontro e as produções teóricas significativas advindas daí. Neste território está o ambiente de reconhecimento das religiões tradicionais africanas, as variedades de práticas religiosas da tradição cristão ocidental que são acima de tudo, humanas e marcadas pelas suas diversidades culturais. A aproximação deste estudo significa compreender o lugar (ou lugares) no panorama religioso afro, reconhecendo os "outros" menos como competidores, mas sim, verdadeiramente, como companheiros de aventura existencial/fé e religiosa.

No universo da pesquisa das produções e sistematizações aqui focadas, queremos aprofundar como se expressam as linguagens e as formas simbólicas manifestadas e/ou camufladas que se apresentam. Tomaremos para verificar o caráter identitário do saber, o que foi experimentado, vivido e como isso pode ser compreendido. Para tanto, exige-se a capacidade de identificar coisas, pessoas, acontecimentos, através da nomeação, descrição e interpretação, envolvendo conceitos apropriados e linguagem.

Atualmente, os estudos sobre religião e religiosidade afro parecem valorizar os fenômenos religiosos de forma diversificada. Há o reconhecimento de que as questões religiosas permeiam a vida cotidiana, como a religiosidade popular, sob as várias formas de espiritualidade, que fornecem elementos para construção de identidades. Elas compõem as memórias coletivas, as experiências místicas e correntes culturais e intelectuais que não se restringem ao domínio das igrejas organizadas e institucionais.

Tendo este reconhecimento como marco referencial, trata-se, portanto, de privilegiar, como objeto central os elementos epistemológicos para uma Teologia Afro-americana, e o diálogo com as discussões teológicas na busca de afirmar a Teologia Afro-americana.

Há na construção de um novo instrumental de interpretação a partir de histórias vividas pelo povo afro na diáspora africana no Brasil, na sua forma particular de ser, saber e estar em meio às adversidades milenares. O respeito à diversidade como um dos valores mais importantes do exercício da cidadania, isso não se pode esquecer. Só com esse respeito absoluto entende-se e supera-se a afirmação de que não existem seitas (pois não existem grandes e pequenas religiões), não existe sincretismo (pois não existe uma religião pura de influências de outras) e, acima de tudo, não existe para o historiador, o filósofo e o cientista da religião uma religião melhor do que outra. Cada experiência religiosa colaborou com uma parte do pensamento religioso; cada sistematização das práticas religiosas expressas uma visão de um grupo e cada atitude testemunhada teve e tem seu valor específico, exatamente por serem e marcarem a diferença.

A reflexão teológica contextualizada nas vivências e práticas afro tem recebido variados conceitos, assim denominada: Teologia Negra, nos Estados Unidos;[7] Teologia Inculturada, em algumas regiões africanas; Teologia Negra da Libertação e Teologia em Contexto, em outras regiões da África;[8] Teologia Afro-americana na América Latina e, no Caribe, a Teologia Antilhana.

Em nível pessoal é imprescindível que o próprio indivíduo se reconheça construtor e ator da sua própria história. Em termos de negritude, isto significa assumir-se como negro e negra. No nível comunitário, a exigência é para assumir as tradições, os mitos, as práticas celebrativas com suas particularidades e similaridades. Assumir é ter o reconhecimento dos embates da vida cotidiana, na pobreza e nas práticas de exclusão.

Apresentamos um olhar "Ser Agente de Pastoral Negro no contexto da realidade brasileira" pelos teólogos Geraldo Rocha e a doutoranda em Humanidades Cristina da Conceição; o teólogo biblista Obertal busca um olhar bíblico-teológico nas práticas dos agentes de pastoral negros e a Bíblia no contexto afro; Cláudio Carvalhaes faz uma leitura interreligiosa e oferece uma possível aproximação entre os cristãos e os povos iorubás a partir da comensalidade convivial: a eucaristia cristã e as oferendas iorubás são lugares de diálogo e convívio quando se comem juntos; Marcos Rodrigues da Silva sinaliza elementos para "uma história afro-americana: caminhos para uma reflexão teológica e epistemológica afro"; Nancy Cardoso e Cláudio Carvalhaes, a partir da religião afro-índigena da jurema brasileira, propõe dialogar com a possibilidade da teologia negra em relação com as matizes dos povos originários como tarefa de toda a teologia da libertação, em especial na vida e luta das mulheres; O Rev. Leontino (Igreja Presbiteriana Independente do Brasil) apresenta um roteiro "Por uma teologia negra no Brasil"; seu olhar tem como ponto de partida a prática contumaz do racismo na sociedade brasileira. Pode-se imaginar a necessidade do desenvolvimento de uma teologia negra que nos chame à reflexão sobre tal fenômeno, à luz de pressupostos bíblico-teológicos de cunho libertador e profético. Silvia Barbosa e Maria Gabriela Hita escrevem sobre a interseccionalidade das categorias de classe, gênero, idade/geração no Candomblé Ilê Asé Ogum Omimkaye na Bahia e nos ajudam a ver novas formas de se entender a negritude nessa religião afro-brasileira. Por fim, o teólogo Ronilso Pacheco indica em seus estudos que "A teologia negra no Brasil é colonial e marginal", posta diante de um contexto de violência, racismo e luta pelo direito à cidadania e ao reconhecimento, que marca profundamente a vida de negros e negras no país.

Assim, os caminhos da teologia afro-americana e caribenha mais do que indicar um itinerário teológico tem o compromisso de refletir, enfatizar e chamar a atenção de todos quantos se deixam sensibilizar pela luta do povo negro. Não se trata de novidade teológica, mas de um aprofundamento calcado numa realidade singular, e que pretende revelar o testemunho, o compromisso e a solidariedade da comunidade negra em vista da mudança da realidade em que vivem no continente latino-americano.

Notas

1. Buarque de Holanda, Sérgio, Raízes do Brasil (São Paulo: Companhia das Letras, 2015).
2. Wilmore, Gayraud S., "Historical Perspective," The Cambridge Companion to Black Theology. Edited by Dwight N. Hopkins and Edward P. Antonio (Cambridge: Cambridge University Press, 2012), 19.
3. Três obras são fundamentos para compreensão deste período. Freire, P., Hassmann, H., Malumba, E., e Cone, J. Teologia Negra — Teologia de La Liberación, Ediciones Sígueme, Salamanca, 1974; Cone, J. e Wilmore, G. Teologia Negra, EP, São Paulo, 1986. ASETT (org.) Identidade Negra e Religião — Consulta sobre Cultura Negra e Teologia na América Latina, CEDI/Edições Liberdade, São Paulo, 1986.
4. Memmi, Albert, Retrato do Colonizado precedido do retrato do colonizador, Civilização Brasileira, Rio de Janeiro/RJ, 2007, p. 55
5. Idem. p. 165-164.
6. Idem, p. 173-174.
7. James H. Cone, assim expressa sua compreensão sobre o fazer teologia negra, na América do Norte:[...] Comenzaré mi exposicións dando uma deficición de libertad, historia y esperanza. Examinaré después las consecuencia steológicas que de ahí se deducen.[...] VV.AA. Teologia Negra-teologia de La liberacion, EdicionesSígueme-Salamanca, 1974, p. 63
8. Na África, desde os tempos do Concílio Vaticano II, Vicente Mulago e outros, já então, refletiam em "Teologia Negra e culturas". Já na década de 70, James Cone mostrou que era não só legítimo, mas necessário e oportuno refletir na teologia em chave de negritude ou vice-versa. Nas últimas duas décadas do século passado, tanto na África como na diáspora, está sendo reconhecida a legitimidades e a necessidade da Teologia Negra.

UMA HISTÓRIA AFRO-AMERICANA
Caminhos Para Uma Reflexão Teológica e Epistemológica Afro

Marcos Rodrigues da Silva

Introdução

Reflexões sobre a histórica da teologia e epistemologia afro foram realizadas no âmbito da Roda de Diálogo Territorialidades Étnicas e Relações Interculturais, enquanto parte da programação do II Seminário Internacional Culturas e Desenvolvimento (SICDES), ocorrido na Unochapecó/SC, em maio de 2014, e no âmbito do Simpósio Temático Questões Africanas, Afro Latino Americanas e os Desafios Contemporâneos, no II Congresso Internacional das Faculdades EST, ocorrido em setembro de 2014. Ambos os encontros possibilitaram momentos especiais de compartilhamento de nossas reflexões e diálogo com pesquisadoras e pesquisadores sobre um tema de uma grandeza significativa para toda a comunidade afro-americana.

A partir disso, nossa tarefa consiste em apresentar um inventário da história do pensamento afro-americano, a partir das contribuições oriundas dos movimentos negros que surgiram nos anos 70, 80 e 90 do século XX. A reflexão teológica afro-americana terá nestes momentos de encontros, estudos e reflexões uma base de dados e elementos significativos para fundamentar a produção teológica e dar seguimento para uma reflexão capaz de sinalizar novos cenários aos primeiros anos do século XXI.

Os Congressos de Cultura Negra das Américas
A iniciativa de organizar os Congressos de Cultura Negra das Américas surgiu da preocupação de vários profissionais: historiadores, sociólogos, antropólogos, artistas, escritores, teólogos e cientistas da religião para atuarem conjuntamente. O objetivo era fazer um exame multidisciplinar da problemática continental sobre a realidade social e cultural dos afro-americanos (ACTAS..., 1989). A realização dos Congressos foi motivada por linhas temáticas que surgem das variadas realidades da América Latina e Caribe.

O primeiro Congresso sobre Cultura Negra das Américas ocorreu em Cali, na Colômbia, no período de 24 a 28 de agosto de 1977. Esse congresso foi convocado e respaldado pela Fundação Colombiana de Investigadores Folclóricos (ACTAS..., 1989). O objetivo foi promover uma reflexão feita por afro-americanos, e sobre estes com a finalidade de superar entraves e barreiras políticas, culturais, econômicas e religiosas, impostas pelos colonizadores e ainda mantidas. O tema do Congresso foi "A realidade social e cultural dos afro-americanos". Os participantes do Congresso foram divididos em quatro grupos de trabalho. O primeiro grupo tratou das questões políticas, religiosas, estéticas e morais. O segundo grupo se ateve às questões das estruturas socioeconômicas. O terceiro grupo ficou com a análise das artes e tecnologia. Enquanto o quarto grupo refletiu as questões pertinentes à "Etnia e Mestiçagem".

Nos diversos países, afirmaram os congressistas, por todos os meios tentam diminuir a população negra, inclusive utilizando a mestiçagem como artifício. A mestiçagem é algo interessante e bem quista desde que seja resultado da deliberação das pessoas. Não é o caso de reportar aqui toda a Ata do Congresso, mas nos parece de fundamental importância recordar as duas recomendações aprovadas pelos congressistas. Primeira: a denúncia de que a maioria dos textos de história, sociologia, economia e política dos países americanos omite, mutila e deforma a participação autêntica do negro no desenvolvimento dos distintos países dos quais é parte fundamental. Segunda: a constatação de que a história do negro na América não pode seguir se difundindo, escrevendo e interiorizando-se simplesmente a partir das crônicas da escravidão (ACTAS..., 1989). Além do substancial conteúdo, o Primeiro Congresso de Cultura Negra foi importante por tratar-se de um acontecimento realmente histórico.

Com o tema a "Identidade Cultural do Negro nas Américas", o segundo Congresso foi realizado na cidade do Panamá, nos dias 12 a 21 de março de 1980. O evento reuniu mais de trezentos delegados, provenientes da América, África e Europa. Foram debatidos nesse Congresso quatro subtemas de questões relacionadas com a comunidade negra: (1) identificação social na estrutura de classe; (2) a identidade cultural do negro na educação formal e informal; (3) pluralismo cultural e unidade nacional; (4) as perspectivas do negro no futuro das Américas.

Dentre os temas tratados, teve maior relevância a questão cultural das afro-américas, da qual emergiram três pontos: (1) a urgência de se formular um projeto pedagógico, através do qual a participação da cultura negra da diáspora seja tão relevante na construção da identidade negra quanto tem sido a cultura dominante na fragmentação e negação da identidade social do negro na diáspora; (2) resgatar a visão de mundo subjacente a estas manifestações culturais, tendo presente a atualização das experiências de resistência negra; (3) articular uma ação política que tome a dimensão cultural como ponto de partida.

A questão dos movimentos sócio-políticos foi debatida no Congresso, indicando algumas áreas onde a reflexão e a ação se fazem necessárias, como por exemplo: a marginalização socioeconômica e cultural, os menores abandonados, a política partidária, a questão agrária, o desemprego, a situação da mulher, a violência policial, o extermínio do negro (ACTAS..., 1989).

Foram discutidas também nesse mesmo Congresso, quatro outras questões: (1) um projeto de organização internacional dos negros; (2) a criação de uma associação internacional de negros; (3) as relações África e Afro-América Latina; (4) a presença da mulher negra. A propósito, sobre este último tema, as mulheres presentes no Congresso assim se manifestaram:

> Nós mulheres negras, em particular, somos o melhor exemplo de separação pessoal, forma de caráter e integridade moral, apesar de viver em sociedades completamente hostis, que nos exploram como força de trabalho, como sexo e como raça. É, portanto, momento de se reconhecer nossos méritos, já que a tendência das minorias no poder, nas sociedades dominadas, é de nos ignorar ou de não nos prestar a devida atenção. É hora de reconhecer o papel

fundamental que desempenhamos na transmissão dos valores da cultura de nossos antepassados, bem como nossa participação decisiva na acumulação de riquezas das novas sociedades americanas. Damo-nos conta de que a luta da mulher negra africana, caribenha e latino-americana, é parte da luta por uma nova ordem social e pela destruição de todas as formas de privilégios econômicos que têm origem nas discriminações racial, sexual, intelectual e de classe. Nossa luta, portanto, tem por objetivo a destruição total da dominação exercida pelos povos imperialistas sobre os povos colonizados (ACTAS..., 1989, p. 111–112).

Ao retomar os registros e avaliar os resultados, pode-se dizer que os Congressos de Cultura Negra sinalizaram uma fase importante do movimento afro-americano. Ao mesmo tempo em que representaram a mobilização dos movimentos negros em cada país, também, foi fator de animação destes movimentos. Representaram ainda, o crescimento da consciência negra em nível continental.

O Movimento Negro Brasileiro: experiências significativas no contexto latino-americano e caribenho

O Movimento Negro no Brasil, por certo, não é homogêneo. É, na verdade, um conglomerado de muitas práticas e posições, tendo em comum o combate ao racismo e a luta pela plena participação da população negra na sociedade. Há que se chamar a atenção para três experiências significativas na fase mais recente dos períodos do surgimento e reconhecimento público do Movimento Negro Brasileiro. São eles, Movimento Negro Unificado (MNU), Grupo de União e Consciência Negra (GRUCON) e os Agentes de Pastoral Negros.

O MNU surgiu no contexto do final do século XX. É reconhecido como um marco histórico de luta por uma consciência negra nacional na década de 70. Quando do seu surgimento a situação geral era de violência policial contra a população empobrecida. Tinha-se intensificado e estava generalizada nas periferias das cidades de São Paulo e Rio de Janeiro, como também, em outras grandes cidades. É indispensável dizer que em tal situação os mais atingidos eram os negros responsabilizados de antemão pelos assaltos a bancos, pelos roubos a indivíduos, e por todo tipo de práticas marginais, neste contexto sócio histórico e econômico. Prevaleciam os dizeres: "Ser negro é ser suspeito até que se prove o contrário".

A intensa perseguição policial incidindo sobre as crianças e jovens negros fizeram com que os sentimentos de revolta da população negra aflorassem. Mais de três mil pessoas se organizaram em ato público nas escadarias do Teatro Municipal de São Paulo na tarde do dia 07 de julho de 1978. Esta manifestação de protesto contra a violência e a discriminação racial deu origem a uma prática mais orgânica assumida, o que originou o Movimento Negro Unificado.

Uma das bandeiras do MNU no final da década de 70 foi fazer do dia 20 de novembro — data do assassinato de Zumbi, líder do Quilombo de Palmares — o dia Nacional da Consciência Negra e de luta contra a discriminação racial. Esta ação surtiu efeito e teve como consequência a mobilização da população negra em direção à retomada da consciência de ser negro no Brasil.

O MNU tem como público os negros universitários e aqueles ligados aos movimentos estudantis. Isto mostra ao mesmo tempo o seu alcance e os seus limites. Não foi uma prática de penetração popular em sua fase inicial. Entretanto, com a ajuda das ciências sociais e políticas os militantes do MNU procuraram estabelecer uma leitura dialética das relações de classes e aprofundar a reflexão sobre os mecanismos de exploração e violência que pesam sobre a mulher negra e o homem negro. Apesar do seu caráter acadêmico o MNU reuniu na década de 70 e o início da década de 80 muitos adeptos, chegando mesmo a ser a expressão maior do movimento negro brasileiro naquele período.

Outro grupo de igual importância foi o Grupo de União e Consciência Negra (GRUCON), que esteve diretamente vinculado com a preparação da Conferência de Puebla.[1] De fato, é através de uma necessidade, que era exigida à Igreja do Brasil, de apresentar uma análise sobre a situação vivida pelos afro-brasileiros, que um grupo de estudiosos (sociólogos, antropólogos, teólogos, pastoralistas e agentes de pastoral) se reuniu na cidade de São Paulo/SP.[2] Neste clima de troca dos conteúdos adquiridos por meio de observações extraídas dos mais diversos ângulos científicos, o grupo chegou à seguinte conclusão: (1) o importante não era olhar o negro, enquanto indivíduo que pratica um culto não-católico. (2) nem era tão importante já buscar métodos para trazer esse indivíduo à Igreja; (3) o importante era olhar a realidade global do negro brasileiro, enquanto grupo social, política, econômica e religiosamente; (4) importa também, conhecer os antecedentes históricos das atuais realidades.

Diante dessas conclusões, os participantes deram por terminada uma primeira etapa da tarefa a eles proposta, que na verdade era o início de um novo e longo processo. Percebendo o grau de dificuldade que envolvia o tema o Grupo escolheu dar passos que o identificasse com a realidade do negro. Pelo caráter mais acentuado para atividades do campo eclesial e pastoral, os participantes entenderam a amplitude do problema e o compromisso evangélico que os desafiavam, e optam por uma análise do contexto geral, onde se procurava recuperar a identidade do negro como pessoa. Também desse modo, não se corria o risco de uma análise na superficialidade dos dados e fatos.

Houve ainda a retrospectiva histórica, que ajudou na compreensão da caminhada realizada. Muitas vezes, foram passos dados pela hierarquia que pouco influenciou na caminhada das comunidades locais. Mesmo assim, uma avaliação social, política, cultural e religiosa a partir das comunidades negras, é possível destacar a presença da mensagem e a vivência evangélica em todos os seus gestos e atitudes. Além disso, pode-se perceber a presença das religiões tradicionais africanas que respeitadas, praticadas, se dispuseram a oferecer orientação com os ensinamentos dos Orixás, principalmente nas religiões tradicionais africanas da diáspora.

Com o surgimento do GRUCON, ocorrido no dia 05 de dezembro de 1978, houve a formação de um Grupo de Reflexão e Estudo, que aprovou um bloco de atividades e projetos a serem assumidos a partir da Conferência Nacional dos Bispos do Brasil (CNBB). Ressalta-se também que a história do Grupo na sociedade brasileira e na Igreja Católica teve um desenvolvimento crescente em vários estados da federação, por meio da realização de encontros temáticos, nacionais, estaduais e local. A partir desse grupo, a Linha II da CNBB[3] assume essa atitude profética e encaminha uma ação conjunta, apoiada pelos representantes dos agentes de pastoral negros.[2]

Em 1979, o Grupo-Tarefa reuniu-se em São Paulo, para planejar a execução do projeto. Além de um encontro de Agentes de Pastoral Negros, agendado para fevereiro de 1980. Nesta ocasião decidiu-se que o encontro não se limitaria a padres e religiosos(as), mas também a leigos e Agentes de Pastoral Negros. Como as reuniões anteriores, esta foi de consulta sobre a realidade da comunidade negra. Outra situação urgente foi a necessidade solicitada pelos agentes de pastoral negros de uma reflexão sobre a realidade das comunidades negras, tradições religiosas afro, e religiosidades afro nos diversos lugares do Brasil. A princípio a preocupação foi com a situação e a prática do negro na Igreja. Mas, ao longo das colocações foram sendo acentuadas as ações de organização do povo negro nos diversos setores da comunidade.[4]

Outro grupo de extrema importância para ampliação das reflexões afro foram os Agentes de Pastoral Negros (APNs). No seu primeiro encontro, os agentes reuniram pessoas de várias regiões do Brasil e apresentaram como conclusão os elementos motivadores, que proporcionaram novas opções para a caminhada. Assim o grupo propôs à pastoral da Igreja Católica algumas sugestões concretas:

1 criar motivações suficientes para estimular e incentivar os contatos com outros companheiros que já tem produções sobre o tema do negro;
2 criar um grupo com a tarefa de: recolher noticia e fazer circular entre os grupos as experiências e informações; ajudar e incentivar a reflexão junto aos núcleos;
3 formar grupos negros de estudos e ação nos Estados;
4 fazer contatos com grupos negros já existentes e participar deles;
5 descobrir, valorizar e incentivar lideranças negras na comunidade e na ação pastoral;
6 contatar africanos residentes no Brasil, com a finalidade de integração e intercâmbio.[5]

O caminho para a formação de um grupo, que se autodenominou de Agentes de Pastoral Negros se tornou irreversível. A semente se espalhou rapidamente, por todo o território nacional. Uma mensagem convidando a uma tomada de consciência da negritude começou a ser refletida desde o setor eclesial, passando pelo cultural, político e nas organizações populares. Em todos os lugares o debate na ótica da negritude começou a ser acentuado e enriquecido pela prática do militante. É a partir do respeito à organização de base e do povo negro que esses passos passaram a ser realizados.

Outro fato significativo é que o movimento conseguiu resgatar a luta do negro dentro da Igreja, desde os antepassados chegando às Comunidades Eclesiais de Base (CEBs). Além disso, os grupos de Agentes de Pastoral Negros foram se o abrindo ao compromisso de trabalhar junto aos demais segmentos negros já existentes no país e buscaram também e, sobretudo, os movimentos populares.

As primeiras atividades iniciam em São Paulo (SP) com características bem identificadas com o movimento de cristãos negros. Logo encontraram seu sentido de abertura para a necessidade de refletir a partir das experiências das CEBs, onde o negro esteve presente em sua maioria. A partir do anúncio e da organização desta novidade, a mulher negra será a protagonista em destaque na ação de organizar os grupos de reflexão e mobilização de ações públicas.

Os APNs[6] realizaram nos dias 14 e 15 de março de 1983 o seu primeiro encontro, tendo como local as dependências da Igreja Imaculada Conceição, em São Paulo (SP). Estavam presentes 70 pessoas. A maioria era agente de pastoral e lideranças das comunidades católicas. O tema do encontro foi A realidade vivida pelos negros e sua participação na Igreja do Brasil.[7] Dois blocos dividiram os trabalhos deste Encontro: o primeiro O negro na Igreja do Brasil, apresentado pelo Pe. Antonio Aparecido da Silva[8] que procurou situar a realidade do povo negro nas igrejas do Brasil. No segundo bloco, o tema foi Igreja, poder e negritude, coordenado pelo Pe. Mauro Batista,[9] que procurou localizar a experiência do povo negro na sociedade e na Igreja, tecendo uma análise da experiência do povo negro na sociedade capitalista, e sustentando a tese de que toda a comunidade negra é produto que retrata a realidade do não ter, não ser, não poder e não saber.

Como pontos da conclusão deste primeiro encontro dos APNs foram apresentadas algumas propostas de encaminhamentos: (1) privilegiar o trabalho de base como forma de ação conscientizadora e libertadora; (2) como agente de pastoral, ficar atento às discriminações para denunciá-los e assumir a negritude; (3) reunir pessoas, formar grupos e passar adiante as experiências adquiridas, visando a conscientização; (4) ampliar as discussões sobre as discriminações e marginalizações do negro, nos ambientes familiares, de trabalho, de convivência, etc.; (5) despertar a consciência do branco enquanto depositário de uma herança discriminatória e racista; (6) conhecer as origens através de estudos e aprofundar criticamente os acontecimentos; (7) procurar conscientizar os casais negros e, sobretudo as crianças, levando-as a assumir a negritude; (8) incrementar os encontros locais e regionais e os de maiores proporções; (9) criar uma equipe para elaborar subsídios sobre a realidade do negro;

(10) realizar dois encontros anuais para agentes de pastoral, preferencialmente negros, para aprofundar a questão da negritude.

Após seis meses, houve o segundo Encontro de APNs, realizado nos dias 6 e 7 de setembro de 1983, tendo como local novamente a Igreja Imaculada Conceição, em São Paulo (SP). Neste, estiveram presentes aproximadamente 100 pessoas, compostas por agentes de pastoral, leigos, padres, religiosos e religiosas e, representantes de outros movimentos negros. As discussões giraram em torno de como encaminhar e solucionar as ações frente a uma pastoral libertadora. E ainda, a preocupação concreta de como o agente de pastoral deve trabalhar para assumir com seus irmãos a identidade e a libertação integral.

Na ocasião, foi realizada uma exposição sobre a noção do Candomblé, onde foi constatado um profundo desconhecimento e preconceitos por parte dos agentes de pastoral negros, em relação aos cultos afros.[7] Outro momento significativo foi a formação de grupos de reflexão que deram origem a três questões básicas: qual a tarefa específica dos agentes de pastoral negros? O Cristianismo é religião para o negro ou a coerência com a negritude exige a conversão ao Candomblé? Como iniciar um grupo de negros?

Um indicativo que serviu como ajuda na caminhada foi encontrada na formação de uma catequese libertadora, onde o negro fosse contemplado e situado a partir da sua realidade, sob os seguintes pontos: (1) ligar a luta do negro com as diversas lutas populares; (2) conscientizar os padres, pastores, religiosos e seminaristas a assumirem sua negritude e a luta do negro; (3) utilizar a pastoral como espaço de conscientização sobre a questão negra; (4) aproveitar os períodos fortes na ação pastoral para uma conscientização mais ampla, como por exemplo, a devoção a Nossa Senhora Aparecida, no mês de outubro; (5) incluir a questão do negro na novena de Natal, na Campanha da Fraternidade, etc.; (6) promover missas e celebrações com rituais litúrgicos afro-brasileiros; (7) dar ênfase ao dia 20 de novembro – Dia da Consciência Negra – convocando as bases para denúncia contra o racismo; (8) elaborar subsídios para o trabalho nos grupos; (9) aproveitar o mês da Bíblia para, por meio de subsídios, fazer uma releitura dos fatos, tendo como tema central o cativeiro do povo negro e suas esperanças de libertação; (10) contribuir para que a Igreja possa enegrecer-se assumindo a luta do negro e enegrecendo também os seus quadros (animadores de comunidades, seminaristas, freiras, pastores, padres e bispos negros); (11) que os encontros de agentes de pastoral negros continuem sendo um espaço de partilha de experiências.[10]

No ano seguinte foi realizado, o terceiro Encontro de APNs, entre os dias 30 de abril a 01 de maio de 1984. O número de participantes aproximou-se de 150 pessoas. Os temas debatidos foram: (1) o educando negro no sistema educacional brasileiro; (2) o negro na história do Brasil e os livros didáticos oficiais, (3) a educação formal e não formal atuando no educando, (4) criança negra na catequese renovada e, (6) religiosidade popular a partir das experiências vividas no norte de Minas Gerais e Bahia.

Nos dias 07 a 09 de agosto de 1984 aconteceu o quarto Encontro de APNs, dando continuidade à proposta de encontros de formação para os agentes participantes. Com trabalhos de grupos e painéis foram aprofundados os seguintes temas: (1) a crise econômica do Brasil e o Negro; (2) a realidade do negro; e (3) a situação da mulher negra nos meios populares. Utilizando sempre a dinâmica de apresentações com debates e reflexões, a proposta do encontro alcançou seus objetivos: a formação e abertura para a presença do negro nas situações concretas da Igreja Católica e na sociedade em geral; o dinamismo e a organização das comunidades eclesiais de base e do movimento popular. As conclusões do encontro foram sintetizadas nas seguintes propostas: (1) aprofundamento dos temas; (2) ampliação da reflexão sobre as religiões africanas; (3) discussão do sentido e vivência da cultura afro-brasileira; (4) o negro na sociedade atual e a violência policial com a prática do racismo. A cada encontro mais os agentes iam se mobilizando, ampliando suas reflexões, além de abrangendo mais pessoas.

Dessa forma realizou-se o quinto Encontro de Agentes de Pastoral Negros (APNs). Na abertura do mesmo foi realidade uma homenagem especial ao Pe. Antonio Aparecido da Silva, um dos responsáveis pelo crescimento e solidificação das propostas do grupo, na Direção da Faculdade de Teologia Nossa Senhora da Assunção, em São Paulo (SP). Sua presença nesta instituição possibilitou a realização dos próximos encontros dos APNs. Neste quinto encontro, foi gestado um curso de formação para os APNs, com o objetivo de analisar em profundidade os elementos que envolvem a questão racial. Estes cursos, diferentes dos encontros que eram semestrais, foram realizados anualmente.

O primeiro encontro aconteceu nos dias 04 e 05 maio de 1985, cujo tema foi "Constituinte e Negritude". Com uma presença aproximadamente de 250 pessoas, o evento teve uma presença significativa de novos participantes. Eram agentes de pastoral negros que pretendiam explicitar suas interrogações sobre o tema discutido na ótica da comunidade negra. Houve uma reflexão sobre uma proposta pedagógica acessível para as dificuldades que encontravam esses agentes nos trabalhos pastorais junto à comunidade negra. Uma sugestão foi a elaboração de uma cartilha de linguagem simples e acessível e que transmitisse noções básicas sobre o processo constituinte e o papel do negro nesse campo da política. O encontro foi muito participativo e fortaleceu a atuação dos agentes em suas comunidades, assim como nas discussões sobre a nova constituinte, que seria promulgada em 1988.

O sexto Encontro de APNs ocorreu nos dias 15 e 16 de setembro de 1985, nas dependências da Faculdade de Teologia Nossa Senhora da Assunção, com a presença estimada em 300 pessoas. A metodologia e as temáticas foram distribuídas para três grupos distintos: o primeiro buscou um aprofundar os temas "A realidade do negro no Brasil" e "Liturgia e negritude". O grupo de trabalho estava destinado àquelas pessoas consideradas novas no movimento. O segundo grupo aprofundou o tema Negritude e Constituinte, como continuidade do quinto Encontro. O terceiro grupo estava destinado aos mais antigos, com o debate sobre o tema Negritude e reforma agrária. Nesse encontro foram dados mais reforços para a implementação de um espaço de contato e articulação do grupo, o Quilombo Central, instalado posteriormente.

Na sequência houve o sétimo Encontro de APNs nas dependências da Faculdade de Teologia Nossa Senhora Assunção, nos dias 19 e 20 de abril de 1986. Os temas foram refletidos a partir do seguinte esquema: (1) o negro e a terra (no cortiço, na favela, zona rural); (2) os mártires da caminhada; (3) identidade dos agentes de pastoral negros. Aos debates e estudos em grupos somou-se a alegria de mais uma experiência que reforçou o projeto de luta contra o racismo e o resgate da negritude em cada um. No encerramento celebrou-se uma rica experiência litúrgica.

O Curso de Formação para APNs aconteceu nos dias 29/06 a 03/07 de 1985, nas dependências da Faculdade de Teologia Nossa Senhora Assunção. Os trabalhos de estudo foram desenvolvidos obedecendo às dificuldades comuns dos agentes de pastoral negros, devido aos contatos frequentes nos trabalhos pastorais ou de CEBs com temas envolvendo as religiões afro-brasileiras. Assim o tema do curso foi "Culto e fé:

comunidade negra celebra a fé". As reflexões estiveram a cargo do Pe. Mauro Baptista, que procurou atualizar a questão da religiosidade afro-brasileira a partir da complexidade que é a religiosidade popular. Houve também a participação efetiva do Pe. Antonio Aparecido da Silva, que fez destaque às manifestações religiosas negras no Brasil dentro do catolicismo popular.

Como praticante do Candomblé, a Profª. Dra. Maria de Lourdes, da Universidade Federal da Bahia (UFBA) aprofundou os valores que estão presentes dentro do rito, e os segredos das religiões afro-brasileiras. Concluindo os trabalhos, o Pe. Edir, teólogo e fundador dos APNs, complementou os estudos com o tema "O negro e a celebração litúrgica".

Os resultados, seguindo os encontros anteriores, foram apresentados como propostas para que as comunidades aprofundassem e, à sua medida, concretizassem em suas ações pastorais ou no movimento popular. Assim foram especificadas as propostas: (1) aprofundamento sobre o candomblé; (2) liturgia negra em nossas comunidades e nas casas; (3) procurar as datas festivas; (4) procurar fazer um trabalho com os padres; (5) preparar subsídios para a liturgia negra; (6) promover debates nas comunidades; (7) aproveitar as outras liturgias além da Eucaristia; (8) aprofundar a problemática do negro; (9) procurar refletir sobre a história do negro nos grupos de base.[11]

Em paralelo aos encontros, que eram semestrais, houve o segundo curso de formação de APNs, ocorrido de 28 a 30 de junho de 1986, com a participação de aproximadamente 120 pessoas. Os temas para estudo foram distribuídos em painéis assim relacionados: (1) o negro na atual conjuntura sócio-política e econômica; (2) a negritude e fé a partir do Candomblé; (3) negritude e fé a partir da Igreja Metodista; negritude e fé a partir da Igreja Católica. Uma agenda foi construída indicando os passos e etapas vividas pelos agentes de pastoral, lideranças das CEBs, lideranças dos clubes negros, irmandades, congadas e associações de moradores de comunidades negras. É nesse caminhar que o Centro Atabaque é criado com uma síntese de conteúdos propostos para serem pesquisados e elucidados.

Os APNs, atualmente, são reconhecidos como uma instituição afro-brasileira orgânica na sociedade, de maior difusão em todo o país. Tem como definição ser constituída por pessoas que atuam em diversos setores da sociedade e na Igreja com o objetivo primeiro de refletir sobre a situação do negro, o compromisso de somar com os demais empobrecidos que buscam a transformação social. Assumem a missão de enegrecer a Igreja, ou seja, trabalhar a fé cristã a partir das culturas e práticas religiosas afros nas comunidades de fé espalhadas por todo o Brasil.

Os Movimentos da Pastoral Afro na América Latina, Central e Caribe
Os Encontros de Pastoral Afro-americana (EPA) surgiram do desejo e da necessidade de uma articulação das iniciativas do trabalho realizado com as comunidades negras em alguns países e regiões da América Latina, Central e Caribe. Embora, o termo pastoral dê a conotação de uma iniciativa ligada à Igreja Católica, os encontros ocorreram por decisão e vontade das lideranças de grupos de pastoral afro atuantes nos diversos países, não vindos e orientados pela hierarquia eclesial.

O primeiro EPA discutiu a temática "Religiosidade Popular e Cultura Negra" e foi realizado em Buenaventura, na Colômbia, em 1980. Embora a representatividade não tenha sido tão ampla, estava iniciado o processo, que paulatinamente foi tendo maior participação oficial da Igreja. Entre as conclusões deste encontro, destacaram-se: (1) necessidade da pesquisa científica sobre a cultura afro-americana; (2) o valor da tomada de consciência frente à problemática cultural das comunidades afro-americanas; (3) interpelar as Igrejas para assumir um compromisso pastoral junto à Comunidade Negra; e (4) procurar formas adequadas para o uso das expressões religiosas provenientes das culturas negras. Os participantes alertaram também para o perigo de superficialidade e folclorização da cultura afro-americana.[12] Em decorrência do encontro, foram elaborados relatos que acabaram sendo distribuídos aos países participantes, como também houve publicações com as discussões que fizeram parte dele.

O segundo EPA foi realizado em 1982, em Esmeraldas, Equador, com o tema "Identidade e história do povo afro-americano à luz da história da salvação". Os participantes, já em maior número em relação ao primeiro, debateram e aprofundaram o fato histórico da negação generalizada da identidade do negro e dos demais oprimidos do continente. Insistiu-se na necessidade de colaborar com os processos de afirmação da identidade afro-americana. Constataram que havia muita desinformação sobre o negro e evidenciaram a importância de uma reflexão mais profunda sobre o modelo de integração dos povos e culturas tendo em vista uma sociedade igualitária.

Como a reflexão foi feita a partir da história, por certo, houve a consideração dos valores e anti-valores a serem discutidos. É preciso considerá-los. Esse segundo EPA reafirmou que era preciso aprofundar e descobrir a força libertadora da Palavra de Deus na comunidade afro, para perceber na história e no presente os sinais de salvação. Como encaminhamento, surgiu uma proposta aos teólogos que elaborassem uma teologia a partir do Evangelho e que revelasse o rosto afro-americano de Deus.[13]

A realização do terceiro EPA, aconteceu na cidade de Porto Belo, no Panamá, em 1986. O tema escolhido foi "Identidade afro-americana e pastoral". Constatou-se que a população negra contribuiu enormemente com a religiosidade popular difusa em toda a América Latina e Caribe, dando-lhe um aspecto de alegria e festa. Os participantes afirmaram a importância de manter a identidade das comunidades negras através da valorização da memória histórica, para que não se dissolva e perca a sua especificidade afro-americana e caribenha.

O quarto EPA, aconteceu na Costa Rica, na cidade de Puerto Limón, em 1989. O tema escolhido foi "A família afro-americana", visando o aprofundamento sobre o modo de viver e de ser família nas comunidades negras, bem como as suas características próprias, específicas e singulares. A família negra possui valores que revelam seu profundo empenho na defesa da vida, apresentando algumas características principais: (1) relação de consanguinidade (pais, filhos, parentes e compadres, etc.); (2) escuta e respeito aos mais velhos; (3) compreensão ampla de família; e (4) abertura ao coletivo. Estes elementos característicos da família negra devem constituir a base para a ação pastoral. Embora marcada duramente pela escravidão no passado e pela marginalização do presente, a família negra é um dos marcos de resistência dos povos afro-americanos.[14]

O quinto EPA foi realizado em Quibdo, na Colômbia, em junho de 1991. A presença de duzentos e vinte delegados provenientes de diversos países, representando diferentes organizações negras foi muito significativa. O tema do encontro foi "Pastoral e educação afro-americana". O objetivo era motivar a elaboração de um projeto de educação afro-americana, chamando à discussão da causa negra as igrejas e os governos. Outro objetivo do encontro foi o de aprofundar a reflexão numa dimensão autenticamente latino-americana aos EPAs. Na avaliação dos participantes, o encontro foi de grande proveito e bastante positivo no sentido de que os debates foram esclarecedores.[15]

O sexto EPA aconteceu novamente em Esmeraldas, no Equador, entre os dias 19 a 20 de setembro de 1994. Esse encontro teve a participação de 180 pessoas de 14 países: Brasil, Colômbia, Costa Rica, Equador, Haiti, Honduras, México, Peru, Republica Dominicana, Benin, Moçambique, Uganda e Zaire. O tema abordado deu continuidade às questões tratadas nos encontros anteriores. Ao aprofundar o tema da espiritualidade afro-americana, o encontro contribuiu para o fortalecimento das comunidades cristãs com rosto negro, assumindo suas próprias vivências espirituais enraizadas nas tradições culturais e religiosas de origem africana.[16]

Podemos concluir que Movimento Negro afro-americano e brasileiro, nas décadas de 80 e 90, chamou a atenção para as formas distintas de organização da comunidade afro-americana. Também ficou como marca desta fase, a inesquecível Frente Negra na história do movimento negro brasileiro, justamente quando a ditadura militar agiu coercivamente sobre as organizações negras, prendendo e fechando as salas de reuniões destes movimentos.

Das Consultas Ecumênicas de Teologias e Culturas Afro-Americana e Caribenha têm-se o conceito de que a população afro-americana é o rosto vivo e desafiador do servo sofredor que está interpelando as igrejas cristãs, sob o seu estado de resistência permanente e sofrimento diante das práticas de exclusão a que é sistematicamente submetida nas relações intrincadas da sociedade latino-americana.

Nas últimas três décadas do século XX, as igrejas cristãs encontraram nas suas experiências pastorais novos desafios e paradigmas, vindos das comunidades afro-americanas que as interpelam para um novo modo de anunciar e viver o Evangelho. Entre os novos desafios e paradigmas aparecem as práticas de racismo, preconceito, segregação, discriminação e da violência antinegro, de certa forma, já institucionalizada e internalizada no cotidiano das relações das pessoas.

Esse encontro com a realidade vivida nas comunidades aparece nos documentos e nas atitudes das lideranças leigas cristãs e de uma parcela crítica dos membros da hierarquia eclesiástica, de forma muito pontual dentro das igrejas cristãs. Assim, são dados os primeiros passos, ainda que tímidos e receosos para colocar à luz do dia escândalos presentes no interior e fora das igrejas.

No espaço da reflexão teológica-pastoral foram colocadas questões que levam a compreender e a buscar a atitude evangélica pertinente à superação dos males que reduzem o direito de cidadania das populações afro-americanas. Sabemos que a teologia acontece na experiência gratuita da revelação de Deus, mas que ela se completa com a palavra humana quando procura mostrar as razões que possui a fé, dom de Deus. Toda reflexão teológica acontece a partir dos limites percorridos pelas pessoas — as comunidades de fé —, buscando a compreensão dos desígnios divinos.

É a partir das experiências de fé vividas nas comunidades afro-americanas que podemos colocar algumas questões com um olhar das Ciências da Religião sobre a reflexão teológica afro-americana: como facilitar e oportunizar que as populações afro-americanas reafirmem seus espaços e territórios de autonomia nas práticas de fé, culturas especificas e direitos de cidadania plena? Que mediações podem ser estabelecidas para que seja vivido um diálogo ecumênico entre as religiões tradicionais africanas: Candomblé, Tambor de Mina, Reisados, Congo, por exemplo, e as Igrejas Cristãs? Que práticas litúrgicas ecumênicas podem responder a essa vontade comum das comunidades de fé de querer celebrar o Deus da vida? Quando poderemos participar do grande banquete do Senhor congregando os valores comuns das tradições afro-americanas? Que atitudes proféticas devem ser assumidas para por fim, definitivamente, nas igrejas, com as atitudes que pretendem inferiorizar as mulheres em todos os níveis, principalmente nos ministérios?

Estas são algumas das questões pertinentes que perpassam o diálogo e as práticas de sincretismo e de ecumenismo, de um olhar e vivência afro-americana e afro-brasileira. Assim, as agendas das igrejas serão ampliadas para que elas assumam uma nova prática pastoral e se insiram junto às realidades afro-americanas. Deve-se garantir e reconhecer as especificidades dessa população. É deste modo que as comunidades afros estarão afirmando o valor da autoestima como sinal da dignidade da população afro-americana.

Em um processo de busca para a afirmação destes ideais surgiu o Centro Atabaque — Cultura e Teologia Negra[17], através das reflexões dos seus membros num espaço de discussão, reflexão e proposição a partir das experiências vividas por todos estes movimentos orgânicos da comunidade negra no Brasil. Ao Atabaque ficou uma tarefa importante de realizar as Consultas Ecumênicas de Teologia e Culturas Afro-Americana e Caribenha. A Primeira Consulta foi realizada de 8 a 12 de julho de 1985, em Nova Iguaçu, um subúrbio na periferia do Rio de Janeiro, lugar de concentração das comunidades negras no sul do Brasil. Estas, além de sofrerem grande discriminação racial, eram vítimas da violência policial (NEVES, 1986). Por ser uma Consulta Ecumênica, num período que o tema afro começa a ser frequente nas agendas de discussão e celebrações comunitárias — nos espaços de formação teológica, nos ambientes de ação pastoral e nas hierarquias das igrejas — sentem-se na obrigação de refletir o seu papel histórico e institucional frente a esta população afro-americana.

> O encontro teve a participação de trinta pessoas, das quais vinte e cinco eram negras (dezoito homens e sete mulheres) e cinco brancas. Além dos cristãos (entre os quais estiveram presentes católicos romanos, metodistas, presbiterianos, batistas, luteranos e episcopais) também participaram pessoas que praticam Vodu, Candomblé e Lumbalu. Vieram pessoas do Haiti, República Dominicana, Curaçau, Costa Rica, Panamá, Colômbia, Peru e Brasil (NEVES, 1986, p. 13-14).

O objetivo da Consulta foi de precisar o papel que a Igreja desempenhou na sujeição e dominação do setor afro-latino-americano. Desta avaliação pretenderam deduzir o papel atual que cabia à Igreja nas tarefas de justiça social aos povos.

A segunda Consulta Ecumênica aconteceu em São Paulo nos dias 06 a 12 de novembro de 1994. Espelhando-se no êxito da Primeira, esta pretendeu somar esforços de pesquisa e produção nas áreas das Ciências Sociais, da Religião e da Teologia da Libertação para, à luz das práticas vividas nas Comunidades Afro-americana, aprofundar, discutir e elaborar conteúdos sobre o tema "Afro-América: Cultura e Teologia I". Os objetivos da Consulta foram: (1) colocar em comum os diversos aspectos sociais e teológicos a partir da realidade das Comunidades Afro-americanas e Caribenhas emergentes nas últimas décadas; (2) analisar e aprofundar, à luz da reflexão teológica, os grandes desafios que apresentam a realidade pastoral dos povos afro-americanos e caribenhos em cada realidade nacional ou regional; (3) propiciar uma maior articulação entre as iniciativas de reflexão teológica que têm surgido nas várias regiões do continente, referente à questão afro, fazendo um intercâmbio com propostas similares em outros continentes; (4) iluminar, em nível teológico, os desafios lançados pelas Igrejas Cristãs e pela Conferência de Santo Domingo, no sentido de aprofundar as exigências de uma evangelização inculturada; (5) fazer uma avaliação sobre os aspectos teológicos emergentes da Pastoral Afro-americana e Caribenha; e (6) aprofundar a reflexão sobre ecumenismo e macroecumenismo a partir das culturas e religiões de origem africana (Silva and Santos 1997).

Participaram desta segunda Consulta cientistas sociais, teólogos e teólogas, pastoras e pastores, sacerdotes, babalorixás e ialorixás, pesquisadores e pesquisadoras das questões e temas afro-americanos representando 11 países latino-americanos e da África do Sul e dos Estados Unidos. Foram constituídas seis oficinas que trataram dos seguintes temas: (1) Teologia negra feminista latino-americana; (2) Negritude, projetos políticos e nova ordem mundial, (3) Teologia da Libertação, fé e práticas afro-religiosas; (4) Ecumenismo das comunidades de fé negras; (5) Vivência litúrgica; e (6) Bíblia e comunidades negras (Silva and Santos 1997).

A terceira Consulta Ecumênica de Teologia Afro-americana e Caribenha, foi realizada em São Paulo (SP) nos dias 20 a 25 de outubro de 2003. Como ocorrido nas edições anteriores, reuniram-se teólogos e teólogas, cientistas sociais, educadores e agentes de pastoral de diversos países latino-americanos e caribenhos. Também estiveram presentes representantes dos Estados Unidos, República do Congo e Angola. Como tema foi discutido Teologia Afro-americana: avanços, desafios e perspectivas, proporcionando aos participantes a continuidade das conclusões das Consultas anteriores, bem como ampliando-as de modo significativo. Nessa edição, os resultados oferecidos aos leitores foram uma variedade de textos temáticos que oportunizaram uma valiosa ilustração sobre a teologia afro-americana.

A Consulta foi realizada com quatro eixos temáticos: (1) leitura da conjuntura afro-americana; (2) contexto da produção teológica; (3) oficinas temáticas; e (4) avanços e desafios. O objetivo da Terceira Consulta alcançou seu êxito com um excelente documento publicado e sua pertinência junto aos espaços de discussão sobre o tema teológico afro-americano e caribenho, o qual repercute até hoje. Houve participação efetiva nessas consultas dos membros de vários grupos do movimento negro, inclusive do Atabaque. Nesse sentido o grupo foi se organizando, se estabelecendo e foi sendo estruturado.

Considerações finais

Ao longo do tempo, o Centro Atabaque foi deixando um grande legado. Seus membros tiveram uma dimensão muito significativa na formação, capacitação da identidade do ser negro e negra nas comunidades da América Latina e Caribe. Em um olhar analítico sobre o processo de intervenção e elaboração dos membros do Centro Atabaque reconhecemos elementos epistemológicos pertinentes. Podemos sinalizar a elaboração de uma teologia negra a partir do reverso da história, isto é, uma reflexão teológica que em sua totalidade contempla práticas de inserção no dia-a-dia da comunidade negra.

O espaço da comunidade negra ofereceu aos membros do Centro Atabaque um ambiente potencial de elementos históricos, religiosos e de uma economia diferenciada, capaz de problematizar e ser problematizado no sentido de responder aos pressupostos de uma teologia afro-americana e caribenha. Essa prática de inserção sócio-histórica e teológica não pode ser abstrata. Deve estar ligada a ações vividas no contexto histórico-eclesial-comunitário. Nesse ambiente escolhido, busca se fazer uma releitura bíblica comprometida com mediações e condicionamentos que devem traçar um rosto de Deus, cada vez mais enegrecido e comprometido com as práticas de libertação das populações afrodescendentes.

Não são poucos os empecilhos para o êxito da tarefa proposta pelos membros do Centro Atabaque, quando as dificuldades estão por todas as partes, pela dimensão e extensão do tema. Há que eliminar os preconceitos contra as religiões tradicionais afro-brasileiras e africanas. Há que buscar convergência, nunca generalização, nos fundamentos da fé e na expressão desses fundamentos.

Nas religiões cristãs a fundamentação da fé é buscada em Jesus Cristo e na história vivida pelo povo hebreu, cujos testemunhos estão registrados por escrito, na Bíblia. No caso das religiões tradicionais africanas e afro-brasileiras esta fundamentação acontece na história dos Orixás, cujos testemunhos são transmitidos dentro de uma tradição rigorosamente oral.

Os estudos desenvolvidos pelos membros do Centro Atabaque acontecem com o exercício pedagógico de estudar, cuidadosamente, as expressões das congadas dos moçambiques, dos quicumbis e dos ensaios dos tambores de crioulas, entre outras tantas manifestações praticadas pelo povo negro. Os caminhos para uma Teologia Afro-americana e o aprofundamento de uma epistemologia negra latino-americana está posto no conjunto das reflexões das ciências especializadas.

Notas

1. A III Conferência Geral do Episcopado Latino-Americano realizou-se em Puebla de los Angeles, México, no período de 27 de janeiro a 13 de fevereiro de 1979, sob o tema: Evangelização no presente e no futuro da América Latina.
2. Encontro de Agentes de Pastoral Negros, Capão Redondo, São Paulo/SP, 1980, mímeo, p. 1.
3. Assim era denominada na estrutura organizativa da CNBB a Linha de Ação Missionária.
4. Ibidem. p. 2.
5. Ibidem. p. 3.
6. APNs é como são chamados os membros efetivos e simpatizantes deste movimento social reconhecido pelas organizações do Movimento Negro Brasileiro quando se referem à organização como Agentes de Pastoral Negros.
7. Cf. I Encontro de Agentes de Pastoral Negros, São Paulo, mímeo, 1983.
8. Foi ordenado padre em 1976. Por dez anos foi pároco da Igreja Nossa Senhora da Achiropita; Diretor Provincial da Congregação Padre Orionitas. Reitor na gestação da Faculdade de Teologia da PUC-SP; presidiu a Sociedade de Teologia e Ciências da Religião (SOTER); Fundador do Centro Atabaque — Teologia e Cultura negra; Assessor e incentivador, junto à CNBB; Esteve presente na criação dos Agentes de Pastoral Negros (APNs) em 1983; Batalhou pela visibilidade e pelo combate ao drama do racismo nas assessorias que prestou ao episcopado durante as Conferências de Puebla e Santo Domingo, e foi uma principal liderança da Pastoral afro nos últimos 30 anos.
9. Foi padre na Paróquia Nossa Senhora de Fátima, Vila das Belezas, durante 32 anos, de 1963 a 1995. Membro da congregação do Verbo Divino, foi ordenado em 1959, em seguida passou quatro anos em Roma aperfeiçoando em teologia. Foi o primeiro brasileiro com doutorado em missiologia pela Universidade Gregoriana. Negro consciente, seu amor pelo povo afro brasileiro se expressou em seu trabalho doutoral, a primeira tese de teologia dedicada à religião afro no Brasil, cujo título é "Um olhar na realidade da população afro na diáspora africana." Foi um dos primeiros a propor elementos epistemológicos para uma Teologia Negra Afro Americana e Caribenha, durante a Consulta sobre cultura negra e teologia na América Latina, em 1986.
10. Ibidem, p. 26-27.
11. Cf. Relatório do 5º Encontro de Agentes de Pastoral Negros, mímeo, 1985.
12. Cf. Relato do primeiro Encontro de Pastoral Afro-americana. In. Palenque – Boletim Informativo, Quito, 1980.
13. Cf. Relato do segundo Encontro de Pastoral Afro-americana. In. Palenque, Boletim Informativo, Quito, 1982.
14. Cf. Relato do terceiro Encontro de Pastoral Afro-americana. In: Palenque, Boletim Informativo, Quito, 1989.
15. Cf. Relato do quarto Encontro de Pastoral Afro-americana. In: Palenque, Boletim Informativo, Quito, 1991.

16. Cuadernos de Pastoral Afroamericana 5/6, Quito, 1995, p. 25.

17. Em 1990, foi fundado em São Paulo, o Atabaque, um grupo de reflexão interdisciplinar sobre teologia e negritude que reúne pessoas ligadas à teologia, filosofia, pedagogia e outras áreas, negros e brancos, mulheres e homens, de igrejas cristãs e de religiões afro-brasileiras. O grupo está vinculado ao Programa de Teologia e Culturas Afro-americanas da Associação Ecumênica dos Teólogos do Terceiro Mundo (ASETT/EATWOT). Sua finalidade é trabalhar com mais intensidade os desafios e as práticas de fé e luta das comunidades negras no Brasil. O nome Atabaque expressa o desejo de se fazer veículo de comunicação entre as várias comunidades de fé, uma voz que convoca para o louvor e a justiça, a dança e a fraternidade, para uma sociedade sem discriminação.

Referências bibliográficas

Actas del Primer Congreso de La Cultura Negra de las Americas. In: Cuadernos Negros Americanos. Quito: Abya Yala, 1989.

Neves, Amélia Tavares C. (org.), 1986, Identidade negra e religião. São Paulo: Associação Ecumênica de Teólogos do Terceiro Mundo (ASETT); CEDI/Edições Liberdade.

Silva, Antonio Aparecido da, and Sônia Querino dos Santos (Orgs.), 1997, Teologia Afro-americana: II Consulta Ecumênica de Teologia e Culturas Afro-americana e Caribenha. São Paulo: Paulus/Atabaque/ASETT.

CROSSCURRENTS
POR UMA TEOLOGIA NEGRA NO BRASIL

Leontino Faria dos Santos

Tendo em vista a prática contumaz do racismo na sociedade brasileira, pode-se imaginar a necessidade do desenvolvimento de uma teologia negra que nos chame à reflexão sobre tal fenômeno, à luz de pressupostos bíblico-teológicos de cunho libertador e profético. Tomamos como referência a teologia negra, que se desenvolveu nos Estados Unidos, como movimento teológico, que surgiu entre os cristãos negros, na segunda metade da década de 60, concentrada na reflexão teológica sobre a luta dos negros norte-americanos sob a liderança de Martin Luther King. No Brasil, a grande referência para se conhecer melhor sobre esse movimento teológico, são as obras publicadas por Edições Paulinas, de autoria de James H. Cone (O Deus dos Oprimidos, 1985), um dos trabalhos mais importantes sobre a Teologia Negra; e a coletânea de documentos sobre a primeira fase da história da Teologia Negra de 1966 a 1979, de Gayraud S. Wilmore (Teologia Negra, 1986).

Lamentavelmente constatamos que a Teologia da Libertação que se desenvolveu no Brasil e na América Latina (apesar de seu enfoque estar mais concentrado numa análise mais social-econômica marxista do que na libertação de uma raça oprimida) na década de 80 e 90, explorou como se esperava, uma teologia negra de caráter relevante; que fosse impactante e que despertasse a atenção dos cristãos no Brasil. As iniciativas com um viés libertador não foram suficientes para fazer a sociedade pensar sobre os problemas de negros e negras na sociedade brasileira. É louvável considerar o fato de que os líderes da teologia negra norte-americana procuraram manter um certo diálogo com os líderes da libertação latino-americana e asiática. Os efeitos desse esforço não foram suficientes para impactar os segmentos religiosos cristãos nem a sociedade brasileira. É oportuno considerar, portanto, que a Teologia Negra se distingue da Teologia da Libertação Latino-Americana ao evitar o uso da análise social-econômica marxista e ao concentrar-se na libertação de uma raça oprimida ao invés de uma classe social-econômica.

Merece menção positiva, contudo, a luta empreendida pela Igreja Católica Apostólica Romana, que sempre foi mais comprometida, no século XX, com os problemas da negritude, do que as Igrejas protestantes. E, entre estas, há aquelas onde a questão negra nunca foi satisfatoriamente abordada, a partir de uma reflexão libertadora e profética.

Pressupostos básicos que justificam uma Teologia Negra no Brasil

Retrospecto histórico do racismo no Brasil

O racismo no Brasil resulta das mesmas causas que o determinaram na América espanhola. Diferente do que ocorria na Antiguidade, na qual a discriminação baseava-se em diferenças religiosas, de nacionalidade ou de linguagem, essa discriminação, no Brasil, era feita em relação à cultura e ao diferente, incluindo-se aqui as diferenças marcantes de traços físicos e cor da pele. No começo do século XVI, os colonizadores que chegaram ao Brasil (portugueses), trouxeram em sua bagagem cultural, ideologias do ponto de vista social, político, econômico, teológicos, pseudo-científicos, explicações consideradas lógicas, para justificar a origem do racismo. Tinham as mesmas características, fundamentos e princípios já usados na Europa, também baseados em equívocos teológicos baseados em textos bíblicos do Antigo Testamento, que se transformaram em doutrina tendenciosa que se desenvolveu entre teólogos fundamentalistas.

O equívoco teológico dos europeus sobre a discriminação racial, tornou-se forte motivo para se defender a escravidão do negro no Brasil. Já em 1520, dizia-se que os ameríndios não eram descendentes de Adão e Eva. A fundamentação bíblica estava na história de Noé que se embriagou excessivamente com vinho e ficou nu diante dos filhos. Cam, um dos filhos de Noé, por ter visto o seu pai nessa situação e por ter caçoado dele, foi, por isso, amaldiçoado juntamente com toda a sua descendência. Os teólogos racistas concluíram, então, que os negros são descendentes de Cam, consequentemente, amaldiçoados e condenados à servidão e à escravidão permanentes. Outras citações bíblicas (Efésios 6.5 e Eclesiástico

33.26-28) também foram objeto de exegeses equivocadas, sempre com a finalidade de justificar a escravidão dos negros e a necessidade de serem dóceis e serviçais.

Tornou-se válido no Brasil, o que já acontecia na Europa, desde o fim da Idade Média, início do século XVI, isto é, a divisão da população em "limpos de sangue" e "infectos". Os negros, mestiços, cristãos-novos e indígenas foram impedidos de ocupar cargos de confiança ou de honra, sob a alegação de não possuírem tradição católica e títulos de nobreza. Os argumentos quase sempre eram de natureza teológica e social. Os negros pertenceriam a uma "raça impura", cujo sangue se encontrava "manchado". O desdobramento de tudo isso no Brasil, resultou numa prática já conhecida entre europeus, que exigia que, para exercer certas funções públicas na sociedade brasileira (escrivão de justiça, coletor de impostos, juiz-de-fora, vereador, entre outras funções), todos deveriam comprovar que eram "limpos de sangue", isto é, que não tinham na família qualquer membro pertencente às raças consideradas impuras.

No século XIX também prevaleceu no Brasil o que se chamou de "mito ariano", com raízes na Península Ibérica, quando foram realizados em meados desse século, experimentos considerados científicos com cérebros de humanos e de símios, que deram origem a um certo número de tratados sobre as diferenças raciais. Aqui os africanos são apontados como seres biologicamente inferiores.

Houve uma incorporação na sociedade brasileira da teoria do Conde Arthur de Gobineau[1] que tivera grande impulso na Europa. Na obra de Gobineau, vale ressaltar, que a raça ariana é considerada superior em relação a outros grupos raciais. Desta forma, Gobineau classifica a raça semita como inferior à ariana, que seria o puro europeu. A ideia de que o judeu é semita, e como tal uma raça estrangeira e inferior, tornou-se um princípio básico dos arianos anti-semitas. Aliada à teoria de Goubineau estava a contribuição de Houston Stewart Chamberlain, que aplicou o conceito de "raça superior" aos alemães a fim de apoiá-los em suas aspirações nacionalistas e proclamou os judeus como uma raça degenerada. É nesse contexto que Adolf Hitler se apropriou dessas ideias e as usou para demonstrar a superioridade dos nórdicos e para justificar o extremo anti-semitismo do nazismo, que foi responsável pela morte de mais de seis milhões de judeus. As ideias de Goubineau e Chamberlain tiveram efeitos significativos nos Estados Unidos e no Brasil onde serviram para exaltar e "afirmar a superioridade dos americanos brancos sobre os negros, justificar a segregação e a sujeição dos negros ao grupo branco dominante.

Vale ressaltar, porém, antes de tudo, que a América já estava povoada de negros que foram enviados para os Estados Unidos e para o Brasil. O chamado "tráfico de negros", iniciado em meados do século XV pelos portugueses primeiramente na Europa e, em seguida nas terras recém-descobertas do novo mundo. como escravos, ao mesmo tempo "abençoados" pela Igreja, graças às interpretações e exegeses equivocadas dos teólogos fundamentalistas do século XVI. A Igreja legitimava a colonização e a escravidão com suas práticas e pregação da resignação e subserviência. Leigos e religiosos, teólogos e hierarquia chegaram a justificar a escravidão e dela usufruíram. Alguns documentos pontifícios da época, especialmente dos Papas Nicolau V (1452) e Leão X (1514), autorizavam a Coroa portuguesa e, depois, a espanhola, a conquistarem as terras dos sarracenos, pagãos e incrédulos, escravizando seus habitantes. A falsa noção de "guerra justa contra os inimigos de fé", trazia consigo a legitimação da escravização dos vencidos.

Não se pode negar que vozes proféticas dentro da Igreja Católica Apostólica Romana também se levantaram contra a escravização de indígenas e negros. Frei Antonio de Montesinos, Bartolomeu e las Casas, o Bispo Antonio de Valdivieso, os Padres Manoel da Nóbrega, José de Anchieta e Antonio Vieira estão entre eles. Um desses padres, referindo-se aos omissos em relação ao problema, escreveu: "Os padres que vão ao Brasil não vão a salvar as almas, mas condenar as suas." Vale ressaltar o ensinamento de Paulo III contra a escravidão dos índios; mas a escravização dos negros nem sempre foi rechaçada com a mesma intensidade!

Os protestantes somente se firmaram no Brasil a partir da segunda metade do século XVI. Em sua maioria missionários enviados à América Latina eram norte-americanos. Principalmente os procedentes do Sul dos Estados Unidos, chegaram ao Brasil defendendo a escravidão e utilizando negros para trabalhos domésticos em suas residências. Vale lembrar que, de alguma forma, esses sempre foram a favor da escravidão negra, uma das bandeiras de lutas na Guerra Civil Americana, entre Estados do sul e Estados do norte dos Estados Unidos.

É importante considerar que entre os protestantes brasileiros, o Rev. Eduardo Carlos Pereira, pastor presbiteriano, notabilizou-se, entre outras, pelo seu veemente protesto contra o racismo e a escravidão. Em 1886 Pereira publicou um livreto sob o título "A Religião Cristã em suas relações com a escravidão", no qual faz críticas severas às interpretações fundamentalistas da Bíblia sobre o racismo; chama a atenção dos presbiterianos em relação à sua omissão frente ao problema; desafia o púlpito a deixar o silêncio; pede aos fiéis que restituam a liberdade aos escravos. Isto porque na época estava comprovado que metodistas, batistas e presbiterianos eram donos de escravos.

Como vimos, as ideias de Goubineau também tiveram muita influência no Brasil. Entre 1869 e 1870 ele visitou o Imperador brasileiro, Dom Pedro II, oportunidade em que fez grande amizade e discutiu, inclusive, a questão da abolição da escravatura e a política de imigração. Foi nessa época que previu para menos de duzentos anos o desaparecimento dos habitantes brasileiros, condenados pela crescente miscigenação.

Tavares Bastos, um deputado alagoano, defendeu a necessidade de uma renovação da população brasileira através do incentivo à imigração branca. Entendia que acabar com a escravidão não era uma questão de compaixão; era uma forma de afastar os prejuízos que o negro trazia ao Brasil. Sustentava que a ciência já havia confirmado que o negro era a raiz dos males da nação e mau trabalhador. A vinda do branco, seria um passo para o progresso e símbolo de civilização. Ele é mais produtivo, afirmava o deputado!

Além dos negros, os orientais (de raça amarela) também foram vítimas do racismo no Brasil. Em 1880 discutiu-se ardentemente sobre a permanência de chineses no Brasil. Políticos paulistas questionavam a culinária chinesa; alguns achavam que gatos, ratos, lagartas, larvas faziam parte de seus pratos típicos. Os chineses eram chamados de "cara quadrada" e aos jovens brasileiros aconselhava-se evitar o casamento com essas pessoas orientais. Também os japoneses sofreram discriminação, principalmente durante a Segunda Guerra Mundial. Foram considerados, além de raça impura, traidores, espiões, inimigos.

Principais características do racismo no Brasil

Atualmente há grande diversidade de raças no Brasil. Aparentemente é dito que há uma convivência pacífica entre as raças, chamando-se essa convivência, inclusive, de democracia racial. Todavia, na prática, é notória a discriminação, principalmente em relação aos negros. A bem da verdade, as estatísticas demográficas ainda fornecem dados imprecisos sobre as diversas etnias no Brasil. Por conta das pressões sociais muitas pessoas da raça negra, negam sua identidade e se definem como "pardos" e até como "brancos". Isto relativiza os dados coletados pelos órgãos oficiais.

Embora os dados oficiais nem sempre reflitam a verdade dos fatos, podemos afirmar que a população afro-descendente na atualidade aproxima-se de 50%. Isto faz do Brasil o segundo maior país do mundo com população negra, superado apenas pela Nigéria. De qualquer maneira, são pessoas que vivem em situação de inferioridade em relação a outras raças.

O negro no Brasil de hoje vive situações preocupantes. Do ponto de vista socioeconômico, é muito desigual o seu rendimento financeiro no mundo do trabalho. Ainda é mais frequente a presença do negro em funções subalternas e mais desqualificadas, socialmente. Na construção civil, por exemplo, os negros são maioria enquanto os brancos, geralmente atuam como mestres de obras.

Quanto à situação de escolaridade e de cultura, percebe-se que o grau de escolarização dos brasileiros reforça a situação de desigualdade em que se encontra a população negra do Brasil. O índice de analfabetismo da população negra economicamente ativa é muito alto em relação à situação da população branca. A média de anos de estudos dos brancos é bem superior em relação aos anos de estudo dos negros. Para exemplificar, registramos que atualmente (2016) os negros são menos de 1% nos cursos considerados de ponta da Universidade de São Paulo (USP). Em aproximadamente 5 anos, os cursos de Medicina, Direito e Engenharia da USP matricularam apenas 77 alunos negros. Estes dados referem-se a 0,9% das matrículas realizadas entre 2005 e 2011, segundo fonte da Universidade de São Paulo.

Para piorar a situação de menosprezo e desigualdade em relação à raça negra, muitos livros didáticos reforçam a posição de inferioridade do negro. Nos livros de História do Brasil, quase sempre escritos na perspectiva do branco, o negro aparece quase exclusivamente associado à escravidão. A ideia que fica na mente de quem estuda essa história, é a de que negro é igual a escravo, consequentemente, negro é considerado inferior. Nos relatos históricos, na galeria de seus heróis, o negro quase nunca é lembrado. A citação de Zumbi dos Palmares como líder de um movimento de resistência contra a exploração dos brancos, por exemplo, quase nunca é feita!

Vale ressaltar que os destaques culturais em relação à raça negra, quando aparecem, estão quase sempre ligados a aspectos tidos como periféricos ou folclóricos, como ocorre com manifestações musicais, hábitos alimentares, contribuições linguísticas. Reconheçamos que em muitas situações, tendo como padrão a cultura do branco, os traços negros são considerados como subcultura e expressão do exótico.

A discriminação inclui os padrões de beleza, cultura e civilidade em relação aos padrões do branco. Nem mesmo a cultura do indígena é levada em consideração. De igual modo, em relação ao negro, a cultura indígena também é considerada exótica, própria de quem é incivilizado. É evidente a maneira como os meios de comunicação social, formadores de opinião, confirmam o que afirmamos. As novelas, reportagens e filmes mostram quase sempre os negros em funções subalternas, como empregados domésticos, em papéis secundários, ou praticando atos que ferem a ética social.

Não há como esconder a situação da mulher negra, provavelmente uma das maiores vítimas de toda essa história de discriminação. Exerceu diversos papéis sempre na condição de subalterna. Foi escrava, objeto de prazer dos senhores nos engenhos, reprodutora, para aumentar o capital humano dos escravagistas, explorada nas atividades domésticas, nos serviços do campo.

Na condição de reprodutora, a mulher foi aviltada em sua dignidade e estimulada a produzir mais de 10 filhos a fim de que obtivesse sua liberdade. Apesar desse aviltamento à sua honra e o desrespeito, resistia heroicamente e se negava a conseguir sua liberdade dessa forma. É o que diz Roger Bastide, em "As Religiões Africanas no Brasil": "o branco estimulava a procriação de seus escravos: a mulher que tinha posto no mundo 10 crianças era libertada; posteriormente o número foi diminuído para 7".[2] Apesar da vantagem, as mulheres quase sempre negavam-se a produzir filhos-escravos para a sociedade em troca dessa liberdade. Muitos abortos voluntários foram praticados como forma de resistência. Em muitos casos essas mulheres, sem qualquer assistência médica, durante a prática desse aborto, também eram vitimadas com a morte. Por isso o índice de natalidade entre as mulheres negras era baixo. O resultado desse tipo de tratamento, em nossos dias, ainda é ver as mulheres negras formarem o maior contingente da população que vive em favelas ou "comunidades", além de serem mal remuneradas como domésticas, operárias ou camponesas. Continuam sendo três vezes vítimas da discriminação: como mulheres, como pobres e como negras.

De acordo com a Agência Brasil, com dados publicados em 25/06/2012, negras e pobres são mais vulneráveis ao aborto com risco. Segundo pesquisas feitas em 2010, 22% das brasileiras de 35 a 39 anos, residentes em áreas urbanas, já fizeram aborto. "As características mais comuns das mulheres que fazem o primeiro aborto é a idade até 19 anos, a cor negra e com filhos", diz em artigo científico a antropóloga Débora Diniz, da Universidade Nacional de Brasília e do Instituto de Bioética, Direitos Humanos e Gênero (ANIS), e, de igual modo o sociólogo Marcelo Medeiros, também da Universidade Nacional de Brasília e do Instituto de Pesquisa Econômica Aplicada (IPEA).

A discriminação também ocorre com as crianças negras quando, em situação de risco, são abrigadas em casas-lares, na expectativa de alguma adoção. À espera de alguma família caridosa, muitas dessas crianças sempre acreditam que alguém chegue, credenciado pela Justiça, para levá-las. Mas adoções de crianças negras são mais raras! Quando não são adotadas, muitas ficam nos abrigos até os 17 anos e 11 meses e, dependendo da situação, são obrigadas a deixar esse ambiente, ficando assim, sujeitas à indigência, à delinquência, à prostituição, ao desequilíbrio psíquico e social, a uma vida sem futuro!

Influências do racismo na cultura do povo

Todo esse passado de violências contra a raça negra, deixou na sociedade brasileira heranças históricas que ainda permanecem. Em relação ao trabalho, os negros continuam em segundo plano. Por causa de sua baixa escolaridade, não têm tido grandes chances. Como vimos, poucos têm acesso à universidade ou concluem um curso superior. A maioria dedica-se a trabalhos manuais grosseiros, e, geralmente, são vítimas das injustiças do salário. O preconceito racial, sob novas formas, e zelosamente guardado, está presente na linguagem (muitos ainda se referem ao negro dizendo "um homem de cor"), nos livros didáticos, na educação, nas manifestações religiosas dos cristãos, nas músicas populares, na cultura brasileira em geral.

Na religião protestante, por exemplo, a mensagem dos púlpitos continua trazendo em sua retórica expressões como "o negro e rude pecado"; nos cânticos aparecem frases como "negros batalhões", "meu coração era preto; mas Cristo aqui já entrou; com seu precioso sangue; tão alvo assim o tornou." A Aliança pró Evangelização de Crianças (APEC), por exemplo, adota em seu trabalho didático, o chamado "Livro sem Palavras".[3] Entre as cores referidas nesse material, está o uso do preto, que pode induzir a criança a rejeitar-se, quando negra. O preto aparece aqui como símbolo do pecado. Considerando as críticas em relação a essa posição, a APEC substituiu a palavra "preto" por "sujo". Faz-nos pensar que preto equivale a sujo, sujeira! Em livros de ética cristã e teologia a frase "homens de cor" continua aparecendo, até mesmo em textos escritos contra o racismo.[4] Certamente há autores e tradutores que acreditam que existem homens sem cor, os brancos!

Outros termos como "mulato", "negro", "preto" e "negritude" têm gerado sentimentos e complexos de inferioridade, dando ao indivíduo a sensação de não-ser e de não ser igual ao outro. Como se percebe, uma mudança significativa na linguagem e na literatura permitiria, cremos, alterações no sentido da palavra "negro" a fim de se conseguir um sentido positivo e digno desse termo "negro".

O preconceito racial tem sido uma prática permanente que cria obstáculos à participação social de um determinado grupo étnico e ao exercício de seus direitos como cidadão. Ele aliena o negro e, de maneira mascarada, às vezes o faz acreditar na tão falada "democracia racial". Esta, tem a finalidade de esconder as desigualdades que existem entre negros e brancos. Os que defendem a "democracia racial" fazem uma leitura a-histórica do período escravista e acreditam na chamada "cordialidade nata" dos brasileiros, na ideia de que as oportunidades são iguais para todos, negros e brancos e que, portanto, não existe distinção de raça, cor, sexo, religião. Uma visão parcial, ingênua de tão complexo problema!

Movimentos de resistência contra o racismo

Apesar de tudo isso, grandes esforços têm sido feitos pelos negros e simpatizantes, para que haja mudança na situação racial no Brasil. A luta pela consciência negra diante dessa realidade, aos poucos vai conseguindo impor-se sobre a sociedade. Ainda que não seja como deveria, busca-se o reconhecimento do registro em relação às representações ideológicas que continuam mascarando a discriminação da raça negra. Faz parte da luta dos negros por sua dignidade e direitos na sociedade. Trata-se de uma luta necessária para a conscientização da sociedade. Reconhece-se como fundamental que os negros tenham consciência do que representam na sociedade e que se garanta a todos o acesso à informação específica e a criação de "uma massa crítica" para que a luta seja viabilizada.

Várias formas de articulação da "consciência negra" têm surgido nas comunidades afro-americanas.[5] Vale destacar o movimento "Frente Negra Brasileira" (FNB), que surgiu em 1931, com os objetivos de denunciar o racismo, lutar pela igualdade de direitos principalmente no mercado de trabalho, pelo direito à educação e pelo direito da terra e à moradia. Outra frente de luta, que surgiu na década de 50, é o Movimento Vento Forte Africano, sob a liderança de Solano Trindade, que defende a ideia de se juntar a discussão racial com a luta de classes. Acrescente-se aqui a participação de Abdias do Nascimento, com uma visão mais negro-africana, trabalhando a ideia do quilombismo, que era um espaço negro de reinvenção da própria cultura negra e um diálogo de negociação e confronto com a sociedade.

Especificamente no Brasil, convém lembrar três experiências importantes ligadas ao Movimento Negro. O Prof. Marcos Rodrigues da Silva, em estudo sobre "Comunidades Afro-Americanas", cita o "Movimento Negro Unificado (M. N. U.), que surgiu no final dos anos 70, que enfrentou perseguições policiais a jovens negros, muitas vezes responsabilizados por assaltos a bancos, roubos e práticas marginais, sem a devida apuração. Foi esse Movimento que conseguiu que o dia 20 de novembro fosse considerado o "Dia da Consciência Negra" e de luta contra a discriminação racial, em homenagem a Zumbi, do Quilombo de Palmares. O Prof. Marcos cita também o "Grupo de União e Consciência Negra", organizado em 1981, sob a liderança de leigos, religiosas e padres da Igreja Católica Apostólica Romana, ligados ao trabalho missionário da Conferência Nacional dos Bispos do Brasil. Finalmente o Prof. Marcos faz menção ao trabalho dos "Agentes de Pastoral Negros", na década de 80, tendo como característica a abertura ecumênica para acolher, valorizar e entender melhor as religiões e cultos afro-brasileiros.

O Prof. Antonio Olimpio de Sant'Ana, um dos articuladores do movimento de combate ao racismo na Igreja Metodista do Brasil e um dos organizadores da Comissão Ecumênica Nacional de Combate ao Racismo

(CENACORA), em seu verbete sobre "Racismo" no Dicionário Brasileiro de Teologia, acredita que "um ecumenismo forte, objetivo, inclusivo, incentivador da verdade, da reconciliação, da justiça, que resulte numa espiritualidade que fortaleça o amor ao próximo"[6] pode ser uma das saídas para se combater o racismo. A propósito, vale também ressaltar o trabalho da CENACORA — Comissão Ecumênica Nacional de Combate ao Racismo, organizada em 1987, por representantes de Igrejas Evangélicas, da Igreja Católica Apostólica Romana e da Igreja Católica Ortodoxa Siriana, tendo como objetivos discutir, bíblica e teologicamente o racismo; refletir sobre a espiritualidade negra e indígena; promover e incentivar atividades que capacitem pessoas a combater e eliminar o racismo; desafiar as igrejas a examinarem a existência do racismo em suas comunidades.

Outras organizações da sociedade civil surgiram para fortalecer os movimentos já existentes, com ações de certa relevância na sociedade brasileira. Mencionamos a Comissão Nacional Contra a Discriminação Racial (CNDR), da Central Única dos Trabalhadores, no Brasil; o Instituto Sindical Interamericano Pela Igualdade Racial (INSPIR), organizado em 1995. A finalidade desse Instituto é formar e capacitar dirigentes sindicais na temática da discriminação racial e prepará-los para negociar cláusulas referentes à promoção da igualdade racial e incentivar a organização dos trabalhadores negros. Estão envolvidas nessa luta as três organizações de trabalhadores brasileiros (CUT, CGT e Força Sindical).

Fragmentos para uma Teologia Negra no Brasil

A certeza de que Deus ouve o clamor dos oprimidos
Na história do povo de Israel, Deus é Aquele que vê e ouve o clamor do Seu povo. Faz-nos lembrar, nessa história, o sofrimento dos israelitas sob a opressão dos egípcios; estes tratavam o povo de Deus como escravos. Falando com Moisés no deserto, assim disse Deus: "Eu vi a miséria do meu povo no Egito. Ouvi o seu clamor por causa dos seus opressores. Eu conheço suas angústias. Por isso, desci, a fim de libertar meu povo das mãos dos egípcios..." (Êxodo 3.7-8). Percebe-se aqui a insatisfação de Deus diante da opressão e angústia em que se encontrava o povo de Israel. Deus promete libertação para aquele povo e deseja contar com a colaboração humana na luta pela libertação. Fica explícita a condenação de Deus a qualquer tipo de exploração!

Acredita-se que Deus continua querendo intervir em toda a realidade social onde haja opressão, discriminação, miséria e ameaças de morte. Porque Deus, tanto na história da libertação de Israel como no ministério de Jesus, sempre aparece ao lado, na defesa dos pobres, marginalizados, discriminados, dos oprimidos!

No ministério de Jesus, Ele é visivelmente solidário com as vítimas da discriminação como ocorria com a situação da mulher na sociedade de Seu tempo; também agiu contra os que discriminavam os pobres, os órfãos e as viúvas, os estrangeiros e outros marginalizados naquela época como ocorria com os doentes, com os escravos, com os de outras raças.

Vale lembrar na história da libertação, o evento de Pentecostes (Atos 2. 1-12) na vida da Igreja. Ali temos exemplos de como deve ser o novo mundo. O Espírito Santo desce sobre a Igreja reunida em Jerusalém e derruba as barreiras culturais de língua e de raça, e todos, ao mesmo tempo, são capazes de entender e aceitar a mensagem do Reino de Deus! Ali ocorre o grande sinal da possibilidade de vida, da unidade na diversidade, contra a negação total de qualquer tipo de discriminação, seja de povos, raças ou nações.

O testemunho dos cristãos do I século também é exemplo para a nossa prática contra a discriminação. Um dos exemplos mais marcantes talvez seja o do conflito entre judaizantes e universalistas, quando se deu a conversão do centurião romano, Cornélio. Cornélio é gentio, mas sobre ele desce o Espírito Santo; Pedro é convencido por Deus que não se deve fazer acepção de pessoas, discriminando-as (Atos 10. 17-18); a ação do Espírito Santo foi decisiva naquele momento da história da Igreja para que as portas se abrissem para os não-judeus na experiência do batismo. Nas Cartas paulinas aos Romanos e aos Gálatas fica clara a recriminação a qualquer tipo de discriminação, fosse cultural, religiosa, de gênero, de classe social ou mesmo a escravidão.

Escrevendo aos Gálatas o Apóstolo Paulo diz: "...Vós todos sois filhos de Deus pela fé em Cristo Jesus, pois todos vós fostes batizados em Cristo, vos revestistes de Cristo. Não há judeu, nem grego, nem escravo nem livre, não há homem nem mulher; pois todos vós sois um só em Cristo Jesus" (Gálatas 3. 26-28). Em outras Cartas, aos Coríntios e aos Colossenses, além da Carta aos Romanos e Gálatas, Paulo é incisivo, repetitivo até, sobre este ensinamento.

A pergunta e a resposta a esta questão: até que ponto a Igreja de Cristo tem ouvido o clamor dos oprimidos?
Temos que reconhecer que, apesar das evidências das Escrituras Sagradas sobre a discriminação, tem sido difícil a superação do problema. Em determinados momentos da história da Igreja, ela mesma tornou-se agente de discriminação e de projetos missionários de caráter opressor. É o que se percebe quando se faz a leitura da história da Igreja na Idade Média e, nos tempos Modernos, quando os judeus foram discriminados. Também missionários que acompanharam as expedições colonizadoras de portugueses e espanhóis tiveram dificuldades na aceitação sem discriminação em relação aos povos a serem evangelizados. Muitos líderes cristãos foram defensores da escravidão dos negros trazidos da África.

Em "O Racismo na História do Brasil", a historiadora Maria Luiza Tucci Carneiro, da Universidade de São Paulo (USP), Brasil, diz, referindo-se à situação do Brasil durante o período colonial:

> As ideias segregacionistas foram veiculadas através de sermões, contos, canções, crônicas, poemas, anedotas, textos teatrais e pintura. Em todas essas formas de expressão a figura do negro emerge como a de um ser inferior, animalizado, serviçal; e o judeu surge como inimigo da humanidade, identificado com a encarnação do demônio, com o 'Anticristo'.[7]

Não se pode negar, em tudo isso, a existência da força da mentalidade discriminatória, de caráter ideológico, nem a cumplicidade da Igreja (tanto no catolicismo como no protestantismo).

A luta para que os equívocos teológicos sejam condenados
Do ponto de vista bíblico e teológico, não há fundamento para a afirmação de que a raça negra, por exemplo, resulta da "maldição" que Noé lançou sobre Canaã, ao se refazer da embriaguez com vinho e diante da ironia expressa de seu filho quando o viu sem roupas: "Maldito seja Canaã; seja servo dos servos a seus irmãos" (Gênesis 9.25). Não há fundamentação bíblica, para que teólogos racistas acreditem que todos os negros não só descendem de Cam como estão condenados à servidão e à escravidão permanentes. O sacerdote espanhol Juan Bautista Casas alegava em 1869 que a raça negra sofre da maldição, conforme o Pentateuco e que essa inferioridade se perpetuava através dos séculos. Mas é

oportuno o comentário de Gardner em "Fé Bíblica e Ética Social", a respeito dessa interpretação errônea, quando disse:

> Leitura cuidadosa desta passagem, em seu contexto próprio, mostra que foi Noé e não Deus que lançou tal maldição sobre o filho, Cam, e que Noé estava em péssimas condições para ser o porta-voz do Senhor naquelas circunstâncias (E. C. GARDNER, 1965, p. 406).

Se a maldição fosse estabelecida por Deus, seria complicado acreditar em Sua vontade redentora em relação à vida humana e nas possibilidades divinas para mudar e transformar as relações intra-grupos. Deus seria incoerente e contraditório em relação à Sua natureza redentora.

Os movimentos religiosos de resistência contra o racismo, no Brasil, entendem que é necessário denunciar profeticamente a falácia do chamado "racismo científico"

Esta denúncia se faz necessária porque muita gente ainda acredita que tudo que é aparentemente científico é digno de crença. Ainda é sustentada por muita gente as teses dos primeiros cientistas sociais. Estes foram conclusivos na defesa de que o homem original era branco; em contato com o trópico, porém, sofreu um processo de degeneração, tornando-o negro. Vários pensadores defenderam este tipo de pensamento falacioso: Voltaire, Linneo, Kamper, Buffon, tendo em vista demonstrar a hierarquização das raças. Tudo isso, embora sem fundamentos sustentáveis, visava a sacralização da dominação colonial.

Até o final do século passado (1995), várias publicações circularam apontando para a intolerância multicultural. Em "A Nação Estrangeira" ("Alien Nation"), Peter Brimelow defende rígido controle da imigração para os Estados Unidos na defesa da hegemonia dos brancos naquele país. Dois outros autores, Richard Hernstein e Charles Morray, publicaram um ano antes, em "A Curva do Sino", a afirmação de que em virtude de fatores genéticos, o QI de negros é inferior ao de brancos e asiáticos.

Até o século XIX prevaleceram os pretextos teológicos para a justificação do racismo. A ciência avançou suficientemente para desqualificar os argumentos dos que acham que há superioridade entre as raças ou os que lançaram mão da teoria da evolução de Darwin, deturpando-a, para justificar o racismo. Mas, como diz Maria Luiza Tucci Carneiro (USP, 1994):

Apesar de não condizerem com a realidade comprovada cientificamente, as teorias racistas serviram para justificar a irritação da sociedade contra os grupos "indesejáveis", encobrindo interesses econômicos, políticos e sociais. Podemos afirmar então que o preconceito baseia-se em falsas ideias, levando à configuração de perigos imaginários.

É preciso desmascarar a ideologia do racismo

Sua origem está no passado, quando se pretendia justificar a desigualdade em relação ao desenvolvimento dos povos. Essa ideologia serviu aos ideais do colonialismo, para tornar legítima a escravidão e a opressão dos povos negros, do aborígene australiano e do indígena americano. Serviu, de igual modo, para negar o acesso igualitário desses povos aos bens culturais (materiais e espirituais) de todos os grupos étnicos e nações.

Tem sido considerada como inequívoca a ideia de que *a Igreja precisa reconhecer e confessar que colaborou com o desenvolvimento do racismo na história da humanidade*. Católicos e protestantes são cúmplices nessa história. Não basta à Igreja reconhecer que em muitas situações foi omissa e, em determinados momentos, seus membros defenderam a servidão. O Cardeal Gonzalvi, representante papal (1815), por exemplo, negou-se a censurar o tráfico de escravos a fim de não ofender os "Estados Católicos" onde tal comércio era permitido. O Papa Leão XIII, em pastoral enviada aos bispos brasileiros, em 1888, quando se deu a abolição dos escravos no Brasil, declarou que a escravidão não é essencialmente má e que pode, inclusive, ser construtiva, desde que o senhor seja "bom".

Muitos protestantes, a exemplo dos católicos, também estiveram a favor da escravidão. Moravos, metodistas, anglicanos, batistas, presbiterianos, quakers da Europa, eram donos de escravos.

Mais do que confessar, os cristãos precisam pedir perdão aos povos negros e indígenas por não terem lutado contra a discriminação das raças e por sua libertação dos poderes opressores em toda a história humana!

A Igreja tem sido encorajada a aceitar o desafio da inculturação a partir das comunidades negras

Tomamos como base o texto do Padre Antonio Aparecido da Silva (Padre Toninho)[8] , publicado em "Comunidade Negra: Desafios atuais e perspectivas" (Atabaque — ASSET, São Paulo, 1995). Neste texto o Padre Toninho faz menção à "indisposição cultural na comunidade europeia" em relação aos imigrantes negros desde o século XIII. Destaca que para a Europa, embora considerada moderna, o mundo não europeu foi classificado de "selvagem" e pré-histórico.

Diante desse quadro, por ocasião das reflexões sobre os 500 anos de conquistas da América (1992), a questão cultural tomou vulto, com destaque para o estudo sobre o encontro entre as culturas europeias, indígenas e negras e os problemas dele decorrentes. Reconhece-se que a cultura negra, em particular, é emergente na América Latina e que, apesar da predominância de um padrão cultural ocidental estabelecido a partir da colonização, não há apenas um só povo e uma só cultura. Há uma pluralidade cultural que se tornou evidente, principalmente a partir das culturas de negros e indígenas.

Considerando essa realidade cultural na América Latina, a Igreja, em particular, está desafiada a desenvolver uma pastoral inculturada, principalmente a partir da comunidade negra. E justifica o Padre Toninho:

> Para que a Igreja chegue a ser uma reunião de povos, diferentes, mas unidos e harmônicos, é preciso assumir e intensificar um diálogo profundo, sincero e respeitoso entre Evangelho e Culturas, visando preservar a legítima identidade dos diversos povos.

Este tem sido um dos grandes desafios com sérios problemas a serem superados na caminhada em direção à cultura negra, nem sempre reconhecida em seus vários aspectos como legítima para ser assimilada pela Igreja, principalmente entre as igrejas protestantes no Brasil.

O Pe. Toninho vê a inculturação como um processo dialético, onde a proposta evangélica "...vivida e assumida através, inclusive, de formas culturais não incompatíveis com o Evangelho, é devolvida, expressa ou re-expressa segundo o modus-vivendi (cultura) daquele determinado povo". Conclusivamente, o Pe. Toninho diz que o povo negro na diáspora assimilou a partir daquilo que já sabia antes; e integrou a proposta evangélica na sua própria trajetória". Desta forma, o processo de inculturação havido na comunidade negra mostrou que a evangelização não é a simples comunicação e recepção do legado histórico do cristianismo, mas "O receptor do Evangelho somente pode recebê-lo recriando dentro de si próprio, por si próprio".

Em síntese, a Igreja tem sido questionada a aceitar o permanente desafio de caminhar na direção dos negros e sua cultura, para que eles conheçam a ação salvífica e de libertação de Deus, com um novo olhar sobre si e sobre o mundo.

Reconhece-se na atualidade que a Igreja tem tarefas a cumprir nas relações raciais

A Igreja tem "a responsabilidade de tornar clara a relevância da fé cristã para as questões de interesse social, em geral, e para as relações intra-grupos", diz Gardner. A Igreja é testemunha e, como tal, deve ser fiel na proclamação e interpretação de sua fé ao mundo. Ela não pode furtar-se a ações concretas que envolvam aspectos da vida econômica, política, moral e religiosa na sociedade. Mais do que retórica, a Igreja precisa ser prática, assumir posições, denunciar o mal que comprometa o bem-estar e a dignidade de irmãos na sociedade.

A missão da Igreja perante o mundo precisa ser clara, objetiva, transparente. Seu discurso deve ser profético e estar presente na vida dos oprimidos como "sal da terra" e "luz do mundo". As pessoas vítimas da discriminação precisam ver e sentir isso! É tarefa da Igreja manifestar em sua própria vida a unidade e a fraternidade que proclama.

Como parte de sua responsabilidade, a Igreja precisa trabalhar para a implantação da justiça de maneira integral na realidade social. Movida pelo amor, deve buscar a mudança, a renovação ou mesmo a reconstrução das estruturas institucionais através das quais as necessidades humanas poderão ou deverão ser atendidas. São muitos os problemas que emergem da discriminação racial. Qualquer que seja, porém, o caráter desses problemas, a Igreja não pode deixar de lado a obrigatoriedade de ações concretas que combatam a discriminação. Vale o exemplo dos missionários e Igrejas negras da Jamaica, em 1783, definidas como centros de subversão pelas autoridades colonialistas da época. Igrejas foram queimadas e missionários foram presos e condenados à morte, mas o movimento emancipador não morreu.

Por uma Teologia Negra no Brasil, faz-se necessário fortalecer o esforço ecumênico

O problema da discriminação racial esteve na pauta da Assembleia do Conselho Mundial de Igrejas (CMI), desde sua reunião em Amsterdam.

Vários documentos chamaram a atenção, na época, para o fato de que era preciso a erradicação da discriminação e do ódio raciais. O apelo era para que as Igrejas eliminassem de suas práticas qualquer forma de racismo. Em 1961, três Igrejas da África do Sul retiraram-se do CMI, por discordarem dessa posição antirracista. Em 1969, O CMI recomendou o boicote às companhias com investimentos na África do Sul e em seguida criou o Programa de Combate ao Racismo.

Já em Amsterdam ficou claro que a segregação racial na Igreja é "escândalo" no Corpo de Cristo. A Igreja que quer ser "Igreja de Jesus" no mundo, não pode ser segregacionista como vários grupos cristãos continuaram sendo ao longo da história.

Em 1957 os bispos católicos da África do Sul reconheceram que havia racismo no seio da Igreja; em 1967, o Papa Paulo VI pronunciou-se através da encíclica *Populorum Progressio* com censura ao racismo, referindo-se às práticas do passado, do presente e do futuro.

Apesar desses esforços e muitos outros, reconhece-se que o racismo não deve ser considerado apenas o problema de poucos religiosos, lutando isolados contra tal evidência. Como escreveu o Rev. Antonio Olímpio de Sant' Ana, "A luta contra o racismo depende... de um ecumenismo forte... que incentive as igrejas a se sentirem parte do sofrimento, da angústia e da miséria dos despossuídos..."[9] Lamentamos, porém, que o ecumenismo em nossos dias não esteja tão forte e atuante para determinar a mudança de mentalidade e de rumo na história da humanidade, com a participação efetiva das Igrejas Cristãs pelos ideais do reino de Deus.

Que a Teologia Negra no Brasil tenha caráter libertador

Para uma Teologia Negra no Brasil, de caráter libertador, faz-se necessário, a princípio, uma *releitura das Sagradas Escrituras*, a partir da realidade dos negros no processo histórico, tendo em vista os textos bíblicos que são os fundamentos da fé cristã, numa dimensão relevante na dimensão da libertação. Com um novo olhar, perceber que os negros, quando oprimidos pelos poderes rebeldes deste mundo, personificados nos dominadores que a si mesmos se bastam, têm sido vítimas de sistemas capitalistas abusivos. Desta forma, os textos escriturísticos revelarão que os negros historicamente oprimidos devem ser considerados como sujeitos e não objetos no ideal de libertação do Reino de Deus. É preciso reconhecer, nessa nova atitude, que até aqui a leitura das Escrituras Sagradas tem sido de tipo sacerdotal, a partir de interesses dos poderosos deste mundo ou simplesmente daqueles que participam dos bens da civilização capitalista (muitos deles também representados nas estruturas eclesiásticas do nosso tempo). Vale considerar que a releitura das Escrituras a partir dos negros oprimidos, de caráter profético, será, ao mesmo tempo de caráter libertador.

Com a releitura das Escrituras Sagradas sob a ótica do negro oprimido, impõe-se a *releitura dos conteúdos da Teologia*, em busca de sua libertação. Essa releitura deve ser de caráter profético, o que será determinante para que esses conteúdos se tornem também impactantes, pois deverá levar em consideração a análise da realidade do negro e seus anseios de libertação.

A Teologia Negra na sociedade brasileira deve levar em consideração a realidade do negro nessa sociedade, que contemple os conteúdos da Teologia naquilo que eles têm de libertação. É fundamental, portanto, que se leve em conta a dimensão social e até mesmo utópica, que contemple no contexto sócio-político, aspectos que sejam relevantes para o processo de libertação. Sob esse viés libertador deve-se reler valores da fé cristã que dizem respeito à vida do ser humano oprimido como o mistério de Deus, de Cristo, da Igreja, da graça, do pecado, os sacramentos, a escatologia, a antropologia e a noção de Reino de Deus num mundo de poderes rebeldes e ameaças de morte. Essa releitura nos aproximará do caráter libertador do Evangelho de Cristo, tão presente em Seu ministério ao proclamar e realizar a libertação de todo tipo de marginalizados (mulheres, enfermos, estrangeiros, endemoninhados, escravos, samaritanos), de qualquer raça, classe social, origem religiosa, cultura.

Reproduzindo considerações dos irmãos Boff (Leonardo e Clodovis Boff)[10] , parece-nos pertinente observar a necessidade de uma *releitura da história* a partir da ótica dos marginalizados, incluindo-se entre eles os negros. O objetivo é a descoberta de novas fontes, novas interpretações e perspectivas, a fim de conferir consciência histórica a esse povo para fortalecer a luta de libertação em todas as dimensões.

Haveria como construir uma teologia negra sem levar em consideração uma *releitura das Escrituras Sagradas*, uma *releitura dos conteúdos da teologia cristã* e uma *releitura da realidade histórica* na luta pela libertação de uma raça oprimida?

Notas

1. Gardenr, E. C. Fé Bíblica e Ética Social, São Paulo: ASTE, 1965, p. 4001.
2. Bastide, Roger, "As Religiões Africanas no Brasil," Volume I, p. 98.
3. dos Santos, Leontino Farias, "Educação: Libertação ou Submissão", p.118.
4. Gardner, Veja-se em E. C., "Fé Bíblica e Ética Social", São Paulo, ASTE, 1965, p. 402. Também no texto "Albert Schweitzer por ele mesmo", publicado pela Martin Claret Ltda., São Paulo, 1995, p. 29, entre outros.
5. dos Santos, Leontino Farias, In "Dicionário Brasileiro de Teologia," ASTE, 2008, p.182.
6. de Sant'Ana, Antonio Olímpio, "Racismo" in Dicionário Brasileiro de Teologia, São Paulo: ASTE, 2008, p. 845.
7. Carneiro, Maria Luiza Tucci, "O Racismo na História do Brasil", São Paulo: Ática, 1994, p.11.
8. da Silva, O Padre Antonio Aparecido, também conhecido como Padre Toninho, é Mestre em Teologia Moral pela Pontifícia Universidade Alfonsiana de Roma; Mestre em Filosofia-PUC/SP; Sócio Fundador da Sociedade Brasileira de Teologia (SOTER) e do Grupo ATABAQUE.
9. de Sant'Ana, Antonio Olimpio, Dicionário Brasileiro de Teologia, 2008, p. 845
10. Boff, Leonardo e Clodovis, Da Libertação — o teológico das libertações sócio-históricas. Petrópolis: Vozes, 1980.

A TEOLOGIA NEGRA NO BRASIL É DECOLONIAL E MARGINAL

Ronilso Pacheco

O lugar do Êxodo

Êxodo sempre foi uma referência importante para a Teologia da Libertação. A história do povo hebreu explorado e martirizado no Egito, tornou-se o ponto de partida, a hermenêutica por excelência de teólogos que queriam um compromisso, na América Latina, com a libertação do continente das explorações modernizadas do capitalismo; explorando trabalho, criatividade, terra, produção, natureza, tudo pondo o lucro e a manutenção do poder no lugar central. Aí vem a compreensão de comparação com o Êxodo. Mas o Êxodo deixa de ser a compreensão de uma narrativa que fala de um deslocamento, uma travessia de um ponto a outro. É preciso chamar a atenção para o que constituía o período de servidão no Egito, o que aquela exploração lá lembra nossa condição aqui.

A Teologia Negra é incluída como uma das "teologias da libertação". O nome passou a ser usado no plural porque o que era unicamente a chamada Teologia da Libertação, abriu caminhos para uma pluralidade de perspectivas teológicas, que vieram reivindicar lugar e vozes emancipadas. Para a Teologia Negra, que surge nos Estados Unidos na década de 60, o lugar do Êxodo é central também pela condição de oprimidos, de exploração, mas um agravante a marca: a ênfase no racismo e na escravidão. Não estamos falando só de povo cujo trabalho e força de trabalho é explorada. Estamos falando de escravidão, e tudo que isso pode significar em países como Estados Unidos, Haiti, Colômbia e, evidentemente, Brasil.

A Teologia Negra é ainda incipiente no Brasil, mas vai mostrando sua necessidade e lugar, revisitando, a partir de novos esforços de uma pequena nova geração de teólogos, as reflexões postas por James Cone, Jacquelyn Grant, Cornell West, Gayraud Wilmore, Allan Boesak, Desmond Tutu (os dois últimos no contexto sul-africano), entre outros e outras. As reflexões de muitos destes teólogos que foram pensadas aqui por gente como Peter Nash e Nancy Cardoso, começa agora a ser retomada, aos poucos, com novos rostos que, mais presentes em um contexto de ação política, prática de rua, envolto em sublevações de resistências em defesa da vida e da dignidade de negros e negras no contexto de violência e racismo do Brasil, vão apontando a contribuição da Teologia Negra para problematizar as diversas desigualdades no país em tratos com corpos e territórios. Aqui o Êxodo segue sendo ponto de partida, entre outras coisas, porque o grito do povo preto, dos jovens negros, das mulheres negras, seguem sendo gritos de dor e de silenciamento.

Também porque o período de servidão do povo hebreu na terra do Egito e narrada no Êxodo, não deve ser pensado mais como uma história romântica de heroísmo e onde Deus é protagonista operando milagres, sinais e prodígios. Antes, deve ser pensado no contexto das dores e violações que estão presentes na condição de um escravo, ou da vida do que é tornado escravo em território colonizado. Isto significa que o contexto histórico do povo hebreu no Egito guarda semelhanças com o processo de colonização empreendido pela Europa que também chega ao Brasil. No território colonizado, como o Brasil se tornara começa sua história, homens e mulheres são assassinados cotidianamente, mulheres violentadas, corpos negros chicoteados, torturados, desaparecidos, subjugados. O silêncio mantido sob o peso da violência e do medo, nunca sem a investidura religiosa cristã. Como bem descreve Riolando Azzi:

> Embora as populações negras já vivessem na África num estágio de maior desenvolvimento, gerado pela vida sedentária e pela prática da agricultura, a redução à situação de escravos na colônia brasileira havia diminuído em muitos deles a capacidade de resistência e de luta pela dignidade da vida. Poucos horizontes se abriam para pessoas que se viam tratadas como animais expostos ao mercado, e

como "peças" na grande engrenagem do engenho. Para elas o trabalho perdia o seu valor, pelo caráter impositivo e forçado, sendo considerado como castigo injusto, ou, numa perspectiva mais católica, como uma forma de expiação do pecado.[1]

É neste sentido então que uma hermenêutica negra passaria necessariamente pelo Êxodo. Na identificação com uma narrativa que começa no território de subjugação, captura, opressão e a construção de uma mentalidade, e as várias formas de resistência, surge um outro horizonte hermenêutico, que fomenta outras narrativas e olha para outro lugar e pensa a partir de outro lugar.

No Egito, Faraó faz uso de seu poder. Faz uso da sua governamentalidade. O povo hebreu se tornou uma ameaça. Se continuassem a crescer, o temor do governante era que eles ameaçassem o seu poder, subvertessem a ordem e, se delinquentes fossem, o pânico tomaria conta da sociedade egípcia. Evidentemente havia alternativas. Eles poderiam ser integrados à sociedade, não como escravos, não à margem, não desde cedo confinados nos territórios de contenção e cerceados pelo controle social, mas sim como sujeitos com um leque de oportunidades muito mais amplas. Poderiam ainda assim transgredir, é verdade, mas não seria uma possibilidade muito distinta dos jovens legitimamente egípcios. Mas era trabalho demais.

Então a solução de Faraó foi reduzir a maioridade penal a zero — a primeira idade "penal" era a idade em que um hebreu, escravo, já tinha forças para trabalhar pesado. Nasceu menino, deve morrer. Não valia correr o risco de ter uma criança que, ao crescer, tinha no horizonte a possibilidade de ameaçar a segurança dos egípcios, matando, quem sabe, por ódio de sua condição escrava. Mas duas parteiras se constrangeram quanto ao decreto de Faraó. O decreto contrariava o próprio ofício delas, que era a defesa da vida, aquelas que davam as boas-vindas aos nascidos, aquelas que ouviam de perto o choro, o grito, o misto de dor física e alegria da alma das mães. Sefra e Puá, num livro em que mulheres e personagens subalternos são, em grande parte, anônimos, têm nome e têm rosto. Subverteram uma ordem e inspiram uma consciência de resistência e luta pela liberdade e a vida, que culmina no êxodo.

É possível então pensar o êxodo não apenas como uma saída, mas também como um resgate, uma condução do povo que sai do local da centralidade do poder de um império para às margens. O êxodo vem a ser então, antes de tudo, uma figura para as margens. Deus o poder simbólico do império do seu potencial coercitivo, controlador e explorador das gentes, ao fazê-los sair em direção à periferia. Portanto aqui é mais que uma geografia, o episódio retratado no Êxodo também é uma espécie de locus enunciativo, pois a saída, a fuga resistente dos lugares sob controle e intervenção da opressão do império, é condição necessária para a construção de novas alternativas e possibilidades de vislumbrar liberdade e autonomia.

Aqui o Êxodo bíblico e as comunidades quilombolas se encontram. No contexto da luta e da resistência do povo negro no Brasil, os quilombos[2] foram "a terra prometida" cujo simbolismo teve a força de mover negros e negras para fora do lugar de controle e opressão do "império" colonial de Portugal. A fuga para os quilombos, território de esperança de uma vivência livre, autônoma e comunitária, não foi uma travessia sem dor, artimanhas, conflitos e perdas pelo caminho. Não foi uma travessia sem traições e investidas constantes de sabotagem (de dentro e de fora), mas foi o movimento que instigou a liberdade possível, o levante, o movimento de desencaixe da opressão do centro, para a reconstrução a partir da margem.

Tem portanto Êxodo a sua forte narrativa de trajetória no deserto em que, por ser deserto, tudo deve ser repensado, ressignificado, reposto, criado coletivamente, e onde a distribuição diária do maná que caía do céu é a metáfora perfeita de crítica a não acumulação e ao mesmo tempo o fomento da partilha em igualdade. Essa partilha que une na resistência, que sente a mesma dor foi fundamental para o povo negro sobreviver enquanto povo à exploração e às execuções que aconteceram no regime escravocrata.

A *Multidão* que se refugia em Jesus, nova fuga à margem

Outra narrativa que se torna modelo importante para pautar uma Teologia Negra é aquela que vem inspirada no episódio famoso pela multiplicação dos pães e dos peixes, em Marcos capítulo 6. E aqui é inspirador por pelo menos três momentos:

O primeiro é a morte de João Batista, assassinado a pedido do imperador. Aqui é emblemático por João Batista morrer por um motivo "banal", uma gratuita demonstração de força e violência do império contra um sujeito que denunciava, que era um errante periférico, corpo independente da gestão do império. A morte de João Batista vem problematizar também essa capacidade que o poder tem de decidir sobre a vida e sobre a morte. Essa mentalidade típica do poder colonial, um corpo negro sabe bem o que é isso. No Brasil, o corpo de João Batista poderia muito bem ser substituído pelo corpo do pedreiro Amarildo.[3] Poderia ser substituído por lideranças negras camponesas que afrontam "colonos" latifundiários. A morte de João Batista causa frustração, medo, desânimo. É a ameaça desse poder homicida e torturador que também afugenta a população negra periférica. Aqui é o momento do desamparo.

O segundo momento é a retirada de Jesus com os discípulos e a multidão, que os seguiam, para um lugar retirado, afastado (volta novamente a perspectiva da fuga, do êxodo). Com Jesus, uma multidão composta de homens desamparados, mulheres desamparadas, uma fuga e retirada de uma multidão de invisíveis, sem muitas esperanças cercados e pressionados por um império opressor. Aqui, uma nova saída da centralidade do império e de onde ele mantém o seu poder, para a construção de outras possibilidades de vivência e experiências de resistência a partir das margens. Diante da multidão sem muito rumo, os discípulos sugerem a Jesus que dispense a multidão para que possam buscar comida, se alimentarem e voltarem depois. Mas a proposta é rechaçada por Jesus, com uma frase simples: "dêem vocês mesmo a eles de comer". Em outras palavras: não forcem a multidão a voltar à dependência do controle do império que condiciona o acesso à comida à exploração do trabalho, impostos absurdos e obediência silenciosa. O enfrentamento e a superação do poder colonizador passa necessariamente pela resistência comum, a capacidade desagregadora das investidas do poder colonial, uma espécie de "sujeito coletivo" não dado à fragmentação. Este é o momento do fortalecimento da comunidade, e este é o momento em que este episódio lembra muito da estratégia quilombista de resistência do povo negro.

Como terceiro momento a ser destacado, o episódio então da multiplicação dos cinco pães e dos dois peixes que são apresentados a Jesus como os únicos alimentos existentes na comunidade para serem consumidos. Mas, mais do que a sua literalidade de ter alimentado ou não cerca de cinco mil pessoas, torna-se a grande metáfora da potência criadora e inovadora da multidão que é capaz de surpreender o império. Surpreender o império, a colônia, o Estado, o senhor e seu engenho e as muitas formas institucionalizadas ou não de reprimir a coletividade. O milagre da multiplicação é o inesperado, que pode ser a luta, a comunhão que sustenta os rebeldes na luta, mas também pode ser a subversão de hermenêuticas dadas, prontas, sustentadoras do status quo. Na multiplicação de pequenos peixes hermenêuticos, a Teologia Negra alimentou negros e negras famintos, famintas, confundiu e confrontou hermenêuticas engessadas, históricas e hegemônicas. Ou, citando Peter Nash:

> Ao falar de um tipo europeu de pensar teologicamente, é claro que se está falando de um estereótipo, porém, estereótipos tem frequentemente as suas origens em alguma forma de realidade. Poucos e poucas de nós, no lado ocidental do Atlântico, tem lido as obras de todos os teólogos europeus, mas aqueles/as, cujas obras são disseminadas nas Américas, acreditam e ensinam que há um absoluto desincorporado ou uma verdade universal independente das experiências diárias. Teologias pós-coloniais, em geral, se opõem a esta rejeição de dados teológicos humanos.[4]

Teologia Negra e Decolonialidade

Aqui podemos iniciar um diálogo com uma proposta (ou seja, não dada como definitiva e estabelecida) da Teologia Negra como uma teologia decolonial. Seguindo a definição de Ramón Grosfoguel,[5] a decolonialidade potencializa não apenas a pura reflexão, mas a resposta epistêmica dos subalternos ao projeto eurocêntrico-estadunidense, hegemônico, seja na teologia, na política, seja nas relações sociais e formas de presença no mundo, mas que, sempre, se encontram na fronteira (nas margens). Na perspectiva do projeto decolonial, as fronteiras não são somente um espaço onde as diferenças são inventadas, são também lócus enunciativo de onde são formulados conhecimentos a partir das perspectivas, cosmovisões ou experiências dos sujeitos subalternos.

Mas essa "resposta epistêmica", esse "lócus enunciativo", esses "conhecimentos formulados" não devem ser entendidos a partir da viciante apreensão acadêmica. Tudo isto está presente nas margens, nas periferias, nos territórios cotidianamente oprimidos e silenciados, em cidades como o Rio de Janeiro e São Paulo. Este conhecimento é formulado, por exemplo, a partir da resistência das mães, quase todas negras, cujos filhos foram vítimas da violência do Estado. Aqui, o lócus enunciativo se torna a dor. É a dor territorializada, do lugar de quem fala a partir da perda, do enfrentamento, da saudade que é força, da memória que é fé e perseverança.

Tive a oportunidade de acompanhar algumas mães vítimas de violência no Rio de Janeiro, e reproduzo aqui um dos relatos ouvido em uma roda de conversas de um grupo de defesa de direitos humanos e uma rede de mães vítimas de violência:

> Todos os dias eu penso que se eu morasse por perto da ponte Rio-Niterói, eu já teria me jogado de lá, pra acabar com esse sofrimento. Desde que o Estado tirou a vida do meu filho, minha vida em casa, com meu marido, é um inferno. Apenas no meio de vocês, em atos, manifestações e encontros como esses, eu tenho um pouco de felicidade.

Chega a ser constrangedor, para quem ouve constantemente os relatos delas e acompanha a luta, ter de ouvi-la repetir as mesmas histórias de perda, nos diversos encontros em que participam, que também parece ter o efeito de um ciclo que parece não ter fim. A gente ouve, se indigna, chora — eu chorei em uns dois ou três relatos — e se sente habitando um inferno materializado ao nosso redor. Então chega a ser constrangedor ter de ouvi-las falar mais uma vez sobre a morte de seus filhos. Dos tiros que atravessaram a cabeça; da tortura com o saco e o afogamento; da humilhação antes de morrer, e o corpo ignorado; da cena do crime violada e forjada para simular um confronto; da acusação precipitada pela sociedade de "bandidinhos" e "envolvidos com o tráfico"; do funeral decente negado; da recusa de socorro. Cada vez que essas mães narram o que aconteceu, elas morrem um pouco. Mas a ressurreição delas vem cada vez que a memória dos seus filhos clama por justiça.

Quando o braço armado do Estado mata um, a gente não faz noção de quantos mortos (vivos sem vida) ele deixou em volta. E cada vítima da "guerra às drogas" nunca é apenas "uma" vítima. Jovens pretos da favela. Jovens policiais pretos residentes nas mesmas favelas. O Estado mata onde, quando e como quer, sem sujar as mãos, já que usa as mãos (e os rostos) de outros para apertar o gatilho e bradar enquanto atira. O choro de cada mãe na violência genocida que consome a juventude nas periferias brasileiras é gerado a partir do Estado. Quem vai parar o Estado? Com essas mulheres, a academia precisa aprender a ser afetada, para além da sua racionalidade instrumental, dos dados, dos Power Points bem elaborados, dos conceitos bem explorados e interpretados. Com elas, as igrejas precisam aprender a ter fé, perseverança e indignação, mediante um ambiente alienador que não aproxima os seus membros do mundo real, precisam chorar, sentindo a mesma dor. Com cada uma dessas mães, as ONGs precisam aprender a não se acomodarem, a não serem pautadas pelo Estado, mas pautá-lo, exigir dele, enfrentá-lo. Com elas, todos nós precisamos aprender a ser solidários, menos ideológicos, mais subversivos, mais firmes, e pelo amor e pela justiça, termos a coragem de olhar nos olhos do Estado — com seu racismo fundante — e dizer a ele, com a força de uma mãe: "Nós vamos te derrubar". É a mesma reação das parteiras hebreias. É a mesma reação das mães negras escravizadas ou inseridas numa sociedade racista, que protege filhos e filhas da dor, e prepara para a dor, para a hostilidade que vêm.

A Teologia Negra no Brasil, embora não tenha prosperado contemporaneamente ao que prosperou e influenciou nos Estados Unidos e África do Sul, por exemplo, está sim inserida num conjunto de "reações" com novas leituras feitas a partir das margens. Ela está junto de outras narrativas que estão a disputar a libertação das subjetividades vigiadas e condicionadas. Na perspectiva decolonial de Grosfoguel, tudo deve ser provincializado, ou seja, perder esta centralidade que empurra para o controle totalitário, para a homogeneidade sufocante e repressora. Eu usaria também aqui, mais próximo de nós, latino-americanos, tudo deve ser *periferizado*, tornado periférico, sem lugar ao centro, aliás, crítico da centralidade, da hierarquização dos lugares de poder e suas formas de acesso. A Teologia Negra está nesta disputa narrativa, consciente de que uma hermenêutica hegemônica, "do centro", vai sempre lhe exigir veracidade, legitimidade, ou, em outras palavras, "explicações". Mas responderia serena, como James Cone:

> É óbvio que, pelo fato de os teólogos brancos não terem sido escravizados nem linchados e de não terem sido colocados em guetos por causa da cor, eles não pensam que a cor seja um importante ponto de partida para o discurso teológico.[6]

Conclusão

Gostaria de concluir propondo então um convite para um esforço, nada novo, talvez semelhante ao que Rudolf Bultmann definiu como a *"desmitologização"*. Provocado então pela Teologia Negra, inspiro-me a desmitologizar os muitos mitos que temos e construímos numa sociedade de "funcionamento colonial", centralizadora, totalitária, de pensamentos hegemônicos, que pautam nosso cotidiano.

Desmitologizar a segurança pública, e sua áurea de defensora de "manutenção da ordem". Os programas de segurança pública, no Brasil em particular, são a continuidade da perspectiva do controle e da intimidação dos corpos negros e pobres, do cerceamento e do confinamento em territórios precários e igualmente criminalizados. Devemos: Desmitologizar a grande mídia e sua construção e manutenção de estigmas contra a juventude negra pobre favelada. Desmitologizar as eleições, que seguem sendo a única forma de participação popular, que, em seu nome, restringe, bloqueia e neutraliza toda outra forma de participação popular. Desmitologizar a esquerda, quando revestida de purismo intelectual, pautadora da organização e dos rumos dos oprimidos que pretende defender sem se permitir afetar por suas narrativas. Desmitologizar a Justiça e como ela é usada em defesa dos interesses de quem concentra o poder, de quem se aproxima da centralidade e é instrumento de opressão e controle dos que estão à margem, uma permanente judicialização da vida. Desmitologizar a primazia da economia, que torna todo sujeito ou um produto, ou um consumidor, ou inválido, descartável, ou produtivo, necessário, a primazia do tecnicismo produtivista, a seletividade das vidas que importam (daí a necessidade de movimentos como *Black Lives Matter*).

Notas

1. AZZI, Riolando. A Cristandade colonial: mito e ideologia. Rio de Janeiro, Vozes, 1987, pág. 111.
2. No Brasil, Quilombo é o nome dado aos locais de refúgio dos escravos fugidos de engenhos e fazenda dos senhores durante o período colonial e imperial. Nos quilombos os escravos experimentavam uma vivência em liberdade e de práticas comunitárias. No Brasil, o quilombo mais famoso foi o de Palmares, localizado e preservado ainda hoje no Estado de Alagoas, região nordeste do Brasil. Palmares teve o seu auge na segunda metade do século XVII, resistiu por mais de um século e sua figura mais lendária é o negro Zumbi.
3. O conhecido "caso Amarildo" é a história do homem, negro, Amarildo, morador da Favela da Rocinha, uma das maiores favelas do Rio de Janeiro, que, em 2013, foi abordado por policiais na frente de sua mulher, foi levado pelos policiais e nunca mais apareceu. As investigações apontaram para uma morte e desaparecimento do pedreiro após tortura dos policiais, que acreditavam que ele fazia parte do, ou tinha informações sobre, o tráfico de drogas na favela. A frase "cadê o Amarildo?" ganhou repercussão internacional e foi uma das

mais reproduzidas durante o famoso "Junho de 2013", quando uma série de manifestações gigantescas tomaram conta do país inteiro.
4. NASH, Peter. Relendo raça, bíblia e religião. São Leopoldo-RS, Cebi, 2005, pág. 33.
5. GROSFOGUEL, Ramón; BERNARDINO-COSTA, Joaze. Decolonialidade e perspectiva negra. In: Revista Sociedade e Estado — Volume 31, número 1 Janeiro/Abril 2016. Pág. 15-24.
6. CONE, James. O Deus dos oprimidos. São Paulo, Paulinas, 1985, pág. 64.

Referências bibliográficas

Azzi, Riolando, 1987. A Cristandade colonial: mito e ideologia. Rio de Janeiro: Vozes.

Cone, James, 1985. O Deus dos oprimidos. São Paulo: Paulinas.

Grosfoguel, Ramón, and Bernardino-Costa, Joaze, 2016. Decolonialidade e Perspectiva Negra, in Revista Sociedade e Estado, vol. 31.

Nash, Peter, 2005. Relendo raça, bíblia e religião. São Leopoldo-RS: CEBI.

CROSSCURRENTS
SER AGENTE DE PASTORAL NEGROS NO CONTEXTO DA REALIDADE BRASILEIRA

José Geraldo da Rocha and Cristina da Conceição Silva

A nossa pertença aos Agentes de Pastoral Negros significou criar um canal de conexão conosco mesmos e com nossas histórias da fé ancestral. Os APNs, na caminhada eclesial, gestaram um espaço privilegiado de crescimento na fé e na negritude, propiciado por pessoas envolvidas no processo de transformação do mundo, tendo como base os elementos constitutivos da Justiça. A consciência negra opera nesse espaço, como elemento fundamental no fortalecimento das lutas contra o racismo, embora seja enorme o desafio da sua construção no Brasil. A história dos APNs nos tem ensinado que as conquistas da negritude necessitam ser alimentadas a cada dia, considerando sempre os diversificados contextos sociais e políticos. Ser APNs encerra um compromisso cotidiano com as implicações da fé em um Deus dos pobres com seu rosto negro, cujos espaços de manifestação estão também associados aos terreiros. O comprometimento com os valores das africanidades descobertos nos terreiros vai impulsionar um novo modo de estar no mundo, um novo jeito de lutar pela justiça do Reino.

Introdução
Ao pensarmos sobre o convite e desafio propostos pela Associação Ecumênica de Teólogos e Teólogas do Terceiro Mundo (ASETT) (EATWOT— Ecumenical Association of Third World Theologians), a primeira coisa que nos veio na mente foi um dos cantos que embalou e alimentou a caminhada dos Agentes de Pastoral Negros. "Eu sou negro sim, Como Deus criou. Sei lutar pela vida cantar liberdade e gostar dessa cor."[1]

Neste canto, cujo autor é desconhecido, o primeiro dado trata-se da afirmação da negritude. Tal realidade era muito difícil em função do racismo e da associação da cor negra com tudo o que de mais feio e ruim possa existir. Daí a consciência negra eclodir como um clamor de justiça. E com ela a certeza de que somos filhos de Deus, pois somos criados por Ele desse jeito, com nossa cor negra. E a partir dessa realidade que se engendrará a luta pela vida, pela liberdade, sem negar a cor.

No intuito de responder ao desafio proposto, o presente texto foi elaborado em três seções. Na primeira são elucidadas as dificuldades encontradas pelos Agentes de Pastoral Negros no Brasil no início de sua caminhada em virtude do racismo e dos preconceitos em relação a tudo o que pertence aos negros. A segunda seção aborda um pouco da história da entidade e seu processo de organização sublinhando a relevância da Teologia da Libertação no fomento da esperança dos pobres e consequentemente dos negros. Por fim, a terceira seção apresentamos uma panorâmica da situação atual dos Agentes de Pastoral Negros e a relevância da atuação dessa organização no processo de combate ao racismo, à discriminação e à intolerância religiosa. Caracterizamos assim o sentido de ser APNs na atualidade.

É preciso consciência

O subtítulo sugere que, as primeiras constatações no presente texto, necessário dizer, são: não é fácil ser negro no Brasil, não é fácil ser negro nas Américas, e não é fácil ser negro na diáspora. Talvez não seja fácil ser negro em lugar nenhum no mundo. Portanto, a nossa proposição nos impõe pensar as dificuldades da afirmação como negros na sociedade brasileira, e não apenas negros, mas negros agentes de pastoral em um contexto eclesial onde o cristianismo, envolto no manto da cultura eurocêntrica, supravalorizou uma concepção de Deus, que relegou a segundo plano as demais concepções de Deus presentes nas diferentes culturas, e de modo particular, nas culturas de matrizes africanas. Então ser Agente de Pastoral Negro, no contexto da realidade brasileira, é uma questão de afirmação de identidade. Tal identidade é marcada pela fé atuando como elemento norteador da ação contra o racismo e em prol da promoção da igualdade racial. Ser agente de pastoral negro nesse contexto, demanda o aguçamento ou a sublevação da consciência, que segundo Ardunini pode ser assim compreendida.

Consciência é saber que se sabe. É autoreconhecer-se. Há seres humanos que sabem que são seres humanos. E há os que não sabem explicitamente que são seres humanos. O que faz a diferença é a consciência. (...) sem a consciência, os seres humanos se nivelam às coisas. São trocáveis como objetos. (Ardunini 2002:84)

A consciência propicia a passagem de objeto a sujeito da história. Os negros atuando na história como sujeitos e não mais como simples objetos é resultante do aprimoramento da consciência trabalhada nos grupos de negros. Essa consciência negra adquirida pelos agentes de pastoral negros tornou-se um grande incômodo na vida eclesial. O tornar-se sujeito da história, coisa que a consciência negra nos tem ensinado, nos faz nos posicionarmos de modo diferenciado diante das situações de racismo e discriminação existentes nas igrejas e nas práticas cotidianas da sociedade brasileira.

Nosso Deus é um Deus que faz História conosco. É a certeza da presença de um Deus próximo, caminhando de mãos dadas conosco que nos alenta no dia a dia em meio às adversidades vividas pela comunidade negra no Brasil e nas Américas. A situação de racismo e de discriminação são atentados à dignidade humana que afrontam a magnitude do Deus que se expressa nas feições dos negros na diáspora. O clamor que nasce do chão da comunidade negra ecoa como um grande gemido do espírito. O significado de ser APNs encontra nessa realidade acolhimento das aspirações humanas mais profundas. Isso fortalece a luta, pois a certeza de que tal qual em Êxodo, Deus ouve o clamor dos negros. Assim sendo, como sujeitos da história, os APNs passam a se autocompreenderem como um povo que tem uma missão, cujo significado contem e expressa a beleza e a riqueza da negritude manifesta na identidade negra. A negritude passa a ser compreendida como um dom de Deus.

> Esta descoberta da negritude como dom recebido de Deus despertou os Agentes de Pastoral Negros para a necessidade de colocá-la à serviço da causa do Reino entre os empobrecidos. Os valores que brotam da negritude são frutos da bondade divina e ninguém recebe um talento para si mesmo e sim para servir à causa do Reino de Deus através da comunidade. Agir na perspectiva da negritude como dom é agir movido pelo Espírito Santo de Deus. (Rocha 1998: 156)

E como dom, a negritude, deve estar à serviço da coletividade da comunidade negra. Afirmamos assim que a "apeenidade" é uma dimensão profética da negritude. Ser APNs no contexto atual da sociedade brasileira é enfrentar com coragem os desafios para a concretização da justiça de Deus em meio aos pobres, e em particular em meio à comunidade negra, envidando todos os esforços para suplantar a discriminação, o racismo e todas as formas correlatas de intolerâncias.

Retalhos de nossa história

Um pouco da história nos ajudará compreender o sentido e o significado dos APNs na sociedade brasileira. A história dos Agentes de Pastoral Negros nasce no início da década de 1980. Sua inspiração máxima se fundamentava na fé que tinham os negros atuantes nas igrejas e movimentos sociais, realidade nem sempre considerada no conjunto das lutas sociais do movimento negro. Era a maioria desses negros pessoas atuantes nas Comunidades Eclesiais de Base, lugar privilegiado de articulação da vida e esperança dos pobres na América Latina, fundamentadas e sustentadas pela Teologia da Libertação.

Os APNs, são inicialmente, aprendizes da Teologia da Libertação. Ela nos ensinou a despertar para os direitos e para os desafios que a nossa fé colocava no contexto socioeclesial. A partir daí desencadeiam-se muitas descobertas importantes, dentre elas a grande riqueza presente no universo das comunidades negras. A descoberta das riquezas da negritude foi algo que desencadeou um grande crescimento na entidade Agentes de Pastoral Negros. Essa realidade demandou uma organização meticulosa em grupos de base, comissões estaduais, comissões regionais e comissão nacional, além da eleição de uma diretoria para responder institucionalmente pela organização. Foi o tempo da descoberta da "boa nova da negritude", que passava pelo negro é bonito e negro tem valor. Foi um tempo de enegrecimento da fé e da igreja.

Inicialmente a condução desse processo de reflexões e organização esteve mais ao zelo dos padres negros. A fé e a negritude, o lugar e o papel do negro nas igrejas, sempre estiveram presentes nas discussões iniciais da entidade. O crescimento da organização demandou encontrar formas de responder às demandas em caráter nacional. Daí a necessidade de constituir uma coordenação nacional, uma diretoria, que inicialmente ficou muito vinculada aos religiosos negros, sendo inclusive eleito Padre Toninho, para ser o presidente da organização Agentes de Pastoral

Negros. Dado a pertença religiosa dos padres presentes na coordenação da entidade, e seus vínculos com as suas Congregações Religiosas, as dificuldades na obtenção de recursos para tocar a entidade eram minoradas, pois as congregações religiosas bem como as relações estabelecidas pelos padres negros influenciava tal tarefa. Os APNs se estruturaram nos grandes quilombos regionais como forma de avivar a fé e a negritude nas comunidades e grupos negros. Esse foram os nossos espaços de educação e formação para a negritude.

Os tempos foram mudando, as compreensões acerca da entidade também, o papel dos leigos na entidade foi tomando cada dia mais impulso e com isso pessoas, que não padres, assumiram a presidência dos Agentes de Pastoral Negros. Alguns padres negros com isso se retraíram e sem eles, de certo modo, algumas fontes de recurso também se retraíram. Isso demandou novos tempos para a instituição. Os grandes encontros que nos primeiros anos aconteciam sistematicamente, tornaram-se pesados economicamente, uma vez que nossa gente não gozava, e nem goza até os dias atuais, de recursos disponíveis para a sustentação da entidade. Inúmeras tentativas de modificações no modo organizacional da entidade têm sido buscadas no intuito de minorar os custos. Entretanto a tão sonhada sustentabilidade, todavia se nos apresenta como um desafio longe de ser resolvido. Essa dificuldade associada a tantas outras acabaram influenciando na organização dos grupos de base da entidade.

Uma panorâmica atual dos APNs
Na atualidade os Agentes de Pastoral Negros encontram-se organizados em 14 Estados da federação. O contexto das políticas de ação afirmativa implementadas no Brasil a partir de 2003 fez com que muitos atores sociais das lutas antirracismo galgassem maior notoriedade e reconhecimento, e assim o foi também com os APNs. Atualmente a atuação dos APNs se faz notar em diversificados contextos das lutas sociais na sociedade brasileira. Entretanto, nos últimos anos é perceptível a retração das conquistas e as dificuldades de navegabilidades políticas onde os interesses da comunidade negra apareçam como algo relevante na política nacional.

Essa nova conjuntura nos insta à reflexão. São fatores como a mudança no cenário eclesial, mas também mudanças de cenário político no país. Muitas questões básicas pelas quais os negros lutavam, acabaram sendo incorporadas nas demandas sociais das políticas implementadas pelo Estado. O ingresso de muitos de nós no mercado de trabalho modificou sensivelmente nosso tempo de militância. Não se pode negar que isso é bom, entretanto esse novo quadro fez com que muita gente já não mais se reunisse para discutir a necessidade da água encanada, pois já têm. Os que buscavam conquista da luz elétrica, do asfalto, do emprego, do saneamento entre outras, também já conseguiram. Ademais algumas pessoas do nosso meio acabaram assumindo cargos nos poderes executivo, legislativo, ou mesmo na iniciativa privada, gerando uma cisão com a organicidade dos APNs. Paralelo a isso, muitos de nós nascemos para a luta nas comunidades eclesiais de base sustentadas pela Teologia da Libertação. Essa prática eclesial foi detonada pelo conservadorismo da igreja, dado que desestimulou muitos negros a discutir direitos nos grupos eclesiais. Por fim, nos dias atuais os grupos de base quase que se extinguiram em muitos lugares. O esfacelamento dos movimentos sociais atingiu também os APNs. A consciência de APNs permaneceu nos indivíduos, pois uma vez APNs, sempre APNs, mas a dinamicidade requerida no fortalecimento da luta já não se dá nos moldes dos tempos iniciais.

Em função desse novo tempo, a entidade demanda encontrar novos modos de se organizar. Talvez não seja mais pensando em organização de "massa", mas quem sabe em um modo de manter acesa a chama dos indivíduos nos seus espaços de atuação na luta de combate ao racismo, à intolerância religiosa, à discriminação e a promoção da igualdade racial no país, considerando como elementos balizadores da luta a nossa fé e nossa ancestralidade. Cabe aqui considerar que o fio condutor da luta dos APNS sempre foi constituído de um pensar que, nossa atuação enquanto negros deve ser em todos os espaços em que atuamos cotidianamente. Isso inclusive foi tema de grandes debates na entidade por ocasião da fundação da pastoral negra na igreja, cuja concepção delega um espaço particular para trabalhar a negritude segmentadamente, não comportada na concepção dos APNs. Ora, se existem APNs na Pastoral da Terra, na Catequese, na Pastoral Operária, nas Filhas de Maria, nas Cebs e em tantos outros lugares na igreja, bem como nos Terreiros, nas escolas, nas universidades, nos órgãos públicos etc., não poderia ser em forma de gueto o modo mais adequado de pensar a ação e intervenção dos APNs.

As marcas de uma fé ancestral, cada vez mais se tornam uma realidade na cotidianidade dos grupos negros no Brasil. O Deus da Vida se revela e se expressa por meio das práticas e vivências religiosas nas culturas afro-brasileiras, cujo lugar privilegiado de manifestação é o terreiro. O reconhecimento dos terreiros como espaço de manifestação de Deus, agregou à prática dos APNs novos significados da luta de combate ao racismo e à discriminação no Brasil.

Por muitos séculos a ação eclesial foi pautada na necessidade de evangelizar os negros. A caminhada dos APNs, no entanto, tem demonstrado que os negros são os verdadeiros evangelizadores nas igrejas. Deus já está no meio dos negros. As vivências nos grupos de agentes de pastoral negros nessas décadas têm sido testemunhos evidentes da presença do Deus da vida fazendo história conosco. Os sinais da presença desse Deus podem ser percebidos por todos aqueles que conseguem desvencilhar dos preconceitos étnicos, culturais, religiosos e sociais e se colocam abertos à ação do Espírito, que capacita a cada um a compreender e discernir o que fala o outro, em sua própria língua.

A caminhada dos Agentes de Pastoral Negros tem significado um avanço das lutas antirracistas, propiciando aos negros, fundamentalmente, um mergulho para dentro de si mesmos, tomando para si a história. Com ela a consciência da pertença afroétnica, que encerra tradição cultural ancestral, do ponto de vista histórico, cultural e religioso; e consequentemente a qualificação dos diferenciados olhares sobre os negros nas suas relações na sociedade brasileira.

O cristianismo na América Latina, e particularmente no Brasil, vive um certo desconforto em relação às comunidades afro-brasileiras, principalmente no tocante ao modo como, historicamente, tem se relacionado com as matrizes religiosas africanas. Segundo a compreensão de Hoonraert o modo como as religiões cristãs têm se relacionado com a comunidade negra no Brasil caracteriza-se como um sistemático processo de violência institucionalizada. Desde o primeiro "gesto religioso" do catolicismo ao batizar os negros que chegavam nos portos brasileiros para serem escravizados no período colonial (Hoonaert 1978, 1983), até os dias atuais com as mais diversificadas formas de intolerância religiosa, os negros têm sido desrespeitados em suas religiosidades e diminuídos em sua dignidade humana.

O projeto político do Estado brasileiro, associado à religião, não mediu esforços para implementar o sistema de escravidão, uma das mais abomináveis práticas de violência que a humanidade tem notícia. O regime escravocrata, enquanto sistema político, lançou mão de métodos e práticas violentos para submeter e subjugar os negros aos trabalhos forçados. Nesse processo de subjugação dos negros imposto pelo sistema político as expressões religiosas vinculadas às tradições africanas foram vistas e tratadas como afronta aos interesses do branco colonizador, uma vez que funcionavam como elemento de fortalecimento físico e espiritual dos negros escravizados.

O modo como os negros vivenciavam suas religiões no período colonial, significava uma ameaça ao sistema vigente, razão pela qual se entendia como uma necessidade a sua perseguição, o seu combate e o seu extermínio. Autores como Hoonaert (1978) entendem estar aí a fundamentação ideológica que fez com que nunca houvesse propriamente missão na América Latina e sim conquista, e implantação da estrutura da religião dominante. Nesse contexto socioeclesial a ação dos APNs, que desde dentro das igrejas cristãs elaboram duras críticas ao comportamento racista e discriminatório das igrejas, vão explicitar e acirrar conflitos. Por outro lado, o reconhecimento dos valores da negritude presentes nos terreiros acaba levando agentes de pastoral negros a participar efetivo e afetivamente nas religiões de matrizes africanas.

O significado da presença e vivências de muitos APNs nesses espaços têm contribuído substancialmente para a abertura de novas possibilidades de diálogos. Agora não mais como evangelizadores, mas sim como herdeiros e partícipes de uma tradição ancestral dessas africanidades. Essa compreensão impulsiona uma nova mística, onde os valores religiosos das africanidades atuam como elementos de fortalecimento da luta. A fé ancestral, tantas vezes negada e silenciada na história do país, e preservada com zelo africano nos terreiros, passa a ser assumida, pelos APNs, como uma dimensão da sua própria existência enquanto negros e negras.

O comprometimento com os valores das africanidades descobertos nos terreiros vai impulsionar um novo modo de estar no mundo, um novo jeito de lutar pela justiça do Reino. Nasce uma fé enegrecida e consequentemente novas implicações pastorais, eclesiológicas e teológicas. A necessidade de aprofundamento dessa fé enegrecida faz surgir no meio dos APNs as reflexões teológicas também à luz dos processos da negritude. A compreensão de que o Deus da vida, não só é o Deus dos pobres, mas é também o Deus dos negros, nos desperta para a dimensão profética de nossa presença no mundo.

Considerações finais

Como iniciamos com uma música, faremos o final também com outra música. "Estamos chegando, chegamos cantando, sambando revolta, nós somos humanos, ouvi o clamor, desse povo negro, que clama e que luta por direto e justiça, um clamor de justiça está no ar".[2] Esse clamor de justiça envolve a dinâmica da ação dos APNs na perspectiva da promoção da igualdade racial. O ser Agente de Pastoral Negro no contexto latino-americano e de modo particular no Brasil é sobremaneira estar focado nos dramas vividos pela comunidade negra e buscar incessantemente práticas alternativas de humanização.

Constata-se que na sociedade, as mulheres negras, ainda que maioria, continuam sendo vítimas do machismo e dos modelos patriarcais e eurocêntricos; a juventude negra vive em situação de vulnerabilidade absoluta, sendo a maior vítima dos processos de extermínio e exclusão social; as comunidades religiosas de matrizes africanas vivem os dilemas em função da intolerância religiosa que recai sobre si e suas práticas religiosas, além de todas as mazelas secularmente impostas pela pobreza. Nesse cenário, um APN faz cotidianamente um pacto com a Justiça do Reino. Um clamor de justiça está no ar! E a certeza de que Deus ouve o clamor de seu povo por causa de seus opressores, alimenta a luta, engendra esperança e garante a vitória.

Notas

1. Canto de animação da caminhada dos Agentes de Pastoral Negros.
2. Canto de animação dos grupos negros composto no ano de 1988 por ocasião da Campanha da Fraternidade sobre o Negro no centenário da abolição legal da escravidão no Brasil.

Referências bibliográficas

Ardunini, Juvenal, 2002, Antropologia, ousar para reinventar a humanidade. São Paulo: Paulus.

Hoonaert, Eduardo, 1978, Formação do Catolicismo Brasileiro 1500/1800. Petrópolis: Vozes.

Hoonaert, Eduardo (org.), 1983, História da Igreja no Brasil. Primeira época. Tomo II. 3ª Edição. Petrópolis: Vozes.

Rocha, Jose Geraldo, 1998, Teologia e Negritude: um estudo sobre os Agentes de Pastoral Negros. Santa Maria: Editora Pallotti.

AGENTES DE PASTORAL NEGROS E A BÍBLIA NO CONTEXTO AFRO
Uma Hermenêutica de Anos de Encanto

Obertal Xavier Ribeiro

Introdução

Para refletir os 32 anos da presença e atuação dos Agentes de Pastoral Negros é necessário pensar a articulação entre a Palavra e a vida.

Em meio a tantos sofrimentos um encanto permanece: a certeza de fé que o Deus que cremos Libertador, caminhou com os nossos antepassados e caminha conosco. Ele se revela nas diversas e diferentes manifestações presentes na comunidade negra, nas religiões e culturas, o que provoca a necessidade do diálogo e do encontro. Isso que marcou o que celebramos e recordamos da atuação do povo negro nesses anos de história e vivência, nos lugares e espaços que ocupamos, nas nossas origens, no presente e no futuro.

Interpretar esses anos indica um caminho, uma postura de valorização dos passos dados, que não iniciaram conosco, mas que continuamos firmemente nesse tempo recordando, cantando, dançando, celebrando e finalmente vivendo.

Da vida para o canto

Parte desse texto foi pensado e pode ser afirmado vivido, a partir do cotidiano de idas e vindas para o trabalho. No transporte de massa, no cotidiano da Baixada Fluminense, junto com tantos outros negros e negras de Nova Iguaçu, no trem da Central. Inicialmente nos perguntamos: lugar dos negros e dos pobres?

Nessas idas e vindas é claro que a memória era dos Navios Negreiros. Transporte tão desumano que trouxe o nosso povo negro da África e que de maneira parecida, não mais pelos mares, mas pela ferrovia, em terra, conduz pelos trilhos as trilhas da vida, sofrimentos e lutas dos que vão para o Centro do Rio, saindo das periferias para produzir riquezas.

Assim pensamos a teologia, neste lugar concreto, a partir desse referencial que é a Baixada Fluminense. Lugar de tantos que vêm de outros cantos do Brasil, marcadamente experimentados pelo que é o Êxodo com suas cicatrizes da escravidão, que embalados não pelas ondas, mas pelo saculejar, sonham Quilombos de libertação.

Vale lembrar Solano Trindade:[1]

> Trem sujo da Leopoldina correndo, correndo,
> parece dizer tem gente, com fome
> tem gente com fome, tem gente com fome... Piiiiii
>
> Estação de Caxias de novo a dizer de novo a correr
> tem gente com fome, tem gente com fome, tem gente com fome.=
>
> Vigário Geral, Lucas, Cordovil, Brás de Pina, Penha Circular
> Estação da Penha, Olaria, Ramos, Bom Sucesso, Carlos Chagas
> Triagem, Mauá trem sujo da Leopoldina correndo, correndo
> parece dizer tem gente com fome, tem gente com fome, tem gente com fome.
>
> Tantas caras tristes, querendo chegar em algum destino, em algum lugar
> Trem sujo da Leopoldina correndo, correndo
> parece dizer tem gente com fome, tem gente com fome, tem gente com fome
>
> Só nas estações quando vai parando lentamente começa a dizer
> se tem gente com fome dá de comer, se tem gente com fome dá de comer,
> se tem gente com fome dá de comer
>
> Mas o freio de ar todo autoritário manda o trem calar,
> Psiuuuuuuuuuuu.

Isso nos leva a pensar e a recordar o canto tão comum entre nós, Agentes de Pastoral Negros, quando nos organizávamos para preparar nossa formação e nossas celebrações nas comunidades. Cantado tantas vezes na roda em nossos encontros pelo Brasil afora: "Sou de lá da África". Vale resgatar a letra, simples e significativa para nossa experiência.

> Sou de lá! De África!
> Se eu não sou de lá, os meus pais são de lá, de África.
> Sou de lá! De África!
> Se eu não sou de lá, os meus avós são de lá, de África.
> Sou de lá! De África!
> Se eu não sou de lá, os meus ancestrais são de lá, de África.
>
> Pela minha cor, pelo meu sorriso!
> Pelo meu andar, pelo meu sambar!
>
> Sou de lá! De África!
> Se eu não sou de lá, os meus pais são de lá, de África.
> Sou de lá! De África!
> Se eu não sou de lá, os meus avós são de lá, de África.
> Sou de lá! De África!
> Se eu não sou de lá, os meus ancestrais são de lá, de África.

Canto e memória comum entre os Agentes de Pastoral Negros, que nos possibilitam pensar sobre o que nos encanta, saber as origens e lugar no mundo e consequentemente na Bíblia, como a seguir.

Do canto para o encanto

Não era somente para cantar, mais do que isso, nossa organização estava em uma fonte comum que era a leitura da Palavra de Deus. Os Agentes de Pastoral Negros descobrem a partir dos encontros ao redor da Bíblia Sagrada que esse povo tem Missão. Essa encanta de beleza nossa atuação e nossa inserção nas CEBs, chegando até Santa Maria, Rio Grande do Sul. Já na conquista da Campanha da Fraternidade 1988 — A fraternidade e o negro: "Negro um clamor de justiça!". Cantamos e marcamos o lugar e o tempo — "Negros, mulheres, índios ... Na Igreja de Santa Maria, as culturas oprimidas vão aparecendo".

"De lá da África", que a vinda não foi à toa, nem por nada. Explorados sim, mas também identificados com o povo de Deus que saiu do Egito, que fica na África, nada é por acaso. Vendo nas duas histórias um encontro verdadeiro com Deus da Vida e da Libertação, surge a descoberta da necessidade da participação não só no espaço das igrejas cristãs, mas para além, ao encontro com aqueles que são de outras religiões de matriz africana, encontro com as tradições dos nossos pais e mães, nossos ancestrais, nos terreiros e também nos espaços da resistência que foram a capoeira, o maculelê, o samba, o pagode e outras expressões que encantam a vida de nossa gente.

Esses novos lugares se tornaram referências para um testemunho de libertação, de resistência que não passava somente pelas comunidades católicas e pelo espaço da profissão de fé cristã. Brota do encontro e do testemunho verdadeiro da presença do Deus que caminha em outros espaços. Disso resultou a grande formação do lugar em que se quer fazer teologia. Nesses anos algumas coisas mudaram, tantas aquisições.

Do encanto para fora do canto
Encantados com a certeza da presença de Deus na nossa vida e na nossa história, partimos para a leitura e a interpretação desta presença e o significado para a nossa própria identidade de teólogos e teólogas negras. Necessariamente, assim começamos a pensar também na nossa realidade a possibilidade da Teologia Feminista Negra. Daí o grupo das mulheres negras APNs.

Essa teologia é certamente a partir dos pobres de forma ecumênica e pluralista. Porém para além do ecumenismo, percebendo a necessidade de um diálogo inter-religioso, pois as lideranças religiosas de matriz africana não são reconhecidas dentro do processo e espaço ecumênicos. Considerando a própria condição histórica, sabemos do não reconhecimento dos Pais e Mães de Santo desde o passado pela sua religiosidade, mas sabemos o quanto, sofredores, perseguidos e marginalizados, são resistentes e vencedores.

A identificação veio a partir da própria fala de Deus no Êxodo:
> Iahweh disse: Eu vi a miséria do meu povo que está no Egito. Ouvi seu grito por causa dos seus opressores, pois eu conheço as suas angústias. Por isso, desci a fim de libertá-lo da mão dos egípcios e para fazê-lo subir desta terra para uma terra boa e vasta, terra que mana leite e mel, o lugar dos cananeus, dos heteus, dos amorreus, dos ferezeus, dos heveus e dos jebuseus. Agora o grito dos israelitas chegou até mim, e também vejo a opressão com que os egípcios os

estão oprimindo. Vai, pois, e eu te enviarei a Faraó, para fazer sair o meu povo, os israelitas."²

Ao recordar e recuperar estas histórias, cresce no coração e na memória a certeza da presença amorosa e cúmplice de Deus, do Deus do Êxodo nesse caminho de libertação. Como é importante e bom ainda hoje reafirmar a fé no Deus libertador que vê a miséria de seu povo, ouve seu clamor e desce para libertá-lo.

As mulheres negras, nessa tradição libertadora recuperam a figura de Agar. "A Iahweh, que lhe falou, Agar deu este nome: "Tu és El-Roi", pois disse ela, "vejo eu ainda aqui, depois daquele que me vê?"³ . A matriarca de um povo sabe que Deus a vê e afirma a sua visão feminina de Deus, conhece a sua situação, determina o seu lugar e o lugar de encontro com seu Deus.

A escrava africana, que também teve descendência numerosa, a insubmissa e outras vezes submissa que busca seus direitos, aquela a quem Deus se revelou é a mãe libertadora que nos ajuda a crer "naquele que vive e que me vê".

Criadas e criados à imagem e à semelhança de Deus, reconhecemos que a ação libertadora de Deus leva o povo à busca de vida em comunidade e com dignidade. Olhando para os primeiros capítulos de Gênesis, encontramo-nos com um Deus que cria o ser humano à sua imagem e semelhança. Quantas vezes não escutamos e refletimos sobre este texto?

Com o passar dos anos chega o momento em que estas palavras são ouvidas desde outro lugar, as escutamos com ouvido e alma coletivos, como negras e negros que têm seu rosto e seu corpo discriminados, explorados por uma ideologia que afirma sua inferioridade. Somos criados e criadas à imagem e semelhança de Deus, criados/as da terra, com cor e cheiro de terra, saímos com a cara de nosso Pai-Mãe. Temos um rosto parecido com a divindade que nos criou. Isso nos faz levantar a cabeça, reconhecer a dignidade e fortalecer a autoestima, caminhar em busca da libertação, fazer êxodos na busca de novos lugares ano após ano.

É Deus quem ocupa os espaços, sai do seu canto e toma a atitude, pelo encanto que tem com seu povo. Ele cria e recria continuamente, suas atitudes e suas ações que se destacam. Ele vê, ouve, conhece e desce e envia. Ele se mostra, deixa ser visto. Esses devem ser também os passos da teologia afro-brasileira de se colocar a caminho e se ver. Isso provoca o caminhar no tempo, tempo este de liberdade religiosa.

A consciência da necessidade de fazer a caminhada pela liberdade religiosa e proclamar com outros: "Eu tenho fé!", tem marcado a nossa trajetória. Já caminhando para o sétimo ano, a presença e participação na caminhada pela liberdade religiosa, expressa esse lugar que queremos ocupar teologicamente. Junto com outros líderes religiosos que dialogam com outras e diversas expressões de religiosidade, porém, que se colocam no espaço social numa perspectiva de construção de liberdade e democracia.

Fomos descobrindo uma grande sabedoria do encontro com o outro. Sabedoria que possibilita a gente receber e integrar a presença do Deus vivo nesses novos espaços. Assimilar e cultivar a possibilidade da troca, do dar e receber. Resgatar e receber a transmissão de um conteúdo tão antigo presente na oralidade dos "nossos mais velhos", que provoca e garante uma espiritualidade da escuta de Deus, necessariamente pela escuta do outro em nosso tempo. Esse texto se tornou um referencial fundamental, voltar às origens da libertação oferece um direcionamento, no sentido de voltar às origens da nossa gente.

Voltando para as origens
É necessário afirmar que a religião e cultura africanas deixaram um legado importantíssimo e fundamental para compreender os valores do povo negro que veio da África e que construiu sua história nessa terra.

De uma forma própria, com elementos inteiramente originais, resistindo a toda imposição cultural e religiosa, ao preconceito e ao racismo homens e mulheres de terreiros, Babalorixás e Yalorixas, formaram uma tradição religiosa, cultivaram espaços de fé e de culto, de preservação, de resistência e de teimosia desde o período da escravidão. Por essa persistência e criatividade, por sua autenticidade e identidade é que valores fundamentais para a formação cultural do povo brasileiro se tornaram conhecidos e reconhecidos.

Oferecem uma forma de cultuar a Deus e de encontro com a natureza que devem ser vistos como formadores de uma consciência religiosa e social transformadora e revolucionária, de uma mística de encontro com a criação e o com Criador, ultrapassando os espaços religiosos, atingindo o sagrado. Assim como na capoeira, no samba, no carnaval a cosmovisão tem uma importância e significado, em que a vida e a existência se unem ao divino, como bem expressou o samba de enredo, entre outras belezas, como dizemos "Oh que coisa bonita, oh que coisa bonita, Deus Pai criador, criar negra cor. Oh que coisa bonita!"

> Bailou no ar
> O ecoar de um canto de alegria
> Três princesas africanas
> Na sagrada Bahia
> Iyá Kalá, Iyá Detá, Iyá Nassô
> Cantaram assim a tradição Nagô
> (Olurun)
> Olurun! Senhor do infinito!
> Ordena que Obatalá
> Faça a criação do mundo
> Ele partiu, desprezando Bará
> E no caminho, adormecido, se perdeu
> Odudua
> A divina senhora chegou
> E ornada de grande oferenda
> Ela transfigurou
> Cinco galinhas d'Angola e fez a terra
> Pombos brancos criou o ar
> Um camaleão dourado
> Transformou em fogo
> E caracóis do mar
> Ela desceu, em cadeia de prata
> Em viagem iluminada
> Esperando Obatalá chegar
> Ela é rainha
> Ele é rei e vem lutar
> (Ierê)
> Iererê, ierê, ierê, ô ô ô ô
> Travam um duelo de amor
> E surge a vida com seu esplendor[4]

Saberes como possibilidade da construção de conhecimentos universais oferecendo uma qualidade de vida diferenciada, que resgata o humano, masculino e feminino, na proximidade do divino, rainha e rei. São referenciais na luta pela sobrevivência do planeta e na busca de uma qualidade nas relações entre sujeitos, grupos e sociedade. Construção de valores a partir da História e Cultura do Povo Negro, da forma bela e encantadora de cantar e contar. Isso nos oferece alguns indicativos para pensar a experiência agrupada nesses tantos anos.

Novas formas de experiência de Deus

Consideramos que não há uma só experiência com Deus. Nas práticas de fé, nas várias manifestações religiosas e culturais, na vida cotidiana, no enfrentamento com uma sociedade de exclusão, há também outros lugares de experiência com Deus.

Um Deus que não só se revela como pai, mas também como mãe, como terra, como irmã e irmão, como amiga e amigo. Um Deus que come e se faz comida, dança, festeja, celebra a vida e luta, se manifesta na natureza e na vida simbólica. É um Deus que também é mulher negra, criança, corporeidade.

Esta maneira, muito rica e simples, de viver e expressar as experiências com Deus, nos ensina a não absolutizar a experiência cristã como única experiência com Deus. Isso nos provoca a pensar alguns indicativos, a partir da experiência vivenciada e sistematizada de alguns elementos para uma hermenêutica que deve ser atualizada nesses tantos anos.

Indicadores para uma hermenêutica negra

O caminho feito nesses 32 anos nos indica algumas direções. Traçar uma hermenêutica negra não é uma tarefa fácil, porém a certeza é que o caminho ensina. Portanto, o que aqui colocamos são alguns pressupostos, que partem de nossas experiências de releitura bíblica e trabalho popular com as comunidades negras.

Uma hermenêutica bíblica a partir das realidades do povo negro exige um enfrentamento com as eclesiologias tradicionais na busca de novas maneiras de ser igreja, com uma cristologia que historicamente tem sido construída a partir de uma ideologia branca e masculina.

Com efeito, este modelo de cristologia, onde a pessoa de Jesus Cristo é o único pressuposto da revelação, com uma liturgia que não leva em conta as manifestações religiosas do povo negro e que ignora suas expressões corporais, sua mística, e suas tradições míticas, considera como único ponto de partida para a celebração os pressupostos ocidentais europeus.

A leitura negra da Bíblia exige um posicionamento político. Não se trata de ser negro ou negra para ler a Bíblia desde nossa realidade. A hermenêutica negra não pode ser entendida como problema de cor da pele, mas como uma causa política. Assumir a causa negra é assumir um processo de libertação que implique em transformações sociais radicais onde todas e todos possamos participar com nossas particularidades culturais e nossas contribuições fundamentais para uma sociedade que não discrimine nem marginalize a causa do sexo, da idade, da raça, da opção sexual. Esse posicionamento necessariamente se confronta com a teologia colonial e busca novos caminhos.

Teologia pós-colonial
Desde o período colonial até os nossos dias a resistência do povo negro foi o elemento importantíssimo garantido pela oralidade e pelas práticas dos nossos antepassados. A oralidade e a transmissão de conhecimentos dentro dos espaços religiosos de tradição de matriz africana, assim como das tradições culturais garantiram um legado importantíssimo. Neste contexto é que pensamos a teologia afro-brasileira, considerando a religiosidade africana e as expressões culturais.

Hoje já se discute academicamente e se reconhece um legado histórico e cultural riquíssimo, de valor inegável na construção social e religiosa do povo brasileiro, porém se deve afirmar que foi construído inicialmente com a vida e a prática e nesse contexto se inserem os APNs.

Entende-se hoje a possibilidade do pensar teológico e de considerar a questão negra que se colocam na perspectiva da reflexão e questionamento pós-colonial para a África, para a América Latina, em especial no nosso contexto brasileiro, considerando o aspecto cultural e social, ideológico e religioso afro-brasileiro.

A questão fundamental se apresenta a partir do pensar que considera a necessidade de viver e criar teologia e hermenêutica que reconhece valores religiosos pessoais e comunitários, modo de ser e pensar no lugar africano, ou no nosso caso afro-brasileiro. Isso se resume numa expressão de profunda importância, ou seja, do "lugar da vida".

A questão inicial que se coloca é: A teologia europeia é a teologia?

A produção teológica africana precisa ser considerada a partir de suas origens, sua concepção e sua mentalidade. Assim como tradicionalmente afirma a relação da filosofia com a teologia, encontramos um questionamento relevante ao pensar a mente e a concepção europeia diante da africana que herdamos.

> Uma das principais foi o projeto de negritude de Leopoldo Senghor, que buscava revelar a identidade africana pela distinção das características mentais de europeus e africanos. De acordo com Senghor, a mente europeia diferencia-se do seu objeto e o considera desapaixonadamente como um sistema ordenado e determinado, com leis que podem ser (?) tornando-os inteligíveis a um observador indiferente. Por outro lado, Senghor pensa que é mentira (?) africana não se diferencia do mundo, mas desenvolve seu conhecimento das coisas tornando-se tanto sujeito quanto objeto ao mesmo tempo, e sentindo compassivamente as coisas por meio da participação.[5]

Temos um outro lugar para pensar a teologia, mas também outra maneira apaixonada, próxima, envolvente e participativa. Evidente na prática da roda e de igualdades de posições. Apoiado nesse argumento podemos pensar com Bruce Janz que afirma que é importante compreender não o que a tradição significa de abstrato, mas o que é no pensamento africano e como pode um entendimento local e anunciado pela tradição capacitar africanos e afro-brasileiros a entender por si mesmo, a vida africana, a si mesmo e o outro, a realidade e o universo. Tradição não é objeto de pensamento, mas um modo de pensar. É um marcador de mundo-vida. O pensamento de Bruce Janz ao tratar a situação da filosofia africana, entre os temas da obra Filosofia contemporânea em ação, contribui para essa compreensão da teologia.

> [...] "O que significa fazer filosofia neste lugar (africano)?". Essa questão é fenomenológica e hermenêutica, em vez de essencialista. Ela assume que já há um significado contido em um mundo-vida, em vez de supor que ele tem de ser criado ou justificado. Isso não significa que a filosofia africana deva ignorar a tradição, razão, linguagem, cultura e praticidade como conceitos-chave - bem ao contrário. Mas cada um desses conceitos comporta-se como todos os outros conceitos como marcadores de um território viajado de uma paisagem habitada.[6]

A tradição aponta para o que importa, e para o modo como importa. A teologia afro-brasileira tem de cuidar disso, do seu potencial conceitual criativo, que tem suas raízes. Isso significa tornar-se parte da cultura, de suas ideias não como conceitos sobre a tradição, mas a própria tradição e religiosidade. O que está em questão é "O que é a teologia africana e afro-brasileira?". A compreensão é possível quando é "voltada ao lugar". Decorre disso a necessidade de se perguntar, entre outras tantas questões nesses anos passados e que fica para o futuro:

De onde que a teologia vem?

Qual a sua relevância para a vida e a história?

Qual seu lugar para essas pessoas?

Os comprometimentos étnicos e raciais, nacionais e até mesmo internacionais, culturais ou mesmo religiosos, políticos e ideológicos dos teólogos afetam a forma como a teologia é feita. O pensamento teológico é afetado pelo lugar em que é praticado e pelo tempo em que é elaborado. No curso dos 32 anos de APNs quanta coisa mudou, até mesmo o lugar que ocupamos nas igrejas e fora delas, na sociedade e na academia.

Muitas conquistas foram realizadas e muitos lugares ocupados. Nesse sentido entende-se a questão hermenêutica, que vai possibilitar interpretar os próximos anos. Não é hermenêutica puramente teórica, mas sim do lugar da vida, "mundo-vida", da história, da sensibilidade, do religioso, do corpo, da poesia, da música, da dança, do espaço natural, da cosmovisão etc.

Trazer a vida negra para a teologia e refletir sobre ela, criando novos territórios e estendendo o âmbito da vida é que nos refaz e nos projeta no caminhar dos próximos anos. Aqui neste lugar, situados ao mesmo tempo em outros espaços que a história poderá nos colocar, que reconhecemos o presente, olhamos o passado e projetamos o futuro. É necessário pensar uma postura hermenêutica crítica que considera os saberes na sua origem, onde e como aparece e se expressa, para que propósito é usado, para onde caminha.

É importante compreender não o que a tradição significa de abstrato, mas o que é no pensamento africano e como pode um entendimento local e anunciado pela tradição capacitar africanos e afro-brasileiros a entender por si mesmo, a vida africana, a si mesmo e o outro, a realidade e o mundo. Tradição não é objeto de pensamento, mas um modo de pensar, de interpretar. É um marcador de mundo-vida, do lugar. Uma certa tradição os APNs já tem construída.

Considerações Finais

Considerar a ação libertadora de Deus na história de homens e mulheres com um referencial tão antigo que é a história e luta do povo negro no Brasil e na África, assim como na Bíblia é referir-se necessariamente a uma história salvífica de construções ano após ano.

Os 32 anos dos APNs se inserem numa busca de identidades, de encontros, de compreensão da ação de Deus pelos caminhos, pelos mares, estradas e trilhos em que passaram nossos pais e mães, nossos ancestrais e deixaram como grande legado a ser seguido e passos para serem dados.

Isso nos provoca a uma nova postura frente à continuidade de tradições e expressões presentes na história e cultura brasileira, do povo afro-brasileiro. É fundamental considerar a necessidade de ressignificar a Bíblia a partir de novas perguntas, de novos lugares interpretativos e de novos sujeitos, de novos tempos.

O que aqui está se afirmando são apenas algumas representações, entre tantas outras, de indicadores de possibilidades de leitura, vivência e releitura da experiência histórica no lugar da vida do povo afrodescendente, no encontro com teólogos, poetas, sambistas, gente de grande experiência e sabedoria. A África está na Bíblia e na vida do povo afro-brasileiro que fez e faz Êxodo que cria e recria a existência e festeja mais um ano.

Notas

1. Solano Trindade foi cidadão politizado e apontou problemas de desigualdade e injustiça na vida social brasileira. No debate da questão racial no país, tornou-se precursor. Ao longo da vida se envolveu com a poesia, as artes plásticas, o teatro e o folclore. Mas foi, sobretudo, o poeta do povo. Mas, por causa desta música, em 1944, Solano foi preso e teve o livro "Poemas de uma Vida Simples" apreendido. Além disso, em 1964, um dos seus quatro filhos, Francisco Solano, morreu numa prisão da ditadura militar. Com a arte e o artesanato que se espalhavam pelas ruas, a cidade ganhou outros contornos e deu origem ao novo nome do lugar, que passou a ser conhecido como Embu das Artes."
2. Bíblia de Jerusalém. São Paulo: Paulus, 2003. Êxodo 3, 7–10.
3. Bíblia de Jerusalém. São Paulo: Paulus, 2003. Gênesis 16, 13.
4. Neguinho da Beija-flor, Mazinho e Gilson. Samba Enredo do terceiro título da Beija-Flor de Nilópolis. 1978. A criação do mundo na tradição Nagô.
5. CAREL, H.; GAMES, D. Filosofia contemporânea em ação. Porto Alegre: Artmed, 2008, p.102.
6. JANS, Bruce. A filosofia como se o lugar importasse: a situação da filosofia africana. In: CAREL, H.; GAMES, D. Filosofia contemporânea em ação. Porto Alegre: Artmed, 2008. p. 111.

Referências bibliográficas

Bíblia de Jerusalém. São Paulo: Paulus, 2003.

Carel, H.; Games, D. Filosofia contemporânea em ação. Porto Alegre: Artmed, 2008, p.102.

CROSSCURRENTS

JUREMA AFRO-INDÍGENA
O Máximo Divisor Comum da Religião Mínima Brasileira

Nancy Cardoso e Cláudio Carvalhaes

> *para Afonso Maria Ligório Soares, que nos ensinou a fazer teologia peregrinando, de tenda em tenda, na provisoriedade, porém animados/as porque nosso próprio corpo peregrino já é templo e morada do Espírito.*

A pergunta por uma religião mínima brasileira (RMB) foi debatida e respondida por diversos pesquisadores/as ao longo das últimas décadas acompanhando a consolidação do campo de estudos da religião ou de ciências da religião. Um dos exercícios mais significativos foi articulado por André Droogers reunindo diversas contribuições nas décadas de 70 e 80 do século passado na Revista Religião e Sociedade (1987). Num país como o Brasil que teve que superar no final do século XX uma visão de si mesmo como país cristão católico e assumir a polifonia religiosa para além dos modos de controle da(s) Igreja(s) como consenso na cultura, esta tarefa se mostra importante ainda hoje, uma vez que esta superação ainda não foi concluída e o campo religioso se complexificou neste período.

Se para Carlos Brandão existiria "uma grande matriz simbólica de uso comum, sobre a qual cada grupo religioso faz seu próprio recorte e combina seu repertório de crenças".[1] Pedro Ribeiro de Oliveira pondera que "...deve haver mais de um estoque de elementos religiosos à disposição das diversas religiões" sugerindo que uma possível RMB se alimentaria principalmente do catolicismo popular;[2] Ruben César Fernandes prefere falar de um "substrato comum que ponha de acordo as várias tradições", dizer de "elementos de conhecimento geral" comuns às diversas religiões com variação no "relacionamento entre as partes" (que seriam Deus soberano, natureza, seres humanos, almas mortas e divindades positivas e negativas).[3] Debatia-se também em especial o papel do "clero" e sua função — de acordo com Ruben César — de "tradutor" na relação com uma massa religiosa "poliglota" mas incapaz de traduzir ela mesma seus conteúdos; para Droogers a RMB não depende de intermediários (sacerdotes tradutores) nem precisa de reconhecimento por parte das assim chamadas religiões institucionalizadas.[4]

A partir do debate Droogers propõe a seguinte concepção de religiosidade mínima brasileira (RMB):

> Trata se de uma religiosidade que se manifesta publicamente em contextos seculares, que é veiculada pelos meios de comunicação de massa,, mas também pela linguagem cotidiana. Ela faz parte da cultura brasileira. Existe no nível nacional e pode, inclusive, servir a fins nacionalistas.[5]

Desde então este debate se atualizou de muitas maneiras mantendo a pergunta por uma cultura brasileira ou o que seria próprio de tal cultura –o que também serviria para a questão religiosa. Neste processo de atualização da questão seria possível reconhecer dois caminhos da pesquisa resumidamente: uma pesquisa descritiva pautada pela ciência e os instrumentos da antropologia, sociologia, história, etc. e uma pesquisa pautada pela pertença dos modos de crença em sua relação com sujeitos (mulheres, negros e negras, gays, etc). Enquanto o primeiro caminho aprofundava as intuições dos "patriarcas" dos estudos da religião, o segundo caminho reconhecia a divergência no trato mesmo com o religioso e suas representações de poder (classe, gênero, etnias...).

Dois exemplos importantes dessa segunda trajetória de pesquisa merecem ser mencionados aqui: a teologia feminista e a teologia negra no Brasil.

Ivone Gebara vai apontar para a situação das mulheres pobres, negras, indígenas, prostitutas, abandonadas pelos maridos, etc., na América Latina, apontando a prioridade da opção da mulher por ela mesma como primeiro passo para consideração do papel e função da religião para as mulheres. Neste sentido não haveria um "mínimo" em si mas deveríamos perguntar no "mínimo" para-as-mulheres. Num texto de 1998 Ivone relativiza todos os esforços de uma assim chamada "leitura popular da Bíblia" das mulheres identificando um conjunto de realidades e relações de poder que seriam mais significativas.[6]

Do mesmo modo Afonso Maria Ligório Soares vai desconstruir o debate sobre sincretismo e inculturação religiosa apontando que boa parte do esforço de estabelecer um "mínimo" possível de sobrevivência acaba reforçando a religião "máxima" e sua capacidade de anexação. Para Afonso o deslocamento para a questão da inculturção como resolução do sincretismo degradado e defeituoso não lida com as questões de poder no âmbito mesmo das religiões.

> Africanos e indígenas corromperam o catolicismo português ou foi este que violentou as tradições ancestrais dos primeiros?[7]

Essa pergunta ressalta uma relação ambígua, mas que perde seu paradoxo na medida em que a religião máxima ocupa o espaço público, definindo os modos de crenças aceitáveis por sua capacidade de visibilidade e ocupação de meios, confundindo e/ou fazendo desaparecer, nesse espaço público, as relações complexas de poder existentes, quase sempre privilegiando formas com pretensão de hegemonia que a religião máxima postula.

Nesta lógica as formas consideradas mínimas perdem de vista as mínimas formas existentes e resistentes; perde-se de vista também as disputas e conflitos e os modos de crença contidos na luta de classes mais ampla na cultura e na sociedade. São modos de acesso ao próprio espaço, de acesso ao lugar, à nomeação do lugar e suas coisas – visíveis e invisíveis.

Os esforços descritivos e analíticos que identificam a RMB com os aparatos do espaço público acabam reforçando as vozes que se pretendem "maximizadas" e "maximizantes" em especial na teologia. Três procedimentos poderiam ser identificados nesse processo de controle da religiosidade "mínima":

1 subordinação das expressões "mínimas", a partir das religiões "maximizadas" num processo de tolerância de práticas localizadas sem o risco de ampliação de influência;
2 usurpação e cooptação de certos elementos rituais, linguagens, objetos com quebra das autonomias funcionais e deslocamento teológico de experiências e vivência que não são facilmente toleradas e que apresentam risco de ampliação de influência;
3 proibição e combate de práticas religiosas e crenças com possibilidade de ampliação de influência e manutenção de autonomia funcional.

As relações entre sistemas formais e informais de religião não se reduzem às investidas de subordinação, cooptação ou abominação por parte dos sistemas institucionalizados — nem sempre eficientes —, mas são marcadas por uma ambivalência que transita entre acomodação e resistência por parte das religiosidades populares gerando este aparente consenso mínimo, ou um resíduo simbólico ambivalente que vai ser acomodado como RMB.

Neste sentido a busca por elementos comuns, ou partilhados ou deslocados dos diversos registros religiosos entre nós não podem ser "minimizados" a partir da logica descritiva e analítica e muito menos cabem num ecumenismo de bolso que pretendendo manter um lugar público para a religião (teologia) pressiona registros diversos e divergentes. O campo da religião assim como o campo da cultura entre nos é campo de conflito, de disputa, perpassado por relações de poder violentas e legitimadoras de subordinação. Qualquer pretensão de apaziguamento elegante destas arestas nada mais é do que recauchutagem das formas "máximas" da religião cristã e suas pretensões de manutenção de poder no espaço público.

O espaço público não é o apaziguamento das formas de colonização, escravização e dominação que persistem entre nós. Só mesmo um pensamento particular, que se auto-proclama universal, normativo e superior — porque apaziguado! — pode pretender olhar para os modos de conflito e identificar o "mínimo" de outros(as) não tão ilustrados quanto eu.

Se é para falar das coisas "mínimas" falemos não de resíduos pasteurizados controlados pela voz patriarcal, branca e colonizada da ciência e da teologia.

> dois elementos ajudam a compreender a postura de rejeição radical de um processo sincrético no sistema cristão. O primeiro é a auto-compreensão do cristianismo como religião possuidora da única e verdadeira revelação de Deus. Na base de tal pretensão estaria um conceito de revelação estático (a-histórico) que, partindo, desde o início, dos dados da fé, imunizaria essa tradição dos vários níveis de sincretismo que constituem todo e qualquer grupo religioso no seu desenvolvimento histórico. Tal posição desemboca, inevitavelmente, em um conflito artificial (ideológico, a-histórico e idealista): querigma revelado (diretamente por Deus) à comunidade cristã versus demais religiões, subjugadas às leis sociológicas.[8]

De modo especial este desconforto é importante para a teologia feminista latino-americana de libertação de não se deixar cooptar ou reduzir nas fórmulas fáceis da "teologia-quero-ser-pública". Ainda entre nós o desafio da desigualdade social dramática e o racismo estrutural não autoriza nenhuma nem qualquer forma de redução.

Tomando a sugestão de "religião mínima" podemos perguntar também o que seria uma Religião Máxima Brasileira. A religião máxima seria um dado anterior à interpretação, com pretensão de plenitude, pureza, autenticidade, organizadora de mundo, democrática e universalmente representativa. Já a religião mínima vista (porque interpretada), como parcial, não oficial, desorganizadora do formal, perigosa, desestabilizadora, e não representativa somente de setores da sociedade.

Polifanias multi-odorificas-pluri-tacteis-hipergustativas da Jurema
As mulheres da Teia Agroecológica dos Povos da Bahia[9] se reuniram para rodar antigas rodas, torés e batuques persistentes que não desistiram de encantar o território do sul da Bahia e seus seres. Encantar aqui é povoamento de memória, de ancestrais não derrotados pela morte, a invasão e o esquecimento. Todo o sul da Bahia é habitado por Encantados e Encantadas, Orixás e Caboclas. Ali no litoral, entre o mar e a mata, as primeiras comunidades nativas se encontraram com os invasores faz 515 anos. Tanta desmesura nos modos de tomar a terra, arrancar a mata e escravizar as gentes des-evangelizou para sempre o povo do lugar e tornou seus deuses e deusas mais belos e necessários. Esta é uma história de radical permanência de povos e seus modos de crença na luta pela terra e o território. No círculo. Na roda. Nada se perde. Somos Cabruca.

Era a primeira vez que as mulheres da Teia se juntavam e tínhamos como horizonte o IV Encontro de Agroecologia do Sul da Bahia que aconteceria 2 meses depois em dezembro de 2015. Esta era uma oportunidade de 60 mulheres conviverem e conversarem. A Teia Agroecológica do Sul da Bahia entende

> a necessidade de articular nossas lutas para combater o racismo, a violência religiosa e demais práticas colonizadoras e eurocêntricas que chegaram nas naus do descobrimento e até hoje se repetem, dia após dia, como se não houvesse jeito, como se fossem irremediáveis... é tempo de preparar os solos onde as alianças

serão cultivadas e com sabedoria e alegria nos UNIR para a defesa de nossas culturas, cosmovisões e territórios.[10]

O que juntava as mulheres no encontro da Teia eram as práticas e debates sobre agroecologia num cenário político difícil e conflituoso e num processo de avanço da florestas artificiais de eucaliptos, pastagem para o gado e empreendimentos turísticos. A Cabruca é o sistema de mata e vida dos povos tradicionais do sul da Bahia. A Cabruca é tudo misturado de árvores grande e antigas com formas de plantio recente que combina o cacau com as frutas e matas do que ainda resta de Mata Atlântica. Da Cabruca e na Cabruca o povo da mata retira seu sustento, mantém seus gostos e sabores e se agrada da vida.[11]

A articulação das lutas de povos tradicionais por terra e território na região juntava a materialidade da Mata Atlântica e a materialidade da Jurema e seus rituais. Entre uma conversa e outra sobre agroecologia encontrávamos sobre a sombra da Jurema e suas pluralidades afro-indígenas.

Alternando entre batidas negras e indígenas uma fumaça fumegava as mulheres e convidava para a roda. Na roda nós tecemos Teia, na articulação necessária, urgente e extremamente bela dos povos em luta pelo território e a Jurema criava para nós e em nós a oportunidade e os modos. Dançamos cada uma seu ritmo aprendido mas nos esbarrávamos, nos tocávamos e uma alegria enorme tomou conta do lugar. Entre uma conversa e outra eu perguntava para as mulheres: o que é a Jurema? como funciona? As respostas vinham misturadas com casos e exemplos que diziam do corpo pessoal, do corpo social e do território: a Jurema abre o corpo, abre caminhos, dá alegria para as festas e rituais; a Jurema fecha o corpo, protege de doenças e perigos, prepara para as tarefas, dá força para os trabalhos, protege nos processos de luta e dificuldades.[12]

O encontro de pastorais sociais do campo: uma teologia do Bem Viver e a Jurema
No Encontro Nacional das Pastorais do Campo em 2015[13] — que junta CPT, CIMI, Pastoral de Pescadores, Quilombolas, Pastoral da Juventude Rural e Caritas — conversou-se sobre a experiência do SumakKawsay — o Bem Viver. Mais do que um conceito ou uma expressão o SumakKawsay é uma experiência de ancestralidade das comunidades indígenas andinas que se atualiza na forma de projetos de vida. A pergunta que se fez é se o Bem Viver expressava também para os povos tradicionais no Brasil esta ancestralidade que se projeta como elemento aglutinador de lutas e até

mesmo nas Constituições de Bolívia e Equador. Temos um SumakKawsay: Seria o "Terra Sem Males"? alguém perguntou. A conversa corria solta quando alguém do nordeste afirmou — "temos a Jurema!"

Cada um/uma disse do que sabia da Jurema e do que representa para os povos tradicionais no Nordeste. Antigas perguntas e intuições foram despertadas — remédio, elemento ritual, emplastro, bebida, tantas possibili-dades de uma mesma planta que fazia parte do imaginário e do cotidiano de muitos grupos no campo e nas cidades. É indígena e é afro. É uma relação com a natureza, com o lugar, com os ancestrais.

> A jurema é uma religião tipicamente encontrada no nordeste brasileiro. Sua presença estende-se entre áreas do sertão e urbanas. É recente o interesse acadêmico sobre o tema, no que diz respeito ao encontro da jurema no espaço urbano, que envolve a confluência de vários outros tipos religiosos, como a umbanda, o catolicismo, o candomblé e o vodum maranhense. Seu nome, de origem tupi, liga-se a espécies de árvores encontradas no sertão. São elas a Mimosa hostilis, hoje reclassificada como Mimosa tenuiflora, a Mimosa verrucosa e também a Vitex agnus-castus, conhecidas como jurema preta, jurema mansa e jurema branca, respectivamente .A jurema preta é utilizada na fabricação da bebida que dá nome a esse universo religioso. Sua origem remonta a pajelança e ao toré, ambos regimes religiosos que fundamentam a estrutura indígena do sagrado.[14]

A Jurema como hibridização defumadora

No encontro de mulheres da Teia Agroecológica dos Povos do Sul da Bahia o paradigma do pluralismo cultural e religioso foi essencial, foi o tecido sobre o qual tecemos a unidade de mulheres camponesas, indígenas e quilombolas com estudantes e agentes de organizações ambientais.

Os modelos econômicos do sul da Bahia sempre privilegiaram as grandes fazendas de cacau, o gado e agora as florestas artificiais de eucalipto fazendo deste trecho do Brasil — o sul da Bahia — um corredor de 500 anos de exploração e de extermínio de gentes e seres.

A chegada de homens e mulheres de tantas Áfricas reforçou no território seu desespero sem pertença. Desaprendidos da palavra e do lugar, as gentes negras sequestradas e escravizadas trataram de guardar na forma do canto, da reza e memória o que insistia em continuar. Demonizados e silenciados pela fé dos senhores, as gentes negras tiveram que aprender o lugar muito depressa e aprender a nomear pedras, rios e árvores com os antigos nomes trazidos na raça. Des-evangelizados pelo amor do livro e as ladainhas que obrigavam a espelhos europeus nos quais não se podiam ver, abriram ouvidos de resistência e souberam escutar o canto dos torés e se reconhecer neles sem se perder, sem desaparecer mas vendo na cara das gentes índias janelas de se reconciliar com o lugar.

O exato momento em que a fumaça de Jurema atravessou o espaço de um toré para se esparramar cheiroso e significativo numa batucada de religião africana reinventada no Brasil... ninguém sabe. Pode ser que antigos quilombos de gentes índias e africanas fugidas da escravidão acolheram fomes e forças e estendeu um tanto de convivialidade entre as danças de roda de um e de outro e a fumaça da Jurema se ofereceu como ar de comum viver e algum tempo depois as coisas da Jurema e suas infinitas formas de estar na mata e as práticas juremeiras eram partilhadas por torés e catimbós. E fez-se o Brasil... esse que ainda não é. Será.

As práticas políticas e as articulações de luta se fazem acompanhar de um processo de articulação também do cultural e religioso desses povos desse lugar. O sul da Bahia conheceu uma das primeiras iniciativas de colonização de portugueses e também marcou um dos processos mais acelerados de expulsão e violência contra os povos nativos num processo demorado que misturou extermínio, assimilação e a alienação do território. Mas foi também na Bahia que a mão de obra escrava foi ferramenta dos diversos momentos econômicos sempre deixando o povo negro em cima da terra mas longe dela. O povo sem terra era o povo da roça, empregado das fazendas aprisionado pelas formas do coronelismo que extrapola os romances de Jorge Amado[15] e se impregna as relações de poder na região.

Se durante muito tempo cada grupo resistiu na terra e lutou por ela de seu modo, com suas forças, com o fortalecimento dos processos de retomada da terra e acirramento do preconceito e repressão os movimentos foram se aproximando e se reconhecendo. No encontro das mulheres celebramos este movimento de aproximação e de reconhecimento. Para além dos objetivos organizativos e políticos os modos de resistência e lutas projetava os modos de mística e a sabedoria que vem desta fonte e integrar as descobertas e intuições profundas na teologia no nosso caminhar teológico e espiritual. Este é um caminho desigual, marcado por violências, incluindo a violência das invisibilidades estratégicas que ainda deixam cicatrizes no cenário religioso brasileiro.

Neste ponto, desejamos destacar que muito provavelmente os motivos dessa invisibilidade residem na dicotomia magia/religião como juízos valorativos. A perseguição sofrida pelos terreiros, principalmente durante os anos do Estado Novo, os coloca sob a tutela da polícia acompanhados do jargão 'charlatanismo'. Em 1933, é criado em Pernambuco o Serviço de Higiene Mental, liderado por Ulisses Pernambucano e tendo entre seus intelectuais Gilberto Freyre, Gonçalves Fernandes, René Ribeiro, entre outros. De forma bem simplificada, o SHM foi uma tentativa de elevar o candomblé à categoria de religião, colocando-o como um componente na formação do Brasil e retirando-o da alçada policial. O mesmo não aconteceu com a jurema, que continuou a ser reconhecida como magia e, principalmente, acusada de charlatanismo e falsa medicina por realizar trabalhos de cura. Essa postura frente à jurema fez com que seus altares fossem escondidos nos terreiros.[16]

O lugar da mística

A Jurema é assim uma antiga conversa do povo negro e indígena que persiste na história brasileira. Um ajuntamento litúrgico feito como resposta à opressão. A mística se faz a partir da luta, vem depois da luta e assim se forma e se transforma na identidade plural dos povos indígenas e negros em contínua transformação. A mística, a espiritualidade do povo e seu possível caminhar teológico vem como resultado da luta pela vida continuar, sua sobrevivência mesmo.

Em suma, em vez de proporcionar uma "sua" representação, a Jurema é multiplicadora de representações. Não é uma única planta, abrange a (polissemia da) mata inteira. Os seus pés são cidades. Afigura-se mulher, cabocla, morena, linda, índia... Poderosa, não obstante fruto de uma cultura oral, enraíza-se em letras: os "seus" índios ora se revelam seres espirituais assemelhados a construções literárias românticas ou a imagens de comemorações cívicas (Santos, 1995), ora, quando efetivamente pessoas e comunidades indígenas, pelo menos em parte, estas receberam tal identidade a partir de critérios disponíveis na literatura antropológica.[17]

A memória da violência que dilacerou e ainda dilacera a carne dos povos originários e negros no Brasil cria trincheiras, rezas, movimentos, visitações e cura. Uma mística solidária, companheira, com-panis, comum, capaz de recriar o mundo conhecido e desconhecido, categorias de pensamento e movimento sagrados desconhecidas pelo opressor, guardados e revividos na mata e nos encontros necessários pra se viver, mínima e maximamente. A viração espiritual entre índios e espíritos, negros e encantados, assim como sua oralidade, é a mística maximizada no momento, exaurida em uma imediatez de vivência plena, necessária para fortalecer os povos celebrantes. Com isso, confunde, ensurdece e bagunça o cânon metafísico-farpado cristão.

A mística se faz não pelos compêndios de doutrinas ou confissões de fé, mas pela materialidade das danças e da fumaça que cruzam espaços não autorizados e mistificam povos que se juntam contra a lei da violência. Mistificados, vivem e sobrevivem, rearranjam seus espaços e seus símbolos. A mística flexibiliza identidades, cores de pele, histórias, legados, tradições e o que for preciso. Os encantados e os espíritos se mobilizam pela sobrevivência do povo. O que era distinto agora é junto, o que estava separado vive da sua relacionalidade, o que se preconizava autônomo agora acontece na dança das intersecionalidades, numa contínua re-descoberta que se mistura e refaz mundos de vivências e sabedorias milenares.

Quando o povo diz: temos a Jurema, eles dizem: temos régua e compasso e não precisamos da tua precisão. Na luta pelas terras tomadas, pelas vidas ceifadas, pelos direitos reivindicados, corpos descolonizados vivem sua luta de vida e morte, tentando voltar para o que era seu, a sua casa.[18]

Possuídos pela encanto

Ao contrário dos controles obsessivos do Cristianismo, as religiões indígenas e de matizes africanas são tomados pelos Orixás e pelos encantados. Perde-se o controle e ficam-se todos entregues às diretivas e encantamentos dos encantados e orixás. Essa possessão define o que era e o que virá, transfigurando-se identidades e estados da consciência. Um poder que a tudo toma, orienta e organiza. A possessão dessas maravilhas está para além do estudo formal, das teologias descritivas e definidoras que vem antes do vivido. Ao contrário está preocupada com a composição de energias e sinergias, na compensação do bem com o mal, da preservação do bem e também do cuidado com o que é mal, sem as particulares polaridades da Cristandade. O espaço do encontro é sempre sagrado e é no transe, no corpo, que a comunicação mais profunda entre diferentes realidades acontece.

A Jurema e o espaço

A mística de Jurema não é atemporal mas conta o tempo pelo espaço, pelo chão que dá vida e fruto. Assim, Jurema é árvore e bebida, usadas para uso religioso e medicinal, como cuidado com o povo reunido. Entidade, local de culto e ritual, uma índia metafísica, uma linha de encantados e caboclas – homens e mulheres, e sertaneja e de beira d'água, um objeto, mata, tronco. Com a vinda dos negros da África vários Orixás vieram acompanhando seus filhos e filhas. Quando aqui chegam se juntam com as entidades locais porque as religiões negras são religiões de adição, de ajuntamento. Assim que Jurema expande o panteão africano assim como os orixás se expandem na vivência com Jurema e os encantados. Nessa confluência de profunda solidariedade, mas também de especificidades, o espaço da mística se estabelece na comunhão dos índios, negros e caboclos.[19] Jurema está localizada em assentamentos. Com o roubo e grilagem das terras dos índios e negros, sua vivência passou da mata para os espaços da Umbanda. Vive da alternância com os ritos umbandistas. Mas a noção de assentamento se conecta com o assentamento do povo excluído em terras roubadas de índios. Os negros foram assentados nessa terra e agora é preciso retomar a terra. Desenraizados, as raízes da Jurema no assentamento criam a noção de pertença, mesmo que o banzo ainda seja seu canto mais primordial. Cosmogonias entrelaçadas e transformadas. Assentados na terra-vida. Jurema faz a ressignificação do espaço público, do que e a quem pertence. Essa ressignificação se faz no refundamento misturado das cosmologias indígenas e negras. As entidades negras-indígenas vivem da profunda relação com a natureza. Assim que a luta das mulheres da Teia na Cabruca é essa simbiose entre espíritos e árvore, semente, frutos, tribos e quilombos.

Jurema como re-definidora de classe

Nesse sentido, a acolhida da Jurema no meio da diversidade dos povos oprimidos re-cria as formas de classe. A expansão da noção e do acesso ao sagrado é plural e não se faz pelo acesso monetário ou de valor. Ao contrário, quebram-se e equilibram-se as diversidades, redefinindo-se assim as classes. Sentam-se todos à mesa de Jurema e sua mesa se expande por toda a mata. Como a Cabruca.

Paralelos e Des-Conexões com o Cristianismo

Na complexidade da religiosidade tupiniquim, a Jurema é religião mínima-máxima, uma des-religião que desbanca as formas ocidentais de se pensar. A noção mesma de religião se coloca à prova, visto que o conceito mesmo de religião é uma invenção cristã, que simboliza o *religare* da criatura afastada pelo pecado com o Deus que a criou. A Jurema não se encaixa nessa noção de religião ou de religião alguma. Ela é um conjunto de saberes e práticas e sabedoria que nasce da terra, da biodiversidade, e se entranha na vida comum dos índios e negros em suas múltiplas formas, cheiros, cores e desafios. A Jurema não reivindica nem quer um estatuto, seja de mínima ou máxima religião. Ao contrário, Jurema é a fazeção da vida, o sagrado sem dicotomia, imerso na vida e nas coisas, e que não se organiza nem se realiza a partir da definição de secular como oposicional e definidor do sagrado. Para os povos originários assim como para os Africanos, tudo é sagrado, habitação dos espíritos. Assim, o corpo, também sagrado, se dá na con-vivência dos encantados, vida do corpo em sua plenitude, sem negação ou culpa. O corpo é elevado quando em transe, e se encontra com os espíritos, ao contrário do Cristianismo que nega o corpo como aproximação do sagrado. A espiritualidade/mística se faz pela materialidade das danças, o ritmo dos côcos e congas, e da fumaça. Tudo enuviado, talvez como misterioso é o Deus *absconditus* da teologia Cristã negativa. Como conjunto de saberes e práticas, o mínimo-máximo não se encaixa em Jurema, porque Jurema é mínima e máxima ao mesmo tempo, escapando as definições pseudo-cristãs.

A liturgia Mestiça de Jurema

Jurema é comensalidade, convivialidade, relacionalidades e alternâncias de poder. O Maracá e os ritmos marcam os rituais. Jurema é o lugar da celebração, o mundo encantado manifestando seus encantamentos e produzindo uma espiritualidade híbrida, mestiça, "brasileira," mas desafeta e assustadora às religiões mínimas e máximas que se reproduzem por autenticações completamente estranhas aos movimentos de Jurema. A

Jurema é marcada por sua singularidade a multiplicidade. Lugar de múltiplas representações, Jurema acolhe e se expande, se re-significando nas necessidades dos povos oprimidos. Povos comungados por deuses não comuns mas que se tornaram comuns para o bem da vida do povo e sua sobrevivência. Jurema, árvore-raiz-tronco que, na vivência com o povo, torna-se potencialidade para a sobrevivência dos povos oprimidos: índios e negros.[20] A mestiçagem de Jurema vem de sua organicidade, de sua capacidade de mutação e mútuo envolvimento. Nesse sentido é canibalista e simbiótica, tornando-se, a partir de sua originalidade, algo outro, além de si mesma porque em si mesma. A pluralidade mesmo de Jurema e suas múltiplas formas são feitas não somente de espíritos mas de coisas e lugares, uma materialidade de movimentos encantados e encantadoras.[21] Assim, confunde e desafia a trindade que se pretende unificadora do Cristianismo. Mais do que três pessoas, Jurema é muitas outras coisas. Suas representações se assemelham mais ao conceito de sacramentalidade múltipla na teologia Cristã Ortodoxa do que a sacramentalidade Católica-Protestante Ocidental feita de dois ou sete sacramentos. Realidade e representação se misturam em várias realidades, espirituais, mentais, corporais ou naturais mesmo que as vezes não se corporificam. Jurema pode ser bebida. A casca de sua raíz ou de seu troco se bebe, talvez como o Deus que se dá no pão e no vinho. Contudo, a Jurema pode criar alteração da consciência, enquanto na eucaristia ainda se tenha o controle total de Deus nas formas do rito e nas possibilidades de sentido.

Conclusão: aportes para uma teologia da libertação negra brasileira

Assim, para se pensar a teologia negra no Brasil é preciso se partir de uma perspectiva mais ampla. Porque a libertação não está na negritude somente mas na coloração composta da teologia. Nenhuma teologia vivida de si mesma se sustentará diante da força colonizadora dos brancos. A pulverização das identidades no *que hacer* teológico nos parece mais uma forma de provisão do ideário da conquista do que de modos de pensar autóctones e auto-determinantes. O que propomos é a possibilidade da teologia negra a partir de suas matizes mais profundas, em uma ideia de pan-africanismo Latino-Americano e suas histórias em relação com as matizes dos povos originários. Essa co-relação, baseada num profundo pluralismo religioso, nos parece mais profunda, mais congenial e capaz de oferecer não só resistência anti-colonial mas também novas formas de se viver e reproduzir a vida.

Diego Irarrázaval nos dá quatro pontos no diálogo do Cristianismo com religiões africanas: 1) Celebrar e pensar, nas formas africanas de se recrear o mundo; 2) Identificar a nós mesmos e nosso continente como Afro-Americano; 3) celebrar o mistério de uma forma Africana, onde o corpo é lugar fundamental da revelação e do sagrado; 4) Engajar sincretismos s pertenças.[22] O que falta aqui é o que Gebara nos lembra: o bem comum que é a vida da terra e todo o ecossistema.[23] A vida mesmo das nações originárias e dos Africanos é toda plasmada no movimento da biodiversidade. Da mesma maneira, precisamos celebrar e pensar as formas indígenas de recrear o mundo, identificar a nós mesmos como indígenas e considerar nosso continente como pertencente originariamente aos povos indígenas que aqui estavam, relacionar o corpo, a comunidade e o meio ambiente como lugares do sagrado e se envolver com sincretismos.

A reconstituição de uma teologia negra latino-americana seria assim um resgate de um paradigma pluralista cultural, religioso e de classe que visa a libertação dos povos originários e também dos povos excluídos, mas também da vida do planeta como lugar epistemológico plural fundamental.

Nenhuma teologia negra se sustenta ou deveria se sustentar como unicamente cristã na América Latina. Tentar fundamentar uma teologia negra que se faça somente a partir de recursos cristãos será o desempoderamento da pluralidade negra latino-americana. Assim que uma teologia negra só se faz possível se profundamente imbricada com todas as religiões de matizes africanas, índias e cristãs. Por isso que o movimento inter-religioso é fundamental e Jurema pode ser um espaço concreto onde essa convivência acontece.

Enfim, acreditamos que: (1) qualquer teologia da libertação negra na América Latina precisa se fazer a partir das relações com os povos originários; (2) qualquer teologia da libertação negra na América Latina precisará se fazer mestiça, híbrida, a partir das mulheres, gays e povos oprimidos. Porque toda teologia negra é feita de inter-secionalidades e misturas, onde povos oprimidos se juntam para se pensar na luta de resistência e transformação juntos; (3) qualquer teologia da libertação negra na América Latina deverá ser sempre uma teologia de assentamento, de luta de classes: de invasão, de tomada de posse, e de fazeção de pertença na marra e na luta, com toda a força de todos os símbolos das místicas e espiritualidades dos povos oprimidos; (4) qualquer teologia da libertação negra na América Latina começará do chão, da biodiversidade vilipendiada e saqueada dos povos excluídos; (5) qualquer teologia da libertação negra na América Latina usará de quaisquer recursos que quiser usar, misturando ou não o que quiser e com quem quiser. Não haverá mais busca de mínima-máxima religião.

Notas

1. DROOGERS, André. "A Religiosidade Mínima Brasileira." In Religião e Sociedade, Rio de Janeiro, 14/2, 1987, p.77.
2. Ibid., p.64.
3. Ibid., p.65.
4. Ibid., p. 64.
5. Ibid., p. 65.
6. GEBARA, Ivone. "Que Escrituras são autoridade sagrada? Ambiguidades da Bíblia na vida das mulheres na América Latina." In Concilium. Revista Internacional de Teologia, Petrópolis, n° 276, 1998/3, p. 10–25.
7. SOARES, Afonso Maria Ligório, Impasses da teologia católica diante do sincretismo religioso afro-brasileiro, in:
   http://ciberteologia.paulinas.org.br/ciberteologia/wp-content/uploads/2009/05/impassesda teologiacatolica.pdf (acesso em 15/12/2015).
8. Ibid., (acesso 15/12/2015).
9. A Teia Agroecológica dos Povos foi criada a partir dos diálogos continuados da I Jornada de Agroecologia da Bahia, realizada em 2012, no Assentamento Terra Vista. Em formato de rede, ela tem o papel de traçar a agenda de ações anuais que auxiliam no desenvolvimento, empoderamento e emancipação das comunidades e elos que a integram. Participam e constroem a Teia assentados(as), quilombolas, indígenas, mestres de tradição oral, campesinos (as), estudantes, pesquisadores, educadores, crianças, juventude do campo e urbana, in: http://jornadadeagroecologiadabahia.blogspot.com.br/p/blog-page_11.html
10. VIII Encontro Afro-Ecumênico da Comunidade de Caxuté, in: http://jornadadeagroecolo giadabahia.blogspot.com.br/ (acesso em 20/1/2015).
11. CABRUCA, "Cabruca é um sistema agroflorestal tradicional da região o qual maneja culturas a sombra das árvores nativas da Mata Atlântica. Na cabruca se aproveita os remanescentes arbóreos de grande porte florestal original. Parte da cobertura original é preservada por isso exige grande confusão no processo de classificação que quiser ou tentar diferir cabruca de floresta densa porque as plantações de cacau acabam herdando características espectrais da Floresta Ombrofila Densa. Nesta lógica a floresta precisa ficar de pé e ser preservada porque as outras culturas de cacau, café e outras dependem da sombra das antigas árvores criando um sistema intrincado de permanência e novidade.", Planeta Orgânico, in: http://plan etaorganico.com.br/site/index.php/cabruca/ (acesso em 20/12/2015).

12. Articulação das Pastorais do Campo, 2015, http://www.cptnacional.org.br/index.php/publicacoes/noticias/acoes-dos-movimentos/2482-articulacao-das-pastorais-do-campo-realiza-encontro-sobre-desafios-pastorais-no-campo (acesso em 28/11/2015).
13. Ibid.
14. RODRIGUES, Michelle Gonçalves; CAMPOS, Roberta Bivar Carneiro. Caminhos da visibilidade: a ascensão do culto a jurema no campo religioso de Recife. Afro-Ásia, Salvador, n. 47, p. 269–291, 2013. In: http://www.scielo.br/scielo.php?script=sci_arttext&pid=S0002-05912013000100008> (acesso em 31/12/2015).
15. COELHO, Alexandra, O culto de índios e negros que chegou a Portugal. In: http://www.publico.pt/sociedade/noticia/o-culto-de-indios-e-negros-que-chegou-a-portugal-1665703 (acesso em 20/11/2015).
16. RODRIGUES, Michelle, CAMPOS, Roberta, op.cit., (acesso em 20/11/2015).
17. BAIRRAO, José Francisco Miguel Henriques, Raízes da Jurema, Psicol. USP, São Paulo , v. 14, n. 1, p. 157–184, 2003. In: http://www.scielo.br/scielo.php?script=sci_arttext&pid=S0103-65642003000100009 (acesso em 31/12/2015).
18. Aqui nessa casa Ninguém quer a sua boa educação Nos dias que tem comida Comemos comida com a mão E quando a polícia, a doença, a distância, ou alguma discussão Nos separam de um irmão Sentimos que nunca acaba De caber mais dor no coração Mas não choramos à toa / Aqui nessa tribo Ninguém quer a sua catequização Falamos a sua língua, Mas não entendemos o seu sermão Nós rimos alto, bebemos e falamos palavrão Mas não sorrimos à toa / Aqui nesse barco Ninguém quer a sua orientação Não temos perspectivas Mas o vento nos dá a direção A vida que vai à deriva / É a nossa condução Mas não seguimos à toa Volte para o seu lar Volte para lá. Arnaldo Antunes, "Volte Para o Lar," Álbum Um Som, BMG Brasil Ltda, 1998.
19. ANTHONY, M., Des plantes et desdieuxdans lés cultes afro-brésiliens: Essai d'éthnobotaniquecomparativeAfrique-Brésil. Paris, apud.: BAIRRAO, op.cit., "Jurema é uma cerimônia religiosa (diversamente celebrada por índios ou caboclos) no âmbito da qual aquela bebida é comungada. Às vezes distinguida como uma religião específica no complexo cenário da espiritualidade brasileira, mais comumente o culto da Jurema apresenta-se difuso em práticas religiosas nas quais pode ter um papel mais ou menos central: pajelança, toré, catimbó, umbanda, candomblé de caboclo etc.", (acesso em 20/12/2015).
20. JUREMA MEDICINA SAGRADA, Aldeia de Shiva, "A jurema sagrada é remanescente da tradição religiosa dos índios que habitavam o litoral da Paraíba, Rio Grande do Norte e no Sertão de Penambuco e dos seus pajés, grandes conhecedores dos mistérios do além, plantas e dos animais. Depois da chegada dos africanos no Brasil, quando estes fugiam dos engenhos onde estavam escravizados, encontravam abrigo nas aldeias indígenas, e através desse contato, os africanos trocavam o que tinham de conhecimento religioso em comum com os índios. Por isso até hoje, os grandes mestres juremeiros conhecidos, são sempre mestiços com sangue índio e negro. Os africanos contribuíram com o seu conhecimento sobre o culto dos mortos egun e das divindades da natureza os orixás voduns e inkices. Os índios, estes contribuíram com o conhecimento de invocações dos espíritos de antigos pajés e dos trabalhos realizados com os encantados das matas e dos rios. Daí a jurema se compor de duas grandes linhas de trabalho: a linha dos mestres de jurema e a linha dos encantados.", http://www.aldeiadeshiva.org/medicinas/jurema.html (acesso em 6/1/2016).

21. Para mais informações RODRIGUES, CAMPOS, op.cit.
22. IRARRÁZAVAL, Diego, "Salvação Indígena and Afro-Americana," in Teologia Pluralista Libertadora Intercontinental, Vigil, José M., Tomita, Luiza E., Barros, Marcelo, (Organizadores), ASETT, EATWOT (São Paulo: Paulinas, 2008), 69.
23. GEBARA, Ivone, "Pluralismo Religioso, Uma Perspectiva Feminista" in Teologia Latino-Americana Pluralista da Libertação, op. cit. 298.

Referências bibliográficas

Alves Jr., Antônio Marques, Tambores para a Rainha da Floresta, a inserção da Umbanda no Santo Daime, dissertação de mestrado, PUC São Paulo, 2007, http://www.sapientia.pucsp.br/tde_busca/arquivo.php?codArquivo=5712

Amado, W., Bertazzo, J., Aldighieri, M., and Lopes, S. A religião e o negro no Brasil, Loyola, São Paulo, 1989.

ATABAQUE-ASETT. Teologia afro-americana: II Consulta Ecumênica de Teologia e Culturas Afro-Americana e Caribenha. São Paulo: Paulinas, 1997.

Bairrão, José Francisco Miguel Henriques, Raízes da Jurema, Psicol. USP, São Paulo, v. 14, n. 1, p. 157–184, 2003, in: http://www.scielo.br/scielo.php?script=sci_arttext&pid=S0103-65642003000100009&lng=en&nrm=iso

Brandão, Carlos Rodrigues, da Fronteira da fé – Alguns sistemas de sentido, crenças e religiões no Brasil de hoje, Estudos Avançados **18** (52), USP, 2004, http://www.revistas.usp.br/eav/article/download/10035/11607

Coelho, Alexandra,O culto de índios e negros que chegou a Portugal, in: http://www.publico.pt/sociedade/noticia/o-culto-de-indios-e-negros-que-chegou-a-portugal-1665703

Camargo, M.T.L. Arruda, Contribuição ao estudo Etnofarmacobotânico da bebida ritual de religiões afrobrasileiras denominada "vinho da Jurema" e seus aditivos psicoativos, Revista Nures, Ano X, Número 26, janeiro-abril de 2014 http://revistas.pucsp.br/index.php/nures/article/download/24694/17574.

Droogers, André. "A Religiosidade Mínima Brasileira." In Religião e Sociedade, Rio de Janeiro, 14/2, 1987.

Estermann, J., Cruz y Coca - hacialadescolonización de lareligión y la teologia, LibreríaArmonía, Instituto Superior Ecuménico Andino de Teología (ISEAT), 2013.

Frisotti, H., Passos no diálogo: igreja católica e religiões afro-brasileiras, SP, Paulus, 1996.

Gebara, Ivone. "Que Escrituras são autoridade sagrada? Ambigüidades da Bíblia na vida das mulheres na América Latina." In Concilium. Revista Internacional de Teologia, Petrópolis, n° 276, 1998/3, p. 10–25.

Grunewald, Rodrigo de Azeredo, Toré e Jurema: Emblemas Indígenas no Nordeste do Brasil, Cienc. Cult. vol. 60 no.4 São Paulo, 2008. In: http://cienciaecultura.bvs.br/scielo.php?script=sci_arttext&pid=S0009-67252008000400018

Irarrázavl, Diego, "Salvação Indígena and Afro-Americana," in Teologia Pluralista Libertadora Intercontinental, Vigil, José M., Tomita, Luiza E., Barros, Marcelo, (Organizadores), ASETT, EATWOT, São Paulo: Paulinas, 2008.

Mota, Clarice Novaes, Barros, José Flávio Pessoa, "O complexo da Jurema: representações e drama social negro-indígena", in Clarice Novaes da Mota, Ulysses Paulino de Albuquerque (orgs.), As muitas faces da Jurema: de espécie botânica a divindade afro-indígena, Recife: Bagaço, 2002.

Mota, Clarice Novaes, Considerações sobre o processo visionário através do uso da jurema indígena Anais 2008. In: http://www.abant.org.br/conteudo/ANAIS/CD_Virtual_26_RBA/grupos_de_trabalho/trabalhos/GT%2006/clarice%20novaes%20da%20mota.pdf

Oliveira, Marco Davi, A religião mais negra do Brasil, São Paulo: Mundo Cristão, 2004.

Pádua, Jorge Hage, Teologia negra da libertação - Expressão teológica dos oprimidos na América Latina, Estudos Teológicos, v. 39, n. 2, p. 143–166, 1999, in: periodicos.est.edu.br/index.php/estudos_teologicos/article/.../715/650

Rodrigues, Michelle Gonçalves; Campos, Roberta Bivar Carneiro. Caminhos da visibilidade: a ascensão do culto a jurema no campo religioso de Recife. Afro-Ásia, Salvador, n. 47, 2013. In: http://www.scielo.br/scielo.php?script=sci_arttext&pid=S0002-05912013000100008

Santos, Jocélio, O poder da cultura e a cultura no poder - a disputa simbólica da herança cultural negra no Brasil, Salvador: EDUFBA, 2005. In: http://static.scielo.org/scielobooks/hqhrv/pdf/santos-9788523208950.pdf

Sena, José Roberto Feitosa, Maracatu rural: uma herança religiosa afro-indigena na capital pernambucana, SOTER, Anais 22 Congresso, volume 3, 2009, http://www.soter.org.br/documentos/documento-t1xF1HqaxcboGYi.pdf

Silva, Silvia Regina de Lima, AbriendoCaminos, Teología Feminista y Teología Negra Feminista Latinoamericana, Revista Magistro, UNIGRANRIO, vol.1, num.1, 2010, in: http://publicacoes.unigranrio.edu.br/index.php/magistro/article/viewFile/1055/618

Silva, Wagner Gonçalves, Religião e identidade cultural negra: católicos, afrobrasileiros e neopentecostais, cadernos de campo, São Paulo, n. 20, 2011. In: http://www.revistas.usp.br/cadernosdecampo/article/viewFile/36804/39526

Soares, Afonso Maria Ligório, Impasses da teologia católica diante do sincretismo religioso afro-brasileiro, in:http://ciberteologia.paulinas.org.br/ciberteologia/wp-content/uploads/2009/05/impassesdateologiacatolica.pdf

Soares, Afonso Maria Ligório, Sincretismo afro-católico no Brasil: lições de um povo em exílio, Revista de Estudos da Religião – REVER, PUC SP, 2002. In: http://www.pucsp.br/rever/rv3_2002/t_soares.htm

Tromboni, Marcos, Índios e caboclos na formação da nação brasileira - A Jurema das ramas até o tronco: ensaio sobre algumas categorias de classificação religiosa, in: CARVALHO,

MR., and CARVALHO, AM., org. Índios e caboclos: a história recontada [online]. Salvador: EDUFBA, 2012, https://books.google.com.br/books?isbn=8523212086

Páginas consultadas

VIII Encontro Afro-Ecumênico da Comunidade de Caxuté, in: http://jornadadeagroecologiadabahia.blogspot.com.br/

Teia Agroecológica do Sul da Bahia, http://jornadadeagroecologiadabahia.blogspot.com.br/p/blog-page_11.html

Articulação das Pastorais do Campo, 2015, http://www.cptnacional.org.br/index.php/publicacoes/noticias/acoes-dos-movimentos/2482-articulacao-das-pastorais-do-campo-realiza-encontro-sobre-desafios-pastorais-no-campo

CENTRO ATABAQUE DE CULTURA NEGRA E TEOLOGIA, in: http://atabaque-cultura-negra-e-teologia.blogspot.com.br/

Cabruca, Planeta Orgânico, in: http://planetaorganico.com.br/site/index.php/cabruca/

Jurema Medicina Sagradas, Aldeia de Shiva, http://www.aldeiadeshiva.org/medicinas/jurema.html

CROSSCURRENTS

OS CRISTÃOS E YORUBÁS COMENDO JUNTOS
Eucaristia e Oferendas[1]

Cláudio Carvalhaes

> Só vivemos para fazer. Sem fazer, apenas existimos.
> Padre Vieira

> Só me interesso pelo que não é meu.
> Oswald de Andrade

> As religiões e as diferenças religiosas são um elemento ativo e indissociável das dinâmicas cultural e política que estão |transformando o sentido das conexões sociais e políticas do nosso tempo, quando vindas de baixo, como emancipatórias.
> Joanildo Burity

> Eu diria que não pode haver diálogo entre cristãos e muçulmanos se não há uma prática comum. Qualquer outro diálogo fora de uma prática comum não passa de discussão. Nonsense bizantino.
> Frei Betto

Este capítulo apresenta a possibilidade de uma forma mais ampla de hospitalidade eucarística, que se baseia nas práticas da igreja primitiva e é consoante com o trabalho em curso da nossa fé *reformata semper reformanda* (reformada e sempre se reformando). Nele, ao explorar uma possível relação entre duas religiões presentes no Brasil, o cristianismo (mais especificamente o seu ramo reformado) e o candomblé (uma religião afro-brasileira), tento expandir os vocabulários inter-religiosos, raciais e globais, práticas e noções das orações eucarísticas de hospitalidade. As questões relevantes da realidade brasileira e o formato da práxis aqui proposta podem talvez ilustrar a crescente necessidade do envolvimento das igrejas de todos os lugares com estranhos, através de novas formas de diálogo teológico e práticas litúrgicas capazes de proporcionar, em certa medida, diálogo, justiça, paz e hospitalidade. Além disso, nosso mundo globalizado continua a disseminar em todos os lugares muitas formas de religião, e os cristãos devem aprender como se relacionar, dialogar e conviver com outros tipos de credos, práticas e visões de mundo.

O candomblé é uma dessas religiões aptas a sobreviver nesse mundo globalizado por apresentar grande capacidade de adaptação e flexibilidade para se ajustar a novos lugares e situações. Os deuses do candomblé viajam com o seu povo e incorporam deuses locais onde o povo do candomblé é recebido. Saído da África, o candomblé se transformou e adotou uma nova configuração no Brasil. Rachel E. Harding define assim o candomblé:

> O candomblé é um rico e complexo portal de ações rituais, cosmologia e significado com profundas e óbvias raízes em diversas tradições religiosas do oeste e centro-oeste africano, especialmente yorubá, aja-fon e bantu. É uma (re)criação dessas tradições, e outras, utilizando a matriz formada pela escravidão, colonialismo e mercantilismo que caracterizou o Brasil e outras novas sociedades do hemisfério ocidental desde século dezesseis ao século dezenove.[2]

Escolhi o candomblé como representante do que chamo de práxis-dialógica inter-religiosa por três razões: (1) o candomblé não é um tipo de religião, como o hinduísmo ou o islamismo, habitualmente escolhido por outros estudiosos para analisar o diálogo ou a práxis inter-religiosa, sendo assim uma oportunidade para novos insights no trabalho inter-religioso que precisamos fazer; (2) é uma religião, um pouco como o cristianismo, na qual a comida e a refeição em comum têm um papel central no culto, fornecendo um excelente estudo de caso inter-religioso para reflexão sobre as fronteiras da prática eucarística; (3) o candomblé é uma religião que, ao longo da história do Brasil, tem sido alvo de grande desconfiança e ataques da parte dos cristãos. Ela se tornou um outro radical, sobretudo para os cristãos protestantes, e minha própria fé foi profundamente definida pela negação e condenação do povo do candomblé e suas atividades religiosas. Explico:

O candomblé não faz parte dos livros sobre as chamadas religiões do mundo. É uma religião sem fundador, textos sagrados ou tradições normativas como o hinduísmo, o budismo ou o islamismo, que atraem a maioria dos cristãos interessados no diálogo religioso. Assim como o cristianismo e as outras já citadas religiões mundiais, o candomblé está alicerçado primariamente na história oral e práticas desenvolvidas em comunidades locais que interpretam o universo a partir da sua própria estrutura social. Contudo, o candomblé não deu o passo seguinte para constituir textos sagrados. Ao invés disso, continuou seu movimento e formação contínua pela transmissão do seu próprio segredo (*awó*) através da história oral para aqueles que pertenciam o grupo. Quanto às suas várias tradições, estas não se definem primariamente por dogmas, ideias teológicas ou religiosas, mas sim pelas suas práticas determinadas pelos grupos sociais (tribos, na África) que movem, transformam e estruturam o seu mundo. É por isso que só faz sentido para nós, cristãos, estabelecer uma relação prático-dialógica como povo do candomblé. Além disso, o candomblé curiosamente é uma religião, um pouco como o cristianismo, na qual a comida e a refeição em comum ocupa um papel central no culto, fazendo dessa religião um excelente estudo de caso inter-religioso para a reflexão a respeito das fronteiras eucarísticas.

Na história do Brasil, tanto cristãos católicos romanos quanto protestantes combateram ferozmente as religiões africanas. Em geral, os cristãos consideravam essas religiões como produtos de civilizações menos avançadas e seus praticantes menos humanos, comprometidos com práticas religiosas envoltas em magia e superstição que pertenciam ao Diabo. Portanto, o candomblé e outras religiões africanas pareciam ser uma ameaça à cultura cristã e ao bem-estar da vida religiosa "livre" no Brasil. Além do mais, uma vez que a maioria dos membros dessas religiões era de negros, não se pode desassociar essa visão desfavorável das religiosidades africanas do sistema com fortes conotações racistas que estruturava as visões, conceitos e percepções cristãos.

O medo, a raiva e desconfiança disseminados na cultura brasileira em relação às religiões africanas fizeram dessas religiões um campo missionário a ser conquistado pelos cristãos. Mais tarde, esse medo, raiva e suspeita apresentaram-se até mesmo em formas mais violentas. Para citar apenas um exemplo, ialorixá Dulce deixou a Assembleia de Deus para se tornar mãe de santo no Candomblé. Ela me contou que os cristãos foram até sua casa, onde ficava também o seu terreiro, e ficaram cantando em alta voz músicas cristãs e mesmo atiraram pedras para interromper e acabar com o culto do candomblé.[3] Esse ataque, devo dizer, não foi uma exceção na história brasileira de racismo e de argumentação teológica cristã.

Finalmente, o candomblé se tornou um "outro" religioso e radical envolvendo a fé cristã no Brasil. Certa vez, o Prof. John Makransky fez a seguinte pergunta a um grupo de estudiosos envolvidos no diálogo inter-religioso: "Qual a sua motivação (pessoal) fundamental para fazer esse trabalho e como isso influencia a sua teologia? É alguma coisa que vem das suas predileções ou é algo mais profundo em você?"[4] Minha fé só pode ser compreendida quando eu olho para trás e vejo que a maioria das coisas que eu afirmava estavam fundamentadas na negação e na recusa de outros povos e outras crenças, incluindo as religiões africanas. Na escola, na igreja e nas ruas de São Paulo, aprendi que o candomblé era uma religião dominada por demônios e controlada pelo diabo. Eu não podia cruzar a porta da frente de um terreiro, um local de culto do candomblé, por medo de ser capturado por esses demônios. Muito cedo na vida eu me tornei um evangélico fervoroso, e minha missão era converter essas pessoas endemoniadas que haviam sido capturadas pelo diabo e estavam condenadas ao inferno.

Foi muito mais tarde que comecei a aprender que o povo do candomblé não era o povo do Diabo, mas meus irmãos e irmãs. O movimento de me distanciar do medo em direção a um lugar de confiança e admiração não foi rápido nem fácil. Eu tinha que me encontrar com eles, visitar os seus locais de culto, me envolver, observar os seus rituais, comer a sua comida, convidá-los para fazer parte da minha própria vida. Assim, comprometendo-me com novas formas de relacionamento, aqui eu queria encontrar e promover um espaço seguro onde cristãos poderiam se relacionar com o povo do candomblé e, através de movimentos práticos, criar um processo de restituição do povo do candomblé e um espaço de compartilhamento de alegria, cuidado, respeito e hospitalidade.

Este capítulo sustenta a crença de que, ao buscarmos por possibilidades sacramentais através do diálogo/práxis inter-religioso e ao explorarmos o relacionamento entre cristianismo e candomblé, podemos encontrar um espaço para o diálogo, reconciliação, vínculo, desmantelamento do racismo, paz curadora e hospitalidade. Portanto, minhas questões iniciais são: dada a história brasileira de escravidão e racismo, nós poderíamos providenciar um local de reconciliação e hospitalidade através de rituais comuns à mesa, de oração e dança? Poderíamos oferecer comida sagrada uns aos outros e comermos juntos? Pode a mesa eucarística conter comida oferecida aos Orixás, os deuses do candomblé? Os Orixás permitiriam que os cristãos comessem a sua comida? Como fazer essas coisas respeitando nossos próprios limites e ao mesmo tempo expandindo nossas possibilidades?

É legítimo perguntar: por que precisamos trazer a história da colonização e da escravidão para mesa da eucaristia? Como vimos também, a mesa eucarística estabelece não só as fronteiras teológicas, litúrgicas e eclesiásticas, mas também os limites sócio-econômico-políticos que delimitam as maneiras pelas quais a comunidade define-se a si mesma, encarrega-se de questões de poder e determina as normas e padrões da sua própria identidade e valor. Em uma só palavra, a mesa eucarística oferece uma certa compreensão da humanidade. Ao explorar como o cristianismo no Brasil lidou com os negros e a sua religião, a questão do que significa ser humano é novamente aberta. Nós, que estamos à mesa, também somos responsáveis não só por nós mesmos mas também por aqueles que não estão aqui conosco e pelo que está acontecendo em nossa sociedade.

Escravidão e candomblé no Brasil
A história do Brasil é a história de índios, europeus, africanos e suas religiões. Em volta desses encontros, as culturas e identidades do Brasil se formaram. Os povos africanos foram fundamentais para essa polidoxia cultural, religiosa e identitária. Os africanos enriqueceram a forma de pensar e de se relacionar, a literatura, a música, a culinária e as religiões brasileiras. Contudo, a história do Brasil é também bastante manchada pelos quase 400 anos de escravidão perpetrados por Portugal. Os portugueses, insatisfeitos com o trabalho dos povos nativos, importaram povos africanos das suas colônias na África. Em 1590, o número de escravos no Brasil chegava a 36 mil; em 1817, eles eram 1,9 milhão, e somavam 3,5 milhões em 1850. "No total", diz o historiador brasileiro Luiz Felipe de Alencastro,

> mais de 4 milhões de africanos foram deportados para o Brasil entre 1550 e 1850, fazendo deste o país do continente americano

que recebeu o maior número de escravos enviados ao Novo Mundo. Se comparado com os Estados Unidos durante o mesmo período mencionado acima, o Brasil recebeu 43 percent de todos os africanos trazidos para a América, enquanto os Estados Unidos receberam, de 1650 a 1808, apenas 5,5 percent."[5]

Em 1888, o Brasil foi o último dos principais países do mundo a aprovar uma lei acabando com a escravidão. Ainda assim, a escravidão continuou sob muitas outras maneiras, afetando profundamente os povos e religiões dos descendentes dos africanos. O impacto desses 400 anos de escravidão ainda é bastante presente no Brasil de hoje, embora seja apresentado de maneira mais agradável pelo aparato cultural brasileiro. O racismo no Brasil não é um movimento "descarado", com placas em locais públicos informando que "negros não são bem-vindos aqui". Ao contrário: é simpático, convencendo as pessoas de que elas vivem "em harmonia" ao mesmo tempo em que mantém os negros nas camadas mais baixas da sociedade. Esse chamado "racismo cordial" demonstra o mito ideológico da democracia racial no Brasil. Sua palatabilidade é tão perversiva/pervasiva que torna a luta contra o racismo muito mais difícil.[6]

Isso não quer dizer que não houve resistência por parte dos africanos contra esse racismo. Um dos mais significativos movimentos de resistência foi o Quilombo dos Palmares[7], durante o século XVII. Escravos fugitivos criaram essas cidades livres em áreas remotas, às quais se uniam. Mais de 20 mil ex-escravos e outras pessoas rejeitadas pela sociedade, incluindo europeus e índios, viveram livres e soberanos nesses quilombos.

Lentamente, o Brasil começa a lidar mais atentamente com essas diferenças e a aculturação dos povos afrodescendentes. Chegando no Brasil, esses afrodescendentes trouxeram consigo suas religiões. No entanto, os escravos eram proibidos de praticá-las e eram forçados a adotar o cristianismo. Especialmente durante o século XIX, os portugueses fizeram tentativas claras de destruir as práticas religiosas dos africanos e crioulos (negros nascidos no Brasil). Isso porque as crenças e práticas do candomblé eram consideradas um sinal de cultura incivilizada, com seus elementos religiosos mágicos e pré-modernos que não faziam parte do projeto de civilização europeia moderna e cristã desejado para o Brasil. Ferozes ataques ao Yorubá e outras religiões africanas continuaram, de diversas maneiras, até o fim do século XX.

Ainda assim, o candomblé e seu povo conseguiram sobreviver, apesar de toda contínua perseguição por parte do governo brasileiro e repressão sistemática pelas forças policiais até 1975, quando uma lei federal finalmente foi criada para proteger os terreiros de candomblé de invasões, abusos e vandalismos. Desde então, o povo do candomblé, chamado "povo dos santos", continua lutando para sobreviver e viver livremente neste país acolhedor e cordialmente racista da América do Sul chamado Brasil.

Candomblé[8]

O candomblé baseia-se no mistério do *awô*, o segredo que é transmitido oralmente às novas gerações de fiéis ao longo do tempo. A transmissão do candomblé dá-se pelos iniciados à medida que estes vivem juntos os preceitos religiosos. O núcleo da religião é a oralidade não-estruturada, que só recentemente começou a ser transposta para o suporte escrito. No candomblé, a tradição é cantada e dançada. A síntese do processo todo, segundo Alessandra Osuna, seria

> A busca por um equilíbrio energético entre os habitantes do mundo material e a energia desses seres que habitam o orum, uma dimensão espacial que poderia ser chamada de céu, o interior da terra ou um lugar além daquilo que é conhecido, de acordo com diferentes compreensões de cada tribo, povo e tradição. Cada ser humano tem um Orixá que lhe protege; o Orixá pessoal que só pode ser conhecido pela pessoa através de um ritual. Ao cumprir as obrigações prescritas pelo seu Orixá, a pessoa recebe uma reserva de energia e ganha mais equilíbrio.[9]

Da mesma forma que não podemos falar de um cristianismo mas de cristianismos, também precisamos considerar os candomblés, no plural. O candomblé varia de acordo com suas muitas tradições: congo, jejê, nagô, queto, ijexá, angola. Roger Bastide diz que "é possível distinguir cada uma destas "nações" pela forma de tocar os tambores (com baquetas ou com as mãos), suas músicas, o idioma falado, as canções, as roupas litúrgicas, os nomes das divindades e alguns aspectos do ritual."[10] Além disso, " 'cada casa do candomblé é uma sentença', isto é, cada casa de culto descobre noções de certo e errado, suas teologias e compreensões religiosas das suas histórias e antepassados."[11]

Gisele Omindarewá Cossard, uma ialorixá muito respeitada, elenca três tradições africanas essenciais na linha Yorubá: "o aspecto Yorubá das casas de tradição ketu, o aspecto fon das casas de tradição jejê e o aspecto banto das casas de tradição congo/angola... O mundo do candomblé é multifacetado."[12] Contudo, as diferenças nas tradições africanas não quer dizer que os africanos são politeístas. Olorum, Olodumarê, Zaniapombo são nomes diferentes para o mesmo deus criador de tudo. De acordo com Vilson Junior, "o candomblé é baseado em três pilares: (1) religião secreta ou oralidade; (2) respeito — hierarquia; (3) preceito — liturgia."[13]

Pierre Verger, um estudioso francês que veio ao Brasil para entender o candomblé e tornou-se um pai de santo, um babalorixá, define o candomblé assim:

> O candomblé é para mim muito interessante porque é uma religião de exaltação da personalidade do povo. Onde você pode ser aquilo que você é e não o que a sociedade faz você ser. Para as pessoas que têm coisas para expressar através do inconsciente, transe é a possiblidade para o inconsciente se manifestar.[14]

O Candomblé carrega uma visão de mundo conhecido e desconhecido poderosa, incluindo mitos da criação e oferecendo caminhos para que as pessoas possam atingir o potencial e a plenitude das suas vidas. O candomblé é uma forma de balancear a energia do indivíduo, da comunidade e do mundo. O movimento entre os mundos visível e invisível, as conexões com os deuses e entidades (e portanto consigo mesmo, com comunidades, passado, presente e futuro), os caminhos para encontrar cura e proteção, os caminhos que exigem uma vida justa, são todos partes das sessões/rituais privados e celebrações públicas. Tudo acontece ritualmente, e a conexão e as respostas dos Orixás são transmitidas através dos rituais. A composição e as demandas desta religião difícil e engajada representam uma maneira fascinante de compreender a humanidade em toda sua complexidade.

Consideremos alguns dos elementos mais conhecidos do Candomblé:

Hierarquia e estrutura

O respeito à hierarquia baseia-se na estrutura religiosa na qual Olodumarê é o principal deus criador, Orumilá é o detentor de toda sabedoria, e os

Orixás, Voduns e Inquices que habitam entre os mundos natural e supernatural. Dentro da organização social do Candomblé, há uma forte estrutura hierárquica, na qual os babalaôs e ialawôs são os principais líderes dos Candomblés, algo equivalente aos pastores e párocos das igrejas cristãs, os iawôs (os iniciados), e por fim aqueles que participam de uma maneira ou outra mas que não são necessariamente membros. A hierarquia fundamenta-se na linha ancestral do povo africano, que é resultado da maneira como o sistema étnico e sociocultural estabeleceu-se na África: de um lado, reis e rainhas de diferentes nações e, por outro, o sistema religioso, com os Yorubás e Nagôs. Reis e rainhas eram responsáveis pelo bem estar dos povos e comunidades, e controlavam os poderes da natureza. Eles eram tratados como deuses. Quando morriam, seu reino era espiritualizado e tornava-se parte da história, memória e força da comunidade que os considerava sagrados. Estes então tornavam-se seus guias e Orixás.

Culto

Candomblé é culto; é serviço. Apenas os iniciados conhecem o segredo e continuam a se aprofundar no entendimento deste segredo. O candomblé é uma religião que conecta o mundo material e imaterial, dando espaço para o inconsciente revelar-se como parte da totalidade do sagrado. A religião que equilibra as energias destes mundos, luta contra o desequilíbrio gerado pelas nossas atitudes e para restabelecer o equilíbrio do mundo dado por Olodumarê, o deus criador supremo, e Orumilá. Candomblé é servir aos Orixás, deuses que advêm de todas as forças da natureza: terra, fogo, água e ar. Babalorixá Aragão descreve o candomblé como um monastério onde as pessoas estão no mundo, e a função do candomblé e seus sacerdotes (ialorixás e babalorixás) é cuidar dos iniciados e das entidades. Servir é uma troca no candomblé. O deus onisciente, onipresente e onipotente não requer adoração. Os Orixás desejam culto! Muitas celebrações giram em torno do canto, da dança e da comida.

Espaços de culto: terreiros

O candomblé é uma extensão da casa, da família. Esta é a razão pela qual os terreiros são sempre nos fundos ou do lado da casa da ialorixá / babalorixá. Os terreiros muitas vezes ficam na casa da mãe ou pai de santo e devem estar perto de árvores, jardins e plantas, já que o candomblé está fundamentalmente relacionado à natureza, de onde vêm suas fontes. Em cada terreiro, geralmente um Orixá principal é o cabeça do espaço de culto, mas todos os Orixás são bem-vindos e cultuados. É deles a escolha de aparecer ou não. Durante as celebrações e trabalhos específicos, os terreiros são o lugar onde o povo fica, dorme, dança, come e vive. Os terreiros são lugares sagrados onde "Orixás, Voduns e Inquices dançam; a fonte na qual os iawôs (iniciados) se banham, as árvores sagradas onde Iroco e Tempo vivem; as casinhas para Exú e os eguns."[15] Fundamentado nas sociedades africanas, o candomblé tem estruturas social, cultura e religiosa complexas, e suas práticas e crenças são múltiplas, variando de acordo com cada terreiro. Os terreiros tornaram-se espaços de resistência e de luta entre antigas e novas visões de mundo. Nestes espaços, movimentos tênues ou robustos da memória, resistência, engajamento e solidariedade trabalham contra a opressão e a morte. Como colocado por Harding, estes espaços se referem "aos lugares sociopolítico, cultural, psíquico e ritual-religioso dentro da experiência afro-brasileira... lugares contém a implicação tanto da fronteira quanto do movimento." Estes espaços religiosos mantidos pelo povo africanos eram lugares que contrastavam e ofereciam alternativas às ruas (onde viviam os pobres, os que "não valiam nada", os que tinham sido abandonados) e as senzalas, os lugares impostos pela sociedade racista e escravocrata que lhes tirava sua dignidade, valor ou orgulho.[16] Os terreiros, também chamados de axé, a energia vital, eram lugares que ajudavam os africanos e afro-brasileiros a se reposicionarem em relação ao novo mundo da escravidão, destruição e morte. Harding estabelece a relação do candomblé com os povos africanos e de origem africana:

> para estas pessoas e seus descendentes, o candomblé era uma maneira importante de processar o trauma. Representava um processo integrativo — recuperando e (re)organizando o que havia sido dividido: família, identidade e psique... O candomblé providenciava um forma de re-lembrar e re-criar uma identidade preciosa e uma conectividade — com o Espírito, com o passado pré-escravidão, com os ancestrais, com a comunidade. Também providenciava, cultivando materiais africanos e elementos da cultura nos rituais, uma africanidade alternativa, uma identidade alternativa da negritude. E onde a miríade de ignomínias da vida no Brasil gerava crises de

integridade psíquica, o candomblé oferecia música e dança transformadoras, comunidade, cura mágico-farmacológica. No acolhimento mútuo da humanidade e espírito no candomblé emergiram intimações de plenitude-representações de reprocidade da devoção e responsabilidade, o compar-tilhamento dos fardos e das alegrias.[17]

Os terreiros de candomblé eram lugares onde o povo participava integralmente, e essa forma de participação lhes deu uma certa convicção da sua identidade e valor próprio, condições para resistir, recuperando sua força e vivendo suas vidas ainda que debaixo do poder esmagador da escravidão.

Sacerdotes e sacerdotisas

O pai de santo, o babalorixá, está ligado ao Conhecimento, enquanto as mães de santo, as ialorixás, estão ligadas à Sabedoria. Muito antes, babalorixás e ialorixás eram chamados de servos. Eram eles que tomavam conta dos Orixás. Os sacerdotes e sacerdotisas (babalorixás e ialorixás) organizam o evento do culto e certificam-se de que tudo é feito da forma apropriada. São eles que detêm os segredos da religião, e a quem os iniciados devem respeito e obediência. Também, são eles que recebem e transmitem as mensagens dos Orixás (entidades/deuses) e são eles quem decide os atos do culto, as oferendas e trabalhos a serem realizados para o desfrute dos Orixás e para a segurança, bênção e proteção dos iniciados. Os rituais são corpóreos, e a fala dos babalorixás e ialorixás geram energia.

Orixás

Orixás são forças incorpóreas e vivas que sentem e pensam e experimentas as coisas como nós, humanos. A compreensão africana do mundo não faz divisão entre sagrado e secular nem comportamentos humanos e divinos dos Orixás. Os Orixás manifestam-se aos seres humanos possuindo os corpos destes durante os cultos nos terreiros. Uma pessoa escolhida pelo Orixá é um elegum, aquele tem o privilégio de receber o Orixá. Qualquer pessoa pode pedir e conhecer e se relacionar com seu Orixás sem ter de passar pelo ritual de iniciação. Contudo, se a pessoa é escolhida pelo Orixá, ela será convidada a fazer o Orí, ou fazer a cabeça, que é o ritual de iniciação. Aqueles que invocam os Orixás devem oferecer saudações, fazer liturgias, realizar gestos e movimentos, cantar, dançar, e tocar tambor, cozinhar, vestir-se com as suas cores apropriadas, e cumprir as exigências dos Orixás. Eles devem fazer oferendas das comidas desejadas e espalhá-las pela cidade, mas sobretudo nas florestas, como forma de satisfazer os desejos dos Orixás. Em tudo, o crente deve obedecer o Orixá, que em troca vai oferecer milagres, curas e equilíbrio para a vida da pessoa. Os Orixás não podem ser contrariados. Se eles pedem um trabalho que não é feito, o crente irá sofrer consequências.

Festas, sacrifício, comida e oferendas

Festividades no Candombé são eventos poderosos com a participação de muitas pessoas. Entretanto, como Roger Bastide disse, "a festividade pública constitui somente uma pequena parte da vida do Candomblé. Os rituais privados são mais importantes que o cerimonial público. As religiões africanas irá colorir e controlar cada parte da vida dos seus membros, e (pelo modo de viver sua religião) os negros se sentem mais africanos e no final pertencentes a um mundo mental diferente..."[18]

A cozinha é uma parte fundamental do culto nos terreiros. Como colocado por Edson Carneiro:

> A cozinha ritual, cheia de panelas de barro e pedras de amolar, com os noviços e iabassês (os chefes da cozinha), é um ponto fundamental de qualquer terreiro de qualquer nação do candomblé... onde o cozinheiro prepara as obrigações, as comidas para as oferendas e as bebidas para os deuses negros. Tudo é imaculado. Estas cozinhas costumavam ser muito diferentes das cozinhas do dia a dia das pessoas, mas hoje elas são parecidas. Mas tanto antes quanto hoje, estas cozinhas guardam segredos que só os que trabalham lá conhecem. A forma de preparar e de servir deve seguir alguns preceitos.[15]

As cozinhas têm todas as ferramentas necessárias e os ingredientes para preparar as comidas. Há um cargo elevado, por assim dizer, no mundo da cozinha, e a pessoa designada pelo Orixá da casa, chamada de iabassê ou adagam, prepara a comida especial. O babalorixá Luis de Logun Edé diz que "Ninguém pergunta se a pessoa tem estudo formal ou não. O dom é identificado pelo babalorixá/ialorixá e escolhida pelo Orixá para ocupar o cargo. Frequentemente a pessoa nasceu com este dom, e vai ser treinado para aprender como preparar as diferentes oferendas para cada Orixá."[19]

Depois de preparada por pessoas especialmente treinadas para esta tarefa, a comida/oferenda é: (1) oferecida em locais específicos numa procissão ao som de canções; (2) depois é levada para as florestas ou a natureza, onde o Orixá vive; (3) oferecida durante a celebração de todo o terreiro e comida pelos participantes. Além disso, a oferenda de comida aos Orixás é geralmente feita à noite, já que os Orixás não comem depois do sol nascer. É comum as celebrações do candomblé terminarem bem tarde e com muita comida. Gisele Cossard descreve assim o fim da cerimônia:

> Geralmente é muito tarde para as pessoas voltarem para casa... Alguns dos iawôs (os iniciados) ajudam a server a refeição para os presentes. A comida é um oferecimento generoso do terreiro para toda a comunidade que vem para a celebração. No entanto, de acordo com as pessoas mais antigas do candomblé, há outro sentido para este oferecimento: os Orixás apreciam fartura, e desejam que todos os presentes saiam com a barriga cheia.[21]

No entanto, há muito mais no significado da comida para as religiões africanas. Na verdade, foram as mulheres do candomblé quem preservaram e tornaram conhecidas as religiões africanas através da sua habilidade na preparação das comidas e na confecção do seu artesanato: colares, pulseiras, costuras, bordados etc. Os rituais do candomblé envolvem oferendas dos reinos mineral, vegetal e animal; cura, dança e percussão.[21] O sacrifício de animais é parte muito importante da religião. Só os que são membros do terreiro/axé podem assistir o sacrifício. A restrição deve-se sobretudo ao medo de que os não-crentes achem a prática do sacrifício incivilizada ou cruel. Cada animal está relacionado a um Orixá. Em todas as celebrações, se o terreiro tiver condições para tanto, um animal de duas patas deve ser sacrificado para Exú, e outro de quatro patas para o Orixá da casa. O sexo do animal deve seguir o do Orixá. Oxogum é quem realiza o sacrifício. A carcaça do animal sacrificado é levada para a pessoa responsável pela cozinha, que prepara a comida para a oferenda. Depois que a comida é oferecida ao Orixá pelo babalorixá/ialorixá numa sala separada, ela será consumida pelos fiéis e também compartilhada com os visitantes.[22]

Toda comida oferecida a um Orixá tem o poder de mudar a vida das pessoas. Cada um pode receber uma bênção através da comida. A comida que não é consumida é guardada por três dias e depois descartada. Foi a culinária africana preservada pelos rituais religiosos que acabou indo para a mesa de todos.

Vilson Caetano de Souza Junior diz que "durante as festividades, a comida é dividida entre o povo e significa comensalidade. As pessoas compartilham, vivem e memorizam a comida. Comida é memória e evoca emoções. A comida no candomblé tem a ver com o resgate da memória do povo. A comida durante o culto é para energizar o Orixá, o povo e o lugar."[23]

O babalorixá Luis de Logun Edé diz que "os Orixás comem a comida que os humanos comem, mas cada oferenda tem sua própria sabedoria e forma de preparo que incluem: palavras encantadas *(fó)*, orações *(àdúrà)*, evocações *(oriki)* e canções *(orin)* ligadas às estórias sagradas *(itan)*, elementos essencials e vitais para a transmissão do axé. Vida, poder, criatividade é o que usamos para fazer o bem."[19]

Bastide descreve assim a estrutura do ritual da comida: "Pela manhã, o sacrifício é feito; a preparação culinária e a oferenda às divindades acontece à tarde; a cerimônia pública começa quando o sol se põe e vai pela noite adentro."[24] O ato de comer junto é uma parte fundamental da festa. Abaixo, Roger Bastide descreve a experiência de comer junto no final das cerimônias. Ele diz:

> ... e antes de todos se despedirem, uma refeição comunitária permitirá a reunião das divindades, membros da fraternidade e espectadores que ainda restarem no salão de culto. As filhas de santo trazem os pratos de acordo com as cores dos seus Orixás, um pouco de comida, parte da qual foi colocada no peiji: branco para Oxalá, azul para Iemanjá, violeta para Nanã... Eles se sentam ao redor da toalha estendida no mesmo chão em que a comida sagrada foi colocada. Cada pessoa pega um bocado da comida do prato do seu deus, com as duas mãos em concha, e leva a comida à boca. Depois disso, um pouco da comida de cada prato é oferecida aos filhos dos outros Orixás segundo a ordem para cimentar a solidariedade do grupo através da partilha da comida. As sobras são guardadas em folhas de bananeira e oferecidas aos espectadores que estão de pé perto

> das filhas de santo sentadas. As diferentes comidas dos muitos Orixás são fraternalmente misturadas num tipo de bandeja; é obrigatório comer com as mãos. Não se deve confundir este repasto, que é a comunhão, com o lanche que às vezes é servido aos convidados importantes entre a dança de invocação e a dança dos deuses. É uma coisa completamente diferente, uma espécie de solidariedade tripla que acontece antes de se retornar ao mundo material: primeiro, entre o divino e o humano, depois a comunhão entre os membros que pertencem a divindades diferentes e às vezes até rivais, e finalmente entre os não-iniciados, para que um pouco da África que foi perdida possa ser reencontrada e penetre nas suas vidas. O grupo de fiéis vai além da comunhão dos filhos e filhas de santo. Entrar num candomblé é um processo gradual, e há muitos graus de inclusão...[25]

A comida/oferenda é uma parte essencial da vida da religião e da comunidade, uma forma de re-encenar a relação com a natureza, comensalidade, memória, resistência, oferta, alegria e celebração entre as divindades, dentro e fora da comunidade. A partir deste conhecimento superficial do Candomblé, como concebemos esta práxis dialógica? O que está em jogo aqui?

Práxis dialógica inter-religiosa
Na América Latina, tem havido um grande movimento de teólogos trabalhando com "teologias plurais de libertação intercontinental".[26] Esses teólogos estão conscientes da necessidade de se expandir o diálogo e de criar oportunidades para o debate teológico e o compartilhamento da vida uns com os outros. Como resultado, estão tentando expandir o discurso da teologia da libertação para o campo do pluralismo religioso, arregimentando religiões, espiritualidades e visões de mundo indígenas e de origem africana. Esta nova forma de teologia de engajamento tem sido chamada de "novo olhar positivo", "pluralismo como princípio", "nova compaixão" e "macro-ecumenismo", um neologismo para reproduzir uma nova realidade e uma nova consciência.[27] Este diálogo inter-religioso de libertação nos desafia a nos debruçarmos sobre temas ecológicos que afetam a vida e as crenças dos pobres e a incluir as mulheres.[28] No cerne deste trabalho cristão, diz Teixeira, "há uma convocação à hospitalidade,

à cortesia e à aceitação da alteridade".[29] Ao nos empenhamos neste projeto, Marcelo Barros chama nossa atenção para um aspecto importante da sua metodologia:

> Por que de repente os teólogos e antropólogos começaram a ver de modo positivo o que era chamado de sincretismo e que, historicamente, autoridades e intelectuais sempre viram como algo negativo? A única explicação que temos é que tal abertura acontece quando estamos dispostos a examinar esta questão não com nossos olhos confessionais ou a partir da perspectiva da nossa instituição, mas sim com um olhar de amor para com o povo, preocupando-se com sua vida e libertação."[30]

Este apelo é muito importante, já que o pensamento intelectual sem o envolvimento das emoções, sentimentos e do corpo, obviamente, não é capaz de levar a um diálogo inter-religioso verdadeiro. O amor é o pressuposto fundamental para os cristãos, e preocupar-se com as condições de vida do povo e as possibilidades de libertação é mais importante do que qualquer ferramenta metodológica a ser escolhida para trabalharmos.

Este projeto espera contribuir com este campo expandindo o pensamento dos teólogos da libertação a respeito do diálogo inter-religioso na América Latina, trazendo para o centro deste diálogo a necessidade de uma hospitalidade radical descrita nos capítulos anteriores. Desta forma, a relação entre cristãos e o povo do candomblé vai se alicerçar em maneiras pragmáticas de acolher um ao outro. Começando pelo mandamento do amor do Evangelho como uma exigência de hospitalidade radical do outro, esta compreensão dos relacionamentos inter-religiosos pretende ir além passar dos diálogos desvinculados para oferecer ferramentas práticas que possam fornecer contornos e formas discerníveis às noções de multiplicidade, pluralidade e amor infinito conforme imaginados por Gebara, Barros e muitos outros pensadores inter-religiosos.

Teologias do pluralismo religioso e teologias comparativas são baseadas na reflexão e prática. A partir de uma perspectiva Latino Americana, precisamos retornar à noção de Antonio Gramsci de "intelectual orgânico".[31] Teólogos da libertação na América Latina têm considerado o "intelectual orgânico" como um facilitador, alguém que reúne a informação oculta por ideologias, conectando-a com o conhecimento formal que pode servir como ferramenta crítica e envolve-se com a realidade pulsante e a sabedoria do pobre para criar uma práxis diferente que transformará a situação social e trará libertação.³²

O teólogo orgânico assume a necessidade de se modificar os laços sociais no Brasil, especialmente o ódio dos cristãos que coloca em risco a vida e os relevos religiosos do povo Yorubá. Portanto, a partir da nossa perspectiva "religiosa-inter-religiosa", precisamos assumir que o teólogo orgânico deve dar um passo à frente e adentrar outras comunidades religiosas para ajudar a facilitação do diálogo e do compartilhar da vida juntos. Além do teólogo orgânico, o teólogo-litúrgico orgânico em particular deve também fazer o mesmo movimento, já que ele(a) é quem deve estudar os rituais e performances, gestos, posturas corporais, orações, voz, audição, tato, paladar, dança e músicas como "textos" chaves para o diálogo inter-religioso.

Como as religiões Yorubás não possuem textos sagrados, sendo baseadas na oralidade não-estruturada, o teólogo litúrgico orgânico precisa aprender a melhor maneira de estabelecer este diálogo através de práticas religiosas e não-religiosas. Assim, teorias sobre os rituais, raciocínios litúrgicos, estudos performáticos, teorias sobre a vida cotidiana, teorias dos afetos, teologias inter-religiosas construtivas e assim por diante, podem e devem se ocupar das danças, músicas e movimentos corporais para tentar organizar este diálogo inter-religioso. No cristianismo, a norma da oração/*lex orandi* é que o sustenta a norma da fé/teologia-*lex credendi*. Neste diálogo, a norma da dança, dos tambores, dançar e comer no axé, junto com a norma da oração e a música e a comida nos cultos cristãos são a *lex agendi*, isto é, as normas de conduta ética respeitosa. Como resultado, a *lex vivendi* é constantemente reformada, uma vida onde espaços de generosidade, compromisso, amor e cuidado são plenamente ocupados.

É o fazer da religião que está em jogo aqui. Como coloca teologicamente J. Edgar Bruns, "Deus está fazendo alguma coisa."³³ Como podemos entender um ao outro pela nossa prática religiosa, ou, pelo nosso próprio fazer de Deus? Qual metodologia, qual jornada, caminho ou estrada, um teólogo litúrgico orgânico deve seguir aqui?³⁴

Gebara sugere que o ponto da articulação pode ser "o reconhecimento dos princípios pluralísticos fundadores da nossa existência e da própria vida, convidando-nos não só a nos compreendermos a nós mesmos, outra vez, como seres humanos, mas também para criar políticas de diálogo que nos ajudarão a atingir novamente aquilo que chamamos de bem comum".³⁵ Além disso, segundo Diego Irarrázaval, este processo inclui a capacidade de se abrir para e de apreciar os símbolos da salvação presentes em outras buscas religiosas. Pela perspectiva cristã, este processo envolve o reconhecimento da sacralidade da religião do outro e como o sentido do sagrado é fluido e permeável na nossa vida juntos.

> Sacramentalidade (de acordo com a perspectiva católica) corre nas veias da população latino-americana. No entanto, ela não se limita a algumas coisas ou à determinada igreja. Muito do ritualismo latino-americano demonstra a importância dos símbolos que configuram a espiritualidade a práxis da vida diária do povo. Deus é amado na vida de todo dia e as realidades concretas sempre carregam um valor simbólico.³⁶

Ararrázaval enxerga a noção de simbiose como uma perspectiva para uma abordagem dos símbolos do povo negro, que envolvem "elementos distintos que, quando conjugados, abrem espaço para uma vida mais ampla."³⁷ É através deste processo simbiótico capaz de lidar com forças opostas sem dicotomia ou contradições que os africanos e suas crenças e práticas interagiram com sua nova terra, o Brasil. Os cristãos poderiam aprender com este movimento simbiótico.³⁸ O ponto de partida não é a ortodoxia, mas a ortopráxis. A vida de todo dia é o critério da verdade religiosa, e neste sentido toda religião potencialmente carrega a possibilidade de conter um sacramento que é vital, importante e necessário para a viver a sua vida. Assim, embora o candomblé tenha seu próprio conjunto de crenças e sacramentos, ele não precisa desmontar outra estrutura de fé, ou sacramento, para se relacionar e estabelecer diálogo; o candomblé respeita e interage com os sacramentos do outro, pois tudo pertence a todos.

Irarrázaval termina oferecendo quatro pontos de diálogo para as religiões afro-cristãs:³⁹ (1) celebrar e pensar, no sentido de que o jeito festivo das religiões africanas são maneiras de pensar e de construir a vida, e de recriar o mundo; (2) identificarmos a nós mesmos e nosso continente como Afro-América, chamando a nós mesmos de africanos para nos ajudar a aceitar a vida, história e os elementos da religião africana como pontos comuns a todos nós; (3) celebrar o mistério do jeito africano, que é a celebração do sagrado em nossos corpos, e perceber que o corpo é um local privilegiado para a revelação do sagrado; e (4) lutar com o sincretismo e pertenças. Embora Irarrázaval não explique o que pertença significa, ele cita Maria Cristian Ventura para dizer que a religiosidade afro tem o poder de recriar seus mundos a partir das religiões que estiverem disponíveis, à mão. Logo, a disposição desta forma de sincretismo, de recriar nossos mundos a partir a sabedoria e ferramenta de outras religiões, é uma forma de se relacionar com as religiões africanas na América Latina.

Um ponto não mencionado por Irarrázaval mas fundamental neste processo é a ligação com a terra. A ecologia é um aspecto central neste diálogo, pois as práticas religiosas africanas são significativamente impregnadas com os elementos da terra. Todos os Orixás têm uma conexão com algum aspecto do mundo mineral, vegetal e animal, e todo terreiro sempre é cercado de terra, árvores e plantas. Sem o ecossistema, os africanos não poderiam praticar suas religiões (nem os cristãos, diga-se de passagem). Para uma teologia pluralista da libertação acontecer na América Latina entre cristãos e as religiões Yorubás, o comprometimento com paz e justiça deve ser acompanhado da defesa do meio ambiente. "Este é o chão a partir do qual construímos uma comunhão verdadeira entre comunidades religiosas diferentes com seus próprios elementos doutrinários, étnicos, linguísticos e ideológicos."[40]

Ela era pastora metodista, fiel à sua igreja. No entanto, por razões que ela desconhecia, seu coração batia em sincronia com os tambores dos terreiros. Tanto que ela decidiu estudar o Quilombo Zeferina e a presença de mulheres poderosas naquela comunidade. Um excelente e sólido trabalho acadêmico. Contudo, o trabalho levou seu corpo para mais perto de onde estava seu coração, e ela começou a participar das festas do candomblé. Tanto que ela foi convidada a fazer o processo de iniciação. Na época, ela disse não, porque ela era fiel à sua tradição metodista. Então, numa manhã, quando ela estava pregando sobre o Espírito Santo, ela foi tomada pelo seu Orixá e começou a se mover como ela fizera numa noite no terreiro. As pessoas da sua congregação acharam muito estranho, mas ela disse que tinha sido a ação do Espírito Santo; ainda que com ressalvas, as pessoas acreditaram que Deus havia se manifestado nela.

Pessoalmente, ela não tinha problema em transitar entre as duas religiões mas, naquele dia, ela tomou uma decisão: "Não posso continuar desse jeito. Preciso honrar meu Orixá e deixar a igreja. Sempre vou amar a igreja e a Jesus, mas meu trabalho agora é no terreiro."

Cristianismo-candomblé: movimentos e desafios
A abertura para um outro cristianismo não é algo novo nem uma escolha. Antes, é uma exigência incrustada no cerne dos evangelhos e baseada no amor. Como diz Sharon V. Betcher, usando Jean Luc Nancy, o cristianismo tem "uma obrigação de ser 'a grande abertura'."[41] Como parte desta obrigação, que é um espaço desconhecido e imprevisível, os cristãos precisam sempre reaprender a oferecer uma hospitalidade radical, e comer junto com o forasteiro e expandir a mesa de Jesus Cristo tem que ser uma prática comum. Novamente, esta "grande abertura" não significa abandonar as crenças cristãs, pois a Eucaristia deve sempre carregar a poderosa mensagem da memória/anamnese de Jesus Cristo entregue, partido e derramado por todos nós, comida para o mundo. Para o povo do candomblé no Brasil, estas reivindicações teológicas não são estranhas. Eles a ouviram durante toda sua história no Brasil, e ela não os ofende. Por outro lado, os cristãos poderiam aprender quais são as reivindicações feitas pelo povo do candomblé e honrar a fé deles. Nesta encruzilhada, os cristãos têm a oportunidade de viver o evangelho como cultura da hospitalidade, da aceitação e da cura. Como lidamos com as afirmações teológicas do outro será decidido ao longo da caminhada. A única exigência é estarmos perto um do outro, preferencialmente na(s) mesa(s) da eucaristia/oferenda de comida. O que então devemos considerar para uma práxis dialógica possível?

Espírito Santo
Todo começo depende do Espírito, tanto para o candomblé quanto para os protestantes. Nós cristãos reformados não podemos começar nada se não formos antes profundamente movidos pelo Espírito Santo. Nossos atos de louvor e de serviço a Deus são sempre uma resposta ao amor, generosidade e mandamentos de Deus. Para o candomblé, os Orixás e as entidades movem as energias e nos impelem a responder aos seus chamados e demandas.

Para os reformados, a ênfase na Eucaristia não é a mesa ou os elementos mas na assembleia cristã convocada pelo Espírito Santo. À mesa, há comida comum/bem comum e, sob o poder do Espírito Santo, nos ajuntamos como estranhos e nos tornamos uma família. À mesa, fazemos contato com as fontes de poder e cura de Deus que incitam conversa e transformação mútuas. Os reformados são capazes de dizer de boca cheia que "através do ato de comer o corpo e beber o sangue de Cristo na refeição, esta comunidade é fortalecida e preservada na sua tarefa de ser o corpo de Cristo no e para o mundo. Com estes significados em primeiro plano, a refeição se torna um símbolo central desta nova comunidade."[42]

A confiança radical no trabalho do Espírito Santo é concedida para que a mesa de Jesus Cristo torne-se aberta, quebrando os muros de auto-isolamento da membresia e da mesmice religiosa. A presença do Espírito à mesa nos chama para vivermos de maneira radicalmente igualitária, dividindo comida, sabedoria, recursos, amor e cuidado com o mundo. A mesa de Jesus Cristo, incrementada pela presença do Espírito Santo, oferece perdão, cura e reconciliação, ainda que ela seja continuamente interrompida pelo medo, ódio, ansiedade, injustiça, morte e pelos perigos e conflitos do mundo.

Porque Deus é quem se manifesta a si mesmo onde quiser, e faz aliança com quem quiser, somos nós, inspirados pelo Espírito Santo, que devemos criar canais para que a graça de Deus seja experimentada de formas que nunca pudemos experimentar antes. Aqui, estamos tentando encontrar maneiras pelas quais a aliança de Deus pode ser expandida e oferecer hospitalidade às pessoas de outras fés. Somos nós que viramos canais da encarnação de Deus.

Ao redor da mesa, os cristãos têm suas Bíblias, sua comida, suas músicas e suas orações dizendo "vem Espírito, vem." Contudo, nesta oração perigosa, a vinda do Espírito pode se tornar a chegada de um estranho, um hóspede, alguém que não estávamos esperando ou sequer desejando receber. Ao orarmos "vem Espírito, vem", o mover do Espírito não pode mais ser controlado. Talvez, depois da nossa oração, tenhamos que acolher o povo do candomblé vestido com suas roupas brancas, dançando e cantando, pedindo aos Orixás que venham e movam as energias através do axé, a energia primal.[43] Uma vez que o Espírito Santo toma o controle, só nos resta segui-lo. À mesa, compartilhamos a comida e lutamos juntos para achar o equilíbrio na vida dos indivíduos, das nossas comunidades, e do mundo.

O Espírito Santo e o Axé são as forças motrizes que estabelecem, deslocam e equilibram o mundo e todos os nossos respectivos universos. O Espírito Santo e o Axé podem transformar o que quiserem, e são a própria fonte da vida. Os cristãos e os Yorubás são completamente dependentes do movimento destas duas entidades, que são fontes das quais bebemos para chamar uns aos outros à mesa e sermos capazes de expandir nossos horizontes religiosos.

O envolvimento com o Axé e o Espírito Santo pode ser uma resposta teológica vital para o mundo globalizado em que vivemos. O crescente senso de deslocamento marcado pelo aumento do fluxo de pessoas ao redor do globo, o hibridismo da imigração, a acumulação do capital nas mãos de menos de 500 pessoas no mundo todo, o tráfico de pessoas, a brutalidade contra as mulheres, as modificações do mercado de trabalho e o crescimento dos novos bairros diversos locais são apenas alguns dos sinais que exigem que nossas teologias e comunidades lidem com o constante fluxo de identidades e de "personalidades móveis".[44] A força, potência e agência do Espírito Santo/Axé podem nos ajudar a enfrentar os desafios e desmantelar realidades mortais do mundo.

O Espírito Santo/Axé também pode nos ajudar a encontrar identidades plurais, não na des-ritualização dos nossos rituais religiosos mas nos processos renovadores da ritualização (a expansão dos nossos rituais) das nossas crenças à medida que encontramos outros pelo caminho. Numa palestra proferida no Union Theological Seminary logo no início da Guerra do Iraque, a professora Janet R. Walton fez a seguinte pergunta: "O seu culto seria o mesmo se um iraquiano entrasse na sua igreja?" Algumas pessoas acham que a resposta para esta pergunta deve ser sempre "não", pois o que fazemos reflete aquilo que somos e não podemos mudar quem somos. Mas se pudermos admitir a possibilidade de que a resposta seja sim, então precisamos modificar nosso culto. Podemos nos transformar em pessoas melhores com a presença do outro que vem nos contar suas experiências, e podemos começar a tomar cuidado com palavras e gestos que usamos na nossa comunidade. Se um iraquiano está conosco, podemos aprender a respeito de nós mesmos e nos esforçarmos para viver nossa fé de forma mais expansiva, poderosa e acolhedora. Esta atenção dedicada ao outro não significa nos calarmos a nós mesmo para nos afastar daquilo que somos ou acreditamos, mas a presença de um outro pode ser uma oportunidade de ampliar quem somos. O Segundo Conselho Escocês de Igrejas afirmou: "Nós nos tornamos humanos através dos nossos relacionamentos — conosco mesmo, com os outros, com a criação, e com Deus. A espiritualidade reformada está antes de tudo fundamentada naquilo que há de comum entre nós, baseado no que significa ser humano." Embora a preocupação inicial desta mensagem seja com a unidade cristã, ela pode nos ajudar a ampliar nossas liturgias e teologias, bem como nos ajudar a acolher os que, seja por muito ou pouco, são diferentes de nós.

O Espírito de Deus manifesta-se através de movimentos de revelação da abertura e alteridade, movimentos marcados pelo des/arranjamento de generosidades. O Espírito de Deus deve ser visível na minha responsabilidade comigo mesmo, mas sempre em relação a alguém mais, ainda que este alguém me atire num abismo de desafios e mecanismos interiores e exteriores inescapáveis. A presença deste *outro alguém* à mesa de Jesus Cristo me conecta a obrigações inesperadas em relação a este outro e ao povo a que este outro pertence, um povo que talvez eu tenha ignorado até aquele momento. Portanto, o movimento do Espírito em nós pode ser um chamado para prestarmos atenção a outro alguém.

A partir deste lugar de abertura inesperada concedida pelo Espírito, os cristãos podem encontrar pontos em comum para acolher o povo do candomblé. Há elementos comuns para a teologia do Espírito no cristianismo e no candomblé. Eis alguns deles: (1) o Espírito Santo/Axé tem uma ligação profunda com o corpo, e sem nossos corpos não há comunidade. Em ambas religiões, Espírito/Orixás podem possuir um corpo. (2) O Espírito Santo e o Axé/Orixás nos auxiliam não só a levar nossa vida diária, nossas lutas, nossas feridas, mas também nos dão força, sabedoria e visão para viver. (3) O Espírito Santo/Axé sempre nos leva a interagir com um hóspede ou visitante; (4) O Espírito Santo/Axé está intimamente ligado com a criação; (5) O Espírito Santo/Axé é quem cria a sustenta as comunidades de fé; e (6) A manifestação da presença do Espírito/Axé é ao mesmo tempo culto e serviço.

No candomblé, a relação entre o Espírito e os corpos dos humanos é verificada nas possessões que acontecem durante as celebrações públicas e privadas, quando os Orixás escolhem alguns dos iniciados para "montar" nos seus corpos como se os Orixás estivessem *montando cavalos*.

Os fiéis se tornam cavalos das entidades. Nas comunidades cristãs, orações para que o Espírito Santo venha e tome nosso corpo e controle nossas mentes, bocas e gestos são comuns. Ser tomado pelo Espírito Santo é algo que é buscado pelos cristãos quando adoram a Deus. Nas igrejas pentecostais, os corpos são literalmente possuídos e tremem, dançam, se movem e estão à mercê do Espírito Santo. A possessão dos corpos vista tanto entre cristãos pentecostais quanto entre iourubás apresenta praticamente as mesmas posturas corporais, gestos e movimentos.

O Cristianismo espiritualiza o corpo para chegar a um lugar de aceitação por Deus. Baseado na culpa, o corpo necessita ser santificado e para isso, o corpo precisa ser alvo de práticas de sacrifício, como o jejum, abstinência sexual e penitência, assim o corpo, a carne, mortificada, pode então se tornar espiritual e ascender a Deus.

Já nas religiões Afros, incluindo o Candomblé, o movimento é contrário e caminha na encarnação do Espírito. Sem a dicotomia da culpa, o corpo é desejado pelos Espíritos, os Orixás, que visitam o corpo sem formas rigorosas de santificação. A preparação para receber os Orixás não se faz na mortificação do corpo, ao contrário, a visitação dos orixás deve e precisa acontecer no corpo como o corpo é e está. O corpo é assim um lugar de interlocução, de conexão, de comunhão. Possuído pelo maravilhoso, o corpo habita na transcendência.

Os fiéis do candomblé e cristãos pedem ao Espírito Santo e às entidades por orientação e sabedoria para levar sua vida cotidiana. Eles bendizem ao Espírito e vivem tentando agradar ao Espírito Santo/entidades. Ambas religiões estão profundamente comprometidas com a transformação da sociedade através de suas crenças e práticas. Para as duas religiões, Deus está sempre fazendo algo através de nós. Ou, usando as palavras de J. Edgar Bruns, "Deus é o ato de fazer alguma coisa"[45] nas nossas religiões.

É dentro, debaixo, através e ao redor do Espírito/entidades nos nossos corpos e rituais diferentes que podemos re-criar nossa vida diária e em comum, dentro e entre nós mesmos. Em ambas religiões, Deus/Orixás está fazendo algo em e através de nós, e nós também fazemos algo com e através das nossas liturgias/culto recriando o mundo, recriando a vida. Como diz Maraschin: "É no corpo que somos espírito, sobretudo quando nossos corpos estão prontos para recriar a vida. Façamos, então, dos nossos corpos nosso principal instrumento de culto."[46] Abertos para os movimentos desconhecidos do Espírito e do axé, nós nos movemos juntos.

À *mesa*

A reunião de cristãos e fiéis do candomblé na mesa eucarística pode emitir um chamado poderoso para parte da cultura brasileira que odeia e tem medo do candomblé, que continua a demonizar esta religião como forma de destruí-la em resposta à sua "devoção" a Deus. Compartilhar o mesmo espaço e a mesma comida é uma maneira de demonstrar uma versão do evangelho cristão que está comprometida com a manutenção da vida do outro, em amor e cuidado, com o direito de viver e de compartilhar a fé plenamente. Este é um evangelho que continua a exigir que amemos, dia e noite, Deus e nosso próximo, não importando qual é a fé que esse próximo professa e vive.

Cada comunidade irá se abrir para o Espírito e para os chamados tanto ao redor da mesa quanto nas mentes e corações. O batismo sempre será um chamado para o povo do candomblé se envolver mais com a fé cristã. E os Orixás também convidarão os cristãos a "fazer cabeça", que é o ritual de iniciação para se tornar um seguidor do candomblé. Estes chamados nunca devem ser entendidos como ameaças, mas como ofendas de amor aos nossos melhores amigos, em movimentos circulares do Espírito/Orixás um para com o outro para expandir nossos corações e mentes. E cada um de nós decidirá o que fazer. A partir daí as palavras de instituição ou as orações e canções cristãs serão cuidadosa e poderosamente ditas/cantadas, assim como as palavras e músicas sagradas do candomblé ditas pelos babalorixás e ialorixás.

Para o povo do candomblé, a possibilidade de fazer suas próprias reivindicações teológicas livremente num evento capital do cristianismo pode representar um pedido de perdão dos cristãos, uma restituição histórica da própria dignidade do candomblé, bem como a correção do estereótipo histórico do povo candomblé como presença demoníaca no Brasil. Para os cristãos, o diabo não tem lugar à mesa de Deus, onde ele será sempre anulado pela afirmação da verdade, vida, justiça e esperança. Ao sentarem-se à mesa de Jesus com oferendas para os Orixás, o povo e as crenças teológicas do candomblé ganham um espaço novo e privilegiado, tanto do ponto de vista religioso quanto cultural, desfazendo um complexo mal-entendido e a demonização da sua fé nos círculos cristãos e na cultura em geral, porque na mesa de Jesus eles são respeitados por aqueles que adoram o Deus dos cristãos.

Eucaristia e oferendas de comidas

Parte deste conhecimento mútuo tem a ver com nossas respectivas compreensões a respeito da comida e de como devemos interagir uns com os outros a partir da nossa comida sagrada. Muitos discursos religiosos em torno da comida têm a ver com a delimitação do outro de nós mesmos. A comida estabelece a singularidade da nossa fé e cria fronteiras que podem apresentar impurezas ou misturas, ou impedir que algumas trocas aconteçam. Noções do que é estrangeiro e alteridade são muito explícitas nas definições internas das comidas sagradas, e devemos tomar cuidado com estas definições.[47] Em I Coríntios 8:1-13, o apóstolo Paulo discute se é lícito comer a comida oferecida aos ídolos. Ele argumenta que a liberdade que recebemos de Deus não nos impede de comer tais comidas. Ao crescermos no conhecimento da liberdade de Deus, aos poucos perdemos nosso medo de enfrentar as dificuldades para aceitar a comida marcada para usos além dos nossos costumes ou regulamentações religiosas. Assim, precisamos ter cuidado com aqueles que, tanto cristãos como de outras comunidades, são incapazes de compreender esta liberdade e preferem a liberdade de se agarrar às suas normas. Cada comunidade deve discutir essas regras e examinar as suas próprias razões e o sistema de crenças do outro no que se refere à comida e identidade. Como Paulo disse, "Não é esta ou aquela comida que vai fazer com que Deus nos aceite",[48] mas certamente ela pode nos ajudar a aceitar e ser aceito pelo outro. O chamado de Deus vem antes do nosso ajuntamento, aplainando o terreno para nosso ajuntamento e exigindo que nós encontremos uma maneira de viver este amor, que é nossa prática. Uma vez que tenhamos aceitado uns aos outros à nossa mesa/terreiro comum, podemos começar a perder o medo que o outro representa para nós.

Como o apóstolo Pedro recebeu a ordem de Deus para comer tudo o que ele via, nós também recebemos uma ordem para estarmos abertos a participar da refeição do nosso próximo que vai além do nosso limite. "A voz falou de novo com ele: 'Não chame de impuro aquilo que Deus purificou.'"[49] Se Paulo nos diz para nos abrirmos, os sonhos de Pedro mostram Deus ordenando que ele coma. Como podemos nos deslocar de Paulo para

Pedro enquanto refletimos sobre a preciosa comida do candomblé? Uma conversa honesta entre estas duas comunidades irá nos ajudar a rejeitar a noção de que o povo do candomblé come comida feita para o Diabo. Para ser religioso-inter-religioso não basta apenas lidar intelectualmente com as diferenças entre as religiões, mas também comer a comida do outro. O aforismo "somos aquilo que comemos" é especialmente verdadeiro no que se refere à religião e à vida religiosa-inter-religiosa. Além do mais, nós *nos transformamos* naquilo que comemos, e é precisamente por causa desta possibilidade de *se transformar* que o povo dos santos e os cristãos precisam comer juntos: para estabelecer elos de amor e cuidado, para afastar o ódio, para recriar o Brasil num país mais acolhedor do ponto e diverso de vista religioso. No fim, como Paulo disse, "o amor nos faz progredir."[50]

Comer juntos tem a ver com a criação do amor, a construção da comunidade, compartilhar memórias e aceitar o outro como um presente de Deus para mim. Quando estamos juntos, começamos a ver o que as possibilidades teológicas, mas também sociais, políticas e culturais, desta reunião, deste comer junto, podem criar no meio do nosso povo. Acredito que um novo capítulo da história do Brasil seria inaugurado. Perdão e reconciliação viriam não só das autoridades de governo, como aconteceu na África do Sul, mas de dois grupos religiosos se abrindo um para o outro, encontrando caminhos mútuos de reconciliação, pedindo continuamente por perdão, enfrentando nosso racismo cordial, e aprendendo a respeitar a fé do outro.

Como as questões centrais deste texto giram em torno de como as fronteiras da eucaristia podem ser negociadas de modo a permitir que pessoas que geralmente são excluídas possam participar da mesa, acreditamos que demonstrações de generosidade entre pessoas de fés diferentes são possíveis. Quando começamos a conversa, o babalorixá Aragão me disse que precisamos voltar à eucaristia original, que era uma refeição, uma refeição completa. Como ex-seminarista católico romano, ele sabia bem do que estava falando. As refeições dos primeiros cristãos não diziam respeito ao sangue e o corpo de Cristo, mas à memória. Ele diz: "Deus fez-se comida, comida para a comunidade. Não é o elemento mítico que conta no começo da refeição, mas sim a maneira pela qual Cristo escolhe ser lembrado. De todos os jeitos possíveis que os discípulos poderiam usar para lembrarem-se de Jesus, eles escolheram o partilhar do pão. A parte mais divina de Jesus, o momento em que Jesus manifestou-se de forma mais poderosa como o Messias, como ser divino, foi dividir a si mesmo e dividir uma refeição. Mais tarde, foi em volta da mesa que eles lembraram das histórias de Jesus. O cristianismo mais original, o mais carismático, o mais pentecostal, é exatamente isto: o compartilhar do pão e da vida."

No candomblé, entretanto, não existe o mesmo tipo de memória como os cristãos tem de Jesus Cristo, já que a entidade está aqui, presente para servir. Para o candomblé, a presença das entidades não aponta para um evento primal, como fazem os cristãos com a última ceia no cenáculo. Porém, a possibilidade da presença das entidades e da presença de Cristo durante um culto em que a comida é compartilhada é um aspecto teológico comum a ambas as religiões.

O sangue e o sacrifício no candomblé, o sacrifício de animais tem a ver com a expiação, que pode ser comparada ao Dia do Perdão judeu, quando um animal era sacrificado para expiar os pecados do povo. No candomblé, o sacrifício animal é oferecido em causa da comunidade e, neste processo, o animal precisa desejar se oferecer para a comunidade. Se o animal não come as folhas que lhes dão, ele não está pronto para se oferecer, e a celebração só pode acontecer quando o animal se oferece para abençoar a comunidade. Este ritual é importante porque mantém a energia fluindo e em movimento, energia que continua circundando as relações que humanos e animais e entidades mantêm. Os animais são mensageiros das entidades, e servem como conexões.

Babalorixá Aragão me lembra que os africanos não têm problemas com sangue. Para eles o sangue não é sujo ou impuro como alguns de nós acredita. Tudo é sagrado na visão de mundo africana. Sangue é comida e comida preciosa, a melhor oferenda possível. Quando o animal morre, ele transfere a energia do sangue para as pedras e reforça a conexão entre as entidades. O sangue é o canal para comunhão profunda, energia que dá vida à relação entre animal-entidades-comunidade. Neste processo, a interligação da vida é assumida, a participação inter-relacionada se conecta intensamente com dignidade e respeito. Cada sacrifício é feito com cuidado, devoção, libações, objetos rituais devidamente consagrados, e segue uma ordem ritual.

Cada entidade tem sua própria regra quanto à comida. Há dois tipos de comida: seca (grãos) e úmida (sangue). A comida ritual é oferecida aos

Orixás e ingeridas pelos iniciados. A comida ritual que não é comida é devolvida à natureza: ao rio, ao mar, à terra, onde as entidades habitam, completando o círculo da vida. Podemos ofertar nossa comida simples, que o Orixá irá aceitá-la. Os lugares preparados para os Orixás nos terreiros, chamados *assentamentos*, encerram uma percepção intensificada do sagrado. Podemos dizer que estes assentamentos não simbolizam os Orixás; antes, *são* os Orixás. Da mesma forma, o pão e o vinho na eucaristia dos católicos não são símbolos da eucaristia, mas são a Eucaristia. O Deus cristão está presente no pão e no vinho, e no candomblé, a pedra, a casa e o lugar preparado para os Orixás são assentamento, são os Orixás. Por exemplo, a tigela e a comida que são oferecidas ao Orixá não são recipientes dos Orixás, mas são os próprios Orixás.

Ampliando a fé, prática e teologia um do outro pela comensalidade
Comida e bebida são elementos litúrgico-teológicos na vida destas duas comunidades. Ambos celebram a criação e a providência divina. Toda a cosmogonia do candomblé é fundamentada no sentido e importância da terra. Deus e os Orixás estão intimamente ligados à terra e às ervas, plantas, comida, bebida, etc., todas as coisas vindas da terra que fazem a conexão entre este e o outro mundo. Além disso, todos os elementos que marcam os objetos litúrgicos e o culto no candomblé vêm da natureza. Os dois rituais precisam da comida e têm uma profunda ligação com a criação, a ecologia, e apenas podem ser sustentáveis se entendidos como parte de um ecossistema no qual a vida é vivida na mesa e no chão, nas reuniões e nos rios e florestas, no ar e em cada parte da criação de Deus. Juntos, podemos lutar pelo nosso bem comum, os ecossistemas e a biodiversidade, luta que representa uma forma poderosa de trabalhar pela paz.

A sacralidade destes eventos de culto é uma marca comum de ambas as religiões. Através da comida, Deus é manifestado através de Jesus/Espírito Santo, e Olodumarê através dos muitos Orixás e outras entidades. O ato do sacramento da eucaristia é uma forma de adoração a Deus, obedecendo o mandamento para realizá-lo em memória de Jesus Cristo. No candomblé, a comida ritual carrega as promessas e os trabalhos de louvor para agradar os Orixás, para que estes continuem a abençoar as vidas da comunidade.

É interessante ver como as mulheres estão no centro da preparação destas comidas sagradas. O culto só pode acontecer se a comida for preparada de forma adequada. Lembro-me da minha mãe se preparando para pôr a mesa da Eucaristia. Jan Rudolph, uma aluna minha no Louisville Seminary, certa vez mencionou durante a aula como sua avó afro-americana costumava passar a ferro os pedaços de pão para a Santa Ceia. Na Bahia, participei de uma cerimônia para Ogum, e vi as mulheres prepararem, dias antes e com muito zelo, a comida ritual. Bebida e comida boa e bem feita são a chave para que a celebração seja eficaz.

Tanto a eucaristia quando o culto do candomblé são ritos de passagem e atos políticos. Historicamente, enquanto no Brasil podemos dizer que a Eucaristia, por estar ligada aos poderes constituídos, estava mais sintonizada com um ritual para reforçar o poder imperial, no candomblé a comida ritual era um ato litúrgico de resistência e resiliência. Seja qual for a circunstância, ambos rituais encenam episódios recorrentes na vida do indivíduo, da comunidade e do país.

A eucaristia cristã baseia-se na compreensão eclesial da nuvem de testemunhas que cerca a comunidade de fé. A presença dos ancestrais pode também ser relacionada à presença de Cristo na história. Para o candomblé, a crença na ancestralidade oferece a segurança de que esta comunidade de crentes é continuamente ajudada pela presença dos ancestrais, que prepararam o caminho. Ambas as religiões podem compartilhar e convergir suas nuvens de testemunhas e ancestrais.

A eucaristia é celebrada ao redor da mesa, e as oferendas de comida acontecem ao redor da mesa ou no chão. Para os cristãos de tradições reformadas, a mesa lembra o lugar de Jesus naquela última ceia com os discípulos. Para o povo do candomblé, a comida no chão enfatiza a profunda relação da comida com a terra, e os lugares da natureza ligados a cada Orixá. Compartilhar a comida de cada um ao redor da mesa e no chão pode ser uma maneira poderosa de se envolver com o ritual do outro e experimentar as diferenças e pontos em comum entre os rituais.

Na mesa/chão comum, os cristãos terão seu livro sagrado, a Bíblia, enquanto o povo Yorubá trará sua cultura oral. Cada grupo pode compartilhar suas histórias de fé e transformação de diferentes maneiras.

O candomblé tem mais ligações teológicas com a eucaristia quando esta é entendida como um sacrifício, como faz a Igreja Católica Romana. O derramamento de sangue e o evento expiatório de Jesus pode ser relacionado ao sacrifício de animais no candomblé. Se o sacrifício cristão traz o perdão, o sacrifício do candomblé traz proteção. A morte de Jesus como resgate, conforme entendem algumas perspectivas protestantes, também pode se relacionar com o sacrifício animal e as oferendas de comida para honrar/pagar/negociar com os Orixás.

Talvez o povo do candomblé possa ensinar aos cristãos como se envolver mais com a preparação da comida e a relação entre comida, preparo e origem dos alimentos. Para os reformados, a eucaristia não é pensada com frequência como sendo uma mesa aberta e com comida de verdade suficiente para todos. Antes, é uma lembrança de uma refeição completa, uma memória de um banquete e não necessariamente uma celebração de júbilo. As pessoas não comem de verdade a comida da mesa eucarística, mas compartilham um mísero pedaço de pão e um pequeno gole de vinho ou suco de uva. O povo do candomblé também pode ajudar os cristãos a ganhar uma perspectiva de comensalidade sobre as comidas sagradas. As comidas rituais são sempre abundantes nos cultos do candomblé e são oferecidas não só aos Orixás mas à toda comunidade. Para os reformados, a eucaristia não é pensada com frequência como sendo uma mesa aberta e com comida de verdade suficiente para todos. Antes, é uma lembrança de uma refeição completa, uma memória de um banquete e não necessariamente uma celebração de júbilo. As pessoas não comem de verdade a comida da mesa eucarística, mas compartilham um mísero pedaço de pão e um pequeno gole de vinho ou suco de uva. Talvez o povo do candomblé possa aprender com os cristãos reformados sobre o princípio protestante que confronta o poder, as estruturas religiosas hierárquicas desbalanceadas e o compromisso com a mudança social.

No final da nossa conversa, perguntei descaradamente ao babalorixá Aragão se era possível colocar a comida para o Orixá na mesa/altar da eucaristia. Ele respondeu com um sonoro "sim"! E continuou: "Recolhemos a comida com nossa família estendida, e tudo pertence a Deus. Ou melhor, tudo não é Deus?" A resposta de Aragão afirma as condições e as possibilidades para este diálogo, conexões e relacionamentos.

Aprendendo com os ancestrais cristãos: um beijo santo como prática litúrgica para a práxis inter-religiosa

Neste ensaio de um futuro possível para nossas sociedades e religiões, invoquei os cristãos primitivos e seu gesto litúrgico do beijo santo para nos ajudar nesta práxis inter-religiosa. Beijar é uma prática comum em muitas religiões, e eu certamente não estou afirmando que os cristãos inventaram o beijo santo. Ao invés disso, a ideia aqui é aprender sobre o beijo litúrgico com as práticas dos primeiros cristãos, e como ele pode melhorar nossa vida religiosa comunitária. O beijo santo dos primeiros cristãs combina o gesto litúrgico de aproximação do outro, o compartilhamento do fôlego/presença do Espírito e do comer junto e a negociação das estruturas sociais. O beijo santo foi uma prática que permeou várias camadas da vida. Paulo e Pedro escreveram para comunidades diferentes recomendando que as pessoas se beijassem com um beijo santo e um beijo de amor (Romanos 16:16 e 1 Pedro 5:14).

O estudioso do cristianismo primitivo Michael Penn diz que, neste gesto, "Família, espírito, reconciliação — conceitos aparentemente abstratos — o beijo transforma em ações encarnadas." Para o mundo greco-romano, qualquer gesto em público era um "exercício de poder... um beijo ritual (deveria ser visto) como práxis — a combinação entre interpretação e ação... o beijo não era só um objeto de debate, mas também uma ação física."[51] Este gesto litúrgico encarnado pode nos ajudar a passarmos da segurança do diálogo inter-religioso para o espaço mais assustador da práxis.

Mais do que isso, o beijo ritual se tornou um modo de vida, uma conexão entre fé e proximidade familiar, um laço social. Por um breve período, o ritual de beijar o outro quebraria com as fronteiras de classe e condição social, as divisões insuperáveis existentes naquela sociedade. Michael Penn escreve sobre o ritual do beijo como laço social e formador da comunidade que guarda semelhanças com nossa práxis dialógica inter-religiosa. Ainda que ele esteja se referindo às comunidades cristãs, pode-se dizer que o embaçamento das fronteiras daquela época pode ser relacionado ao embaçamento das fronteiras sociais e religiosas do nosso tempo. Ele diz:

> Primeiro, as conotações familiais do beijo greco-romano ajudam a retratar a comunidade cristã como uma família. Em segundo lugar, suas conexões com a troca spiritual enfatiza o laço pneumatológico de um membro da comunidade com o outro. Terceiro, especialmente quando o beijo passou de um selo de oração a uma parte do serviço eucarístico, os líderes cristãos tentaram reduzir as tensões internas fazendo do beijo um ritual de reconciliação. Finalmente, o

beijo como ação física unindo dois indivíduos estava correlacionado com a criação de um corpo unificado.⁵²

Expandindo esta lista, podemos dizer que o beijo litúrgico nos possibilita ampliar a ideia de família para além das fronteiras das crenças cristãs. Como nota Philip Pen, "os parâmetros do beijo podem ser ampliados regularmente para incluir pessoas de for a da família, ou aqueles a quem beijamos durante os rituais cristãos podem ser redefinidos como membros da família."⁵³

Em segundo lugar, como o beijo enfatiza a conectividade pela respiração, a crença de que compartilhamos a própria alma com a pessoa que beijamos, podemos dizer também que a presença pneumatológica do Espírito Santo/Axé pode ser nosso compartilhamento, a oferenda do que temos de melhor. Nesta oferenda que fazemos uns para os outros daquilo que temos de mais precioso, podemos aprofundar nossos laços de afeto e pertencimento ao outro através da troca de beijos. Beijar é levar o coração para dentro do outro, é receber seu fôlego, sua própria vida dentro do meu corpo. Beijar alguém é estabelecer um laço de paz que me impede de retirar meu corpo e a mim mesmo desta pessoa. Estou inevitavelmente ligado a esta pessoa agora. É por isso que um beijo pode ser um gesto assustador, especialmente se estivermos tentando não interferir na vida um do outro, sendo civilizado e respeitoso, pelo menos sob a ótica desta cultura individualista. O "espírito" da nossa cultura é um espírito que não quer dividir, trocar, viver junto. A promessa e esperança de intercâmbio do Espírito é aquilo que estas religiões pode oferecer à cultura brasileira e ao mundo. O beijo santo é uma prática coletiva que vai contra a corrente, uma prática que talvez possa desafiar esta cultura narcisística que empurra as pessoas e as afasta umas das outras.

Em terceiro lugar, o beijo santo como laço, um gesto de profundo comprometimento, de perdão, um gesto familiar de afeição, uma afirmação de pertença, um ato de amor, amor social e comunitário. Eis porque se beijava durante a Eucaristia. Penn nos lembra que "o beijo ritual pode unir as almas dos participantes e fazer os indivíduos esquecerem todos os erros." Algo poderoso acontece quando beijamos uns aos outros. João Crisóstomo escreveu: "O beijo é dado para que ele seja o combustível do amor, para que possamos acender a chama da disposição, para que nós possamos amar uns aos outros como irmãos [amam] os irmãos, como crianças [amam] os pais, como os pais [amam] crianças. Mas muito além, porque aqueles amam por natureza, estes pela graça. Logo nossas almas estão ligadas umas às outras."[54]

Finalmente, o beijo santo é um gesto litúrgico que conecta os corpos dos indivíduos à um corpo maior, o corpo social que podemos chamar de corpo de Deus. Michael Penn diz que "vários autores do cristianismo primitivo estabeleciam uma ligação entre o beijo, a troca espiritual e a coesão do grupo."[55] Quando beijo alguém, dou a esta pessoa uma parte de mim mesmo que só esta pessoa irá conhecer. Mais ainda, ofereço a esta pessoa meu grupo social, abro a porta de entrada para que o outro se torne parte da minha família e da minha vida. Assim, através da participação de diversos grupos de afeto e conexões sociais, tornamo-nos responsáveis um pelo outro. Quando fazemos isso numa dinâmica inter-religiosa, o outro radical muda seu status: de ameaça, o povo do candomblé tornou-se uma bênção para mim, um auxílio para minha vida cristã na sociedade, uma segurança advinda de uma pertença dupla mais ampla, uma expansão da minha alma, um toque respeitoso do meu corpo, um presente para minha fé. E vice-versa.

Povo reformado e do candomblé comendo juntos: um itinerário prático

Se o cristianismo trabalha ao redor da espiritualização do corpo através de atos de santidade como a eucaristia, penitência, jejum, privação, etc., as religiões afro trabalham com a encarnação do espírito pelas entidades que possuem os corpos e dança, comem, celebram, falam, riem, etc. Estas formas diferentes de movimento em torno do sagrado são ao mesmo tempo bênção e desafio, e devem ser consideradas ao planejarmos esta práxis dialógica.

As duas religiões incluíram elementos estranhos em suas estruturas de fé e práticas, adaptando-se ao seu entorno através de diferentes processos. Nem o cristianismo ou o candomblé são religiões puras, autônomas, desvinculadas da cultura e homogêneas. Além disso, houve a presença de uma na outra que terminou por definir como essas religiões são no Brasil. Depois de conviver por quase 500 anos, oferecer uma mesa aberta para compartilhar a comida eucarística com os irmãos e irmãs do candomblé, e os cristãos comendo nas celebrações do candomblé, pode não ser algo estranho ou um ato de fidelidade de ambas as partes, mas uma oferenda mútua de bênção e presente.

Este movimento de ir mutuamente atrás uns dos outros precisa ser cuidadosamente planejado e criado de acordo com as condições das possibilidades que esta reunião impossível pode ser. O itinerário deve ser traçado pelas duas comunidades quando elas estabelecerem entre si um elo de confiança e aceitem que este diálogo/interação acarreta uma grande vulnerabilidade. Os cristãos devem se lembrar do que Paul Knitter afirmou: "para ser leal a Cristo, é preciso estar vulnerável ao outro."[56]

Ao ponderarmos as possibilidades de diálogo e vida juntos, precisamos considerar estratégias que venham da prática através e além das diferenças. Pontos de partida, movimentos do sagrado e resultados finais são completamente diferentes. O que podemos aprender uns com os outros? Ao redor da relação espírito/corpo corpo/espírito, podemos ampliar as possibilidades e compreensões de práticas e fé.

Para que este diálogo aconteça, muitos mal-entendidos irão acontecer. Nosso trabalho teológico é auxiliar uns aos outros para desfazer, tanto quanto possível, estes mal-entendidos, sabendo no entanto que a incomensurabilidade de cada religião sempre nos lembrará deste diálogo impossível.

Da perspectiva das tradições reformadas, este diálogo impossível deve carregar o aspecto do princípio protestante, que questiona qualquer e todo aspecto da fé cristã para evitar se tornar uma comunidade de fé idólatra e continua em perpétuo movimento para "ser" reformada: *ecclesia reformata semper reformanda*.

Sua filha ficou muito doente. Ela pediu ao pastor e à sua amada congregação presbiteriana para orar pela sua filha. Todos oraram mas a menina continuou muito doente. Ela consultou vários médicos e, muitas opiniões depois, ninguém sabia o que fazer com sua filha. Desesperada, ela levou Diane num terreiro de candomblé para ver uma mãe de santo. Seu coração batia tão forte no seu peito que ela mal podia respirar. No terreiro, a mãe de santo lhe pediu algumas coisas, que ela fez. Dentro de uma semana, sua filha estava curada. Depois de receber tamanha bênção, ela começou a se sentir culpada. Toda a sua vida, ela ouvira que o candomblé era um lugar demoníaco. Ela começou a se perguntar se tinha sido o próprio Diabo que havia curado a menina, que agora pertenceria a ele. Ela ficou tão aterrorizada que foi até seu pastor presbiteriano e lhe confessou seu pecado e sua necessidade de se converter e pediu pelo perdão de Deus, ainda que o preço a pagar fosse que sua filha voltasse a ficar doente. O pastor tinha aprendido sobre a soberania de Deus e a providência de Deus com Calvino, e disse a ela: "Irmã, o amor e o cuidado de Deus vão além das fronteiras da igreja ou dos muros da religião. Deus pode agir onde quiser, o Espírito de Deus é livre para fazer o que agradar a Deus. O Espírito de Deus também quebra as regras e faz o que não queremos ou não permitimos Deus fazer. Talvez neste caso nós devêssemos confiar que a soberania e o amor e a provisão de Deus para você e Diane é tamanha que Ele decidiu curar Diane de uma forma muito diferente. Acreditamos que Deus ama a Diane, certo? Então, mesmo que a gente não entenda, devemos agradecer a Deus por seu amor e aos nossos irmãos e irmãs do candomblé que foram uma verdadeira bênção para você e a Diane. Você ora comigo? Que nossos corações se encham de gratidão e se elevem a Deus. E que, depois da nossa oração, ela se alegre quando sair pela porta da igreja chorando, carregando a sua bebê curada e crendo que Deus se move e age de maneira maravilhosa.

Este itinerário imagina Deus vindo depois,[57] após nós nos ajudarmos uns aos outros, mas vindo depois no sentido de aparecer mais tarde, depois que já atravessamos as dificuldades de um diálogo e interação possíveis. Os passos concretos podem ser: primeiro, visitamos os espaços sagrados do outro para enxergarmos um ao outro nos nossos cultos. Depois, nos reunimos para comer juntos uma refeição não religiosa e levantamos questões sobre nossas práticas para iniciar a conversa. A partir daí, começamos a cumprimentar uns aos outros e beijamos as bochechas dos outros. Então, comemos juntos novamente. Antes de comer, o povo Yorubá vai nos explicar porque e como eles fazem o que fazem, principalmente sobre suas oferendas de comida. Depois, os cristãos vão explicar porque fazem o que fazem, explicando a Eucaristia. Cada um mostrará ao outro o que acontece durante suas celebrações e como é viver a sua fé. Então, decidimos o que podemos e o que não podemos fazer/comer juntos por enquanto, e tentaremos formular possibilidades dentro desses rituais fundamentalmente diferentes. E voltamos outra vez para o culto do outro, tentando participar como possível dentro dos limites estabelecidos. Músicas, orações e o beijo de paz serão compartilhados. E comemos novamente e trazemos os elementos das nossas celebrações para mostrar ao outro como fazer. Depois, deixamos aqueles que quiserem ir um pouco além participar na mesa do outro. Começamos com a hospitalidade da mesa eucarística, escrevendo uma oração eucarística que acolhe nossos irmãos e irmãs do candomblé e evoca o axé e a poderosa história do candomblé no Brasil para fazer de nós quem somos. Continuando, a próxima vez que estivermos à mesa eucarística, o povo do candomblé será convidado a se pronunciar e trazer comidas oferecidas aos Orixás. Toda vez que celebrarmos a Eucaristia, comeremos uma refeição completa.

Dentro deste processo, questionar é fundamental: Além das questões sobre práticas, nós, como cristãos, precisamos questionar nosso próprio envolvimento e conhecimento mútuo: (1) se formos comer juntos, como fazer isso? (2) se eu participar de uma refeição Yorubá, o que e como esta participação mudará como eu vejo e pratico a Eucaristia cristã? (3) o que a refeição Yorubá pode alterar da minha compreensão de comunidade, resistência, memória, ancestralidade, comensalidade, ação de graças, possessão pelo Espírito? (4) podemos orar e cantar juntos? (5) o que é comunidade para mim como cristão após esta experiência? (6) qual é o processo de memória aqui e como ele afeta meu próprio entendimento de memória? (7) como cristão, se participo de uma refeição Yorubá, o que esta participação muda na Eucaristia cristã? (8) o que a comida/oferenda Yorubá muda na minha própria compreensão de memória, de resistência, de comunidade? (9) em que se apoia o compartilhar da refeição? (10) quais são os aspectos teológicos disso? Aprender com outras religiões mobiliza totalmente nosso ser. Emoções, sentimentos, corpo, mente e espírito estão todos entrelaçados neste processo. Como podemos informar e re-formar este envolvimento físico?

Neste processo, talvez tenhamos que ensinar uns aos outros a respeito da história da nossa fé e práticas. Ambas comunidades poderão pesquisar a história do cristianismo/religiões africanas no Brasil, enfrentar o "racismo cordial" da cultura brasileira, e encontrar lugares onde a interação entre cristianismo e o candomblé não foi apenas destruição, mas ajuda, proteção e cuidado mútuos. Em outras palavras, procuramos como a realidade suplantou a retórica oficial e como os povos africanos, europeus e indígenas construíram pequenas harmonias e experiências comunais. Zumbi dos Palmares talvez seja um começo. Quais foram as acomodações feitas entre cristianismo e candomblé? Encontrar onde estavam e estão as conexões, simetrias, semelhanças e paralelos. Como processo teológico, uma pesquisa com orientação mais social e histórica pode ser realizada para fomentar uma base teológica sólida.

Alimentamos uns aos outros aqui não só porque moralmente somos obrigados a fazê-lo. Nós nos reunimos e alimentamos uns aos outros porque precisamos criar não só um outro mundo possível, mas um mundo necessário, um mundo que ampliará nossas possibilidades e fará nossas vidas e nosso país maior e melhor para nós e as gerações futuras. Estamos nos alimentando uns aos outros porque temos que curar as feridas da nossa história comum, e nos dirigir uns aos outros com respeito e dignidade. Estamos aprendendo e praticando e nos reunindo porque é mandamento de Deus que amemos e cuidemos uns dos outros. Estamos comento juntos ao redor das mesas e no chão porque estamos oferecendo ao outro uma hospitalidade radical que só pode acontecer se estivermos ligados pelo Espírito.

Conclusão

É impossível oferecer uma introdução lúcida e honesta do candomblé nestas páginas. No entanto, a ideia aqui é dar uma visão geral desta religião para que possamos honrar o povo do candomblé e começar a pensar por que esta prática dialógica inter-religiosa não é apenas possível mas verdadeiramente necessária.

Simbiose e fagocitose podem ser elementos teológicos chave a serem desenvolvidos neste diálogo. Também a noção de ritualizar/ritualização, conforme proposta por Catherine Bell e Ronald Grimmes e explicada no próximo capítulo, é um elemento importante deste diálogo quando acolhermos o outro em nossos rituais e inventarmos outros rituais em comum para enriquecer nosso diálogo e cuidado mútuo. Aprendemos também com o teórico ritual Jonathan Z. Smith que os rituais são formas de se envolver com aquilo que esperamos que aconteça. Quando criamos nossos rituais, estamos numa luta entre a realidade em que vivemos e a realidade que queremos, a realidade que desejamos. Nesta práxis litúrgica dialógica inter-religiosa, também estamos numa luta entre a realidade que coloca estes grupos religiosos em conflito e uma realidade na qual cristãos e seguidores do candomblé comem, bebem, oram e dançam juntos.[58]

Assim como exploramos algo da história da escravidão e da religião Yorubá e identificar novos desafios relacionados à assim chamada diversidade religiosa brasileira e seu "racismo cordial" e nos dedicamos à hospitalidade da mesa eucarística e o compartilhamento do beijo santo, podemos encontrar um espaço comum para transformar a história e romper com a alienação histórica e o ódio religioso. As esperanças se mantêm enquanto tentamos incentivar o diálogo e rituais entre o candomblé e o cristianismo como estratégia para acabar com a violência, interagir valorizando grandemente às escolhas religiosas do outro e possibilitando um ao outro a se tornar plenamente humanos dentro e através dos nossos chamados religiosos mais profundos.

No fim, devemos nos lembrar que nosso compromisso está assentado no amor. Marcelo Barros nos relembra outra vez:

> Evidentemente, todo caminho espiritual é um itinerário de amor e não pode ser explicado intelectualmente. É uma mistagogia. É um mistério que só pode ser explicado através de uma íntima relação de vida... Podemos ser amantes que entregam a si mesmos para servir. Do que é divino, há título de propriedade. O acesso é livre a todo aquele que buscar o que faz seu coração bater. Nenhum mortal pode domar o vento selvagem. Mistério é nossa paz, e os caminhos religiosos, nossas parábolas de amor."[59]

E com Ivone Gebara diz:

> a questão do pluralismo nos convida, novamente, à reflexão, à proximidade da sabedoria, à amizade como diferente, com aqueles de quem estou perto e ao mesmo tempo longe como expressões desta incrível complexidade da vida. E é o mesmo com as nossas teologias porque, no fim, suas certezas têm a ver com a fraco, a incerta, a plural e sempre renovável confiança neste amor que nos sustenta: "Onde há amor, ali Deus estará..."[60]

Então este amor viveu rodeando a comida e as comunidades. Cristãos e o povo do candomblé criando um espaço de cuidado e amor e acolhida que não existe ainda na nossa sociedade. Um lugar onde as pessoas são o que gostariam de ser, onde suas identidades são forjadas, desenvolvidas, transformadas. Como nas igrejas cristãs primitivas ou no Quilombo dos Palmares. Um lugar para sermos não o que a sociedade quer de nós necessariamente, mas um lugar para explorar livremente nossas esperanças, crenças e sonhos. Espaços onde respeito e proteção são intrínsecos e onde reimaginamos nossas vidas e nosso mundo. Um espaço para sambar e cantar hinos e também músicas dos Yorubás. Um espaço um tanto impossível, certamente. Mas nunca saberemos se tal espaço é possível ou não se não tentarmos, realmente, nos aproximarmos uns dos outros.

Notas

1. Este artigo foi publicado em *Sacraments and Globalization: Redrawing the Borders of Eucharistic Hospitality* (Wipf and Stock, Pickwick Publications, 2013), pp. 203–41.
2. Harding, Rachel E. *A Refuge In Thunder. Candomblé and Alternative Spaces of Blackness*. (Indiana: Indiana Univ. Press: 2000), p. xiii.
3. Alguns amigos cristãos me disseram que várias igrejas têm como missão fazer com que um certo número de terreiros feche a cada ano.
4. Esta questão foi feita numa plenária da Cohorte II do Seminário Luce sobre teologias da religião, pluralismo e teologia comparativa, desenvolvida pela Academia Americana da Religião. (Chicago, maio de, 2011).
5. De Alencastro, Luiz Felipe. As Populações Africanas no Brasil. Disponível em http://www.casadasafricas.org.br/site/img/upload/680108.pdf
6. "Homem cordial" é uma expressão criada pelo historiador Sérgio Buarque de Holanda para descrever como vivem os brasileiros. Ver Raízes do Brasil, (São Paulo: Companhia das Letras), 1997. O livro foi publicado pela primeira vez em 1936, mas a expressão "racismo cordial" foi criada mais tarde para descrever o tipo de racismo existente no Brasil e constantemente negado. Como disse Marcelo Coelho: "Talvez esteja aí um dos horrores do "racismo cordial: o preconceito se exprime sempre que alguém diz não ter preconceito. Dizer que "no Brasil não existe racismo é verdadeiro até certo ponto (não há bancos na praça separados para brancos e negros, como havia no sul dos Estados Unidos) e enganador em última análise." Marcelo Coelho, "Estranhamento conduz ao 'racismo cordial'." (Folha de São Paulo, 28 de junho de 1995). Disponível em: http://www.cefetsp.br/edu/eso/comportamento/racismocordial.html
7. Quilombos. Estes lugares ainda alimentam a memória dos negros no Brasil em suas lutas do presente. Como novos quilombos continuam a existir, as religiões africanas continuam sendo bastiões da resistência, autonomia e transformação ainda que praticamente esquecida pelo governo. Para maiores informações sobre o Quilombo de Palmares, veja: Carneiro, Edson. *O Quilombo dos Palmares* (São Paulo: WMF, Martins Fontes), 2011. Gomes, Flávio. *Palmares* (São Paulo: Contexto), 2005.
8. Peço *agô* (permissão) aos Orixás, aos candomblés do Brasil e ao povo dos santos para tratar das suas crenças e práticas.
9. Alessandra Osuna: http://ebomealessandraosun.blogspot.com/2008/04/significado-do-candomble.html
10. Bastide, Roger. *O Candomblé da Bahia* (São Paulo: Companhia das Letras, 2009), p. 29. Este livro é um ótimo recurso para compreender a estrutura, sentido e movimento dos rituais do Candomblé em geral, mas particularmente dos realizados na Bahia.
11. Oliveira, Rafael Soares de. (Org.) *Diálogos Fraternos Contra a Intolerância Religiosa* (Rio de Janeiro: DP&A Editora & Koinonia, 2003), p. 14
12. Gisele Omindarewá Cossard. *Awô, o mistério dos Orixás* (Rio de Janeiro: Pallas, 2006), p.12 (meu trabalho baseia-se largamente neste estudo.)
13. Vilson Caetano de Souza Junior, http://www.youtube.com/watch?v=VuGlStsTVBc&NR=1 (?)

14. Pierre Verger comentando sobre o Candomblé, na Fundação Pierre Verger: http://pierreverger.org/fpv/index.php?option=com_content&task=view&id=14&Itemid=41&limit=1&limitstart=2&Itemid=155
15. Edison Carneiro, op. cit., 20–1.
16. Harding, Rachel E. A Refuge In Thunder. Op. cit., xvi.
17. Ibid.
18. Roger Bastide. O Candomblé da Bahia. Op. cit., 27.
19. Babalorixá Luis de Logun Edé, A Relação da Comida no Candomblé: 25 Anos de Logun Edé." http://www.youtube.com/watch?v=8IxS7vQUQNg
20. Ibid., 123.
21. Maria Helena Farelli descreve os pontos principais dos terreiros de candomblé fundados na Bahia:

"Princesas negras com sorrisos de marfim conduziram seu deus pelas ruas empoeiradas das cidades sob a lua do campo. Para os seus senhores divinos, elas preparam a melhor comida temperada, cozida sob fogo à lenha com os seus mistérios. Não fosse por elas, rainhas e sacerdotisas africanas, trazidas de Benin e Angola como escravas, como seus deuses viriam ao Brasil? ...Comidas para os santos são tradição, necessárias, e elas fazem a beleza das festas religiosas... Ao redor dos terreiros as pessoas vivem para adorar seus deuses e ancestrais e, para eles, preparam bebidas e comidas que constituem uma das ligações entre aiê (terra) e orum (céu) através do axé (a força mágica). Todo o mundo sobrenatural afro-brasileiro gosta de comida. Eles precisam ser alimentados. Sangue, dendê e ataré são parte do cardápio. Se você nunca comeu a comida deliciosa ou bebeu os néctares, você deveria experimentar. Se você seguir os preceitos, a comida será tão bem feita que todos os deuses virão, até da África e do Haiti. Saudemos nosso orixá, o dono da nossa ori (cabeça), e vivamos sem a ideia do pecado, que trouxe tantas coisas ruins para os africanos, que desconheciam o pecado. Axé para meus antepassados brancos, pretos e índios, pois é hora de comida boa da Bahia." Maria Helena Farelli, op. Cit., p.12

22. Roger Bastide, op. cit., 31. Este é o costume em muitos terreiros, mas alguns babalorixás como Luis de Logun Edé não gostam de oferecer comida.
23. Vilson Caetano de Souza Junior. "A Relação da Comida no Candomblé: 25 Anos de Logun Edé. Parte II". http://www.youtube.com/watch?v=VuGlStsTVBc&NR=1
24. Bastide, Op. Cit, p. 34. Bastide, op. cit, p. 34.
25. Ibid., p. 40
26. Vigil, José M., Tomita, Luiza E., Barros, Marcelo (editores). *Teologia Pluralista Libertadora Intercontinental* . ASETT, EATWOT (São Paulo: Paulinas, 2008).
27. Faustino Teixeira. A Teologia do Pluralismo Religioso na América Latina. In: Teologia Pluralista Libertadora Intercontinental, op. cit., 31.
28. Ivone Gebara apela para que este estudo inclua também as mulheres, já que o "princípio estruturante não pode ser apenas masculino. Sua expressão tem que ser múltipla, plural, infinita." Citado em Faustino Teixeira, A Teologia do Pluralismo Religioso na América Latina.
29. Faustino Teixeira. A Teologia do Pluralismo Religioso na América Latina. In: Teologia Pluralista Libertadora Intercontinental, op. cit., 39
30. Barros, Marcelo. Múltipla pertença, o pluralismo religioso. In Teologia Pluralista Libertadora Intercontinental, op. cit., 54.

31. Todo grupo social, nascendo no terreno originário de uma função essencial no mundo da produção econômica, cria organicamente para si mesmo uma ou mais camadas de intelectuais que lhe conferem homogeneidade e a consciência de sua própria função, não apenas no campo econômico, mas também social e político." Gramsci, Antonio, "The Intellectuals: The Formation of the Intellectuals," in *Selections From The Prison Notebooks Of Antonio Gramsci*. Antonio Gramsci. (New York, NY: International Publishers, 1971). p. 5.33.

32. Sacerdotes, pastores, professores como Carlos Mesters, Ivone Gebara, Leonardo Boff, Milton Schwantes, Richard Shall, Nancy Cardoso, Pedro Casaldáliga, Dom Élder Camera, Dom Paulo Evaristo Arns, para citar apenas alguns, dedicaram-se intensamente à vida do pobre e, com eles, organizaram movimentos locais e nacionais de libertação no Brasil (Comissão Pastoral da Terra, Movimento dos Sem Terra, direitos dos trabalhadores, denunciando a violência contra a mulher, etc.) e criaram discursos marcados tanto pela intelectualidade acadêmica como pelas preocupações e necessidades e sabedorias dos mais pobres.

33. J. Edgar Bruns quoted by Sharon V. Betcher, "Take my Yoga upon you: a spiritual pli for the global city" in Keller, Catherine & Schneider, Laurel editors. *Polydoxy: Theology of Multiplicity and Relation*. (New York, London: Routledge, 2010). p 72.

34. José Maria Vigil renova a metodologia da teologia da libertação baseada no trabalho de Paulo Freire: ver, julgar e agir, e enquadra isto nas teologias do pluralismo religioso como "uma nova forma de viver a religião, uma nova prática." Vigil, José Maria. *Teologia do Pluralismo Religioso, para uma releitura pluralista do Cristianismo* (São Paulo: Paulus, 2006), 15.

35. Gebara, Ivone, "Pluralismo Religioso, Uma Perspectiva Feminista". In Teologia Latino-Americana Pluralista da Libertação. Tomita, Luiza E., Vigil, José M., Barros, Marcelo, editors, *ASETT, EATWOT* (São Paulo: Editora Paulus, 2006), 297.

36. Irarrázaval, Diego. "Salvação Indígena and Afro-Americana". In Teologia Pluralista Libertadora Intercontinental, op. cit., 69.

37. Ibid.

38. Esta noção pode ser correlacionada à noção do inclusivismo. Enquanto o inclusivismo cristão reconhece algum valor nas outras religiões, ele se apropria de algumas coisas mas retém apenas aquilo que reconhece, transformando o que foi apropriado no seu próprio sistema, guardando dentro de si noções de salvação, verdade e revelação que são válidas apenas dentro do sistema do cristianismo. Tudo o que não é autenticado é demonizado/destruído e rejeitado. O que Aragão defende no candomblé como inclusivismo é muito diferente e diz respeito à simbiose. O candomblé aceita outras crenças e práticas e as torna parte do seu próprio sistema sem desvalorizá-las ou classificá-las de acordo com suas próprias categorias para destruir a alteridade e até a relevância do outro. Ao invés disso, este processo simbiótico se envolve com realidades distintas de vida junto para lutar contra um adversário mais forte que poderia destruir o sistema maior. Esta forma de se relacionar com outras religiões permite aos crentes Yorubás viver de forma religiosa-inter-religiosamente pois qualquer religião é capaz de dar alento para as agruras da vida cotidiana.

39. Ibid.

40. Barros, Marcelo. "Múltipla Pertença, o Pluralismo Religioso". In Teologia Pluralista Libertadora Intercontinental, op. cit., 66.

41. Ibid., 67.

42. Invitation to Christ, PCUSA - http://www.pcusa.org/resource/invitation-christ/

43. "Axé é a força primal, o princípio da vida, a força sagrada dos orixás... é poder, é carisma, é a raiz que parte dos nossos ancestrais; podemos ganhar e perder Axé; Axé é presente dos deuses...; é, acima de tudo, a própria casa do candomblé, o templo, a rocá (lugar onde você planta para sua família), toda a tradição." Reginaldo Prandi. Os Candomblés de São Paulo. São Paulo: Hucitec-EDUSP, 1991, pp.103–4.
44. Betcher, Sharon V. "Take my yoga upon you. A Spiritual Pli for the Global City,". in *Polydoxy: Theology of Multiplicity and Relation*, eds. Catherine Keller & Laurel Schneider (New York: Routledge, 2010), 58.
45. Citado por Betcher, Sharon V. "Take my yoga upon you. A Spiritual Pli for the Global City". in Catherine Keller e Laurel Schneider (orgs.) *Polidoxy: Theology of Multiplicity and Relation*. (New York: Routledge, 2010), p. 72.
46. Jaci Maraschin, The Transient Body: Sensibility and Spirituality, artigo apresentado no evento "Liturgy and Body;" Union Theological Seminary, New York, October 20, 2003.
47. Para um trabalho fascinante a este respeito, veja David M. Freidenreich, Foreigners and Their Food. Constructing Otherness in Jewish, Christian and Islamic Law. (Berkeley: Univ. Of California Press, 2011).
48. 1 Coríntios 8:8 NTLH
49. Atos 10:15 NTLH.
50. 1 Coríntios 8:1 NTLH.
51. Michael Philip Penn, Kissing Christians: Ritual and Community in the Late Ancient Church, Filadélfia: University of Pennsylvania Press, 2005, 15, 35, 50.
52. Ibidem., 8.
53. Ibidem., 36.
54. John Chrysostom, In epistulam II ad Corinthios 30.2 (PG 61, 607), in Michael Philip Penn, Kissing Christians, op.cit., 34.
55. Michael Philip Penn, Kissing Christians., 39.
56. Knitter, Paul, Introducing Theologies of Religions. Maryknoll, NY: Orbis Books, 2008, p, 209. CHECK IT HE IS CITING J. Fredericks and F.X. Clooney.
57. Taylor, Mark C., *After God (Religion and Postmodernism)* (Chicago: University Of Chicago Press, 2009).
58. "Ritual é uma maneira de executar as coisas da forma como deveriam ser, numa tensão consciente em relação ao modo como as coisas são". Jonathan Z. Smith, To Take Place: Toward Theory in Ritual. Chicago: Univ. of Chicago Press, 1987, p. 43.
59. Barros, Marcelo. Múltipla pertença, o pluralismo religioso. In: Teologia Pluralista Libertadora Intercontinental, op. cit., 60.
60. Gebara, Ivone. Pluralismo religioso, uma perspectiva feminista. In: Teologia Latino-Americana Pluralista da Libertação, op. cit. 298.

A IMPORTÂNCIA DA INTERSECCIONALIDADE NOS ESTUDOS DE GÊNERO E RELIGIÃO
Uma Breve Análise Sobre o Ilê Asé Ogum Omimkayê (Salvador, Bahia)

Sílvia Barbosa

Considerações iniciais

A fim de pensar as articulações entre as categorias sociais gênero, raça, classe e idade/geração, no interior do Candomblé Ilê Asé Ogum Omimkaye, fez-se necessário o conhecimento e análise sobre os debates contemporâneos que marcaram os usos das categorias e suas intersecções dentro das abordagens das teorias feministas e das ciências sociais. Para tal compreendemos que pensar essas articulações significa considerar categorias sem hierarquizá-las, haja vista que a relevância dessas categorias encontra-se diretamente relacionadas com o contexto sociocultural no qual os sujeitos sociais encontram-se inseridos.

O Candomblé não representa apenas um universo em que a distribuição do poder[1] é fruto da hierarquização do espaço físico ou da atuação religiosa, mas, também, representa um espaço onde a distribuição desigual do poder pode ser fruto das disparidades derivadas das relações de gênero, raça, classe e idade/geração. Neste sentido, se faz necessário a maior compreensão dessas categorias sociais articuladas no universo religioso, entendendo que esses elementos compõem a vida social de homens e mulheres candomblecistas.

A análise dessas dimensões sociais e de suas articulações nas relações que envolvem os sujeitos sociais possibilita um maior entendimento das relações de poder, explorando assim, as interfaces existentes entre os sistemas de opressão que se organizam através das categorias gênero, raça/etnia, classe e idade/geração. A distribuição do poder no Ilê Asé Ogum Omimkaye será analisada, portanto, considerando essas categorias —gênero, raça, classe e idade/geração—como sendo constitutivas do processo sócio-cultural a que estão submetidos e a que se submetem os sujeitos religiosos. Entendo que um determinado grupo social não é homogêneo e que os indivíduos candomblecistas têm, como qualquer outro grupo social, as suas especificidades.

Nesse contexto, a discriminação de gênero não se esgota na exploração de classes, mas encontra apoio no sexismo e nas diferenças raciais que a sociedade se encarregou de naturalizar e perpetuar. Assim como o racismo, encontra-se apoiado nas desigualdades raciais também naturalizadas pelas ideologias racistas que hierarquizam os indivíduos e perpetuam desigualdades. Não é diferente no que diz respeito à idade/geração, uma vez que esta categoria também demarca os espaços ocupados pelos indivíduos na sociedade. Embora essas dimensões sejam naturalizadas e universalizadas no intuito de perpetuar as desigualdades sociais, também, constituem sistemas de opressão interligados (Gonzalez 1984, Motta 1999).

Para ilustrar as dimensões que pretendemos alcançar entre gênero, raça/etnia, classe e idade/geração, observados no Ilê Asé Ogum Omimkaye, lançou-se mão de alguns pressupostos teóricos importantes para a nossa análise, destacando algumas autoras como Lelia Gonzalez (1984), Alda Brito da Motta (1999), Kimberlé Crenshaw (2002), Avta Brah (2006). Outras (os) autoras(es) foram utilizadas(os) para dar suporte ao debate, assim como trechos das falas de nossos entrevistados—Ogã[2] da casa, Iya-Egbé[3] da casa e Iyalorixá[4] do terreiro—ambos participantes e ligados diretamente ao campo religioso do Candomblé de ketu através do Ilê Asé Ogum Omimkaye.

Ilê Asé Ogum Omimkaye: relações de poder e interseccionalidades

O Ilê Asé Ogum Omimkaye está localizado no bairro de Fazenda Grande III, Cajazeiras, Salvador na Bahia, de origem ketu, apresentando descontinuidades e continuidades adaptadas dessa tradição, fundado há mais de 20 anos, apresenta característica tradicional e moderna. Possui sede própria onde funciona um barracão e anexos, pelo qual, sobretudo em período de festas, circula em média 120 pessoas. Destas, cerca de mais de um quarto são associados e se constituem frequentadores(as) mais assíduos. Eles(as) se encontram envolvidos nas mais diversas atividades do terreiro, tais como reuniões administrativas, celebrações religiosas.

Neste terreiro predomina a liderança maciçamente feminina, organizada pela Iyalorixá—líder espiritual, pelas ebomis, ekedes e mães pequenas que são detentoras de significativa parcela de um poder que se expressa no exercício sacerdotal, na preservação das heranças culturais e identidade afro-brasileira, assim como na manutenção da autoridade cotidiana das pessoas envolvidas nas cerimônias próprias desse Candomblé.

É importante frisar a participação dos Ogãs—membros do sexo masculino—que possuem cargos de destaque na hierarquia religiosa. Mas, mesmo assim, predomina neste Candomblé de ketu aspecto estrutural e cultural de matrifocalidade, sistema matricentrado, pois as mulheres em geral e as mães em particular são os pontos focais desse sistema de poder.

No Ilê Asé Ogum Omimkaye o sistema de filiação se dá por consanguinidade e por consideração. Este modelo de filiação compactua, portanto, com a ideia de parentesco proposta por Marcelin (1999), que argumenta que a concepção de parentesco—por consanguinidade e por consideração—extrapola a concepção americana de parentesco. Partindo da suposição "de que o sangue é mais denso do que a água", a lógica etnocêntrica privilegia, sobretudo, os laços consanguíneos à filiação.

Marcelin (1999), ousadamente, apresenta a categoria "consideração" como necessária e suficiente para identificar aqueles que são parentes (não necessariamente parentes de sangue), pois, o parente pode também o ser quando reconhecido como tal, pela consideração. No parentesco simbólico das famílias de santo, prevalece o laço de consideração. Portanto, ser "mãe de santo" é antes de tudo reconhecer que o filho é seu filho, a filha é sua, implicando ter consciência das relações de obrigações que este reconhecimento requer.

Tendemos, nas ciências sociais e humanas, a hipervalorizar as análises socioeconômicas e também, tendemos, quando pesquisamos espaços de religiosidade, a colocar o universo místico-ritual como único e "elementar" lugar de formação de identidades e disputas, ainda que este lugar—o religioso—seja atravessado pelas múltiplas identidades individuais e coletivas dos sujeitos que o compõem. Porém, se promove disputas em sentidos mais amplos, que extrapolam o religioso, ou, por vezes, se interconectam a ele, mostrando-se complexos e variados, que não se interligam somente ao conjunto das crenças, também são constituídos por convergências e divergências sociais forjadas nas intersecções de gênero, raça, classe e idade/geração. Scott (1994), p. 18) observa que:

> As identidades de grupo são um aspecto inevitável da vida social e da vida política, e as duas são interconectadas porque as diferenças de grupo se tornam visíveis, salientes e problemáticas em contextos políticos específicos. São nesses momentos—quando exclusões são legitimadas por diferenças de grupo, quando hierarquias econômicas e sociais favorecem certos grupos em detrimento de outros, quando um conjunto de características biológicas ou religiosas ou étnicas ou culturais é valorizado em relação a outros—que a tensão entre indivíduos e grupos emerge.[5]

Ainda que as identidades estejam em perpétua mutação, carecendo de elementos que as consolidem, de acordo com variados tempos históricos, precisamos ter em mente que algumas referências fundamentais são trabalhadas dentro de cada grupo social; porém, não podem ser tomados como arranjos estáticos, pois as identidades são construídas em cima de diferenças sociais, culturais, politicas etc., como bem problematizou Scott, fazendo emergir diferenciadas tensões.

Avta Brah (2006, p. 332–333), observa que o entendimento do termo "negro" adquire diversos sentidos sociais e políticos em contextos diferenciados. Brah, quando questiona "o que há em um nome? o que há em uma cor?",[6] evoca múltiplos sentidos para as variações étnicas e identitárias formadoras de nossas noções racialistas e/ou racializadas. Determinados grupos sociais podem experimentar a construção de sua racialização a partir de condições delineadas pela sua "não brancura"; porém, atravessadas pelas compreensões de classe e gênero que podem ser cambiantes em estruturas sociais diversas. O binômio branco/não branco cada vez mais se conectou, historicamente, ao processo de racialização dos indivíduos, ainda que, em determinadas sociedades, os processos de racialização não tenham sido idênticos.

A partir das considerações acima, podemos perceber que os Candomblés, ainda hoje, são compreendidos como lugares religiosos exclusivamente "negros", ou de indivíduos que derivam etnicamente da afro-descendência. Estes espaços foram forjados pela identidade negra que a posteriori foi racializada, ainda que estes espaços de religiosidade sejam frequentados, em menor número, por outros grupos étnico-raciais; foram inscritos a partir de cruzamentos identitários e políticos específicos que construíram a experiência da racialização, nestes lugares, de maneira diversificada.

Muitos embates políticos giram em torno da construção dos Candomblés como espaços de religiosidade e negritude; ainda que poucos trabalhos versem sobre o assunto, são necessárias reflexões profundas acerca do exposto para que possamos entender como as relações de poder se apresentam a partir do entendimento do "não branco", da "negritude", ou do "ser preto/negro" nestes espaços religiosos.

Na fala de um de nossos entrevistados, Hugo, negro, 40 anos de idade, há 09 anos participante do Candomblé pesquisado, Ogã da casa, podemos perceber tênues conexões entre o "ser negro" e o espaço religioso. Quando perguntado se "poderia ser possível chegar a espiritualidade pela porta da questão étnica?", respondeu que sim, seria possível; porém, ressaltou que não seria apenas a negritude que conformaria um membro do Candomblé, mas a espiritualidade que passa pelo indivíduo e pelo seu Orixá. Hugo ainda reforça que, a partir de seu "estado no Candomblé", foi levado a pensar que não seria só "a questão étnica" o veículo para o ingresso nas religiões de matriz-africanas, ressaltando que "você não tem que ir lá só por isso... entendeu... pode ser até a porta de entrada, mas não é só isso" [...] "você chega lá e percebe que tem mais coisa".[7] Porém, o que poderíamos destacar como coisas a mais que Hugo ressalta?

Nosso entrevistado coloca as relações religiosas e étnicas em posições hierárquicas, entendendo que, no ambiente religioso, as questões raciais são subsumidas pelas questões religiosas e pelas divindades—Orixás— assim como pelas vocações místicas de cada integrante. A partir desta colocação, podemos perceber como estão imbrincados e naturalizados pelos indivíduos a valorização hierárquica do poder religioso na forma de vocação e a partir da força dos Orixás. As relações étnicas e raciais, postas em segundo plano, deixam-nos emergir as sensíveis e complexas estruturas que formam a etnicidade e criam as imagens do "ser negro" nos Candomblés, ou seja, ser negro não seria importante, de acordo com Hugo, para essa organização religiosa, o mais importante seria o seu "chamado", seu ingresso a partir de sua tendência vocacional e religiosa, ou, ainda, a partir de uma necessidade mística não explicada racionalmente, que seria o chamado do Orixá.

O depoimento de Hugo nos remete a uma construção emblemática que circula, historicamente, os espaços religiosos de matrizes africanas que são as conexões feitas entre classe social, raça/etnia e religiosidade. Nos discursos de senso comum, observou-se com frequência relatos que definem os Candomblés como espaços religiosos de ordem subalternizada, religiosidade manifesta por indivíduos de classes populares empobrecidas, negras e etnicamente inferiorizada. Lucinha, negra, 52 anos, Iya-Egbé do terreiro reafirma em sua fala as conexões pejorativas que muitas pessoas fazem ao falarem "que o Candomblé é do diabo", devido aos rituais e as entradas de transe existentes.[8]

Os inúmeros ataques e as violências que os espaços religiosos de Candomblé e seus participantes sofrem no país são reflexos do pensamento construído em torno destes locais, que o apontam como o lugar do incomum, do diabólico, do sujo e dos indivíduos negros. Ainda que diversos trabalhos de pesquisa venham desconstruindo esta imagem, permeia no cenário nacional uma grande tendência ao desconhecimento e a se pensar as religiões de matrizes africanas como ligadas ao submundo da crendice, da inferioridade racial e da superstição. Mesmo que nosso interlocutor—Hugo—não associe diretamente este espaço religioso e a escolha do Candomblé como religião, a partir de pressupostos que marcam a raça/etnia dos indivíduos, estes marcadores sociais estão presentes e demonstram a sua força, sobretudo quando atos de violência atingem candomblecistas em todo o país.

Dona Dulce, negra, 67 anos, Iyalorixá do terreiro, nos dá um depoimento intrigante, quando questionada sobre "o que teria mudado em sua vida após sua inserção no Candomblé?", nos respondeu veementemente:

> [...] mudou muito porque, na verdade, obrigação religiosa eu não tinha, passei a viver aquela vida de crente e... Não tinha aquela responsabilidade com a religião... Porém, depois que eu passei a ter uma história no axé, mudou. Eu tenho responsabilidade a cumprir com meu dever... Aqui, você sabe que veio da senzala e na senzala tem o quê? Trabalho, muito trabalho [...][9]

Na fala da Iyalorixá fica claro suas ligações com a afro-descendência, remete suas raízes mais profundas a "senzala", a escravidão de seus ancestrais e o duro labor que se circunscreve no entendimento de seu "eu", de sua identidade negra.

Não podemos estar como diria Geertz (1997, p. 88)[10] "embaixo da pele do outro"; podemos, no entanto, através de suas falas tentar captar, "com quê?", "por meios de quê?", ou "através de quê?", as pessoas compreendem o mundo em que se inserem e, no caso de mãe Dulce, percebemos que seus valores, sua leitura sobre a sociedade e, fundamentalmente, sobre a construção de si mesma perpassa concatenada a seus elementos étnicos e religiosos; elementos estes constituídos pela singularidade da raça e da etnia, do ser negro, do ser da senzala e do universo do trabalho.

Para a Iyalorixá sua "diferença" religiosa e social está atravessada pela sua ancestralidade, pelo conhecimento que possui de si e de sua constituição como descendente de africanos (as) escravizados (as). Essa fala contrasta com a de nosso outro entrevistado, Hugo, pois possibilita entrever as complexas estruturas que constituem as identidades dos sujeitos dentro de uma mesma unidade religiosa. Mãe Dulce, Iyalorixá do terreiro e Hugo Ogã, possuem perspectivas diferenciadas sobre as questões de raça/etnia que, possivelmente, constituem os indivíduos no Ilê Asé Ogum Omimkaye.

Para a Iyalorixá o Candomblé lhe remete, quase que instantaneamente, para uma realidade passada de escravização, sofrimento e trabalho, que permeiam a sua identidade negra e que subentendem a estrutura de responsabilidades—"pesadas"—que a mesma assume ao adentrar o espaço religioso. Quando a Iyalorixá expressa seu entendimento sobre a sua inserção no espaço religioso, também possibilita entrever insígnias distintivas emergidas de suas experiências.

A experiência-próxima da Iyalorixá se deu através da descoberta de sua religiosidade no seio do Candomblé, experiência esta que não tinha observado em nenhum outro campo religioso que tentou se inserir. A partir de sua maturidade religiosa ou sua experiência distante, seu entendimento mais geral e amplificado da sociedade mudou diante das diversas atribuições e responsabilidades que sua religiosidade lhe propôs. Mãe Dulce permite-nos observar que através de sua experiência-próxima no campo religioso passou a decodificar o mundo em que se insere por prismas variados que perpassam campos da etnicidade e da classe, inserindo a si mesma em uma sociedade concreta, construída pela interpretação de uma afro-descendência marcada pelas conexões do religioso.[11]

Debater as interseccionalidades possibilita perceber a "coexistência de diversas abordagens"; as perspectivas diferenciadas traçam pensamentos diversificados sobre "diferença e poder", refletindo sobre as margens da agência concedida aos sujeitos e suas reais possibilidades de agir mediante as suas fronteiras sociais e culturais. De acordo com Kimberlé Crenshaw (2002, p. 173):

> Assim como é verdadeiro o fato de que todas as mulheres estão, de algum modo, sujeitas ao peso da discriminação de gênero, também é verdade que outros fatores relacionados às suas identidades sociais, tais como classe, casta, raça, cor, etnia, religião, origem nacional e orientação sexual, são diferenças que fazem diferença na forma como vários grupos de mulheres vivenciam a discriminação. Tais elementos diferenciais podem criar problemas e vulnerabilidades exclusivos de subgrupos específicos de mulheres, ou que afetem desproporcionalmente apenas algumas mulheres.[12]

O que Crenshaw (2002) sinaliza tem se tornado, academicamente, um desafio instigante no que tangencia os estudos de gênero. A autora nos alerta para as diferenças existentes nas formas de vivenciar a vida, a discriminação, a vulnerabilidade; as mulheres possuem diferentes prismas que divergem ou convergem entre grupos sociais específicos e criam as condições diversas que também tangenciam a opressão e a discriminação social dentre outros importantes elementos que constroem o "ser" social.

Que configurações de poder podemos extrair destas falas? O poder da "mãe de santo" também se nutre do trabalho, suas diversas responsabilidades no campo religioso, na administração do terreiro e na distribuição das tarefas lhe concedem múltiplos domínios na casa, (re)configurando, constantemente, o poder que lhe foi atribuído pelos Orixás e pela comunidade.

O comprar, limpar, costurar, cuidar, "zelar do santo" são tarefas determinadas, com dias específicos para suas realizações, onde toda a comunidade do terreiro tem suas atribuições específicas; estas atribuições, porém, são determinadas em dois planos, o espiritual e o material, ambos convergindo para que a manutenção dos espaços do terreiro e a salvaguarda dos saberes místicos sejam preservados, mantidos e repassados. A organização do trabalho religioso também reflete as diferenças atribuídas aos gêneros, as vocações, as possibilidades de inserção neste espaço religioso, fazendo-nos refletir sobre as conexões entre gênero/trabalho/geração—três eixos norteadores de diversas unidades sociais e suas organizações.

Lucinha faz uma interessante fala sobre a divisão do trabalho no Candomblé, ressaltando que homens e mulheres possuem postos diferenciados, seguidos de hierarquias a serem respeitadas e funções determinadas a serem desenvolvidas. De acordo com a entrevistada:

> Eu acho assim, [...] cada um deveria ficar nos seus postos, nos seus devidos lugares, assumir o que é seu de direito. [...] e todos deveriam trabalhar juntos. Desde quando a cultura africana veio para o Brasil... Por escravos... Homens e mulheres devem, sim, trabalhar juntos, sendo que tem determinadas funções que são estabelecidas, exclusivamente, pra mulheres; mas isso não quer dizer que os homens sejam exclusos, pois o papel do homem é fundamental no Candomblé, principalmente pra apertar atabaque, pra tocar, porque no Candomblé não se faz nada sozinho, se trabalha com ambos os sexos, os dois precisam trabalhar juntos, pra poder fazer uma soma, pra poder crescer e parar de existir essa discriminação de que aqui não pode, só porque é um homem, ou aqui é de homem, mulher não pode, porque é mulher.[13]

A partir das especificações de gênero podemos perceber que homens e mulheres são convidados a trabalhar, ativamente, no espaço religioso do Candomblé; porém, estes trabalhos são definidos de acordo com o sexo de cada integrante, sua idade e seu tempo no espaço religioso. Por exemplo, como esclarece Lucinha, Iya-Egbé, cargo de extrema importância que a coloca como a segunda na hierarquia após a Iyalorixá, ambos precisam trabalhar juntos—homens e mulheres—porém, a função de apertar os atabaques é exclusivamente masculina. Outra função exclusiva dos homens é a de Ogã, responsável por vários tipos de serviços dentro do terreiro, incluindo tocar as músicas atribuídas aos Orixás. Sobre o ofício de Ogã, Hugo, o Ogã da casa, explica que dentre as suas funções estão:

> [...] consertar a casa do Orixá quando precisar, suspender o santo quando precisar, limpar a casa do santo, realizar os sacrifícios para a obrigação do santo e, se precisar, vestir o santo, cuidar da casa nos momentos da festa, acolher bem as pessoas por algum momento [...][7]

As especificidades do trabalho do Ogã, descritos por Hugo, fazem muita diferença quando vamos observar a natureza do trabalho feminino no terreiro pesquisado. Por exemplo, as mulheres Ekedes são responsáveis pelos Orixás mais diretamente, "cuidam do santo, enxugam o santo, vestem o santo e guiam o filho de santo" quando o mesmo encontra-se incorporado de seu Orixá.[13] As funções da Ekede nos remetem ao ato de "cuidar", lembrando que dentro das organizações sociais mais amplas o ato de cuidar em si sempre foi uma atribuição feminina.

A partir de tais observações, podemos traçar um paralelo entre as funções religiosas específicas, Ogãs/masculinas e Ekedes/femininas dentro do terreiro; as Ekedes estariam ligadas com mais proximidade as funções do cuidar, este cuidado, porém, estaria conectado amplamente aos cuidados dos sujeitos, dos orixás, dos filhos de santo, já os Ogãs estariam mais estreitamente ligados com os cuidados estruturais para o bom funcionamento da casa, cuidam dos instrumentos musicais, da limpeza e manutenção dos espaços dos santos e dos sacrifícios.

As perspectivas de gênero tornam-se importantes para explicarmos as diferentes trajetórias de vida percorridas, socialmente, por homens e mulheres. Homens e mulheres experienciam trajetórias de vida social diferente que permitem a formação de identidades, também, diferenciadas. Os sujeitos sociais vivenciam experiências que lhes dão possibilidades distintas de compreensão dos sistemas de relações sociais como gênero, classe, raça/etnia e idade/geração. E é exatamente o modo como esses indivíduos apreendem esses sistemas e se integram na sociedade que os fazem produzir outras formas de disparidades.[14]

Desse modo, é possível inferir que as relações entre sujeitos no campo religioso também são atravessadas por suas classes sociais, seus gêneros, suas raças/etnias, suas idades/gerações; transformando suas noções de sociabilidade, de compreensão e leitura do espaço religioso, podendo influir para a sua própria inserção no grupo. A inserção do indivíduo no universo religioso promove leituras sobre este espaço que são atravessadas pelas compreensões forjadas nos liames da experiência pessoal e coletiva. Assim, cada indivíduo usará de suas várias percepções sociais para reconstruir estes espaços, de forma diferenciada, como lugares de sociabilidade, alteridade, fé, mística, disputas políticas e relações de poder, dentre outros.

Considerações finais

No presente trabalho pontuamos uma pequena amostra sobre as relações de interseccionalidade que podem ser observadas em nosso campo de pesquisa. As falas de nossos interlocutores, ricas em significados, desvelam as várias superfícies por onde o poder se revela no Candomblé, construindo gênero, raça e classe como anteparos substanciais para a organização social e religiosa do espaço. Observamos que as falas da Iyalorixá, do Ogã e da Iya-Egbé, ainda que possam ter conexões refinadas com o coletivo religioso, apresentam-se independentes umas das outras, demonstrando que cada sujeito compreende e constrói sua participação no espaço do Candomblé de forma heterogênea, única, com pontos de vista pessoais sobre suas atividades, responsabilidades e inserção no meio religioso.

As análises emergidas da compreensão da interseccionalidade como ponto de apoio teórico e multidimensional na formação das relações de poder nos possibilitam apreender conexões mais complexas e dinâmicas nas relações dos indivíduos nos campos religiosos, sem contudo fragmentar sua individualidade ou sua compreensão do coletivo religioso. Entender as conexões possíveis apontadas pelas dinâmicas de gênero, raça/etnia, classe, idade/geração possibilita visualizar, mais profundamente, os indivíduos em suas relações coletivas e sociais, demonstrando que as minucias do ser individual, ainda que impregnadas pela sua coletividade, apresentam formas de ser, viver e conhecer que são inerentes de suas experiências e subjetividades pessoais e podem apontar novas relações sociais, novas formas de interpretar o mundo e de modelar o poder.

Dado os limites de espaço não podemos apontar outras importantes conexões existentes entre as intersecções aqui elencadas, mas podemos assegurar que os arranjos sociais e as relações de poder são permeadas pelas categorias de gênero, raça/etnia, classe, idade/geração, usando estas categorias de forma hierarquizada a fim de contemplar os indivíduos com papeis e lugares específicos nos espaços de religiosidade.

Notas

1. Com base na leitura de Vivaldo da Costa Lima, "A família de santo nos candomblés jeje-nagôs da Bahia", pp. 80–82, acrescida da minha observação participante, cabe mencionar que a distribuição do poder no terreiro pesquisado se estrutura a partir da hierarquia de mando; respeitando os critérios de senioridade e de herança da tradição do Candomblé de ketu. A circularidade do poder se efetiva entre os sujeitos candomblecistas a partir das ações

decorrentes dos cargos e funções religiosas do terreiro. *Iyaloriaxá/Babalorixá*: mãe ou Pai de Santo. É o posto mais elevado na tradição afro-brasileira. *Alagbá*: cargo masculino, chefe dos Oyê. Em algumas casas é também chamado de Ogã. Pode desempenhar diversas tarefas de cunho espiritual e civil e não entra em transe. *Mogbá*: cargo masculino específico do culto a Xangô. Ministro de Xangô. *Tojú Obá*: cargo masculino específico do culto a Xangô. Olhos do Rei. *Iya-Egbé/Babaegbé*: é a segunda pessoa do axé. Conselheira, responsável pela manutenção da ordem, tradição e hierarquia. *Iyalaxé* (mulher): mãe do axé, a que distribui o axé e cuida dos objetos rituais. *Iyakekerê* (mulher): Mãe Pequena, segunda sacerdotisa do axé ou da comunidade. Sempre pronta a ajudar e ensinar a todos (as) iniciados (as). *Babakekerê* (homem): Pai Pequeno, segundo sacerdote do axé ou da comunidade. Sempre pronto a ajudar e ensinar a todos (as) iniciados (as). *Ojubonã* ou *Agibonã*: é a mãe criadeira, supervisiona e ajuda na iniciação. *Iyamoró*: responsável pelo *Padê* de Exu. *Iyaefun* ou *Babaefun*: responsável pela pintura branca das (os) iaôs. *Iyadagan* e *Ossidagã*: auxiliam a *Iyamoró*. *Axogun*: sacerdote responsável pelo sacrifício dos animais. Dependendo do caso, no ritual de iniciação, este sacerdote pode assumir outro cargo, ja que *axogun* é um *ogã*. *Aficobá*: responsável pelos sacrifícios dos animais de Xangô. *Aficodé*: responsável pelos sacrifícios dos animais de Oxossi. *Iyabassê*: (mulher): responsável no preparo dos alimentos sagrados—as comidas de santo. *Iyarubá*: carrega a esteira para o(a) iniciando(a). *Iyatebexê* ou *Babatebexê*: responsável pelas cantigas nas festas públicas de candomblé. *Aiyaba Ewe*: responsável em determinados atos e obrigações de "cantar folhas". *Aiybá*: bate o *ejé* nas obrigações. *Ològun*: cargo masculino (e, em alguns casos, feminino). Despacha os Ebós das obrigações, preferencialmente os filhos de Ogun, depois Odé e Obaluwaiyê. *Oloya*: cargo feminino. Despacha os Ebós das obrigações, na falta de Ològun. São filhas de Oya. *Iyalabaké*: axé e cuida dos objetos rituais. A guardiã do alá de osaala. *Iyatojuomó*: responsável pelas crianças do Axé. *Pejigan*: responsável pelos axés da casa, do terreiro. Primeiro *Ogã* na hierarquia. *Alagbê*: responsável pelos toques rituais, alimentação, conservação e presaervação dos instrumentos musicais sagrados (não entram em transe). Nos ciclos de festas é obrigado a se levantar de madrugada para que faça a alvorada. Se uma autoridade de outro Axé chegar ao terreiro, o *alagbê* tem de lhe prestar as devidas homenagens. No Candomblé Ketu, os atabaques são chamados de *ilú*. Há também outros *Ogãs* como Gaipé, Runsó, Gaitó, Arrow, Arrontodé, etc. *Ogã*: tocadores de atabaques (não entram em transe). *Ebômi*: são pessoas que já cumpriram o período de sete anos da iniciação (significado: meu irmão mais velho). *Ekedi*: camareira do Orixá (não entram em transe). *Iaô*: filha (o) de santo que já foi iniciada(o) e entra em transe com o Orixá dono de sua cabeça. *Abiã*: novato. É considerada *abiã* toda pessoa que entra para a religião após ter passado pelo ritual de lavagem de contas e o *bori*. Poderá ser iniciada ou não, vai depender do orixá pedir a iniciação. *Sarapebê*: é responsável pela comunicação do *egbe* (similar a relações públicas). *Otun* e *Osy Axogun*: são os auxiliares do *Axogun*. *Apokan*: responsável pelo culto de Olwuaye e o Olugbajé.

2. *Ogã* com cargo de *axogun*, sacerdote responsável pelo sacrifício dos animais.
3. *Iya-Egbé* é a segunda pessoa do axé. Mãe Conselheira, responsável pela manutenção da ordem, tradição e hierarquia.
4. *Iyalorixá* é a mãe-de-santo. É o posto mais elevado na tradição afro-brasileira.
5. Scott (1994).
6. Avta Brah (2006, p. 332–333).
7. Entrevista com Hugo, 16 de abril de 2014.

8. Entrevista feita com Maria Lúcia, apelido Lucinha, em 23 de setembro de 2012.
9. Entrevista feita com Mãe Dulce em 11 de setembro de 2012.
10. Geertz 1997, p. 88.
11. Geertz 1997, p. 87–91.
12. Kimberlé Crenshaw 2002, p. 173.
13. Entrevista feita com Maria Lúcia em, 23 de setembro de 2012.
14. Motta 1999, p. 193.

Referências Bibliográficas

Brah, Avtar, 2006, "Diferença, Diversidade, Diferenciação," Cadernos Pagu [online] (26), pp. 329–76.

Crenshaw, Kimberlé, 2002, Documento para o encontro de especialistas em aspectos da discriminação racial relativos ao gênero. Estudos Feministas. 1-2002, pp. 171–89.

Geertz, Clifford, 1997, Do ponto de vista dos nativos. In: _____ O Saber Local: novos ensaios em antropologia interpretativa. Petrópolis: Vozes.

Gonzalez, Lélia, 1984, Racismo e sexismo na cultura brasileira. Revista Ciências Sociais Hoje. Anpocs.

Lima, Vivaldo da Costa, 2003, A Família de Santo Nos Candomblés jejes-Nagôs da Bahia: Um Estudo de Relações Intragrupais. 2 ed. Salvador: Corrupio.

Marcelin, Louis Herns, 1999, "A Linguagem da Casa Entre os Negros no Recôncavo Baiano," Mana [online] **5**(2), pp. 31–60.

Motta, Alda Brito da, 1999, "As Dimensões de Gênero e Classe Social na Análise do Envelhecimento," Cadernos Pagu **13**, pp. 191–221.

Scott, Joan W., 1994, Gênero: Uma Categoria Útil Para Análise Histórica. Educação e Realidade. Recife: SOS Corpo.

CROSSCURRENTS

TEOLOGIA DA LIBERTAÇÃO
História, Temas e Nomes

Cláudio Carvalhaes and Fábio Py

A Teologia da Libertação não é uma teologia de escolha, mais uma dentre outras. Não! A Teologia da Libertação, tal como a conhecemos, é matéria de sobrevivência, uma matéria de vida e morte, um lugar onde fé, discurso de Deus e vida real encontram-se para proteger e expandir as possibilidades da vida, na eco-bio-diversidade do planeta e na possibilidade de justiça para o pobre. Não escolhemos a Teologia da Libertação: fomos escolhidos por ela. É por causa da Teologia da Libertação que estamos aqui hoje. Se tirarem de nós a Teologia da Libertação, ficamos mudos e desenvolvemos afasia.

Somos talvez a terceira geração de teólogos da libertação latino-americanos. Frequentamos igrejas protestantes e tivemos uma criação mais conservadora, e descobrimos a Teologia da Libertação através da resistência social e da nossa formação no seminário. Começamos lendo, ainda que com muita dificuldade para entender o livro, o teólogo católico Gustavo Gutierrez. Apesar das dificuldades, foi um tempo de descoberta e empolgação! Rubem Alves, Richard Shaul, Julio de Santana, Jaci Maraschin, Leonardo Boff, Milton Schwantes, dentre muitos outros, nos influenciaram na época em que a Teologia da Libertação foi amadurecendo. Padres e pastores também contribuíam com o movimento através das suas igrejas e das Comunidades de Base, tomando consciência da sua situação social e de como Deus os chamava para um novo dia! Muitas mulheres também começaram a se envolver no trabalho, redesenhando o mapa da produção teológica. Sentimos a Teologia da Libertação pulsar em todo lugar, com excelente material teológico sendo produzido e experiências fantásticas de transformações políticas e sociais acontecendo em toda a América Latina.

Não é nossa tarefa aqui apresentar um longo relato histórico dos processos e movimentos da Teologia da Libertação na América Latina. Em vez disso, tecemos comentários sobre o trabalho de alguns teólogos da libertação latino-americanos, a saber: Rubem Alves e Ivone Gebara, Milton Schwantes e Nancy Cardoso. A Teologia da Libertação preocupava-se com o pobre e, por isso, envolvia-se com os negros da América Latina. Contudo, até então não havia teólogos da libertação negros fazendo Teologia Negra, nem teólogos da libertação em geral lidaram com a questão da raça como deveria ter sido feito.

Aqui, começaremos delineando os primeiros passos da Teologia da Libertação na América Latina com alguns comentários a respeito dos seus princípios fundamentais. Em seguida, apresentaremos uma pequena parte do trabalho destes quatro teólogos que mencionamos, e terminaremos com algumas palavras sobre o que continua por fazer.

O início da Teologia da Libertação não foi o trabalho de um único teólogo. Não foi Gustavo Gutierrez que deu origem ao movimento, mas sim as pessoas e os movimentos populares que clamavam por justiça, movimentos estes que acabaram aceitando o envolvimento de sacerdotes e teólogos e que modificaram profundamente o modo como as coisas aconteciam na América Latina. Aliás, a melhor forma de entender a Teologia da Libertação é se debruçar não só sobre os livros publicados, mas também sobre o movimento da igreja. Nas décadas de 50 e 60, a América Latina vivia sob profunda influência e controle exercidos pelos Estados Unidos. No auge do Macartismo, os EUA temiam que a Rússia se tornasse a referência para outros países da região além de Cuba. Por isso, a CIA apoiou grupos conservadores radicais que tomaram o poder em vários países da América Central e do Sul: Chile, Argentina, Brasil, El Salvador, Nicarágua e assim por diante. A Escola das Américas foi a instituição colonizadora vigente que deu vazão aos desejos da CIA de controlar a região da América Latina, treinando os locais para matarem sua própria gente e prometendo em troca dinheiro e proteção. O massacre de El Salvador, o assassinato de Oscar Romero e dos padres da Universidad Católica, os golpes militares no Brasil e na Argentina — todos estes eventos podem ser explicados pelo poder e influência letais dos Estados Unidos nos países latino-americanos.

A Teologia da Libertação nasceu da luta contra a dominação externa e a opressão social e econômica. Se quisermos olhar para o começo da Teologia da Libertação na América Latina, precisamos ir até às conferências da CELAM, a Conferência do Episcopado Latino-americano de Medellín, na Colômbia, em 1986, que começou a ouvir os gritos do povo da América Latina. Foi o início de um movimento que, na esteira do Concílio Vaticano II, começou a estabelecer conexões com o povo através das comunidades de base, com os sacerdotes indo onde o povo estava. Foi a expansão da igreja para um novo movimento.

De 1968 a 1979, quando a conferência da CELAM foi realizada em Puebla, México, muita coisa aconteceu na América Latina. O movimento tinha se fortalecido e a CELAM definiu o conceito da "opção preferencial pelos pobres" de Deus. Teólogos, especialistas em Bíblia e em ética, sacerdotes e educadores, junto com o povo, deram forma ao movimento. Neste período, o pensamento acadêmico desenvolvia a "teoria da dependência", que criticava a maneira pela qual a América Latina se tornava dependente demais da colonização dos EUA. Teologicamente, os países do terceiro mundo criavam a EATWOT: Associação Ecumênica de Teólogos do Terceiro Mundo, uma organização fundamental que se engajou nas realidades sociais dos países pobres e amplificou as vozes dos pobres ao redor do mundo.

Este movimento massivo criou estruturas e movimentos políticos e sociais por toda a América Latina que desafiaram a elite desta parte do continente: o Partido dos Trabalhadores no Brasil elegeu Lula, o primeiro operário a ser eleito presidente na América Latina; o Movimento dos Sem Terra tornou-se o maior movimento social do mundo; os zapatistas e o Subcomandante Marcos no México; os sandinistas na Nicarágua; e mesmo a recente rede global chamada Um novo mundo é possível. Todas estas organizações foram influenciadas, em algum grau, pelas crenças e forma de organização originada nas comunidades de base e nas teologias da libertação.

É só a partir deste contexto mais amplo da igreja e da sociedade como um todo que podemos entender o trabalho dos principais teólogos. Do livro de Gustavo Gutierrez, "Uma Teologia da Libertação: História, Política e Salvação", por exemplo, tornam-se a primeira e maior referência prático-teórica a partir deste longo processo de morte e opressão da América Latina e acaba dando forma a muitas das práticas e pensamentos dentro dos movimentos de base.

A primeira geração de teólogos da libertação foi fundamental para que o movimento se desenvolvesse. Muitos deles receberam sólida formação teológica, principalmente na Europa, e foram corajosos em recriar a teologia na América Latina baseada na vida do povo que ali morava. Juan Luis Segundo no Uruguai, Jon Sobrino e Ignacio Ellacuría em El Salvador, Gustavo Gutierrez no Peru, Elsa Tamez na Costa Rica, Enrique Dussel no México, Pablo Richard no Chile, José Miguez Bonino na Argentina, os irmãos Boff no Brasil e muitos, muitos outros. Sacerdotes foram fundamentais neste processo: Dons Oscar Romero, Pedro Casaldáliga, Hélder Câmara, Paulo Arns e muitos outros que capacitaram e deram esperança ao povo para acreditar junto com a fé que receberam de Deus!

Este relato histórico é muito insuficiente, mas ele pretende apenas apontar, em linhas gerais, como a Teologia da Libertação tomou forma na América Latina.

Alguns temas principais da Teologia da Libertação
Primeiro, o método
A Teologia da Libertação expande as fontes da revelação divina. Junto com os documentos da igreja e a Bíblia, as vidas das pobres tornam-se não somente fontes para o discurso de Deus, mas um eixo hermenêutico a partir do qual a fé e a doxa serão compreendidas. A praxis torna-se esta forma complexa de abordar a vida, teoria, tradição e teologia.

Em segundo lugar, salvação
Como consequência, um dos grandes temas da teologia cristã, a salvação, ganha um novo entendimento. A salvação deste mundo desloca-se para a salvação neste mundo. Isto significa que o mundo tem pecados sociais estruturais e a salvação torna-se a libertação destes pecados; a vida encontrada em Jesus Cristo pode ser vivida dentro da história! A esperança de um outro mundo não exclui a concretização do Reino de Deus em nosso mundo. Ao invés disso, há esperança de que o movimento do Espírito possa nos ajudar a viver a vida na sua plenitude aqui! Já nos nossos momentos aqui e não ainda!

Em terceiro lugar, a opção preferencial pelos pobres
Os teólogos da libertação leem a Bíblia a partir da ótica do pobre e descobriram que, ao longo de toda a Bíblia, Deus faz uma clara opção preferencial pelo pobre. Desde a história do Êxodo até os profetas, da encarnação

de Deus em Jesus à vida, morte e ressurreição de Jesus Cristo, na vida da igreja e através das manifestações salvíficas de Deus na História, Deus demonstra claramente sua opção preferencial pelo pobre.

Em quarto lugar, lutas de classe

Ao olharmos para as vidas dos pobres, vemos nossas realidades e vemos que o mundo é marcado pelas lutas por riqueza. Dinheiro/economia é o maior vagão do trem da História. É a sede por dinheiro e acumulação que cria uma distinção entre as pessoas e estabelece as lutas de classe. Em todo lugar que olharmos, veremos disparidade econômica e pessoas divididas na hierarquia de classes sob controle do Estado e da lei. Ao olharmos para as realidades concretas do nosso povo, estamos olhando os aspectos econômicos, sociais, políticos e culturais das nossas vidas, e o que vemos são os pobres sendo engolidos pelos poderes econômicos e políticos controlados por uma elite microscópica. Portanto, não há como ler a Bíblia e entender o amor de Deus senão através das lentes que revelam a injustiça e a morte causadas pelas lutas de classes.

Quinto ponto: consciência

O amor preferencial de Deus pelo pobre não só vê o pobre como receptáculo do amor de Deus mas, além disso, aprendemos a ver o pobre como agentes do amor de Deus no mundo. É Jesus no meio dos pobres, nus, famintos, sedentos e encarcerados, mostrando onde Deus vive e de onde vem a salvação à medida que consideramos a presença de Deus na História. Isso significa que o evangelho lido nas comunidades pobres tem o poder de transformar cada pessoa no sujeito da sua própria história. Conscientes do nosso chamado para fazer a história, nós é quem somos capacitados por Deus para trabalhar com Ele de forma a vivermos a utopia do Reino de Deus em nosso meio.

Sexto, os teólogos se transformam em "intelectuais orgânicos", aqueles que, para fazer o trabalho acadêmico, vivem com o pobre e aprendem com eles sua sabedoria, e ajudam o povo a ganhar, nas palavras de Paulo Freire, consciência do seu poder e a possibilidade de promover transformação neste mundo. Como sujeitos da sua própria história!

A seguir, um rápido olhar sobre quatro dos principais teólogos brasileiros.

Rubem Alves

Se definirmos a Teologia da Libertação a partir dos livros publicados, devemos dizer que ela apareceu pela primeira vez no trabalho de um teólogo e pastor protestante chamado Rubem Alves.

Rubem Alves foi um teo-poeta, educador e contador de histórias brasileiro, um ex-sacerdote presbiteriano que moldou profundamente a história do protestantismo no Brasil, tanto através da sua própria história nos últimos cinquenta anos do século vinte quanto através dos seus múltiplos escritos. Seu livro "Protestantismo e Repressão: um estudo de caso brasileiro", publicado em inglês pela Orbis Books, por exemplo, é um marco da análise do protestantismo no Brasil.

Em 1963, Alves estudou no Union Theological Seminary em Nova Iorque e, em 1964, voltou ao Brasil para pastorear uma igreja no interior do seu estado, Minas Gerais, quando foi preso pela ditadura militar. Alves tornou-se um inimigo do governo, principalmente porque sua amada igreja, a Igreja Presbiteriana do Brasil, o denunciou à ditadura como um pensador perigoso.

Os líderes da igreja à época eram alinhados aos militares e ajudaram o governo a se livrarem das mentes perigosas. Não obstante, com a ajuda de presbiterianos da América do Norte, Alves viveu no exílio nos Estados Unidos, onde fez seu doutorado no Princeton Theological Seminary. O título da sua dissertação foi: "Em direção a uma Teologia da Libertação". Alves conta, no prefácio da edição brasileira, que à época sua ideia de libertação era completamente desconhecida e que a banca examinadora lhe deu um prazo de um ano para reescrever sua tese. Foi Richard Shaull, seu mentor, que impediu que isso acontecesse.

Mais tarde, um editor católico romano interessou-se pela sua dissertação e quis publicá-la. Sua única condição foi mudar o título, porque ninguém iria saber o que era teologia da libertação. Influenciado pela teologia da esperança de Moltmann, o livro foi finalmente publicado com o seguinte título: "Uma Teologia da Esperança Humana", que continha as sementes da agenda da Teologia da Libertação.

Harvey Cox escreveu no prefácio do seu livro e disse que a teologia do norte deveria, a partir dali, fazer teologia *com* teólogos da parte sul da América, e não mais sobre eles. Seu livro foi escrito antes de "Teologia da Libertação" de Gustavo Gutierrez. Mais tarde, Alves tornou-se um grande amigo dos professores James Cone e Walter Wink, formando, nas palavras do próprio Alves, os "três mosqueteiros" do Union. Depois que voltou ao Brasil, Alves trilhou diferentes caminhos na sua vida acadêmica, e trabalhou ativamente na área da educação, tendo vários livros publicados, incluindo histórias para crianças.

Depois de ter sido um teólogo acadêmico, Alves decidiu abandonar a teologia. Pelo menos, aquilo que conhecemos como teologia. Alves passou por uma enorme transformação e abandonou a crença de que o trabalho acadêmico era capaz de realmente transformar as pessoas. Ele começou a acreditar que só era possível transformar as pessoas falando diretamente ao coração delas. A partir desse momento, ele transformou sua linguagem, mudou suas fontes e sua maneira de construir conhecimento.

Ele começou a se basear livremente nos trabalhos de Nietzsche, Gabriel Garcia Marques, Albert Camus, Freud, M. C. Echer, Octavio Paz, Santo Agostinho, Bonhoeffer, Feuerbach, Bachelard, Beethove, diversos poetas, filmes e escritores brasileiros para entrelaçar suas compreensões do mundo feito carne e amor através de uma ampla gama de fontes, como poesia, política, culinária, beleza, teologia, alquimia, memórias e desejos. Teologia para ele assumiu a forma de brincadeiras com as palavras, numa tentativa de compreender o mistério de Deus, este nome que não pode ser nomeado.

O trabalho de Alves situa-se na fronteira na qual teologia e poesia se encontram. Alves tornou-se um teopoeta, libertando a teologia de qualquer tentativa de aprisionamento dentro as jaulas dos discursos teológicos dogmáticos herméticos.

Alves expandiu os horizontes dos teólogos de infinitas maneiras e nos levou a lugares inesperados, oferecendo-nos possibilidades empolgantes para diálogos curiosos e resultados imprevisíveis. A partir da mão e do coração de um dos primeiros e principais teólogos da libertação latino-americanos, recebemos sempre um relato apaixonado sobre Deus e a vida, um relato que ainda carrega um horizonte utópico para um mundo novo, um mundo de poesia, mágica, beleza e libertação.

Ivone Gebara

Filósofa e teóloga, Ivone Gebara é uma freira pertencente à Ordem de Nossa Senhora das Cônegas de Santo Agostinho. Ela trabalhou durante mais de 30 anos com Dom Hélder Câmara, arcebispo de Recife. Só no Instituto de Teologia de Recife, ela trabalhou com ele durante 18 anos, até que o Vaticano fechasse o Instituto em 1989. Numa pequena cidade chamada Camaragibe, perto de Recife, Gebara trabalhou sobretudo com os pobres, principalmente mulheres vítimas de violência doméstica na região de Recife. Seu trabalho como teóloga não pode ser separado do seu trabalho com o povo. Mesmo seu escritório, onde ela escreve sua teologia, era cheio de crianças correndo para lá e para cá. Ela tinha um computador muito antigo. Lembro-me que ela costumava me pedir para não lhe enviar arquivos muito grandes, porque seu computador levava séculos para conseguir abri-los.

Hoje aposentada, ela vive dos seus escritos e palestras que dá em todo lugar. Dois anos atrás, ela ficou muito doente e quase morreu. Tive o privilégio de ser o assistente de duas matérias que ela ensinou no Union Theological Seminary em 2003, e dois anos atrás editei um livro em sua homenagem chamado "Dear Ivone" (Querida Ivone).

Ivone Gebara é uma das vozes teológicas mais importantes da América Latina. Dois dos seus principais trabalhos foram publicados em inglês: Longing for Running Water: Ecofeminism and Liberation, publicado em 1999, e Out of Depths. Women's Experiences of Evil and Salvation, publicado em 2002. Em 2012, ela foi a palestrante principal da reunião da Academia Americana da Religião. O título da sua palestra foi: "Conhecendo o humano, conhecendo o divino para o humano: perspectivas a partir dos cantos vulneráveis do mundo de hoje".[1]

Ela tem uma infinidade de artigos publicados em português, espanhol, inglês e francês. Em 1997, ela publicou "Teologia EcoFeminista" (São Paulo: Olho D'agua, 1997), e apenas dois anos depois publicou um outro novo livro importante em português: "Teologia Urbana — Ensaios Sobre Ética, Gênero, Meio Ambiente e a Condição Humana". (São Paulo: Fonte Editorial, 2014). Em 2014, Nancy Cardoso e eu editamos um livro para celebrar sua vida e pensamento: "Dear Ivone, Love letters of theology and feminism" (Querida Ivone: Cartas de Amor de Teologia e Feminismo). Uma das cartas no livro foi escrita pelo Prof. Chris Tirres.

Em 1989, ela deu uma entrevista para uma das principais revistas do Brasil e, em "off", falou sobre a questão do aborto entre as mulheres que ela atendia. Quando a revista foi publicada, estas revelações foram incluídas, e por isto ela foi silenciada pelo Vaticano e enviada à Bélgica para ser reeducada. Durante este período, ela escreveu "Out of the Depths. Women's Experience of Evil and Salvation". Gebara vive sua vida para os pobres do Brasil. Contudo, ela frequentemente foi bastante crítica a respeito da igreja e sua dominância masculina.

Gebara tem uma compreensão diferente da teologia. Ao invés de considerar Deus uma essência, um ser ensimesmado a quem recorremos em busca de sabedoria, ela vê Deus como um mistério, um mistério que permeia a vida de homens e mulheres e toda a criação. Ela vai além da imagem de Deus fixada num ser que está além de tudo que existe, um ser em si mesmo. Para ela, esta concepção de Deus serve para um grupo de homens controlarem tanto oque se conhece de Deus quanto o povo. Esta compreensão acerca de Deus é usada pelas lideranças patriarcais para proclamar que eles detêm a verdade de Deus, e que todos precisam aprender com eles. Este controle e tutela abafa as vozes das mulheres e daqueles que não cabem nesta compreensão de quem é Deus.

No seu curto livro "What Is Theology?", Gebara afirma que teologia é a roupa que usamos por cima das nossas experiências e sentimentos profundos. O problema é que usamos uma única peça de roupa, que nunca tiramos do corpo.

Ao invés disso, segundo ela, deveríamos tirar nossas roupas religiosas com frequência para que possamos descobrir nossos corpos, nossos sentimentos, e então experimentar roupas diferentes para aprendermos outras maneiras de falar a respeito das nossas experiências com Deus.

Teologia é um processo de conhecimento, e o patriarcado nos forçou a pensar de forma unívoca, providenciando apenas uma única roupa para que possamos entender Deus e nós mesmos. Para ela, as experiências religiosas nascem e vivem dentro e através dos nossos corpos, e são nestes corpos e nas suas relações que podemos encontrar os fios do que Deus pode ser em nosso meio. Há uma tapeçaria de solidariedade e conectividade que nos dá, em corpos diferentes e em sentimentos singulares, uma ideia do que e quem Deus pode ser, este mistério que nos agracia de diferentes formas. É este mistério, vivido nas pluralidades da vida, que suplica por diferentes tipos de conhecimento capazes de oferecer diferentes relatos sobre Deus, sobre nós mesmos e nossa vida juntos.

Somos bios e logos, ela diz, vida e palavra, e é nesta relação entre os corpos da terra e nossos próprios corpos que criamos símbolos, sentido. Este sentido está fundamentalmente ligado à nossa capacidade de ouvir nossos corpos ligados ao corpo da terra. A partir desta interligação profunda, Deus vem até nós, mas não a partir do alto, de um tipo de conhecimento formatado, e sim das experiências que vivenciamos. Quanto menos interligarmos corpos, sentimentos, experiências e movimentos da terra, mais nos distanciamos de Deus, o mistério que vive em nossas experiências.

O pensamento patriarcal não possui este tipo de relacionalidade, já que frequentemente está desvinculado destas fontes: corpo, sentimentos, e a terra. A consequência deste tipo de pensamento desvinculado é a criação de uma estrutura de cima para baixo para definir o logos, de forma a manter oficialmente um conceito homogêneo de Deus para sustentar uma ideia homogênea de poder. Falando na condição de teóloga eco-latina, Gebara defende a diversidade das vozes, com as mulheres incluídas na oficialidade da igreja, bem como uma maior integração entre sensação-conhecimento, com diferentes maneiras de experimentar-conhecer e de se construir o conhecimento. O conhecimento das mulheres é capaz de lidar com a complexidade desta ligação e com os problemas reais do dia a dia das pessoas, incluindo sexualidades e questões de saúde que fazem parte das pessoas reais, fazendo uma ponte entre o distante pensamento dogmático que está exposto no abismo existente entre os poderes temporal e religioso.

O trabalho intelectual das mulheres tem sido capaz de demonstrar como a forma patriarcal do conhecimento associou a origem de um poder absoluto com o desenvolvimento de dogmas referentes à perfeição e à pureza e que servem para refletir a representação absoluta do poder masculino sobre e contra tudo aquilo que não é masculino. Assim, através da história, as representações de Deus, Jesus e o Espírito Santo são sempre masculinas. A presença de Maria, por exemplo, serve apenas para reificar o poder masculino de um sistema de dominação patriarcal.

Para Gebara, um dos novos desafios da teologia é tornar-se plural. Ela tem escrito recentemente a respeito de pluralismos cristológicos e a necessidade do pensamento cristão se envolver em diálogos plurais e diálogo inter-religioso. Diálogos plurais requerem uma variedade de vozes. As mulheres, por exemplo, precisaram lutar contra o sistema patriarcal que as empurrava para a periferia, considerando inapropriado ou até que elas fossem incapazes de pensar teologia. Junto com as mulheres, negros, indígenas e queers também foram relegados à marginalidade. Contudo, eles estão resistindo e fazendo o discurso teológico ser mais plural e mais consistente com nossas sociedades e nossas maneiras de viver. Porém, devido à hegemonia histórica das formas únicas de pensamento, estes grupos continuam sendo marginais. A conversa plural é mais comum fora do domínio oficial da igreja.

O que esta forma única de pensar faz também é evitar formas plurais-comuns de pensamento, o que rouba de nós as formas éticas plurais de avaliar e negociar a vida e respeito na grande pólis-cidade. Gebara diz que o problema das nossas teologias não é o pluralismo, e sim uma falta de modus vivendi baseado na generosidade, afeto e no respeito aos direitos e aspirações.

Quanto ao diálogo inter-religioso, Gebara diz que, novamente, a perspectiva feminina pode se aplicar muito melhor com a vida real das pessoas e suas lutar diárias, criando pontes necessárias para um mundo que está aberto a tipos diferentes de afeto, pensamento, sexualidade e práticas.

Gebara vê o poder das mulheres na criação e recriação da vida, mesmo dentro do patriarcalismo e da corrente opressão econômica, política, de gênero, sexual e social. É na vida das mulheres e suas experiências com o mal e de salvação que ela encontra Deus, este mistério que continua se movendo através e na vida das mulheres pobres. Assim, é através do trabalho das mulheres, da justiça ecológica, da igualdade das relações de gênero, da pluralidade teológica e das relações éticas que a teologia deveria ser feita. Não apenas em causa da teologia, mas também por causa da vida de todos e da vida do planeta.

Milton Schwantes
Milton Schwantes nasceu em 1946, em Tapera, no Rio Grande do Sul. Em 1966 entrou na Faculdade de Teologia da IECLB tendo acesso a varias teologias, contudo, a que mais chamou atenção foi a "Teologia da Revolução" de Richard Schaull[1], ajudando a ampliar a visão além do germanismo na direção revolucionária da década de 1960. Inspirado em Schaull, percebe que a luta social pode ser desencadeada a partir de pequenos grupos revolucionários, como em Cuba. Doutora-se em 1974 na Universidade de Heidelberg incorporando mais ainda a negação do modo à vida capitalista pelo turbilhão de críticas à modernidade por meio do passado idealizado. Ali teve acesso a produção do Círculo de Weber, principalmente dos autores Georg Lukács e Ersnt Bloch.[2] Sua estada em Heidelberg possibilitou não só o incremento exegético, mas também a

ampliação da negação da civilização moderna, incrementando sua Teologia da Libertação. No seu tema de doutorado, o "pobre" da Bíblia hebraica, confirma o interesse pelo reverso da história, pelos desfavorecidos. Diz ele sobre a tese:

> o direito também de receber comida e uma terra da sociedade. O direito é o de obter da sociedade o apoio na necessidade e na crise, em meio aos parentes e à comunidade. Igualmente quis saber quem são exatamente os pobres. O termo pobre é usado no Antigo Testamento e na Bíblia de modo diferente do que nós o usamos. Nós damos aos pobres o sentido de carentes. A Bíblia o entende como quem tem o direito de reivindicar os direitos sociais garantidos. Na tradição bíblica, um pobre não pede (não é pedinte), mas exige sua parcela da sociedade.[3]

Reconhece o "pobre" na Antiguidade como donos de direitos atualizando de forma de direta críticas ao presente, no qual escamoteia os empobrecidos tornando-os mais e mais subumanos. No retorno ao Brasil, lidera por quatro anos o pastoreado na região de Santa Catarina, na Paróquia em Cunha Porã — área rural com cerca de mil e duzentas famílias. Desenvolve junto aos camponeses uma pastoral atenta aos agricultores espoliados nos tempos da Ditadura Militar. Por eles, escreve sobre o "meu povo" em Miquéias, relacionando-o as camadas mais pobres dos campos de Judá, praticando um exercício interessante de, a partir da narrativa do passado sagrado, ajudar na organização dos primeiros acampamentos que começam a se desenhar no Sul do Brasil dos movimentos Justiça e Terra (MJT) e o dos Agricultores do Oeste do Paraná.[4] Em sua passagem por Cunha Porã desperta mais ainda a prática de reflexão bíblica e a ação social confluindo junto as organizações pastorais luteranas do campo.

Entre 1978 até 1988 atua como docente na Faculdade de Teologia da IECLB, em São Leopoldo. Torna-se professor de Antigo Testamento, indo morar na favela, no bairro São Borja. Sempre que podia, entre 1985–1986, auxiliava nas celebrações de suas CEBs, como no acampamento da Anonni, onde surgiu o Movimento dos Trabalhadores Sem-Terra (MST).[5] Acreditamos que cada autor escreve de acordo com as vivências, assim, não se pode retirar suas primeiras obras fora do contexto nos setores agrícolas como os termos que repete nos textos: "Deus acampa entre nós" e "Deus fala para os camponeses". Na sua entrada como professor de Antigo Testamento que passa a colaborar mais ativamente no CEBI, Centro de leitura popular da Bíblia, local articulador das organizações pastorais camponesas da época. Fruto dessas articulações é seu importante estudo do período chamado "Profecia e Estado: uma proposta para a hermenêutica profética"[6] — escrito retratando os problemas dos agricultores que passavam pela espoliação do agronegócio (apoiado pelos militares), que contrariamente a isso se organizam no início dos movimentos sociais rurais. Escreve sobre a organização dos pobres:

> Outro exemplo: torna-se mais compreensível por que Amós fala de modo tão retumbante da exploração dos "pobres", atribuindo a ela, em última instância, o fim do Estado monárquico opressor, enquanto que Oséias, no mesmo Estado e praticamente na mesma época, nem mesmo menciona "pobres". Acontece que o próprio Amós provém deste campesinato empobrecido. Sua contestação à classe dominante e ao Estado está enraizada em sua situação e na fé em Javé, que tinha seu foco justamente nestes setores explorados da sociedade israelita. Resumindo esta tentativa de entender Amós, concluo que sua mensagem não trata do fim total do povo, mas do fim dos totalitários, chegando inclusive a esboçar esperança ainda que de modo pouco explícito, e postulo que este profeta provém do movimento do campesinato (...) O específico da profecia radical deve ser buscado em seu antagonismo ao Estado. Reinado não é um de seus assuntos. É seu tema básico, ao tematizar a ruína das instituições básicas deste Estado/reinado: fim do templo e palácio, da cidade-capital e do rei. Neste antagonismo espelha-se a oposição entre agricultores e cidade, pelo que havemos de buscar as raízes do movimento profético nos vilarejos interioranos de Israel e Judá, em seu campesinato. Assim sendo, o conflito com o Estado não emerge do sacerdócio. Nem brota da pergunta pelo lugar do Estado dentro da ordem ou das ordens existentes. Posso imaginar que, quem olha o Estado sob esta ótica, dificilmente perceberá antagonismos. Justamente neste sentido a profecia vétero-testamentária nos poderá ajudar a redescobrir que não é do templo e nem da estabilidade sacral que provém a contestação à opressão arregimentada sob estruturas estatais. Origina-se justamente na margem, ou

melhor: na luta de quem efetivamente produz, de quem trabalha a roça, em termos de Antigo Testamento. Daí porque será fácil de entender que, se uma igreja não estiver enraizada neste mundo periférico, até mesmo lhe será difícil de entender que existe o conflito profético sofrido contra o Estado.[7]

No fragmento, Schwantes incita não o "o fim total do povo", mas do *modus totalitarius* dos Estados totais e dos opressores e sugadores dos que o cercam. Por meio do texto bíblico, e tragado da realidade social brasileira, o jovem Schwantes deposita sua esperança na profecia que "provém do movimento do campesinato".[8] A realidade se faz em completo "antagonismo ao Estado", no qual, desde a antiguidade, firma-se na urgência do "fim do templo e palácio, da cidade-capital e do rei". Nesse sentido, o chão de sua hermenêutica coloca em xeque o Estado militar brasileiro do período, suas relações com as igrejas (católicas, protestantes) e as relações exploradoras da cidade em relação da alimentação com o campo. Schwantes diferencia sacerdotes e profetas. Para ele, os profetas são os que organizam a resistência nos campos e vilarejos, já os sacerdotes não apresentam críticas direta a ação dos Estados. Diz ele: "nem brota da pergunta pelo lugar do Estado dentro da ordem ou das ordens existentes".[9] A partir da realidade brasileira, pondera que o sacerdócio não é denunciante, ao contrário, se interessa pela promulgação dessas instituições. Diz que, "não é do templo e nem da estabilidade sacral que provém a contestação à opressão arregimentada sob estruturas estatais".[10] A luta, a organização vem de quem originalmente "produz, trabalha".

Deixa para o fim do fragmento o aviso mais sistêmico de contrariedade à igreja, à época. O problema dela era que buscava silenciar o conflito profético. Contudo, a igreja nas organizações populares deveriam destacar as divergências com o Estado e assumir a profecia. Agora, falar de Milton Schwantes sem referendar seu principal livro, "Projetos de Esperanças: meditações sobre Gênesis 1–11",[11] é deixar de lado o que de mais significativo produziu. Schwantes escreve para um encontro das Comunidades Eclesiais de Base que participa em Quito (Equador). Atento ao universo popular, abre mão no livro das notas de rodapé afim de disfarçar suas bases sociais. Por exemplo, entre as linhas destaca a importância das lutas de classes: "os donos do poder tratam de amputar os desejos populares"[12] — opondo os "donos do poder" e os caminhos das organizações populares. Também, inspirado em Marx, a partir da vivência espoliada camponesa, denuncia a lógica do Capital de transformar tudo em formas de consumo: "[os donos do poder] esforçam-se em substituí-los por imagens de consumo, por felicidade televisionadas, por novelas irreais".[13]

Ao analisar Gênesis 4, indica que a aposta do divino se encontra no campo, isto é, em Abel, morto por Caim — citadino, arrogante. Com sua sensibilidade teológica, destaca que Caim só tem chance de sobreviver quando se transforma em agricultor, uma provocação as cidades - estereótipo do capitalismo brasileiro da época. Para ele, as cidades só seriam saída da humanidade se forem reconstruídas junto as formas comunitárias rurais, isto é, "por meio da organização camponesa".[14] O que se justifica por sua vivência camponesa não acreditando que qualquer ideia de transformação social ligada as técnicas e ao maquinário do urbanismo, mas com formas comunitárias do passado pré-capitalista.

Para terminar a parte de Schwantes retornamos a umas de suas metáforas ao tempo presente, e, com ela, mostra-se como a utopia de Marx o comove:

> [os donos do poder] reprimem e matam quem se organiza por um teto ou por um pedaço de chão para plantar. Contudo, por mais que os poderosos destruam flores, esmaguem jardim, não impediram a primavera.[15]

A partir dos solos espoliados do Sul do Brasil pela exploração capitalista, Schwantes, ligando os movimentos de leitura popular da Biblia e as pastorais da terra luteranas, parafraseia a metáfora de Marx sobre a iminência revolucionária da impossibilidade dos poderosos calarem os anseios populares. Cita a "Primavera dos Povos" como lugar sem-igual, de igualdade entre os humanos. Não seria mais divididos entre pobres e ricos. Assume, também, que "terra", "pão" e "vida" são as questões fundamentais da humanidade. Tais formulações são moldura do livro de Gênesis 1–11.[16] Quando trata dos poderosos, Schwantes indica que, estes, fornecem dominação e a alienação, amarrando os projetos populares, comunitários e de luta pelo comum. Sua aposta, inspirado nas organizações pastorais camponesas, era de que a religião seria um dos pontos de luta pela dignidade do homem e de organização comunitária, o avesso ao capitalismo e suas oligarquias modernas.

Nancy Cardoso

Não se pode iniciar o tópico sobre a pastora metodista Nancy Cardoso sem lembrar que seus textos são para serem lidos entre suspiros, transpiros, suor e umidade. De fato, a leitura dos textos de Nancy causam emoções, transgridem fronteiras como um dos seus clássicos artigos para RIBLA: "Ah! Amor em delícias — leitura feminista do Cântico dos Cânticos", "Sem perder a ternura: jamais! Homens amados e mulheres prisioneiras do amor" e "Uma espada atravessada no meu corpo — leituras doloridas sobre a maternidade". Diante da larga produção da Nancy, separamos alguns dos últimos escritos. Antes, destacamos a entrevista, na qual, trata da questão do agronegócio, alimentos, fast-food e a teologia do "Tempo de Criação". Assume o tom profético para denunciar a questão dos alimentos, da desigualdade da distribuição incrementados pelas indústrias. Na reflexão, destaca os interesses classistas por trás das discussões sobre a produção proposital da fome no planeta, justificando a produção alimentícia por meio do "ídolo do agronegócio",[17] aprofundando os lucros dos empresários dos fast-foods. Diz:

> Nunca o mundo teve tanta capacidade de produção de alimentos! Mas a fome continua rondando 1 bilhão de pessoas no mundo. As grandes indústrias de alimentos continuam devorando terras, sementes e águas, fazendo fortuna para minorias do planeta. Os processos produtivos do agronegócio são extremamente destrutivos e não respondem às necessidades de todos e todas. Comemos mal e somos inundados pela lógica do "tempo para o lucro" do fast-food. O Tempo para a Criação é hoje um desafio para repensar os processos de alimentação e de retroalimentação dos seres e da humanidade.[18]

Pelas pastorais, junto aos sem-terra, se preocupa com a produção dos alimentos, exploração da terra/natureza pelo trabalhadores rurais. Por isso, a crítica da Nancy Cardoso volta-se ao agronegócio, herdeiro brasileiro das grandes propriedades monoculturas, empregadoras de tecnologia avançada nos campos por meio de mão-de- obra precária, reverberadora do passado escravizador. O agronegócio se sustenta junto a estrutura fundiária, filha do capitalismo colonial europeu, portanto, a teóloga protestante revolucionária com os pés calejados pelas roças destaca que o "Tempo da Criação é o que pode ajudar a pensar a alimentação fora dos alimentos em série do agronegócio".[19] Entende que a saída seria pela organização das forças camponesas confluindo na composição dos pequenos agricultores.

A partir de 2013, aprofunda seus vínculos pastorais com os seguimentos da terra, passando a se dedicar integralmente a CPT. Desde lá, se dedica com mais atenção a questão da produção dos alimentos, exploração da terra/natureza e a espoliação dos trabalhadores rurais. O texto "Dos filhos deste solo não sou a mãe nezm gentil: do imaginário da Mae-Terra à critica eco-feminista"[20] destaca a união dessas questões denunciando brilhantemente por meio da metáfora da Terra-mãe tão característica dos povos originários das Américas (ou de seu imaginário) Algo que vem sendo utilizado na modernidade brasileira pelas grandes indústrias para indicar que de forma explícita que "a Grande Mãe tudo tolera, que pode seguir sendo desmamada pela humanidade-masculina".[21]

No texto, problematiza que a construção da ideia da "Mãe-Terra" vem sendo naturalizada pelo status quo moderno-masculino, no qual implicitamente apela ao imaginário popular indicando que a "Mãe-Terra" tudo aguenta/atura, mesmo diante da continuidade da devastação do modus do capitalismo brasileiro. Escreve primeiro sobre os usos da ideia de "Terra-Mãe" seriam primordialmente contrários à forma de vida moderna:

> No âmbito deste quadro de crise civilizacional os usos da mãe-terra funcionam ora como elemento de continuidade, ora como possibilidade de ruptura e renovação exigindo assim um esforço de compreensão e crítica. De modo especial, a reflexão crítica precisa desnaturalizar os usos do binário mãe-terra, identificando seus vetores de significado e, a partir de uma perspectiva política feminista, entender as potencialidades e os limites desse imaginário.[22]

Para Nancy, somente a critica feminista mobilizadora de inteligências anticapitalistas pode colocar em xeque a naturalização desse imaginário antigo (mítico) dos povos originários. Percebe que a empresa estaria utilizando a metáfora da "Mãe-Terra", para seguir explorando a Terra — coisificando a relação com a natureza.[23] Com isso, a empresa estaria dizendo que o homem poderia seguir "mamando" a grande "Mãe-Terra" pois ela tudo permite.

Tece sua critica teológica junto a teologia prática, da carnalidade, das reflexões sociais, dos seguimentos que lutam por direitos e/ou por Outro

Mundo. Aponta que a verdadeira dinâmica de construção da metáfora da "Mãe/Terra" deve sobretudo radicalizar junto aos movimentos sociais das mulheres vitimadas pelo capitalismo heteronormativo-masculino:

> Mesmo após muito trabalho de crítica e organização dos movimentos de mulheres e do feminismo, os modelos explicativos que se sustentam nas oposições binárias varão/mulher, cultura/natureza, positivo/negativo, raciocínio/intuição continuam operantes na cultura. Na metáfora do Planeta Mãe Terra, mesmo formatada por conteúdos econômicos e políticos divergentes, a representação da maternidade continua consistente, interferindo em diversos níveis das lutas das mulheres, em especial nas pautas do ecofeminismo. Mulheres e natureza compartilham um desprezo comum nos estudos econômicos de modo geral, consideradas como 'recurso' para a satisfação das necessidades masculinas, em particular, ou humanas em geral com capacidade intrínseca de autorregeneração, o que significa também prescindir de cuidados.[24]

Portanto, para ela, tanto as mulheres, quanto a natureza são utilizadas nas propagandas televisivas, confluindo um profundo desprezo pelo sistema econômico atual. Até porque tais inteligências são condenadas a apenas um recurso, a "satisfação das necessidades masculinas".[25] Portanto, unindo denúncia ante a exploração da Mãe/Terra pelos valores feministas e ecossocialistas, Nancy sugere que a Mãe-gentil permite-se a utilização, ou melhor, sua exploração dos filhos em nome de um amor à pátria. Pelo próprio bem dos filhos, a "Mãe" (na metáfora da Terra) permite-se ser 'usada' pelos filhos para manter a vida. Promulgando, assim, a violência da utilização e exploração ante a desigualdade do solo. Perfeita (pátria) mãe-gentil, como escreve:

> O manejo cultural da "maternidade" permite e precisa dessa resolução fundada na ambiguidade para dissimular o mal-estar das relações de violência e subordinação que fundam a "pátria" e sua circunscrição de "solo". A disciplina dos filhos se baseia na gentilidade da "mãe". O amor pela "pátria" é o amor pela "mãe" que quer dissolver a violência real que funda o Estado, distribui desigualmente o "solo" e funda os imperativos da submissão voluntária. Patriótica.[26]

Nesse sentido, Nancy é representante da Teologia Feminista da Libertação, no qual, a partir das ações da CPT une de forma explosiva a teoria (nos livros, artigos e palestras) e a prática (junto aos movimentos sociais) de forma complementar. Novamente, junto a pastora revolucionária, assumimos que a Teologia da Libertação não seria apenas uma posição (status) na vida, mas sim, um modo de vida, uma forma completa de se relacionar com a sociedade. Por tanto, destacamos a linda teóloga metodista e toda sua conspiração anti-modernidade a fim de incendiar o masculino capitalismo brasileiro ancorado nos latifúndios genocida dos índios, índias, pretos, pretas, mestiços e pobres. Enfim, o caminho do suspirar, transpirar e transgredir de Nancy Cardoso, é da organização das vítimas do setor econômico e socialmente como saída real para dinamitar a vida urbana heteronormativa do mundo moderno.

Conclusão: da Teologia da Libertação e as alternativas nas cidades brasileiras
Junto a esses teólogos e teólogas da Teologia da Libertação, também existe uma linha de composição no Brasil que se articula junto a ela, expressando resistências e organização dos segmentos desguarnecidos socialmente, negros e negras. Antes, porém, assumimos que teoricamente existem mudanças nas humanidades brasileiras, nas quais a própria Teologia da Libertação é parte, articuladas diante a formação do Brasil moderno. Ocorre que o país, desde as décadas de 1950 e 1960, vem passando por mudanças, as quais, não decorrem apenas nas questões político-eleitorais. São transformações que vêem passando a partir das estruturas urbanas ajudando a sociabilidade por meio do desenvolvimento das malhas de cidades, inundando regiões antes apenas compreendidas por agrárias.

É um fenômeno complexo que faz parte as "globalizações nos quais se alastraram pelas geografias do Sul do Mundo", como afirma Boaventura de Souza Santos.[27] Passou-se pelo processo denso de industrialização do campo, ajustando a economia brasileira à substituição das importações, o que vinha desde a República Velha. Assim, entra as décadas de 1950–1960, começa a brotar a Teologia da Libertação numa mistura da teologia política (católica) e a teologia da revolução (protestante). Como se vêm indicando, a Teologia da Libertação surge ancorada nas bases da sociologia, questionando o cristianismo brasileiro e seu capitalismo.

Originalmente suas bases sociológicas fixam-se a noção da totalidade, discurso sobre a evolução, luta de classes. Termos, esses, que faziam parte do léxico da agenda progressista da época. No contexto, a Teologia da

Libertação se embeleceu na mentalidade da solidificação urbana das primeiras cidades, nos termos de Ciro Flamarion Cardoso,[28] que relaciona a geopolítica brasileira e a fixação do marxismo no pais. Também, o discurso totalizante fazia sentido por conta da luta/vitória revolucionária dos agricultores liderados por Fidel Castro e Ernesto Che Guevara, e, por outro lado, unificava o sentido da luta contra o regime ditatorial civil-militar governante no Brasil — inimigo também à época da Teologia da Libertação.

Atualmente, por conta da queda do Muro de Berlim, Ciro Flamarion Cardoso escreve que perdeu "força o marxismo, e as tentativas totalizantes dos saberes das humanidades".[29] Houve expansão da diversidade, da polifonia das vozes, da pluralidade na composição do Brasil a partir da década de 1980 e 1990, com o processo de desilusão do marxismo com a expansão do neoliberalismo globalizante. Como destacam Raquel Rolnik e Jerome Klink, a expansão dos saberes com as variadas pluralidades como pela integração das redes urbanas das metrópoles- pois há um "cenário de reestruturação produtivo-territorial e de abertura econômica sem políticas tecnológicas e industriais compensatórias — se gerou uma dissociação de mentalidades, em prol da pluralidades".[30]

Assim, a partir de 1980 com a desilusão do comunismo viveu-se a ampliação do capitalismo-urbano do território brasileiro produzindo "privadamente, a 'cidade'".[31] O capitalismo se liga mais à cultura brasileira, silenciando sua exploração e permitindo menos resistência à sua brutalidade. Ao mesmo tempo, o Capital no Brasil, demandou uma inserção precária à modernidade com baixas condições de urbanidade — mediante ocupações vulneráveis. As populações mais expostas à urbanidade neoliberal brasileira a partir de 1980 foram os negros, índios, mulheres, gays.

Parte desse seguimento foi precarizado desde a formação brasileira. Na modernidade, foram obrigados a se alocarem nos bairros mais pobres, nas favelas. Formaram os guetos brasileiros que, a partir de sensibilidades, começam a expressar nova agenda de reconhecimento próprio com o aprofundamento do capitalismo. Esse processo se reconhece justamente com o processo de desilusão da Teologia da Libertação, quando passou-se a identificar os pobres com os rostos negros, indígenas, quilombolas, e das comunidades LGBTQ.

No aprofundamento do capitalismo neoliberal brasileiro passou-se a reconhecer a face do pobre, entre os vitimizados do sistema, tonificando as identidades[32] — nexo de seus pensamentos teológicos influídos a partir das metrópoles. A Teologia da Libertação, que tinha afinidades eletivas pela revolução social, passou a se interessar pela resistência, identidades e pelas sobrevivências à exploração capitalista. Centros de formação teológica antes engajados com a teologia política libertadora passaram a ser espaço de vivências das diferentes locuções teológicas, portando-se a partir dos diferentes corpos marginalizados.

A todo esse fenômeno complexo teológico-urbano foi chamado por Faustino Teixeira de "teologia pluralista da libertação"[33] Teixeira, Faustino, *O pluralismo religioso no coração da teologia*, (São Bernardo do Campo: Nhanduti, 2012). que seria uma dinamite de teologias com poucas pretensões universalistas, nas quais, expressam certa conformidade ao capitalismo e defesa da vida mediante ao processo de degradação humana. Para Faustino Teixeira,[34] a Teologia da Libertação seria o horizonte de caminhada da "teologia pluralista da libertação", contudo, essas teologias trabalhariam em prol da justiça dos segmentos sonegados pelo privatismo capitalista. Seriam elas: teologias negras, feministas, ecológica, indígenas, queer, etc. Mas também, desafiados pelo neoliberalismo que a tudo domina, será preciso que essas teologias da libertação e outras que ainda não existem continuem/comecem a trabalhar com os mesmos e outros discursos em novas formas, recursos e movimentos do pensamento e da prática, e que continuem a se envolver nas comunidades sofridas e falar a partir dai, das economia de solidariedade contra a economia de exclusão e do domínio de impérios econômicos, dos espaços e políticas públicas, da educação, das teorias de comunicação e de memórias políticas, da história, das muitas psicanálises, da liturgia, performance e teatro, das teologias políticas e das formas da esquerda política se refazer e oferecer um novo mundo, da amplitude das sexualidades, da pluralidade das formas de negritude, dos diálogos inter-religiosos, das formas de desabilidades, do império das drogas, da militarização, da reforma agrária e de moradia, do tráfico de pessoas e da escravidão, do assalto da terra pelo agronegócio e do genocídio dos nossos indígenas. E tantas outras formas de se decolonizar o pensamento e as realidades injustas da América Latina a partir daqueles que sofrem.

Acerca da teologia negra, que no número esta desenvolvido, indicamos que embora as iniciativas estejam brotando nas terras brasileiras, a teologia negra vêm se fazendo (embrionariamente) presente, desde a década de 1990. Três grupos facilitaram e ampliaram o pensamento teológico negro no Brasil. O primeiro foi a construção do grupo "Identidade" na Faculdade EST, em São Leopoldo, liderado pelo teólogo Norte-Americano Peter Nash. Também, na década de 1990, a Igreja Católica, em São Paulo, criou o Centro Atabaque de Cultura Negra e Teologia.[35] O terceiro grupo, criado pela Igreja Metodista, em Porto Alegre, nasceu o Centro Ecumênico de Cultura Negra — Cecune.[35]

Sobre as atividades desenvolvidas por Peter Nash, como professor da EST, ligou o labor bíblico com a sensibilidade negra, denunciando nas reuniões os enquadramentos dos negros no Sul do Brasil como: "sararás", "de cor carioca", "morenos", "mulatos" e "escurinhos". Desenvolveu um intenso trabalho levando os estudantes a se identificar como negros passando para a auto-aceitação da condição afro e afro-brasileira. A partir de 2000, Peter Nash retornou aos EUA e quem assumu a vaga foi a biblista católica colombiana Maribel Mena Lópes, ficando pouco tempo na EST e na liderança do grupo.[36] Agora, além do trajeto entre os católicos, luteranos e metodistas, outras vias vêm brotando no Brasil. Hoje existe uma quantidade considerável de negros e negras que assumem sua identificação na diversidade do pentecostalismo. Perguntamos: esses sujeitos não produziriam teologias?[37]

Já o grupo Atabaque foi um grupo feito de antropologistas e padres e pensadores que ampliaram o pensamento teológico negro para além dos limites do Cristianismo. A teologia negra no Brasil queria transformar a tarefa hermenêutica (branca) em um oikos negro, uma casa negra, um lugar onde as várias formas de expressões religiosas poderiam ser pensadas a partir de um sentido pleno de negritude, de uma chave diferente, forma, fontes e experiências negros/as feitos pelas negras/os. Reinaldo João de Oliveira perguntou: "Esse pensar hermenêutico, se é que ele existe, é um pensamento de quem é por definição negro/a afro? Ou ainda mais: É um pensamento teológico contextualmente negro, afrolatinoamericano, de fato?"[38]

Portanto fica o questionamento: a teologia negra não estaria sendo gestada no Brasil? Principalmente nas igrejas mais populares, de bairro, pentecostais (ou não), formando e configurando um novo rosto dos movimentos protestantes/evangélicos brasileiros. São rostos leigos e de comunidades locais/populares. Passamos assim, a partir dessas indagações, a pluralidade que muniu a Teologia da Libertação, de leituras e experiências, que hoje condicionam de potencial transformador do seguimento dos pobres e expoliados/expoliadas da América Latina. Não apenas reconhecidos pela Teologia da Libertação como "pobres", mas com a multidão enegrecida dos vitimizados com a pluralidade de linguagens e formas que passaram a produzir significado teológico a partir de seus vivencias e resistências ao engodo da vida meritocrática capitalista.

No entanto, a luta é intensa e cheia de desafios. Não há instituições educacionais religiosas no Brasil, sejam seminários cristãos ou departamentos de religião, que deliberadamente apoiem o pensamento teológico negro. Estas instituições são majoritariamente formadas por homens heterossexuais brancos. Se o negro não tem espaço nas instituições acadêmicas a presença da mulher negra ainda é pior. É muito difícil a luta das mulheres negras pelo seu pensamento autônomo. No Brasil as mulheres em geral, o povo queer/LGBTQA, e as pessoas com deficiência não estão sequer na margem dessas instituições educacionais e da produção acadêmica. O latino-americano ainda mantém uma estrutura patriarcal branca profundamente forte e as Teologias de Libertação conhecidas fizeram muito pouco para chamar a atenção dessas disparidades sociais.

Mais do que nunca, a América Latina precisa de teologias da libertação e que rompam com as teologias presentes, conservadores ou liberais, que servem somente à classe média ou a dominante, e que na maioria das vezes oferecem discursos isolados, auto-imunes, e comprometidos com o poder. A América Latina precisa de novas teologias da libertação que falem e vivam o Deus que (ainda) tem preferência em viver entre os pobres, entre mulheres, crianças, imigrantes, indígenas, portadores de deficiência, camponeses, negros, e todos aqueles que vivem sem condições mínimas de vida e em tantas e tamanhas formas de vulnerabilidade.

Talvez os próximos 45 anos de teologia da libertação corrijam quem falou, o que não foi falado e nem feito. Talvez usando diferentes fontes, bibliografias, experiências, mas sempre comprometidos com aqueles que ainda são colocados nas cruzes do sofrimento e da exploração em nossa amada Pacha Mama.

Notas
1. https://www.youtube.com/watch?v=0u-w0k_tn50

2. Dreher, Martin, "Milton Schwantes: um perfil biográfico", em Carlos Dreher e Isolde Dreher, org., *Profecia e Esperança: um tributo a Milton Schwantes* (São Leopoldo: Oikos, 2006), p. 15.
3. Schwantes, Milton, A teologia e o direito dos pobres — Interview with Schwantes at Unisinos. Acessed at 10.03.2014. Available at: https://www.metodista.br/fateo/noticias/duas-entrevistas-com-o-professor-milton-schwantes.
4. Op. cit.
5. Para saber mais sobre o Movimento dos Trabalhadores Sem–Terra, ver http://www.mstbrazil.org/content/history-mst visited 12/10/16
6. Schwantes, Milton, "Profecia e estado: uma proposta para a hermenêutica profética", Estudos Teológicos, n.22, v.2, 1982.
7. Op. cit, p. 69.
8. Py, Fábio, "The Lutheran rebellion in the Brazilian countryside", Crosscurrents, n.12, 2016, p. 156–8.
9. Schwantes, Milton, "Profecia e estado: uma proposta para a hermenêutica profética", Estudos Teológicos, n.22, v.2, 1982, p. 69.
10. Op. cit.
11. Schwantes, Milton, *Projetos de Esperanças: meditações sobre Genesis 1–11* (São Paulo: Paulinas, 2011).
12. Op. cit., p. 9.
13. Op. cit., p. 9–10.
14. Op. cit., p. 84–5.
15. Op. cit., p. 10.
16. Op. cit., p. 11–8.
17. Pereira, Nancy Cardoso, "Agronegócio & religião: pretensões & profecias". EcoDebate, 19.10.2007. https://www.ecodebate.com.br/2007/10/19/agronegocio-e-religiao-pretensoes-profecias-por-nancy-cardoso-pereira/
18. Op. cit.
19. Op. cit.
20. Pereira, Nancy Cardoso, "Dos filhos deste solo não sou a mãe nem gentil: do imaginário da Mãe-Terra à crítica eco-feminista". Caminhos, v.11, n.2, 2013, p. 123–38.
21. Op. cit.
22. Op. cit., p. 124.
23. Op. cit.
24. Op. cit., p. 125.
25. Op. cit.
26. Op. cit.
27. Santos, Boaventura Souza, *Os processos da globalização*, (São Paulo: Cortez, 2002), p. 51.
28. Ciro Flamarion Cardoso, "Tempo e História", 2001, p. 9–21.
29. Op. cit., p. 13.
30. Rolnik, Raquel; Kilnk, Jerome, "Crescimento econômico e desenvolvimento urbano", Novos estudos, n.89, 2011, p. 109.
31. Op. cit.
32. Cardoso, Ciro Flamarion, "Tempo e historia", 2001, p. 15–20.

33. Teixeira, Faustino, *O pluralismo religioso no coração da teologia*, (São Bernardo do Campo: Nhanduti, 2012).
34. Op. cit.
35. http://atabaque-cultura-negra-e-teologia.blogspot.com/?m=1
36. Leyva, Pedro Acosta; Souza, Ezequiel; Mello, Luis Carlos, "Historia do grupo identidade: uma década de vida e contribuições!" Identidade!, v.9, 2006, p. 21–41.
37. Op. cit.
38. de Oliveira, Reinaldo João, "Existe um pensar hermenêutico-teológico negro?" in http://periodicos.est.edu.br/index.php/identidade/article/view/2202/2099

AUTORES

Sílvia Barbosa é Bacharel em Teologia, filósofa, cientista da religião (UMESP), especialista em Teologia e História Latino-Americana (EST) e doutora em estudos interdisciplinares sobre mulheres, gênero e feminismo (UFBA), com dois livros publicados sobre empoderamento de gênero e raça no Quilombo do Urubu e no Candomblé de Ketu pela editora online Nova Edições Acadêmicas.

silreligare@hotmail.com

Nancy Cardoso, pastora metodista e teóloga feminist, agente da Comissão Pastoral da Terra e membro do Fórum Ecumênico da Palestina e Israel.

nancycpt@yahoo.com

Cláudio Carvalhaes, pastor presbiteriano, teólogo da libertação, liturgista e artista, professor associado de liturgia do Union Theological Seminary em Nova Iorque, EUA.

www.claudiocarvalhaes.com
ccarvalhaes@uts.columbia.edu

Maria Gabriela Hita, Pós-doutora pela Universidade de Manchester e docente do Programa de Pós-Graduação em Ciências Sociais e em Estudos Interdisciplinares sobre Mulheres, Gênero e Feminismo—UFBA.

mghita@ufba.br

Ronilso Pacheco é de São Gonçalo, Rio de Janeiro. Graduando em Teologia na Pontifícia Católica do Rio (PUC-Rio), interlocutor social na organização Viva Rio e presta assessoria para vários movimentos sociais e coletivos de defesa de direitos humanos. É autor do livro *Ocupar, resistir, subverter: igreja e teologia em tempos de violência, racismo e opressão.*

ronilsosilva@vivario.org.br

Fábio Py, doutor em teologia sistemática na Universidade Católica do Rio de Janeiro, é um teólogo protestante que trabalha na relação entre fé e política. Ele é o autor de "Crítica para a Ecologia Inferior". (São Leopoldo e São Paulo: Cebi & Fonte Editorial, 2014). Ele é um membro do conselho editorial do Journal Plura, Studies of Religion da Associação Brasileira de História das Religiões. ABHR—http://www.abhr.org.br/plura/ojs/index.php/plura). Ele é um colunista da Magazine Caros Amigos sob o tema de Religião e Direitos Humanos. (http://www.carosamigos.com.br/).

pymurta@gmail.com

Obertal Xavier Ribeiro é de Nova Iguaçu—Rio de Janeiro. Atualmente é professor auxiliar de ensino na Federação das Faculdades Celso Lisboa na área de Filosofia. Professor de Ensino Religioso no Estado. É Doutorando em Teologia com concentração na área de

Religião e Educação na Escola Superior de Teologia, EST, RS. É Mestre em Letras e Ciências Humanas pela UNIGRANRIO—Universidade do Grande Rio. É especialista em Teologia Bíblica pela Escola Superior de Teologia, EST, RS. Esteve no ministério sacerdotal por 12 anos na Diocese de Nova Iguaçu. Atualmente continua assessorando a Diocese de Nova Iguaçu na área de formação bíblica. Trabalha como assessor pedagógico no CEAP—Centro de Articulação de Populações Marginalizadas com populações remanescentes de quilombos e na formação de professores do Ensino Fundamental e Médio na área da História e Literatura dos afro-descendentes. Desenvolve projetos sociais de geração de renda e trabalho alternativo na área de coleta seletiva de lixo não perecível desde 2004. É bacharel em Teologia pelo IFTPS—Seminário Diocesano Paulo VI—Nova Iguaçu—RJ e Universidade Metodista de São Paulo—São Bernardo—SP. É bacharel em Filosofia pelo IFTPS—Seminário Diocesano Paulo VI—Nova Iguaçu e Universidade Santa Úrsula—RJ. É pós-graduado em licenciatura plena de Filosofia pela Universidade Cândido Mendes—RJ. Endereço para acessar este CV: http://lattes.cnpq.br/7800511322792289.

ribeiro.obertal@gmail.com

José Geraldo da Rocha é doutor em Teologia Sistemática pela Pontifícia Universidade Católica do Rio de Janeiro; professor no Programa de Pós-graduação em Humanidade, Culturas e Artes da Unigranrio. Bolsista de produtividade 1A FUNADESP/UNIGRANRIO. É Agente de Pastoral Negro e mora em Duque de Caxias RJ.

rochageraldo@hotmail.com

Marcos Rodrigues da Silva é Bacharel em Teologia pela Faculdade de Teologia Nossa Senhora da Assunção (1984), mestre em Teologia Dogmática pela Faculdade de Teologia Nossa Senhora da Assunção (1997) e doutor em Ciências da Religião pela Pontifícia Universidade Católica de São Paulo (2014). Pós-Doutorado em Educação e membro do Centro Atabaque de Cultura Negra e Teologia; Pesquisador associado da Associação Ecumênica de Teólogos do Terceiro Mundo.

marcosrit@gmail.com

Leontino Farias dos Santos, de São Paulo/SP, é Mestre em Ciências Sociais e Religião, Pós-Graduado em Gestão Escolar, profissional em Psicanálise Clínica Humanista, doutorando em Psicanálise pela Atlantic International University e professor licenciado em Filosofia, com habilitação em Filosofia, Psicologia e História; licenciado em Pedagogia, com especialização em Administração Escolar; Bacharel em Teologia e Vice-Diretor da Faculdade de Teologia de São Paulo da Igreja Presbiteriana Independente do Brasil (FATIPI).

leontinofarias@hotmail.com

Cristina da Conceição Silva mora no Rio de Janeiro e é professora do

Município de Nova Iguaçu. Doutoranda no Programa de Pós-Graduação em Humanidade, Culturas e Artes na Unigranrio.

cistinavento24@Yahoo.com.br

Marcos Palhano, Fotógrafo, Pesquisador, Educador Social. Atualmente ele mora em São Paulo.

olhodobturador@gmail.com
http://marcospalhano.wix.com/fotografias